The Empty Fortress

The
Empty
Fortress

Infantile Autism and the Birth of the Self

Bruno Bettelheim

The Free Press, New York / Collier-Macmillan Limited, London

Collier-Macmillan Canada, Ltd., Toronto, Ontario

Library of Congress Catalog Card Number: 67-10886

Second printing March 1967

To Ruth Marquis

Acknowledgments

Fɪʀsᴛ ᴀɴᴅ ꜰᴏʀᴇᴍᴏsᴛ I wish to express my gratitude to all staff members of the Sonia Shankman Orthogenic School on whose work this book is so largely based, and to the University of Chicago which fathers this institution. By its very nature, the School is often a troublesome child that survives and flourishes only because of the University's patience and insightful understanding into its unique problems.

I am greatly obliged to the parents of the three children whose stories I have told in some detail, for their cooperation while their children were with us, and for their acceptance of the School as an institution devoted to research. The research itself was made possible by a grant from the Ford Foundation whose contribution is gratefully acknowledged.

Work on this book began some twelve years ago and I have received so many helpful suggestions on various of its aspects, that it is difficult to do them all justice. I am particularly grateful to Jane Watson Duncan, Merton Gill, Morris Janowitz, David Rapaport, Milton Wexler, and Peter

Wolff for having read various parts of this book and given me the benefit of their criticism and thoughts. To all others whose ideas or suggestions have also contributed, I wish to express here my thanks.

I am grateful to Mr. Gerard Piel, publisher of *The Scientific American* for permission to use material and pictures which appeared in "Joey: The Mechanical Boy," and to the editors of the *American Journal of Sociology* for permission to use material from "Feral and Autistic Children."

I am indebted to the authors and publishers who granted permission to quote from the following sources: Gerhard Bosch and his publisher, Springer-Verlag, Berlin, for permission to translate and quote from *Der Fruehkindliche Autismus*, Copyright 1962; J. D. Call and the *International Journal of Psycho-Analysis* for permission to quote from "Newborn Approach Behavior and Early Ego Development" [45:286–298 (1964)]; Emma K. Zingg, widow of Robert M. Zingg, and Harper and Row, Inc. for permission to quote from *Wolf Children and Feral Man*, Copyright 1939, 1941, and 1942 by Robert M. Zingg; Basic Books, Inc. for permission to quote from J. Piaget, *The Construction of Reality in The Child*, Copyright 1954; and Leon Eisenberg, M.D. and *The American Journal of Psychiatry* to quote from "The Autistic Child in Adolescence," volume 112, pages 607–612, Copyright 1956 American Psychiatric Institute.

Contents

Contents

PART THREE
Wolf Children

PART FOUR

A Discussion of the Literature
on Infantile Autism

Illustrations

The Empty Fortress

Part One

THE WORLD OF ENCOUNTER

In the Region
of Shadows

Much of modern psychology seeks to know about others; too much of it, in my opinion, without an equal commitment to knowing the self. But I believe that knowing the other—which is different from knowing about the other—can only be a function of knowing oneself.

One source of knowledge about the other lies in experimentation. A well-designed experiment is intellectually convincing and pleases us esthetically. Unfortunately, the more the object of the study is man himself, and not just some isolated aspects of his behavior, the more questionable the value of the experimental method. The human mind is so complex that experiment can still clarify only some rather simple aspects of its working. If we wish to understand the human being in all his intricacy, we must fall back on the earliest method for comprehending man: to know oneself so that one may also know the other. This is why a deficiency in self-knowledge means a deficiency in knowing the other.

What is also difficult to know, in a given situation, is which of the two to start out with: an observing of others or an introspection into the self. Often introspection will come first and will motivate observation. But the introspecting person must also observe and have others observe. Otherwise he cannot verify as being generally true what, for all he knows, may be only his private uncorrected bias.

Psychoanalysis itself began with introspection. Freud's initial motive was that of all who introspect: the wish to know oneself. But the venture became scientific when to introspection was added his observation of hysteric patients. That is, psychoanalysis proper began with Freud's reflections on his own dreams. But these reflections he then verified through observations, based on what he had learned from introspection.

Still, introspection has its limits. We can only contemplate what is or was part of our life. When we engage in introspection we do not leave behind us our present frame of reference. Try as we may, we cannot find the one firm spot outside ourselves that would move our world of experience outside of our present personality. Even more limiting: we cannot regain by introspection our earliest experience or the origins of our mind—both of which so largely condition all our later development. Slowly, however, some carefully planned infant observations begin to add to our understanding. Even some limited experiments have been attempted in this twilight zone of beginning humanity. Of these, Piaget's studies are rightly among the best known.

Schachtel [1947, 1959], among others, discusses this loss of our early experience and why all we can do thus far is to speculate about it. For example, the experience of the infant is probably more intense in some ways than that of the older child or adult. For one thing, it is dominated by sensations of touch and smell. In the adult's experience these sensations are largely filtered out. But because of it, the very same event may produce a different experience in the very young person than in the older one. Moreover, as Stern [1914] recognized, the whole concept of self and others does not make sense to the infant or very young child—a sign that the distinction between subject and object is a later development. So here too, until about the second year of life, the child's experience of the world differs radically from ours.

But what if there were human beings who retained into a considerably older age this earlier mode of perception and of experiencing the world and themselves? Because infants are not the only ones who live in this shadowy region of mind. Some children remain partly arrested at this stage of emotional and intellectual development, and there are others who return to it in part. These are children suffering from infantile autism, a severe disturbance of childhood first described by Kanner [1943].

Although some autistic children are as solipsistic as infants in their contact with reality, and communicate as little, they are much farther developed in body. Their reactions and expressive movements are complex (unless they are rigidly frozen), and hence more revealing than those of an infant. Since their central nervous systems are fully developed, certain actions and reactions or the absence thereof are not caused by any lack of potential ability, but by the fact that for some reason a potential was not realized. While they probably do not experience the world as the infant does, what they experience is not mediated through a complex personality, or at least not as complex as in normal children their age.

We cannot be sure just how primitive the structure of their personalities may be. But unlike feeble-minded children, whose reactions too are very primitive for their age, personality in autistic children can be developed to far greater richness. And if, under treatment, this eventually happens, it does so at a much later age, and the children can either tell us what is happening to them or give us much richer clues as to why and how personality develops.

The infant, for example, is less able to manipulate objects, and cannot handle those that are very complex. The autistic child's manipulative activity, as it begins to appear, tells us more of what goes on in him as the rudiments of personality unfold. We can better understand, then, what in the preverbal infant is still obscured from our eyes.

What, for example, are the necessary steps in such development? Do the steps build on each other? And in what way? Are there critical periods in which organism and environment must interact to produce a given personality feature? Will those features fail to develop if the interaction does not happen at a critical period? Can certain features of personality develop even if earlier steps in personality growth did not occur?

Since their central nervous systems develop normally (except for the autistic arrest of potentials), autistic children should be able to acquire missing personality features in any sequence. But if, despite their greater chronological age, they can do this only by repeating the sequence in which personality unfolds for the infant and small child, then those steps are not only conditioned by the rate of neurological development but have to follow each other in some order independent of physical maturing.

Again: if in consequence of particular experiences during treatment these children develop personality features they were lacking before, we can be reasonably sure which experiences were missing in earlier life, which environmental events failed to have their effect in the past, and which events accounted for which steps in present personality growth. And if the same or very similar events fail to evoke a personality feature in children of a different age, then we can infer from it which periods are critical for acquiring that particular step in personality development.

Thus however fascinating the problems posed by autistic children, any understanding we gain of their pathology and what makes treatment effective, and why, has implications far beyond the particular disturbance.

Obviously, too, what can be learned from the study of autistic children cannot be applied to personality development without the cautiousness always necessary when inferring from pathology to the normal.

To live with autistic children then, to study them and try to treat them might be termed an experiment. But the complexity of the problems, the vast differences between the individuals (none of whom remains the same from moment to moment), the distance between observer and observed, all this and much more precludes that any such experiment can be carefully planned in detail. It cannot observe the rigors of a "scientific" experiment since it must, in its course, pursue the vagaries of life which are nothing if not unpredictable. Least of all can we expect to end up with unequivocal answers.

Given our present state of knowledge, the nature of the phenomenon studied forces on us many ambiguities, even seeming contradictions. This is apart from any that belong to my own shortcomings as an investigator. For the first I offer no apologies; for the second my honest regrets. On the other hand, without a willingness to risk the ambiguities and possible contradictions, one cannot study infantile autism or earliest personality development, both of which are so largely preverbal and prelogical. Hopefully one day we shall have resolved the ambiguities. But this stage of clarity we have not reached yet, neither I nor my co-workers at the School.

I have said that often it is introspection, a highly personal experience, that motivates observation and search. An "experiment" like that of treating autistic children does not begin accidentally. Beyond the many "scientific" reasons that make it important to study this severest arrest of personality there was also a personal bent to my interest. What first disturbed me and aroused my interest in these children was how deliberately they seemed to turn their backs on humanity and society. If their experience of reality was such that it led to a total rejection, then there was a terribly important lesson to be learned about reality, or whatever part of it provoked their rejection. If we could understand which isolated aspects of reality were so abortive of humanity as to snuff it out, there might be something constructive we could do.

During many years of work with schizophrenic children I had learned how an institutional setting designed especially for their treatment produced unexpectedly favorable results [Bettelheim, cf. Bibliog.]. This led me to wonder if the same setting might not be helpful to far more severely disturbed children, such as the autistic group. So on an exploratory basis a few such children were enrolled at the University of Chicago's Sonia Shankman Orthogenic School beginning in the early 1950's. We found them most interesting to work with and also most difficult. With some we had considerable success. Others improved, but not enough to live in society on their own. Staff members, for their part, had differing reasons for their interest and involvement in these children, of whom we could never have more than six or eight at a time.

Then, thanks to a grant from the Ford Foundation it became possible to concentrate on the study and treatment of autism during the years 1956 to 1962. The considerable help we thus received, and which made this book possible, is gratefully acknowledged. Because of it we were better able to continue in our work with autistic children.

Though my own interest had been great from the start, I only became fully involved at a point where human and theoretical issues crossed a uniquely personal one, and this happened when Anna came to live with us.[1] Although Anna was not a child of the German concentration camps, her life history was such as to bring them sharply to mind. Through her, the phenomenon of the camps which had long occupied much of my personal and theoretical interest [1943, 1960] became somehow linked with my daily work, the treatment of severely disturbed children.

Some victims of the concentration camps had lost their humanity in response to extreme situations. Autistic children withdraw from the world before their humanity ever really develops. Could there be any connection, I wondered, between the impact of the two kinds of inhumanity I had known—one inflicted for political reasons on victims of a social system, the other perhaps a self-chosen state of dehumanization (if one may speak of choice in an infant's responses)? In any case, having written a book on dehumanization in the German concentration camps what next preoccupied me was the present volume on infantile autism.

If one is to fully understand a psychological state one must be capable of considerable empathy tempered by critical judgment. Some people have deliberately subjected themselves to experiences that would enable them to empathize and introspect about the schizophrenic experience and permit others to study it objectively. Recent experiments with sensory deprivation belong in this class. Others have used drugs to induce psychotic-like states in themselves, and possibly something of value may be learned from them too, though I doubt it. But all studies of this kind exclude the one factor that I believe makes an experience extreme: its inescapability.

To know that one can interrupt an experiment at will keeps the experience from being totally overwhelming. It is precisely the irrevocable,

1. Her story, in bare outline, is part of the chapter on feral children entitled "Persistence of a Myth."

more than the prospect of torture or death, that so destroys personality. The very fact that one submits to experiment in order to further a scientific inquiry can be enough. So much does it bolster the self-respect that this alone can keep the experience from being shattering.

For myself it was the German concentration camps that led me to introspect in the most personal, immediate ways on what kinds of experience can dehumanize. I had experienced being at the mercy of forces that seemed beyond one's ability to influence, and with no knowledge of whether or when the experience would end. It was an experience of living isolated from family and friends, of being severely restricted in the sending and receiving of information. At the same time I felt subject to near total manipulation by an environment that seemed focused on destroying my independent existence, if not my life.

There was still another experience that enabled me to observe and to introspect about infantile autism. From 1932 until March 1938 (the invasion of Austria) I had living with me one, and for a few years two, autistic children. To make this a therapeutic experience for them, many conditions of life in our home had to be adjusted to their needs. This was my initial experience with trying to create a very special environment that might undo emotional isolation in a child and build up personality.

Then suddenly, after spending much thought and effort on creating this environment, I found the tables radically turned. Within weeks I was made subject to far-reaching isolation, and to deliberate efforts at personality destruction. Perhaps this sudden reversal helped me first to understand how the camps could destroy personality, and later to resume, with I hope greater insight and empathy, my earlier task: that of creating a milieu which would favor the reconstruction of personality.

Having said this much about my basis for introspecting about infantile autism, I would stress that the contents of this volume do not derive from introspection. They are based on the findings of trained observers, their observations checked against each other, and on inferences drawn on that basis. (Concerning the use of observations in this book, see the discussion "On Writing Case Histories," in my *Truants From Life*, 1955.) At most, what came from introspection was a certain direct feeling for what may have been going on in the mind of the person studied, a feeling that can never rank as more than a hunch. Otherwise the uses of introspection for understanding others would be a projection of one's own experience, with little scientific merit.

Five years after my liberation, in 1944, I returned to where I had been forced to leave off. But I returned on a far different scale, with infinitely larger resources at my disposal. No longer did a private home have to do for creating an environment specially suited to help severely disturbed children toward mental health. There was now the opportunity to create an institution for exactly that purpose at a great university, and in doing so to draw on its wealth of resources.

Since then my life's work has consisted of refining this very special environment. Even more important has been the effort, with the help of the School staff, to provide those general experiences in living and those special therapeutic ones that would help the most severely disturbed children get well. Some of what we have learned from the autistic group among them is in the following pages.

In planning this book some choices had to be made. Most important was which of the more than forty autistic children we had studied extensively would best illustrate our convictions, however tentative still, about the nature of the disturbance, its treatment, and what we had learned about early personality development. It was tempting to think of presenting those youngsters we had helped to entirely overcome their early disturbance. For example, it would have been gratifying to concentrate on stories like that of a young man now happily married who received his Ph.D. from the same university of which our School is part. Though not an autistic child, he was just as arrested in perceiving reality as they are. This temptation passed. But I will at least add here that when I asked him, ten years after he left us, if he would be willing to set down what his experience with us looked like in retrospect, he began as follows:

"Giving battle to terrible fears, wishes and hates had consumed my emotional strength. So when I attended the Orthogenic School this period of my life was marked first with terrible struggle, then delinquency, and finally recognized achievement. The process that I went through in changing and directing my energy into acceptable and productive areas was marked by direct confrontation. No one changes unless he has a desire to do so. The first steps that one takes toward change are directed toward the area of realization that 'you' are the one who is ill rather than the other guy. Once this fact is established the process of reorganization can begin in earnest.

"To realize that one has a life to lead of one's own is a great insight (simple as that statement may seem). However, to be able to act on this information is a great achievement. The School provided the environment in which I could test out my insight."

I could also have told of one of our nontalking autistic youngsters who, after our work with him was concluded, took a job for a time on the assembly line. Soon afterward he decided that he wanted more skilled work, so he put himself through barber school. For several years now he has not only been a successful barber, but is happily married and the father of a delightful child. He is still somewhat tongue-tied; that is, he speaks slowly, with deliberation. The words do not flow easily. But he is a steady worker and a good wage earner. He has established a pleasant home for himself and his family, is as well adjusted to life as the so-called average person, and more deeply satisfied with life than is common.

Having thus toyed with the idea of illustrating from histories that would also show our successes, the conviction won out that it was more important to select those we had learned most from, whether or not they had ended happily. The severest cases were obviously those least likely to end happily, but they were also the ones that showed deepest arrest in personality. They were the cases of children most in need of help. They were also the cases that showed most clearly how many questions still remained, and are therefore the ones that should most invite further study. By selecting children with whom we did not fully succeed we wished also to stress that the treatment of autistic children is by no means a closed chapter, but one that is just beginning to be written.

Since the mute autistic child is even further behind than those who have speech, two of the three histories we chose tell of nonspeaking autistic children: those of Laurie and Marcia. The third history (Joey's) is that of a child who, when he came to us, did not have language in the sense of communication but was at least not entirely mute.

Another decision was whether to include in this volume some of my writings already in print. Quite a bit contained in *Love Is Not Enough* and *Truants From Life* seemed pertinent. But since both books are readily available, it seemed hard to justify repeating them here. As for past papers in scientific journals, only two seemed essential for rounding out this book [1956, 1959]. They were therefore rewritten toward this end, one of them now forming part of the chapter, "Persistence of a Myth." Nevertheless a word here about the treatment philosophy to which I devoted the books named above but which is little spelled out in this volume.

In most institutions I know of the basic approach, even to the psychotic child, is to encourage him to see the world as it really is, which is exactly what the psychotic child cannot do. Instead, our task as we see it is to create for him a world that is totally different from the one he abandoned in despair, and moreover a world he can enter right now, as he is. This means, above all, that he must feel we are with him in his private world and not that he is once more repeating the experience that "everyone wants me to come out of my world and enter his." How, then, is this done?

I speak here of the child's private world, and my former student speaks of "direct confrontation." Each of us is implying in his way that one cannot help another in his ascent from hell unless one has first joined him there, to whatever degree. There is no "direct confrontation" available to the sick child, unless somebody offers himself for the confrontation. This will always, to some degree, mean a descent to one's own hell, however far behind one has left it. It will also, to some degree, become a self-confrontation as one offers oneself to the other. At the same time there is no purpose to such a venture if all that happens is our offering to accept the child in his desolation. What we also have to demonstrate is that together we can make a go of it, even down there—something that he alone at this point cannot do.

Hence at the heart of our work is not any particular knowledge or any procedure as such, but an inner attitude to life and to those caught up in its struggle, even as we are. It is an attitude toward others and why they do what they do, which is first of all an attitude toward oneself and why we do what we do; an attitude that was not even available to us before Freud. Since I have written elsewhere on the nature of this attitude [1966] I shall not repeat myself here. But I hope some day to publish a long-delayed volume on the staff of the School.

As to the writing of this book, in a very real sense I was only one among many co-authors. It was created by all those, staff and children, who were part of the School during the span of years covered in these pages. It was the children who lived out the histories and in large part "wrote" them through what they did and said, or implied through their actions and nonaction. It was the professional staff who enabled them to realize that each of them "has a life to lead of one's own," and who also recorded the children's ascent from hell. These, the written accounts of the staff, plus their thinking about it, and mine, are what make up this book. And even all this would not have sufficed. Ever since its inception Ruth Marquis has been my companion in the creation of the book, more deeply than even in my other writings which owe so much to her; so much so that without her this book would never have come to be.

For the rest, those who contributed most to the writing of the particular histories we chose, and to the children whose stories they tell, will be named at the start of each history. But they too could never have achieved what they did without the many staff members, unnamed here, who made their very significant contributions. And neither professional staff nor children could have gone ahead with their efforts but for our technical staff—the secretaries, the maids, cooks, and janitors—who tendered help daily in the struggles of these most unhappy children.

Since my report, then, rests squarely on the work of the staff, and since in what follows I shall so little refer to their doings, I would like to conclude here with a description of those doings by a master; namely that they

. . . minister to a mind diseas'd,
Pluck from the memory a rooted sorrow,
Raze out the written troubles of the brain,
And with some sweet oblivious antidote
Cleanse the stuff'd bosom of that perilous stuff
Which weighs upon the heart.

I have taken the single liberty here of changing a desperate question to a statement. That this is thinkable now suggests the progress we have made since Shakespeare—not in understanding human needs, because this the poets have known since the beginning of time—but in the art of tendering help.

Where
The Self Begins

First was the golden age . . .
When all were content.
When food came of itself . . .
And spring was everlasting.
Then did milk and sweet nectar
Flow for all.   OVID, *Metamorphoses*

Even in ovid's time what he describes for us here was an ancient
belief. He tells of a world before *Metamorphoses*; a time before change
or development began and when life was eternally good. Each age has
its dreams of a paradise lost, of a golden age once known and enjoyed,
then eternally mourned.

Psychoanalysis teaches that all myths, including those of our beginnings and first home, have their source in the unconscious wish. Often
the same myths are called on to relieve deep anxieties by suggesting that
once we lived without fear or despair and may do so again. Sometimes
the myth contains a kernel of truth, but out of so distant a past that we
can hardly discern, behind the elaborate tales spun around them, what
may once have been familiar historical events.

In Judaeo-Christian mythology this golden age we dream of is the
age of innocence. Long ago, when we were innocent of good and evil
and could never do wrong, a merciful deity stood ready to satisfy our
every desire. But from this brief paradise too, we are fallen forever.

Since then our anxiety, our despair, is that each of us is alone in the world and must fend for himself. Hence our eternal wish for a union that will put an end to our separateness again.

Less obvious is how the same myth tells that man could not stand being less than himself, however briefly. That no sooner was he given everything, without the need to do anything on his own, than he defied the Giver of all things. Man wished to act on his own even if it cost him apartness.

§

The World of the Newborn

This golden age out of the far-distant past is early infancy. And indeed it was an age when nothing was asked of us and all that we wanted was given. This is the kernel of historic and psychological truth in our dreams of a paradise lost. This is when delicious food entered the mouth the moment we opened it hungrily, as the nourishing breast indeed did. Or else the age of eternal satisfaction only seems so when recalled from the immense psychological distance between us and our earliest days.

Though psychoanalysis recognizes the source of our fantasy, it does not always escape the sweeping desire to believe that once in our lives we really had it so good. So while psychoanalysis has more and more to teach us about the anxiety and frustration that may soon be our lot, it continues, for the most part, to view earliest infancy as a time of passivity, an age of primary narcissism when we experience the self as being all.

Actually, others enter our lives in those very first days, and in some minimal ways shatter the solipsistic existence. Equally important, it is an age when the human being just born takes important steps in trying actively to master his fate. True, when viewed from our perspective, his steps seem few and infinitely small, interrupted as they are by long periods of sleep. What is overlooked is that the infant sleeps long perhaps just because the learning is so intense and exhausting. Much as it may seem to the naive observer that little development took place in the millenia when man struggled toward speech, so it only seems to us that the infant does little at the start.

Because of his obvious dependence on others for survival, because there is so little the infant can do for himself, we conclude he does nothing at all. (This conviction his own mother does not usually share.) So far as the outer world is concerned, we assume that either he does not perceive it, or that he responds, if at all, on a purely instinctual level. That is, we assume that psychologically he does not yet exist, or responds only to bodily sensations like hunger.

According to the *American Handbook of Psychiatry,*

Within that twilight stage of early life . . . the infant shows no signs of perceiving anything beyond his own body. He seems to live in a world of inner
stimuli. . . . Whereas the enteroceptive [system] functions from birth, the
perceptual-conscious system, the sensorium, is not yet cathected. This lack
of peripheral sensory cathexis only gradually seems to give way to sensory
perception, particularly to distance perception of the outside world.

In a similar vein Spitz [1962] writes:

From the dynamic point of view the baby's attitude and behavior are anaclitic. . . . Due to the infant's helplessness, the anaclitic relationship encom-
passes the totality of the infant's commerce with the surround.

Thus psychoanalysis creates its own myth of the infant's golden age,
when all his wants are taken care of by others and he neither wishes or
needs to do anything on his own.

We as adults know how helpless the infant really is, but the infant
does not know it. And while our view seems objectively correct, it tells
us nothing about his subjective experience. Yet by thus projecting our
views into the inner life of the infant we are kept from assessing correctly his psychological experience of the world.

Contrary to such views I believe that in his nursing, for example,
the infant is eminently active in what to him is a central event in his
life. At such times he may not feel he is moving mountains, but as if
he were sucking them dry. To regard such an experience as anaclitic,
as utterly passive, contradicts the infant's experience. Because to him it
is not his real dependence that counts, but the conviction that his efforts
are monumental. Fortunately such views are slowly being presented both
in psychoanalytic writings and in academic psychology.

Kohut [1959], for example, suggests that

[the state] of the healthy infant at the breast should be compared with the
emotional state of an adult who is totally absorbed in an activity of the utmost importance to him as, for example, the sprinter at the last few yards of
the 100-yard dash, the virtuoso at the height of the cadenza, or the lover at
the peak of sexual union.

And Josselyn [1962] speaks of how we fantasy "with nostalgic longing
that in infancy manna flowed from heaven."[1]

1. More specifically, she writes: "Our professional language and theories have
not kept up with our knowledge of infant behavior. . . . A striking example of the
inaccurate use of words to conceptualize infant behavior is the description, so often
found in the literature, of the neonate as 'passively receptive.' . . . At no time during
the sucking period is an infant passive. The nursing sequence is characterized by an
active sucking, active seeking for an object to suck, and active participation in de-

While both authors are critical of the dominant psychoanalytic view of the infant's passivity, being psychoanalysts, they stress the infant's being active around the oral experience. This makes good sense insofar as much of his interest seems focused on the nursing which for so long we considered instinctual. But more and more we begin to realize that almost from the beginning of life the infant also takes note of his world, pays deliberate attention.

Psychologists, for example, have studied visual pursuit in the newborn and Fantz [1958] demonstrates that not only do infants observe and follow objects as early as eighteen hours after birth, but that during the very first weeks of life they also discriminate between various geometric shapes. Wolff and White [1965] demonstrate that three- to four-day-old infants not only follow objects with their eyes, but also rotate their heads to follow better. More important, their study shows convincingly that infants do this best if they are "in a condition of quiet alertness analogous to the adult attentive state."

So the infant's paying attention to and observing of the outside world has much in common with our own state of attention. He is distracted, as are we, when emotionally too preoccupied. And how well he can pay attention depends on how often he can be in a state of "quiet alertness." Conversely, the more he finds himself preoccupied or needful at all waking times, or even emotionally perturbed, the less he will be able to observe and eventually understand.

In short, how "quietly alert" an infant is, and how much chance he has to be active in observing the world, may have far-reaching consequences for his later development. This is vastly different from a view of early development that is based, for example, on how well the child's oral needs are being satisfied.

For our own part, we have found, as we worked more intensively with autistic children, that at the core of their disturbance was not (or not crucially) that they lacked for any passive satisfactions. Those satisfactions were very easy for us to provide. Some autistic children accepted the offered satisfactions and remained autistic; others rejected them. None moved out of the autistic position because of them. This they did only if and when we were able to activate them. Contrary to reports on "symbolic realization" [Sechehaye, 1951] which view the patient as much too passive, and which ascribe his improvement to the therapist's actions, we found that neither those actions nor the satisfac-

riving nourishment from that object. . . . The infant's exhaustion ending in sleep, occurring when adequate nutrition is not obtained, is the measure of the actual expenditure of energy." Balint too, in an earlier paper [1949], stressed that "contrary to common parlance the child is not suckled, indeed it sucks actively."

tion of instinctual needs (except the need to be active) sparked the return of these children to life. They came to life only when we were able to create the conditions, or otherwise be the catalysts, that induced them to take action in their own behalf.

It is precisely because nursing is one of the infant's more crucial activities that what happens around it is so important. But so is what happens around his early observation of the world—whether we foster it or squelch it. Nursing, for example, is itself a compound experience of which the actual sucking and intake of food are only a very significant part; other parts of it, too, make a difference. Whether the infant is gently or rigidly held; how securely or anxiously; whether he is carefully "heard," or emotionally ignored—all this and more will make for his comfort or discomfort at the moment, and will influence his later development. But however important, these conditions cannot compare in significance with the central activity they surround: the infant's nursing and being nursed, and how much chance it affords him to actively shape the total experience in terms of his own needs.

Because while the infant can make it clear, through the way he holds his body, whether or not he feels comfortably held, he cannot ensure that this active expression of his feelings will meet with a positive response. That will depend on how the mother reacts. While he can and does act in his own behalf, his view of himself and the world will depend on the failure or success of his efforts. Consistent nonreward for being active may even lead to his giving up trying to shape his interactions and yield to passivity. The same is true for the way he adjusts to being picked up or diapered or bathed. When he is active, be it in nursing, or in watching the world, he is at the height of his encounter with life. But how his activity succeeds, and the response it receives, will significantly color all his later attempts at self-motivated action.

I have said before that recent observations of newborns indicate they are active and are influenced by their environment much sooner than was thought up to recently. We know, for example, that the baby's head movements as he responds to touch on the cheek and the lips are among his most mature behavioral responses. These are present in the fetus as early as at eight and one-half weeks [Hooker, 1952]. And in the newborn, his head movements lead in activity those body parts that relate reflexly to the position of the head [Gesell, 1938]. But none of this guarantees that the newborn baby, on his own, can assure himself of adequate nursing through the movements of his head. If they do not, he may turn apathetic, or fight off the mother.

There are newborn babies who fight (or "box") the mother even with their fists.

This is a typical action of a baby when it is in anoxia. These babies protest as soon as they are put to the breast [if they become anoxic because of] the obstruction of the airway either by the upper lip going up over the nostrils or by the breast covering the nostrils. The curious thing is that no mother or nurse apparently looks to see what this part of the lip is doing, or to notice if it blocks the airway; so when a baby who has experienced nasal obstruction is put to the breast, it cries and boxes itself off. Then the attendant midwife shoves a bit harder to get the baby on and it boxes even more. You have only got to have this fight two or three times and from then on the baby cries as you turn it toward the mother. . . . Usually the whole thing has developed by the second or third day. . . . Generally speaking this is a situation which no mother can endure, it is literally frightful for the mother. Mothers who have endured it lose all wish to feed the baby because they cannot bear being so rejected by the baby [Gunther, 1961].

In thus fighting the mother the infant deals actively with his fate. But Call [1964], in an opposite example, tells of an infant who was seemingly overpowered by his mother very early. She took over the feeding relation so entirely that his anticipatory behavior was squelched.

The mother fed the infant lying down and was extremely skillful in rapidly inserting a large amount of her nipple, areola, and breast into the infant's mouth before there was any opportunity for the infant to do anything other than bring its hands up to its own mouth adjacent to the mother's body, thus accommodating the mother's skillful and rapid breast insertion. Follow-up of this infant three months later revealed the same wide opening of the mouth and forward movement of the head when the infant's mouth was approached with a tongue blade.

These examples show that the infant is as active as the environment and his biological equipment permits. They are further instructive because they show that if things go wrong, the mother and her newborn child may enter a struggle that moves quickly from bad to worse. Soon the baby averts his face or even hits the mother, which the mother interprets as meaning she is not a good mother, instead of investigating to see what went wrong. And partly it is true: she was not attuned enough to her baby to find out what went wrong. Or perhaps she was so insecure that she condemned herself before she could see that nursing was only impeded by the position of her breast, or because the baby's own lip was in the way.

Some babies, according to Wolff's observations, seem to turn away from stimuli like the breast in what looks like an avoidance reaction. If this happens, then what follows depends largely on the mother's response. Some mothers interpret this as rejection; feeling turned down in the best they can offer—mother care and their own body—they in turn reject the infant. Other mothers do not interpret it this way at all. They conclude that the baby has overshot the mark or doesn't know any better, and try patiently to help him find the nipple. Once back on the breast and sucking well, the baby's reaction changes, and from avoiding the stimulus he roots for it avidly again [Wolff, 1964].

All of which may indicate why nursing and what happens around it seems to be the nuclear experience out of which develop all later feelings about oneself and other persons—so important is it, this initial experience of having acted on one's own within a context of mutuality, of having known what it is to be fully active, of having shaped the experience in spite of one's otherwise dependent state.

Conversely, when the infant is kept from being active in the relation on his own terms, or when his actions evoke no response, he becomes flooded with impotent rage, a helpless victim of inner tensions. According to Erikson [1958] this experience is "the ontogenetic source of the sense of evil, a 'basic mistrust' which combines a sense of mistrustfulness and of untrustworthiness."

That is why breast feeding remains the best paradigm of how combined action leads to a sense of trust in oneself and other persons. Too often, however, it is accepted as such unexamined, on faith. For it is neither mother love, nor food, nor the skin contact between mother and child that accounts for its essence. Certainly this essence does not lie in its being an "oral" experience related to a particular mucous membrane or a specific erogenous zone, though all these help the experience along. While mother love is immensely important, it too becomes significant mainly as it conditions what goes on—first in the nursing experience and later in all other interactions between mother and child. What conditions the later ability to relate—which, after all, comes from within us—is our inner experience during these first interactions with the world.

Nursing, then, is an exceptional experience in which combined action, engaged in by two persons out of their separate personal wants, leads to relief of tension and to emotional satisfaction in both. (The same is true of mutually satisfying sexual intercourse.) The pleasure of mothering, the pleasant tactile and kinesthetic sensations, add greatly to the depth of satisfaction. But they only add, they do not account for it.

For breast feeding to be fully satisfying, the child must be hungry for food and the mother must want relief from the pressure of milk in her breast. Then, in the infant's sucking and the mother's nursing, both take action to relieve a bodily tension and also satisfy an emotional need. This process of mutuality is vastly superior to common action for an external goal and contains all essentials of a truly intimate, personal relation. For it is chiefly in personal relations that both outer achievement and inner satisfaction result from combined action.[2]

2. Others have used different terms and examples for the same phenomenon. Spitz

None of the higher mammals has been studied so completely as the dog. What is relevant here is that newborn puppies are as comparatively helpless as human babies, though they develop toward maturity much faster. And for them, as for other higher animals studied, it is not true that the pleasure of eating leads to socialization and attachment. Brodbeck [1954] fed half of his experimental group of puppies by hand, while the other half never saw the person who fed them. But when, apart from feeding times, both groups had the same chance for contact with him, they all developed an equal attachment to him.

Scott and Fuller [1965] summarize evidence from a variety of other experiments. They conclude that however attractive and simple the theory—that feeding creates the emotional bond between mother and offspring, and that this is the basis of the child's later more generalized attachments—the theory does not stand up under scrutiny. What actually happens is that

the process of forming an emotional attachment to members of the parent species is largely independent of outside circumstances. . . . The essential mechanism appears to be *an internal process acting on the external environment.* . . . To state it more clearly: a young animal automatically becomes attached to individuals and objects with which it comes into contact during the critical period [and] there is a high probability that a critical period for primary socialization exists in human development [italics added].

As a matter of fact, breast feeding can even hinder the forming of personal relations. Among the Manus of New Guinea, according to Mead [1958],

the mother's breast is treated as a piece of plumbing entirely under the control of the child. Instead of the mother taking her breast and giving it to the child in what is a complementary interpersonal relationship, here is a mother who happens to have a piece of rubber tubing attached to the front of her

---

[1962] talks of reciprocity and defines it as "the circular exchange of affectively charged action between mother and child." He uses the example of "a mother putting the nipple of the milk bottle into the mouth of her seven-month-old. He reciprocates by putting his finger into her mouth; she answers by moving her lips on his fingers, whereupon he twiddles his fingers and she responds with a smile; all the while he stares at her face with rapt attention."

I prefer the term mutuality to reciprocity because to reciprocate (according to Webster) involves an "alternative moving back and forth," while mutual is defined as "exerted by each with respect to the other." But the difference in viewpoints goes beyond any mere choice of words.

Sander [1962], among others, suggests the terms interaction and interactional. These come closer to what is implied in mutuality, though I think it less appropriate because of the connotation of in-between, as contained in the "inter." His paper stresses what goes on between mother and child, while I wish to emphasize what goes on within each of them. There is no automatic relation between the two—what goes on between people, and what goes on within them—though the one deeply influences the other.

person, which happens to be connected with the milk, and the child grabs it, pulls it, pushes it, yanks it around, and there is a more or less continuous battle over it between the mother and the child.

Conversely, whenever an infant's activity is encouraged within a relation of deep mutuality, even language is not always needed to foster human attachments, though it helps greatly. Along with the cooing and later the infant's prattle, all his expressive movements are a form of communication that go a long way toward establishing his relations with the environment. No less than words, they can frighten or worry or delight us. Most of all they stimulate the mother and permit a reciprocal exchange which will normally develop into social games. This is why, when given both—enough encouragement to be active on his own, and enough part in combined actions, in mutuality—even the mute and deaf child manages to relate and communicate, though he lacks even archaic forms of language.

§

Body Language

How the infant's activity and the mutual give and take between mother and infant can be furthered or squelched becomes readily observable during the supplementary feedings that infants are given nowadays, as early as the second or third week of life. As the mother spoon-feeds her baby, he can be encouraged in his spontaneous efforts to be active in the feeding process. At first he may merely try to finger her moving arm. Later on he may attempt to get his fingers in the food, and eventually make a grab for the spoon.

In this last situation, the mother may prematurely coax him not only to help, but to do it all by himself, a tendency not unusual with the present widespread push to make children independent as early as possible. While activity is thus encouraged, it is done at the expense of mutuality, because the infant is expected too soon to manage on his own. I do not say such a child will become autistic. But his pattern of relating to others may become constricted; again, not by this single experience, but by a totality of parallels that flow from the same manner of rearing.

In other cases the mother inhibits her baby's efforts to do things on his own. Here, too, mutuality is blocked, though in different ways. Since not only mutuality but activity are inhibited, the consequences may be more serious. And if here too the same pattern extends over all or most interactions between mother and child, then infantile autism is a possible outcome.

For example, in later infancy the child may try to grab the spoon his mother feeds him with and experience how she firmly—perhaps even gently—returns his hands to his sides so that food will not spill or the feeding process go on for too long. Not only is he frustrated in trying to do for himself, but also in attempting to make the feeding a mutual process. And if, in addition, the mother carefully wipes his mouth after every spoonful—however gently—the disapproval of how he eats will again not be lost on the child.

I use this example because it has also been observed how the mother of a blind or deaf child will let her infant grab the spoon and hold it with her; will enjoy his clumsy and ineffective efforts at helping her feed him and at feeding himself; will share his enjoyment of food though it gets messy around the mouth. In this way they establish mutuality around spoon-feeding although the blind child cannot see the pleasure on her face, nor the deaf child hear the pleasure in her voice.

A film produced by Mittelman, Malkenson, and Munro [1959] records the expressive movements (or affectomotor patterns) of infancy. In one sequence centering around a feeding situation the child points definitely to the morsel he wants and the mother then feeds it to him. It is fascinating to watch the back-and-forth in the infant's desire to feed himself. It is still much more comfortable to be fed by the mother. Yet her visible delight at the baby's expression of his desire to feed himself leads to a social game around the feeding that makes it more pleasurable to both. It is a perfect example of how good relations between mother and infant permit both of them to find a solution that implies respect for the child's autonomous decisions while still assuring him of dependent care.

Despite all this, the infant does not become active through the experience of mutuality alone. Life is certainly with others. But from the very beginning it is also lived for and with our own selves.

Where, then, does the human personality begin? Normal development happens so smoothly that we take little note of the natural sequence of events. For example, I have suggested that while the infant is active from the start, he is not trying to communicate anything by his action. While he may box himself off from the breast, it is not at all his intention to communicate, "I am suffocating." He is not aware of any listener and intends only to fight free in order to breathe. But if all goes well, things are not this way with the mother.

Whether consciously or not, she senses that she communicates her feelings to the baby by the very way she responds. Though the infant cannot read her message in all its complexity, he may soon react to whether her emotions are mainly positive, negative, or ambivalent. Thus while communication starts from the moment of birth, it begins as a one-sided action. There is no two-way communication as yet.

This is hard to demonstrate for humans from our present knowledge of earliest infant development, but it can be demonstrated for other mammals. The animal mother does something for the newborn baby: for example, she licks it and thus cleans it. The young of some species cannot survive if she fails to do that, and many mammals, if they are separated from the mother for those few hours after birth, will grow up but will not mate, will remain indifferent to others of their kind. Thus in meeting some need of the infant, the animal mother must also communicate something of greatest importance to the baby who obviously receives it, but may not respond yet with a message of his own.

It may be that the baby also begins to relate. For in this action by the mother (or this interaction, if it is such) the infant animal seems to receive the seeds of relatedness from the mother's licking him clean right after birth, though it may be months or years before the hidden seed blossoms as the animal matures.

Typically for the human infant, relating and communicating have their roots in his cooing or crying, and the mother's appropriate and positive response. As she helps him sort out pain from hunger through her different responses, and as different ministrations relieve different forms of discomfort, the infant learns to distinguish between his own feelings of discomfort. As the sense of discomfort becomes less diffuse, becomes located by which part of the body senses it most keenly, the feeling of self (or the body ego) begins to develop.

Once an expression of feelings (crying or smiling) has been accepted as the signal for a specific event by mother and child—and this can be a particular movement or wail of the child responded to by a special reassuring action or noise from the mother—communication has been established. One has left solipsism then, and can join in the experience of another.

Again in normal development, the smooth manner in which a mother cares for her infant in ways that best suit his development often obscures the many separate steps in the process. Only some of these steps have by now become apparent, and of these I will sketch only a few.

For example, the mother's good care—the consistent manner in which she responds to the baby's at first random expressions of vague inner pressures—slowly induces him to shape the expression of his needs, and later also his feelings. This he does first through typical expressions which soon become particular signals that both understand. The connections he then makes between inner pressures and the various signals he gives bring them into some order. They become more concrete, lead to a differentiated awareness of the body. The infant also becomes interested in that part of reality which meets his now more specific needs, and provides comfort.

But even all this is still akin to a conditioning process, although it is an inner signal from the self (cry, smile) that evokes an action from the external world—as opposed to conditioned responses where an outside signal evokes an inner response. There is by no means self-awareness as yet. There is still not a person, aware of trying to get something from another person who is recognized as such. All there is at this point is a striving to gain comfort and avoid discomfort, to observe and take note.

By now the infant has repeatedly experienced that his needs are not always or immediately met. And the manageable frustration that follows is what makes him aware that an outer world even exists. The emphasis here is on the *manageable*. Because otherwise the child is so flooded by unpleasant emotions that nothing else seems to exist. Blotted out is the barely emerging awareness of a world that responds. Thus the child's expectation that something outside of him will satisfy his needs is what powerfully increases his interest in the world and his impulse to learn more about it.

In a next and crucial step he fathoms that he, through his own efforts, through signals or the giving of signs, has been able to influence the external world—and this is the point at which he begins to become a social being. If his efforts keep succeeding, then eventually he wants to make the advantage a permanent one by coming to terms with this something outside him that has the power to satisfy or frustrate. This coming to terms requires a liminal notion of a self evoking, manipulating, influencing a nonself. The wish, on the child's part, to manipulate the nonself is expressed first through efforts at one-sided control. Only when this does not work does he slowly develop a sense of the advantage of mutuality and with it a first conscious responsiveness to others.

Thus while the infant can feel, can observe and give expression to sensations—can in some fashion respond to other persons and objects long before language or some equivalent develops, there is no self as yet, nor can he relate. This happens only after the following sequence: First his own efforts to make contact with others, must have given him some minimal distinction between himself and the nonself. Second, this vague distinction must have been verified by some kind of repeated communication.

Appropriate responses to these expressions of the infant's will soon validate them enough so that crying and smiling become signals for specific events both to him and to others. The damage suffered, if the infant's expression of emotions is not met with validation from the outside, have been described by Spitz and others [Spitz, 1945, Spitz and Wolf, 1949].

This is why artificial feeding times, arranged according to the clock, can dehumanize the infant. The reason is not just that time-clock feeding is contrary to the natural rhythms of the body, or that it signifies a mechanical ordering of time and of the mother-child relation. More important here is that it prevents the infant from feeling that *his* actions (crying, smiling) have a significant effect on this important life experience of being fed.

What humanizes the infant is not being fed, changed, or picked up when he feels the need for it, though they add greatly to his comfort and feeling of well-being. Nor does irregular care necessarily dehumanize, though it will tend to make him dissatisfied with life or may cause poor development or sickness. It is rather the experience that *his* crying for food brings about *his* satiation by others according to *his* timing that makes it a socializing and humanizing experience. It is that *his* smile, or facial grimacing, evokes a parallel or otherwise appropriate response in the mother.

Conversely, the experience that his own actions (cry or smile) make no difference is what stops him from becoming a human being, for it discourages him from interacting with others and hence from forming a personality through which to deal with the environment.

Smile and cry remain crucial examples because through both an emotion is communicated while at the same time an influence is exerted which together bring about the intended result. To act on the environment is hence not enough for developing a human personality. To it must be added the ability to communicate emotions and to experience an appropriate emotional reply. It is an extremely debilitating experience if our emotions fail to meet with a fitting reply. The joke that fails to amuse, the loving gesture that goes unanswered, are some of the most painful experiences. And if we consistently and from an early age fail to meet the appropriate response to our expression of emotions, we stop communicating with others and eventually lose interest in the world.

But even this is not all. Unless we can also influence reality, things are just as destructive for our efforts to develop a personality. If the child's hungry cry met with only deep sympathy for the pain he expressed, and not also with food, the results would be as bad as if there had been no emotional response. This is an unlikely example, since the child must be fed, to survive. But should his smile, inviting to play, be met with even the tenderest smile from the parent but lead to no playing, then too, both environment and the wish to communicate one's feeling lose all interest.

One could argue, of course, that many infants were fed by the clock and eventually grew up to be fine human beings. But this only means that for them the conviction of being able to affect significant aspects of their environment was not acquired around feeding but around other situations. No one situation excludes all others in equipping the infant with the conviction that he can, through his own actions, change the conditions of his life. And so long as we do not have much more knowledge about which experiences are specially pregnant here, compared to others, we must assume that any situation permitting the child to feel "master of his fate" is as good as any other to help him develop into a full human being.

The importance of this entire process for the development of a self can hardly be overrated. With it, the ego expands from one that only acts into one that interacts, that responds to others and becomes slowly aware that it can modify their responses. This is different from the self-contained activity of observing, or paying attention, though the one depends deeply on the other. But first must have come the emotional experience of having something of a self that can act, and of its connection to something outside that responds.

In order for this to happen, the mother must have wished all along to relate to the child in mutuality. But for some time she must not expect the child to contribute, and later must not expect him to do that except in step by small step. If the child has all along known the experience of mutuality, as in nursing, it then helps him to develop it in his personal relations.

Winnicott [1953], among others, recognized the importance of the mother's meeting the child's needs through her own adaptive responses. He writes:

The good enough mother . . . starts off with an almost complete adaptation to her infant's needs, and as time proceeds she adapts less and less completely, gradually, according to the infant's growing ability to deal with her failure. . . . If all goes well the infant can actually come to gain from the experience of frustration, since incomplete adaptation to need makes objects real. . . . Nevertheless at the start adaptation needs to be almost exact, and unless this is so it is not possible for the infant to begin to develop a capacity to experience a relationship. . . . The mother, at the beginning, by almost 100 per cent adaptation affords the infant the opportunity for the illusion that her breast is part of the infant.

Despite the above I feel that Winnicott views the infant as much too passive in this process of adaptation. True, most of the adaptation must come from the mother; at first nearly all of it. But the infant too is active from the start and adapts from the very beginning. The issue here is that mother and infant adapt in radically different ways. The mother adapts to the infant, and ideally her adaptation will end in the satisfaction of his and her needs. The infant, on the other hand, adapts only for his own ends, with only the most limited means, and without any regard for the mother's needs. For the rest Winnicott is correct: growth occurs as the infant, too, slowly begins to adapt to the mother.

Let me cite a typical example of how an instinctive action, based on one-sided need, can lead to an experience of mutuality: the young child extends his arms, and this is interpreted as a signal that he wishes to be picked up. In terms of evolution this is a very old instinctive reaction of the primate baby who feels lost, and would indeed soon get lost, did it not cling to the animal mother. When primate infants cling to their mothers they do so with arms and legs extended, clutching the mother's flank.

Similarly, human infants from a certain age on extend both arms and legs when an adult appears [Bowlby, 1958]. If picked up, the child increases the closeness to the mother on his own, through his clinging. But when the response to him is positive he learns that reaching out to gain closeness increases his well-being. He learns also that whether this happens or not depends on the response of another person, and that his own actions could and did evoke that response. Here the essence of what is communicated is the value of combined action, where one's solitary action might fail.

Later on, communication through spoken language and even more so in silent thought is how we normally grasp and make contact with reality. Even nursing becomes far more effective with language. For out of the one signal of the cry come the separate language symbols for "hurt" (where nutrition would bring no relief) and for "hunger" (where nutrition *would* bring relief).

§

Mutuality

All this and much more happens smoothly where the mother's desire for mutuality does not make her expect it too soon. If she expects her child to relate before enough experience with need satisfaction has led him to recognize that some part of reality (the mother) has positive value for him, she may be too disappointed. If her disappointment is severe her responses will reflect it, and the child may not only fail to develop any wish to relate, he may even lose interest in reality, or at least in trying to influence it. The same may happen if the mother expects too little. If she assumes the infant cannot adapt, she may stymie his efforts in that direction. By not encouraging or responding to his actions she may force him to exist only or mainly as an extension of herself, as the passive object of her care.

Having said all this, it should be stated emphatically that no mother can, even at the start of her baby's life, adapt entirely to his needs, nor later adapt perfectly as he adjusts to her and the world. There will always be times when even the best and most responsive of mothers will expect too much of her infant, and at other times, or in other respects, too little. In the end she is a human being, variable and fallible. Were she not, her child would have little chance to test his adaptive capacities against reality, nor would her behavior ever challenge these to develop. Even the best of mothers is tired after childbirth, is sleepy during night feedings, sometimes picks up the infant too quickly, too forcefully, too gingerly.

Much as I have cautioned against the myth of the blissful infant, so I would caution here against the correlate myth of the perfect, all-giving mother we all wish we had had. Saints may be needed in heaven, but they rarely make good parents. At least we hear little of their having had children or having raised them successfully.

What I am trying to suggest is that since the infant is only capable of small adaptations, what he thrives on are the mother's small adaptations to him. The mother who picks up her infant too vigorously, but quickly relaxes her hold as she senses an unhappy response—she is the mother who provides him with examples of how a very small adaptation can make a great deal of difference. And this he will try to emulate. Conversely, a mother may sense in her infant a small negative reaction to the way she holds him and tense up in fear. She is afraid she is a bad mother who does not know how to hold her baby. Or else she decides that his negative response is directed against her; that he is a bad child who does not love being held in her arms. So she is the mother who is likely to firm up her grip, and in doing so prove to the child that his efforts at bettering his lot, at adapting to how she holds him, have no such results and are better given up.

It seems so unjust, but in regard to motherhood, too, it appears that to those who have will be given, and from those who have not will be taken away. The mother who feels secure as a mother is readily able to adapt her reactions to the tiny cues of her infant, and in doing so support his growing adaptation to her and her ways. The anxious mother, on the other hand, responds defensively to her baby's efforts to adapt to her because for one reason or another they make her anxious. As she stymies his responses and they become fewer, or disappear, she is ever more at sea about how best to care for his needs.

Here, as everywhere in life, fate plays a great and at times decisive role. Infants are born with differing endowments, intelligence, temperaments. However great the influence of our earliest experience, and all later ones that build on them, they can only modify the endowment we are born with. Inheritance is fate in this respect. A very fast mother will find it difficult to gear her rhythm to her very slow child even if she tries, because to move that slowly demands too large an adaptation of her.

Similarly, a hyperactive baby may be too much for a slow-moving mother who cannot speed up her reactions, even if she wants to. Thus the mother and infant whose patterns of reacting are too far apart may have to start from a common base line that is much harder for each of them to reach and maintain than is true for the mother and infant whose temperament, rhythm, and sensitivity mesh together much better. Again life can be very unjust in that mutuality and the rewards for adaptation are so much easier to come by for some than for others.

Normally, however, the infant's reactions will not differ too radically from his mother's, or she will be able to make the needed adjustments. So from the very beginning he will not only seek and respond to body comfort, but will soon interact with his environment. The sooner his actions leave the realm of chance or of random behavior the better. First he has learned to gear them to the environment, however minutely, and to expect certain responses from it. And second, if things go well, he has learned that some consequences of his actions are predictable. These are the basic preconditions for personality development. With it a vague feeling of selfness develops into a self. Or to put it differently, the ego that begins by reacting to inner and outer stimuli slowly engages in goal-directed actions that presuppose some awareness of a goal and how to reach it.

Being active, if this trait is to flourish in the child, must be tested for its value in gaining specific, anticipated results. That there is a critical age when this happens is a decided possibility for some birds and animals, and a well-documented fact for others.

But if this were all I would not be discussing bird behavior. What counts is that the decisive factor is whether, and to what degree, the little bird is active on his own during this time. As Hess [1959] observes of the mallard duck, for example, the more effort he must expend in following the mother (or some experimental substitute), the more successful the imprinting. So even for this comparatively lower species, the infant's acting on his own toward a goal is of crucial importance, above and beyond what was once called instinctive behavior.

Among primates, so much closer to us, parental reaction to the infant's spontaneous activity is also crucial. Carpenter [1934] describes how the howler monkeys care for their very young. At the beginning, their concern goes so far as to react to the mere breaking of a tree limb because it might have been caused by an infant's fall. "The cracking of a limb under the weight of an animal may set the males roaring" and the females rush to pick up the fallen child. This is the early phase of development during which little initiative is expected of the infant. But the next stage of development is one he calls "a transition stage between complete dependence of the infant on the mother . . . and complete independence." During this period "Howler mothers control and condition their infants by facilitating their 'spontaneous' activity at times, and on other occasions by restricting it."[3]

Thus spontaneous action within a social context, and the encouragement toward it, seem crucial to the development of independence, not only in humans but also in primates; while being active in the learning process seems of crucial importance even for the subprimate species.

As I have indicated before, the literature on mother-child relations has in my opinion overstressed the child's need to passively receive. By comparison it has neglected the fact that from the very beginning the infant needs not only to be cuddled and held, but to actively cling. I believe that the need of many young children to cling to a transitional object (a stuffed animal, a baby blanket, etc.) so vividly described by Winnicott [1953] represents spontaneous efforts to provide themselves with the experience of active clinging which was too little present in their relations to their mothers.

Among primates, it is enough that the baby's cry brings the mother's presence. Once he can cling to any part of her body, he can find the nipple on his own. But for the human infant clinging is not so useful a tool because he cannot get at the breast on his own, even if the mother is in reach. And in Western society, with the prevalence of non-nursing mothers, even if the human infant could get at the breast it would not help much. He would still have to cry for his food.

I believe there is another reason why clinging in the human infant cannot affect his development as it seems to in the animal where clinging appears essential for the later mating of many mammals and for the socialization of primates. The reason is that the primate baby clings actively to the mother's fur. This being active in the interchange may be

3. Sander [1962] is aware of what mutuality and adaptation require on the part of the mother. He recognizes five distinct stages which he calls "period of initial adaptation, of reciprocal exchange, of early directed activity, of focalization on mother, and of self-assertion." Crucial in each of them is "to what degree . . . will the mother's behavior be specifically appropriate to the baby's state and to the cues he gives of it?"

as crucial for the monkey as it is for the imprinting of birds. Much as the human baby may wish to be active in holding on to his mother, he has little chance, short of fingering the breast or her face as he nurses, or holding on to her finger in his grasping reflex. Nor is the holding on likely to go with much body or skin contact between them. In this area of experience the human infant seems disadvantaged from the start.

Unfortunately the mutuality of clinging is all too little studied in human infants. Perhaps the nursing experience would be vastly more satisfying if the mother could respond with emotional freedom to feeling large areas of her skin against her baby's skin. Then being held to the mother's body might be as important for the human infant as it seems to be in the animal. Certainly in those societies I have any knowledge about the mother's bodily responses are inhibited enough to rule out a total sharing of the experience of holding on and being clung to.

As the infant grows, he learns that crying is not the only way he can bring about the mother's presence in order to cling. Bowlby [1958], in reviewing the literature, discusses how the infant who tries, through his crying, to bring the mother to his side later becomes very active in seeking out her presence on his own.

The tendency to remain within sight or earshot of their mothers . . . is particularly easily evoked if the child is tired, hungry, or in pain; it is also immediately activated if the child is afraid. . . . In many, a zenith seems to be reached in the period eighteen to thirty months. This late dating may come as a surprise, especially to those who, equating psychological attachment with physiological dependence, presume that attachment must be at its maximum soon after birth."

Bowlby then adds that on the basis of his experience, "fully as many psychological disturbances, including the most severe, can date from the second year of life when clinging and following are at their peak as from the early months when they are rudimentary."

We too have been astonished at how often the history of autistic children showed no obvious deviation or traumatization at the earliest age, though it may have occurred. Instead the children were reported as developing more or less normally up to about eighteen or twenty-four months, matching the ages in Bowlby's report. This is an age when the infant still has many needs he cannot fill by himself, but through walking and talking is beginning to try to get what he wants on his own.

Again and again in the history of our mute autistic children we find the statement, often fully verified, that they began to speak normally. Then after the rudiments of speech were acquired—that is, after they could say a few words—they slowly gave up talking, or dropped it suddenly. That is, speech was developed in an effort to influence the environment, but was given up when it failed in this purpose. The child does not withdraw from all efforts at relating because his needs are not adequately met—though this too will scar the personality. He withdraws when these efforts find him less able to modify the environment than before.

Here, the parental observations of their autistic children are significant. Most of their accounts of the child's first year indicate that the autistic child was quiet, a good child; that in the second year he amused himself on his own, often with stereotyped, empty activity, such as humming to music or turning the pages of a book. But that their behavior was strange, out of the ordinary, did not catch the attention of parents or pediatrician until the second year of life.

Isn't it possible that what these children showed, during the first year of life, was only a lowered level of activity? That they only became autistic at the age when spontaneous goal-directed activity is part of normal development, in addition to the earlier behavior that is no less spontaneous but not consciously purposeful? That is: quiet and isolated children they were, even before their second year; but autistic children they became only when their reaching out to relations led to what they viewed as destructive responses. This, in my opinion, is why they gave up all initiative.

Certainly things happened this way for Marcia. The first activity that brought her out of her total isolation was a chasing game where the important thing was that she initiated all action and we had to passively, but with enjoyment, follow her lead. Above all we were not permitted to touch her.

Just as the primate infant who has fallen from a tree or is momentarily lost must be recaptured, and just as his clinging precedes his nursing, so we had to play at recapturing Marcia for several years before she would deal with any feeding or nursing experience. Our willingness to seek her out so that eventually she could cling to us, and her wish to do that actively on her own, all this had to be regained before she let us nurse her. As with primate babies, mutuality in the clinging response certainly preceded by far any mutuality in nursing for this human child.

The Harlows' experiments, on the other hand [Harlow, 1959; Harlow and Harlow, 1962], show that activity without response can be fatal. Monkey babies raised with terrycloth mothers could do all the clinging they wished. They grew, they gained weight, seemed to be doing all right, until such time in development as they would normally have socialized and mated. This they could not or would not do.

Thus the child's active grasping for mutuality will not do, if the reaching out is not met by a parallel enjoyment in the mother at being clung to; if the result is not a process of mutual interaction. For the human infant, it seems that feeding, cuddling, diapering, bathing, humming, singing, and talking to him will have to achieve what clinging and being held, feeding and being fed does for the baby monkey.

Bottle feeding, for example, can support mutuality nearly as completely as nursing from the breast, provided the culture favors mutuality. Pavenstedt [1965] observed five Japanese mothers of children from thirteen to seventeen months of age, four of whom were still breast feeding and the fifth not. The fifth mother was unable to nurse because of a breast abscess that developed at six weeks. "She was almost tearful about it and hastened to assure me that she tried to make up to the child for the loss." But the way she bottle-fed her child is described as follows:

Mother . . . gives him the bottle . . . She lays him down, drinking, and proceeds to lie down beside him. . . . While he drinks, she holds the bottle and looks directly into his eye—it looks almost hypnotic. She smiles at him tenderly and he smiles back. Very soon he rolls over on his side, facing her, and the tender interchange continues. When he tries to kick, she undoes the blanket around his feet to give him more freedom and does not interfere with his sucking his thumb. She shows no impatience and for an hour continues to try to lull him by stroking his head and face. He begins to explore her face and she allows him to. Eventually he just rolls away from her, off his mattress, and so she takes him downstairs again.

Pavenstedt adds, "I felt I had been a witness of a tender love scene."

In short, how active the baby will be in his early experience with mutuality, to what degree his own contributions are allowed to make it more satisfying—these are apt to greatly influence what autonomy he will later achieve.

§

Autonomy

I thus believe that the seeds of autonomy are sown very early in life. To follow Erikson [1959], earliest infancy is characterized by the psychosocial crisis of trust versus mistrust (the oral stage of classical psychoanalysis); while early childhood (the anal stage) is dominated by the psychosocial crisis of autonomy versus shame and doubt. I fully agree that autonomy, as well as delineation of the infant's world into "I" and "you," is often gained around the mastery of defecation in socially acceptable form. But I also believe that autonomy begins to develop even sooner.

To use Erikson's terms, what happens during the adolescent identity crisis depends in part on how autonomy was gained in early childhood, and how much. Only our experience with autistic children has taught us convincingly that no such crisis takes place in adolescence if the child has not gained much autonomy to speak of in infancy. Autistic children simply have no adolescent identity crisis unless they have left their autism way behind them as they reach the age of puberty.

Despite my large agreement with Erikson, I believe that even he has not paid enough attention to the importance of active strivings in the first stage of development when trust is so central. And he neglected to spell out how autonomy rests on the ability to predict and to act on one's predictions. In describing the issues involved, I believe that he, no less than Spitz and others, views the infant as too passively dependent and as much too subject to the oral experience. These I feel stem from the origins of psychoanalysis in pathology.

Let us say that the infant is prevented from asserting his developing personality through independent responses to parental caretaking—or as much so as his somatic and psychic equipment permits. If this happens, then both dependence and the acting out of problems around the oral experience become the only avenues left open to him, and hence do indeed become of paramount importance. Normally, however, orality and dependence are only *primi inter pares* of the infant's life experiences.

Moving from early infancy to the age of toilet training, psychoanalysis rightly stresses how crucial this is to the child's socialization. But perhaps the emphasis is often misplaced on his becoming a *social* individual, while I believe with Erikson that the greater psychological importance rests on his becoming a social *individual*.

True, it was psychoanalysis that made us aware of how personality can depend on what the individual experiences around toilet training—whether he will, for example, become a compulsive miser or spender. But intent on the morbid, we have not paid equal attention to the role of toilet training in developing a feeling of selfhood, of being a person in one's own rights. It is true that if things go wrong here the person may come to feel he is not in charge of his life since others impose their will on him even to the functioning of his body. But we should not therefore neglect the converse: that this same experience can go a long way toward convincing a person that he *is* in charge of himself; that he can and does have some say in the functioning of his body.

Certainly, his defecation can be a present the child gives to his mother. And that something that was just part of the self can suddenly become nonself stresses the need to delineate selfness. But by stressing these elements, the importance for the child of doing something on his own got buried behind an emphasis on the child's doing something for the mother, or on what society expects him to do. The good mother does not make this mistake and in toilet training she stresses what a big boy or girl it is, who now can go on the toilet. She recognizes that toilet training will proceed without damage if it stresses selfness at first more than socialization.

Again, toilet training is only one among many experiences that help to separate the self from the nonself. But it is impressive, in the treatment of autistic children, to see how differently the separation is made secure around intake than around elimination.

Around intake, it seems paradigmatic that the breast (or the bottle) is not always available and is therefore not part of the self. This begins a delimitation of the self, but through a negative experience; it does not give the self any positive content, does not help to recognize what is self and what is nonself. It is an experience that merely teaches: "Not everything of importance, not everything desirable, is self." Certainly it contains the depressing element of: "I cannot provide myself with a feeding experience exactly when I wish."

However strenuous the nursing baby's activity at this age, he is entirely dependent for his intake on the mother. While it is he who takes in, he cannot provide himself with what he takes in. However active in eating, he is still dependent on others to enable him to be active in the experience at all. So closely interwoven is this twosome of mother and child in the nursing situation that it sets the primordial experience for the twosomeness of people, and with it for the "thou." But for the most part both participants are still experienced as one. This is because the child's perceptual and intellectual faculties are not developed enough for him to recognize that it is *he* who takes in what was nonself, and turns it into self. Thus it fails to provide the primordial experience of the "me"; or of a self that can do, on its own.

In elimination, by contrast, it is clearly experienced that I push something out that was me, and make it non-me. With this action the problem of what is me, and what is not—or the delimitation of self versus nonself—is clearly presented to the child. My guess is, because it entails for the first time both a consciously goal-directed action and a great deal of physical doing: the pushing out of feces.

Therefore as a conscious process it very much provides the experience: "*I* can eliminate exactly when and where I wish," and this can add greatly to the sense of autonomy, of self. But this is true only if the time and place for eliminating is based on the child's decision and if the whole thing begins in a context of mutuality.

If all this is so, how does any child learn to use the toilet without being forced to, or without curbing his autonomy? Simply because it does not lessen our autonomy if we, of our own free will, decide to do something to please a person we love. On the contrary, it enhances self-respect, because autonomy has moved to a higher level. To eliminate where one wants to merely implies there is autonomy over the body. To freely choose to give pleasure to a loved one implies autonomy in one's relations to others. Solipsistic autonomy is then lifted to include autonomy in social relations as well.

In normal development the mother is happy when the child goes to the toilet on his own, when he wants to, without reminder. Her pleasure derives partly from being freed of the labor of diapering, lifting, laundering. But she also rejoices at the pride she senses in her child who can recognize he is now less dependent, more grown up.

The child's pleasure is also twofold. Relief from any bodily tension is always pleasurable. But this pleasure was available before. He could always let go of his feces into the diaper, or even his pants. Recently, however, he has begun to notice that grown-ups do it in the toilet and he wants to do it there too, both to be like them and because his mother would like him for doing it. Parental and child's desires are thus in accord. In addition, the experience of defecation becomes self-enhancing when to these pleasures are added the feelings: "I alone provide myself with this pleasurable experience"; but also, "I, of my own volition choose to have this experience in a way that also pleases my mother."

Unfortunately, this gaining of a heightened self-esteem is too often interfered with in the toilet training of children, because they are told that if they want to enjoy the experience they must conform to parental conditions. The warning that stools are dirty can further detract from the pleasure. Then the child does not think, "I wish to go to the bathroom because I feel a pressure in my body that I want to relieve," but "I have to go so I won't get a licking, or get criticized for soiling my pants." The result is that whatever the child does—whether he goes to the toilet or soils—he will not feel any *pleasurable* relief. If he soils, the pleasure is canceled out by the fear of disapproval or punishment; and if he goes to the toilet it is canceled out because he resents being forced to conform.

How, then, is toilet training achieved without loss of bodily pleasure? Normally, it is only the adult's behavior that prevents such a loss, at least in part. Presumably the enjoyment of two people is better than solitary enjoyment. So the good mother, as she toilet-trains her child, provides enjoyment around his going to the toilet. This she must do if she is not to drive underground the bodily enjoyment of relief. Eventually the wish to do it there becomes so well established that even for him it becomes enjoyable to do it there too. But in the beginning this can come about only through her.

Thus the separation of self from the nonself is greatly enhanced through the experience of "I can provide myself with this relief of tension." But full enjoyment of young selfhood around the experience comes only from mutuality, as the parent joins the child in the pleasure of the act.

Here perhaps, I should at least say what I understand by selfhood, though I cannot presume to define it. Nor is psychoanalytic theory of help. When Freud said that where there was id there should be ego, he implied a distinction between ego and self, since the self includes not just the ego but the id and superego as well. Only the ego can achieve knowledge of the self—but only to the extent that id and superego are accessible to the ego. And this, even at high levels of consciousness, is not very much. Thus psychoanalysis too, implies that man cannot know himself since large parts of the id and superego remain hidden from the ego.

Perhaps, then, to say that the self consists of what one knows and can do must suffice. Certainly selfhood is not a state but a process of becoming. And when the struggle to realize the self is concluded, so is one's life. That is, the more I can do what I find it worthwhile to do, the more I am myself. Nevertheless Goethe, who described the epic struggle of Faust for a self, knew that for self-realization even this was not enough. To be a self means also to interact with others in the world. Faust as a solitary genius ended up in frustration. His true self he found only after going out into the world, after learning to love.

In this sense the more we know and contemplate, the more we act and interact, the more of a self do we have.

Typical of autistic children, selfhood begins when they start to come out of their total isolation and begin to act—both in their own behalf, and to some minimal degree in respect to the other; that is, when they recognize that another person exists within a field of experience that is no longer entirely amorphous. Likely as not, if such a child uses personal pronouns, all the people who move in this field are called "you," and so he calls himself. If we succeed in guiding him outward, it is through his budding recognition of one person among all those others as specially important. It is the person who most consistently performs a good mothering function. Around her dawns the realization that it is not *she* who eliminates, but *he*. In the context of elimination then, comes a separation not only of the self from the nonself, but a separation of the *I* out of the undifferentiated *you*.

For example, Mahler et al. [1959] write:

We found in several instances that recognition, enjoyment, and acceptance of the own stool coincided with giving up the pronominal reversal, as if the recognition of the scybalum which had been within and actively was pressed out helped to establish body-self-identity. This is "I." I made this, but it is not me. More observation and research however, are necessary to ascertain this connection.

Our work with autistic children certainly supports this connection. One extremely bright autistic boy who had full command of language only acquired a feeling of identity at age eight when he mastered the process of elimination. He had been using the toilet for years, though only with great anxiety and many peculiar rituals. But one day he indicated he was ready to have the person most important to him join him in going to the toilet. The issue was to provide himself with the experience that in the presence of this important and hence powerful figure, it was *he* who eliminated, and not she. So he wanted her to grunt, in order to experience that despite her grunting it was *he* who defecated. He wanted her to mimic his body contortions when defecating, to make sure that despite the mimicry it was *he* and not she who produced feces.

Through this single device he provided himself with the twin experience needed for achieving selfhood: that it was *he* who acted, and that he acted within a relation to a most important person.

To others it happens as it did to Brian, one of our nine-year-old autistic boys who had speech but hardly any communication. Brian first began to use the pronoun "I" when he announced, "I want to go to the bathroom." In all other contexts he continued to use the pronoun "you" when referring to himself or to others. Only here, where he realized he could do something himself, did his enhanced feeling of self enable him to say "I."

Quite a few autistic children, having reached this point, choose a particular way to further convince themselves it is really they who defecate. It seems that straining their muscles to push out the feces is not enough of a kinesthetic sensation to convince them that defecation happens only by their decision. So they add a deliberate doing: they dig the feces out of the rectum with their fingers. Our assurance that their bodies are well able to eliminate without manual help falls on deaf ears; they simply do not believe us.

When we first began to recognize the importance of such behavior, we laid it to a distrust of the functioning of their bodies. But further observation, combined with what some of these children told us, showed that the notion of an inadequate body was only a small part of their decision to use their fingers. They did it mainly out of a powerful wish to be sure that defecation was their deliberate doing; as if they needed to undo the experience that some outside force was what made them eliminate. Straining the inner muscles did not seem to give this feeling clearly enough; doing it with their fingers was better. Typically this behavior disappears as the child is convinced he can also do things on his own in other areas of life.

§

The Autistic *Anlage*

While there seem to be particular experiences, such as those around nursing and defecation that can powerfully aid or interfere with the development of a self, there is no time between birth and death—and perhaps even before birth—when personality is not developing. Nevertheless, there are certain times in our lives when specific experiences make more difference than at others, when they can and do have a more lasting and radical effect.

We have learned that personality development may begin before birth, since the mother's personality, experience and behavior during pregnancy may affect the later development of personality in her child (see pages 397–398). With it the question of personality development, the controversy of nature versus nurture, or of genetic endowment versus the impact of the environment becomes more and more moot. To quote Montague [1950],

There is little that is final about constitution, for constitution is a *process* rather than an unchanging entity. In brief . . . constitution is not a biologically *given* structure predestined by its genotype to function in a predetermined manner. The manner in which all genotypes function is determined by the interaction of the genotype with the environment in which it undergoes development.

But while personality develops in a continuous process, students of very early development agree that even under normal conditions there are periods of special sensitivity. Two in particular are frequently mentioned: the age from six to nine months, and again from about eighteen months to two years.

These "critical periods" have been carefully studied in some mammals and birds and it now appears that imprinting in animals does not necessarily take place immediately after birth but at a certain well-defined stage of development specific to the species. Hess [1959] and others have observed of the mallard duck, for example, that the most effective period of imprinting is the thirteen to sixteen hours after hatching. These findings, while they are highly suggestive for humans, are not conclusive. Still, the concept of critical periods is so important that I shall try to present it here briefly.

According to Scott and Fuller [1965],

[It is] a special time in life when a small amount of experience will produce a great effect on later behavior. . . . It is a relative rather than an absolute concept. The difference between the amount of effort needed to produce the same effect at different periods determines just how critical the period is. In the case of the puppy, it looks as if a small amount of contact shortly after three weeks of age will produce a strong social relationship which can be duplicated only by hours or weeks of patient effort at later periods in life— *if, indeed, it can be duplicated at all.*

There may be more than one critical period in the life of the individual. . . . There could be a variety of critical periods in development for different events . . . [but] our evidence on the puppy reinforces the general conclusion that in any highly social species of animal there is a relatively brief period, usually early in development, when primary social relations are established. . . . This law . . . has many implications for the modification of social organization in human beings and the *disruption of organization by disturbances in development.* [All italics added.]

More specifically, Scott and Fuller have shown that the critical period for a puppy is one of "great change and sensitivity" and that what happens to him during this period will "determine which animals and human beings will become his closest social relatives . . . all the rest of his life." It is therefore interesting to note which new achievements occur at this time in the life of the puppy since they may suggest what changes in the human infant may herald a critical period.

According to Scott and Fuller,

Between two and three weeks of age a very large number of changes take place in rapid succession, and all of them modify the capacity for forming a close social relationship. The period of change begins with the opening of the eyes and includes the opening of the ears and the startle response to sound. At its end the puppy is capable of walking, so that it can either approach or avoid another individual. It begins to eat solid food and hence starts to be independent of the mother. It develops the ability to make rapid associations between outside events and unpleasant feelings. This last change is probably the most important one with regard to establishing a boundary for the critical period for forming social relationships, because the puppy is now capable of discriminating between individuals.

I have quoted so extensively from the life of the dog because what in his case is a single critical period seems to be separated, for the human infant, into at least two such periods. In the human being everything is much more spread out, and the boundary lines are by no means so quickly and definitely drawn.

Examining Scott and Fuller's list against our knowledge of human infancy, it appears that during the human infant's first "critical period," but even before then, he makes rapid associations between outside events and unpleasant feelings and is beginning to eat solid foods. But these by no means start him toward independence from the mother. This begins only in his second critical period, when he learns to walk and hence can freely "approach or avoid another individual." However, in the first of these two epochs the human infant can already discriminate between persons, an ability just as important to the baby as to the puppy in the forming of social relations.

Nevertheless, while human beings too, seem to have critical periods of development in which they are specially vulnerable, these differ from the imprinting process in animals in that human beings are not shaped once and for all. Even among animals, imprinting is a very different process for those that can learn a great deal, than for those with small capacity to learn. Scott [1962] suggests that some developments that take as long as ten weeks in dogs are as complete as they will ever be after the first few hours of a lamb's life.

The longer the critical period, the greater the chance of later reversing its impact. Studies of neonatal behavior in humans and of imprinting in animals suggest that many aspects of later behavior that do not appear in the neonatal period or when imprinting takes place will nonetheless be directed toward the imprinted object when full functioning is later achieved. Thus the very early experience can do both: have immediate consequences, or affect a response pattern that will not emerge till much later. The long period required for human development permits a much greater latitude, but not an unlimited one, as to when the effects of the early experience may to some degree be changed.

During the first critical period in humans, it seems that at six months or a bit later the infant is more definite about recognizing familiar persons. At the same time those others who are not familiar are more definitely perceived as alien and hence threatening; perhaps because they threaten his efforts to relate positively to the familiar ones. One cannot very well relate to persons who are nobody in particular, who do not seem different from the rest. All this happens at a time when the infant no longer wants only or mainly to be given to by others (food, stimulation, affection), but wants them from particular persons, in by now familiar ways. People become persons as a few, out of his family and friends, achieve positive valence, as opposed to their interchangeable value as providers.

It is reasonable to assume that as other persons become more clearly defined for the infant, so does he to himself. At this early age he probably functions largely on an all-or-none principle, viewing things as either all-positive or all-negative. If so, then the more he views familiar persons in a positive light, the more he is likely to view others in the negative. Thus by a process of polarization, all unfamiliar persons now begin to appear to him as unfriendly.

This, then, seems to be the period in which real object relations begin. It is also when, for reasons just described or for others still unknown to us, even the happy infant no longer responds to strangers with a smile but with signs of distress; so much so that some call it the period of the "eight-month anxiety." Scott [1963] has compared it to what seems like parallel behavior in animals as they learn to discriminate between friend and foe:

In the animals so far studied there frequently appears one mechanism which establishes positive contact and another which makes later contact with other individuals difficult or impossible. The negative mechanism in ducks, dogs, and human beings appear to be the development of a fear response. The positive behavior mechanisms are more various. In ducks and geese it is a following reaction. In puppies it is social investigation and tail wagging, while in the more helpless human infant it is simply a smile.

So much for normal development, in which the separation of friend from stranger results from the infant's earlier positive relations to those who mothered him. This is when his first rudimentary awareness of self becomes extended to others. But while this enables him to feel himself more of a person, he still cannot fend for himself without help from others.

That first becomes truly possible during the second "critical" period of development, when language and locomotion turn the infant into a child. If the experience of being able to do for oneself is important, this second period makes it doubly so for the child who lacked even the minimal experience of selfhood that the normal infant enjoys during the six to nine months period of his life.

This second "critical" period that begins at around eighteen months is when the child can much more definitely shape his relations to his environment if permitted to do so; when his activity can not only influence others but permit him actual mastery. Like the three-weeks-old puppy, the human infant can now, through walking and talking, "approach or avoid another individual." He can toilet-train himself, as opposed to being trained against his wishes. And again, what happens in this second sensitive period builds to a very large degree on what happened before; on what view of the world he has so far developed and into which he must now fit the newer experience.

Probably these are also the critical periods when autistic withdrawal may appear, and with it a giving up (or nondevelopment) of a self. Weiland and Rudnik [1961] arrived at the same or very similar conclusions though they are less clear about when exactly the second period of damage occurs.[4] But it was Mahler who first recognized that infantile

4. "Therapeutic and other observations on autistic children raised the possibility that such children consist of two distinct groups. The development of the syndrome of one group is attributed to severe traumatic experiences during the period at which object relationships are just 'learned'; the object relationship thereby attains the

autism has a great deal to do with the child's frustrated strivings, that there are two phases involved, and that it comes to full bloom in what she calls the "separation-individuation phase."

As Mahler wrote in 1952,

Children who begin with a symbiotic psychosis will use autism as a desperate means of warding off the fear of losing whatever minimal individual entity they may have succeeded in achieving either through development or through treatment, which they then attempt to preserve by the opposite psychotic mechanism of autism.

This Mahler spelled out more precisely in a later paper [1965] as follows:

If during the symbiotic phase defenses have already been built up against apperception and recognition of the living maternal object world, because it has not been experienced as symbiotic, i.e., need-satisfying, but somehow as unpredictable and painfully frustrating, then retreat into secondary autism dominates the clinical picture. If, on the other hand, disturbances of the symbiotic phase go unrecognized, then the psychotic picture emerges at the chronological age when separation-individuation should begin and proceed. In this case we see the predominance of delusional symbiotic, restitutive mechanisms —separation panic, dread of dissolution of the self, and dread of loss of identity.

As a result of either of these disturbances the complex task of organizing the stimuli that impinge upon the locomoting toddler, a task arising out of the preordained maturational sequence, seems to become so perplexing to these vulnerable infants that the steps of separation-individuation are experienced as a catastrophic threat. This arrests further differentiation and integration of and by the ego. According to our hypothesis, therefore, the psychotic small child is only half an individual, one whose condition can be optimally studied only through as complete as possible a restoration of the original mother-child unit.

As is evident from this passage, Mahler also recognized that autism is a response to a catastrophic threat. Nevertheless, my conclusions as to the nature of that threat, namely about the origin of autism, and even more so its treatment, are at variance with hers. Nor can I accept the idea that the psychotic child is "only half an individual" and that we must therefore, restore for him the mother-child unit whose deficiency led him to break with reality in the first place. Further discussion of these problems I reserve for my review of the literature at the close of this book.

As we see it, then, some children may never develop to any extent in the first place, because of what they experience before and during

---

potential of danger. A second group is composed of children who have failed to experience those particular operations at some 'critical period' essential to the organization of behavior that characterizes object relatedness."

the first critical period of development. Others may only become autistic in about their second year of life, because of what they experience then, or because of demands they encounter only then. But even where autism does not develop till this later time, that it does develop may have a great deal to do with what happened much earlier.

According to psychoanalytic theory the newborn infant views the world as mainly need satisfying, more or less at his command. But this seems true only if good care is at all times provided, and if his own limited activities—a reaching up of arms, a vigorous sucking, later a smile—make him feel he had a great deal to do with securing these satisfactions. Together they give him the impression that the world is his for the asking. How soon, how much, and how lastingly he comes to feel that this is not so, that the world is also frustrating, may deeply condition whether or not he can learn to come to terms with the world.

The necessary frustrations of living, while they shatter the infant's feeling that the world is his for the asking, also challenge him to learn to do something about it. That is, he must learn to manipulate his environment at each stage of his development as well as his capabilities permit. In this way he can still gain his ends in a world that is neither all giving nor at his command. Still, all his later ability to do so may be the consequence of an earlier conviction that the world is "at his fingertips," as the nourishing breast usually was. It simply turns out that the pleasures he wants are not so close at hand. He must go out and capture them first.

I suggest, then, that there may be a critical time to experience the world as frustrating. If this experience hits the infant after the conviction of "a world at his fingertips" is well established—and does not hit him too acutely at any one time—then all is well. Eventually he will try on his own to make his original fantasy come true, at least as much as he can in this less than perfect world. And since his desires and fantasies are simple at first, he will succeed to some degree. Moreover, as his wants grow more elaborate, so will his ability to satisfy them. But things may go terribly wrong if the world is experienced as basically frustrating too soon; before the conviction of its satisfying nature has been established in an *Anlage* that will reappear once the child can do things on his own.

At this point, an endowment of unusually high sensitivity may lead to difficulties in adjustment, a subject I shall return to later on. Here I would like to suggest the possibility that if an infant is unusually intelligent, or unusually early in responding to his environment, a discrepancy may exist between his precocious efforts to "do" for himself, and the physical immaturity that holds him back. Unless the environment is sensitive to the lag, such a discrepancy can lead to a severe imbalance between the infant's wish to reach out and his inability to do so. This too can arouse inner frustrations that are as damaging as any the environment could impose.

In short, the lack of satisfying responses from those who take care of him may force the infant too early to view the world as purely frustrating, before he has had a chance to be fully convinced that the world is essentially good. If so, then his later, more realistic experience will not be neutralized by the earlier one. It will not impel him to invest vital energy in reaching out for what he wants, even when his growth development makes that possible.

Such children stop trying. They see no reason to reach out to a frustrating experience, and this is all the world seems to offer. These, then, are children who suffer from infantile marasmus, are Spitz's vegetating children who suffer from hospitalism. Such children do not develop socially, emotionally, or intellectually, and many soon die physically as well.

But I believe it was not directly the mechanical, impersonal care that was given them, nor even the low stimulation they experienced, that accounts for their shriveling up and withering away. I think it was rather their failure to become active in their own behalf. Though poor nursing care was at fault in not activating them, it was their not becoming active that led to their emotional, intellectual, and often physical death. Otherwise, the observations of Spitz and others would still not explain why some of these children survived and others did not, though all of them were treated alike. Some, either because of endowment, prior experience, or benign accident, became more activated than others and hence put even the mechanical care to better use. More correctly, perhaps, the care seemed less purely mechanical to them because they were more active in receiving it.

There are other children in whom their early experience created an autistic *Anlage,* but whose later encounter with frustration, during their second year, was not their total experience of the world. These are children whose essential needs, both to receive and be active, were satisfied to at least that minimal degree that the world did not seem to them wholly destructive. There are again others who were fairly well cared for, but nevertheless denied the experience that what they did made much difference. To children with either experience, the world appeared to be need satisfying, but wholly insensitive. (This latter experience they share with the first group who hardly developed at all.) Such children remain passive, the "good" quiet infants. They develop up to the point where growth and maturation, as well as society, require them to begin to act on their own, at least to some degree, in shaping their lives. This task they cannot meet. But then the world that seemed only insensitive begins to seem destructive as well, because it asks of them, for their survival, to do what they are unable to do. In reaction to this experience they assume the autistic position.

I can now be more specific about what essentially the autistic *Anlage* consists of: it is the conviction that one's own efforts have no power to influence the world, because of the earlier conviction that the world is insensitive to one's reactions.

Infantile marasmus, then, and Spitz's hospitalism, are due to a combination of the conviction that one can do nothing about the world, and that the world is not need satisfying at all, but only frustrating, destructive: these convictions result in utter passivity.

Infantile autism, on the other hand, stems from the original conviction that there is nothing at all one can do about a world that offers some satisfactions, though not those one desires, and only in frustrating ways. As more is expected of such a child, and as he tries to find some satisfactions on his own he meets even greater frustration: because he neither gains satisfaction nor can he do as his parents expect. So he withdraws to the autistic position. If this happens, the world which until then seemed only insensitive now appears to be utterly destructive, as it did from the start to the child who succumbs to marasmus. But since the autistic child once had some vague image of a satisfying world, he strives for it—not through action, but only in fantasy. Or if he acts, it is not to better his lot but only to ward off further harm. The child with infantile marasmus does not even have a fantasy world.

There is one further possibility. This is where the situation is the same as described for autism, but where the child retains one single access to satisfaction: through the mother. This is the child who, despite all his efforts, cannot gain satisfaction and meets only frustration, but with one crucial difference. If he can involve the mother in doing for him, acting for him, there are some satisfactions to be had—but only through her; never or rarely on his own steam. It is the much more benign symbiotic psychosis of childhood first described by Mahler [1952]. Since the child reaches out toward even one person, the ability to relate has theoretically developed. Hence ambulatory therapy can sometimes succeed in extending this to where it eventually includes other persons and significant aspects of the world.

Thus we may perhaps think of infantile autism as coming from the infant's experience during not only two, but even three or more critical periods. The first may occur during the first six months, the time before the so-called eight-month anxiety, the time before his reaching out to friends is being powerfully reinforced by his fear of the stranger. In order for this normal separation of friend and foe to occur, the baby's prior experience must have enabled him to single some out as friends; that is he must have had the experience that the world is essentially good. If not, then no eight-month anxiety will be experienced either, as it is absent in Spitz's children who suffered from hospitalism. Some children are recognized as autistic at around this age. They are the children who fail to form social relations because they have been too sorely disappointed in the world.

The second time for critical experiences to account for autism may be the period from about six to nine months, the period that normally includes the eight-month anxiety. Other persons are now recognized as individuals, and the child begins to recognize himself as such, too. If, during this period, the infant tries to relate to the other but finds him unresponsive, he may give up trying to relate. But not having found the other, he cannot find the self either.

The third critical time may be the age from eighteen months to two years, when autism is most commonly recognized. It is the age when the child can approach or avoid contact with the world not just emotionally, but by walking away from it all. This, then, may be the stage when to emotional withdrawal from the mother (in the second stage) is added emotional and physical withdrawal from the world altogether.

At best, these are highly tentative suggestions and gross approximations. In each stage, different strivings of the self have been blocked or severely interfered with: in the first with the child's being active in general; in the second with his active reaching out to others; and in the third with his active efforts to master the world physically and intellectually.

§

The Right Side of Time

I have suggested before that correct imprinting in animals is basically a matter of timing, although human beings enjoy an immensely wider latitude for achieving the original steps in developments. As to the nature of those steps—and even more so, their timing—there is some leeway for personal variations within a culture. Variations are even wider between cultures and their study may teach us much about personality formation. For this reason the method of child rearing in the Israeli Kibbutz aroused my interest, since the Kibbutz infant is reared only in part by his mother, and to a very large degree by caretakers assigned to the task.

Israeli society is one very similar to ours, and the children so reared grow up to be stable and competent adults. How this happens is a lengthy tale which I reserve for a forthcoming publication, based on a limited field study. Here I wish only to say that my experience in the Kibbutz convinced me that every infant must have a star to steer by—but that this need not be his mother. To stick with the analogy, a constellation can replace the individual star, on condition that what is lost in intensity is made up for by how definite the directions by which to navigate.

The reason I mention this here is that the Kibbutz method of child rearing develops autonomy in the young child's interactions with others, and in his mastery of the human and physical environment, considerably more than does ours. It is true that the giving of clear directions on how to develop is combined with much else, both desirable and otherwise. The Kibbutz child enjoys only limited leeway on how to adapt to such directions in his own individual way. But he is given ample gratification of his physical and other instinctual needs, with only little pressure to control them at an early age. And these, when combined with optimal conditions for autonomy, seem to go a long way to supplement deficiencies even in the earliest mothering of the child.

Of particular relevance to this book is the Kibbutz toddler's experience. I have stressed before the seeming two- (or more-) phase development of autism, and its appearance, full-blown, toward the second or third year of life. Whatever the Kibbutz child's losses in early infancy, it is exactly at the next stage that he enjoys a height of autonomy, and a height of success in employing it. Each of these advantages is beyond what even the best of parents can offer to his toddler in our society.[5]

Despite which it seems clear that while steps in social development may vary with the culture, there is much less freedom where the inner development of the infant is concerned, whether mental or physical. Crawling typically comes before walking, and while some infants skip crawling, it is hard to imagine an infant who would proceed from turning over to walking, and later from walking erect to crawling as a preferred mode of locomotion.

Autonomy is greatly enhanced by gaining control of the functions of one's body. But so much is man a social animal, that even this development only becomes actual as a result of the social experience. For us

5. I wish to make clear that when I speak here of the encouragement of autonomy this is not to be misunderstood: I am not in favor of having the child, at an early age, shift for himself. This would mean he is overpowered and will end up defeated. There is a great tendency in our society to want children to be independent at an early age and to push them to "do things," particularly those things the parents want them to do. I believe this is most destructive to the development of autonomy, which grows best out of the conviction: it's important to me to do this, and that's why I'm doing it; not because I'm told I should (or must), and not because (even worse) I must consider important what others want me to consider important.

humans, both autonomy over the body and in the external world can be gained only through a relationship, and it cannot be made secure unless we have also mastered our emotions. True, these will always overwhelm us at times, but so will the functions of the body. Control of our elimination does not free us never to empty our bowels. Autonomy requires that we, and nobody else, shall decide when we empty them, and how and where; it cannot possibly require that we shall not empty them when our body feels it must.

To submit the body's demands to a rigid control by the mind does not lead to autonomy. It only means that submission to the parents has been traded for a submission to even more crippling compulsions because their source is our own anxiety. And this—until relieved by the corrective emotional experience—is always with us, while the parents are not.

Thus autonomy is neither dependent on nor helped by an absolute control of our feelings. That would only lead to a compulsively depleted personality. Our emotions, like our bowels, must be free to assert their right to satisfaction and discharge. Autonomy does not require that we are in total, but in sufficient control of our emotions. Most important, as with the bowels and bladder, it means that no one else should have control of them, though other people may have an influence. We must certainly be in sufficient control of our emotions so that they do not lead us to damage ourselves or other persons.[6]

6. Extreme situations, such as combat, present specific problems. But even then, one would hope it was a person's autonomous decision that made him want to defend his country even at the risk of his life.

A situation we are all too familiar with may clarify my point. I believe the anxiety felt about nuclear war, above and beyond what any war will evoke, relates to exactly this issue of autonomy. Each of us, after all, can die only once, and it should make little difference to us whether we die in a nuclear blast or from a conventional bomb that falls on our house. The bomb might also wipe out one's spouse and children— but I doubt that love of mankind in general, or its survival beyond one's family and friends, is a great concern to many. Yet conventional war seems (but only seems) to permit decisions on whether to fight or take flight. The image of the sudden atomic blast seems to have done away with the autonomous or semi-autonomous decision about how to meet the danger of war. Thus it seems more destructive, because it gives us even less margin than other types of war for meeting danger in our own way.

Strangers to Life

ANIMALS KNOW: and they can learn to pull levers and even to count. They know how to build elaborate structures and find directions over thousands of miles. They communicate with each other, as in the dance of the bee telling other bees where honey can be found. This and much more they know, and only because we do not know how they know, we call it instinct. If we teach them they can learn to run complex mazes or to recognize and pick from among different forms. They can also be taught to run machines we have built. But even without our teaching, some birds have learned on their own to open milk bottles, for example, as did the great titmouse in Britain.

Animals can also act unselfishly and with devotion as when two baboons together killed a leopard to protect their own horde, though both of them died in the process [Marais, 1940]. This is by no means remarkable, since many a dog will fight and die to protect his master.

But I doubt very much that animals *know* they are doing such things, either when they do them or afterwards. Because if the rest of the baboons had known of their defenders' heroic deed, they too might have evolved a war tactic against leopards, and eventually had epic songs to commemorate their ancient heroes.

Animals can also predict the results of their actions. Thus they can predict, and they can act. Otherwise the dog that chewed up the rug would not fear the return of his master and cower in a corner. But does the dog know that he "caused" his punishment or has he only learned, through something like a conditioned response, which events follow which others? Whatever the case, the dog cannot influence the course of events: he cannot sew together the now chewed-up rug. Neither can he clean up the rug, once he has soiled it. And there's the rub.

What I believe to be missing is the knowledge, or conviction, that through his own interference he can change a course of events, once set in motion. I believe it to be a distinctly human experience to feel with conviction: *I did it, and my doing made a difference.* It is this conviction that leads to a spontaneous building up of learned experience and personality, till complex series of events can be modified, mastered, stopped and controlled as the particular personality decrees.

§

A Reason to Act

The human experience is built up on our sense of space, time, and causality, Kant's *a priori* categories of mind. The sense of time and space in many animals far surpasses our own. But our ability to extract, from contiguity in time and space, a sense of causality took us into the human adventure. What made us what we are was not simply that we recognized causal relations, but what followed from it: the conviction that a sequence of events can be changed through our influence. That by injecting a new link in the chain of causality we can so change a course of events that the outcome is entirely different from what it would have been without this, our spontaneous action. That is why I so stressed, in the preceding chapter, that artificial feeding times can dehumanize the infant: because it prevents him from feeling that *his* actions (cry or smile) are what bring about his being fed.

It is when we feel we cannot influence the most important things that happen to us, when they seem to follow the dictates of some inexorable power, that we give up trying to learn how to act on, or change them. In time we may come to associate this seemingly inflexible order with some kind of an influencing machine, and later to believe that all events are produced by this or some other mechanical contrivance. Since so much of the child's life seems to be regulated by arbitrary schedule, this power may come to be identified with a clock. But that happens much later.

Normally, however, as the child grows so does his conviction that through personal efforts he can alter a given chain of events. If so, then new importance is added to his ability to order and predict them, because a correct ordering of events in space and time helps him to understand their causal connection.

The ability to act with purpose is based on a grasp of the likely consequence of our actions. It cannot be achieved without orientation in space and time, or without organizing these so observed events in causal terms. But not even the ability to predict future events from correct clues makes for full humanization. Prediction as such has no value unless I feel that by acting on its basis I can change an expected sequence of events. If I cannot, then it may seem pointless to even pay it attention.

If this is the case, then even startling events may not reach my attention because I can do nothing about them. Then prediction might only lead to trembling before the inexorable bad event. Better not to tremble ahead of time, if we cannot prepare for, or change it. Better then, to give up predicting and correct ordering of events. Better to withdraw all attention from the world, as we see it typically in the autistic child's deliberate disinterest in a world he feels he cannot change.

To begin to function, then, as human beings, one must have learned how to arrange one's own life in terms of time, space, and causality. These categories of mind are not just metaphysical; there is a definite historical-genetic sequence in which they appear.

Orientation in time and space precedes a sense of causality. Certainly the infant's feeding is a crucial time experience, bringing some order into life at a very early age. I do not know if the time-ordering of the world (according to feeding, sleep-and-waking, the rhythm of day and night) takes precedence over an ordering in space on the basis of visual, auditory, and kinesthetic experiences (the infant's recognition of events within his body or in space outside himself, as in response to moving objects). According to Genesis, the ordering of space (the separation of chaos into an up and down of heaven and earth) preceded the ordering of time (the separation of day and night).

I am in no position to argue whether or which of these two parts of human experience came first—orientation in space or in time. But I do know that our autistic children have so alienated themselves from the experience of time that only space and its emptiness remains. And this they try to master through sameness or boundary behavior.

Actually the two are so closely knit to begin with that in the natural experience of the world it makes little sense to distinguish between them. It is one of our first tasks, with autistic children, to help them reestablish this unity. I do not know how important their separation is in the rational order of things. But had Minkowski and Einstein not recognized it long before us, our schizophrenic children would have taught us that space-time is a unity that precedes any separate understanding of either category; just as grasping this unity is a precondition for understanding causality. Without exception our autistic or severely arrested schizophrenic children achieve a fairly clear concept of space-time long before they can conceive of either one distinctly; and long, long before they can understand causal relations.

Their day, for example, when it finally becomes ordered, is not organized in terms of morning, noon, and night, nor their space in terms of the location of rooms. Instead, a space-time concept is acquired rather early and given misleading names like "dining room" or "school." These concepts cover a unitary experience comprising both the time of day when they go from the dormitory to the dining room or class room, and the movement through space required to get to these places. This they show by many types of behavior, one of which may illustrate: "School" to them means the time of day they go there, the place, and the person of their teacher. A holiday is "no school," and this throws them into severe panic: if they do not go to the usual place at the usual time they are lost. Their time-space orientation does not work.

Whatever the sequence of learning to find one's place in time and in space, a correct ordering of events must precede prediction, and prediction must precede action, because otherwise it would be random action without plan or any hoped for results. In the normal course of events all this takes place without much conscious effort, unless we are engaging in scientific inquiry. But it does not change these facts that for most of us all this ordering and predicting takes place on a semiconscious level. It seems generally true that the less we are able to act where the results are important to us, the more we predict. And the less we can act and predict, the more inclined we are to order. That is, if the next step in this sequence—from ordering to predicting to acting—is impossible, the more energy we seem to expend on the earlier step. Yet without the ultimate one of goal directed action, none of the preceding steps make much sense.

This is true not just for children or emotionally disturbed persons but for all of us. Any parent knows that the less the child can act successfully, the more assertive are his predictions of what is going to happen. This is partly an effort to deny that one is unable to act. Hence the person who feels most incompetent may also be the one who makes the most grandiose assertions. (The deeply depressed person is another story.)

In the severely disturbed children we work with we can certainly observe an absence in all cases of any goal-directed action, or at least of action that would get them what they want, given the society they live in. Combined with it goes an explosive rage, usually without specific content, and a total unwillingness to indicate what caused it, or indeed any other of their emotions—because they are certain there would never be a satisfying emotional response. The autistic child's withdrawal goes much further. Most of them have not only given up goal directed action and communication of feelings, but also prediction. Beyond this stage they divide themselves into at least two groups: one that simply never moved out toward, or withdraws even further from the world, and another group that combines withdrawal with the creation of a private world, one that often parallels our own.

In the first group we see children who seem to have given up predicting what will happen but without having given up prediction of what will *not* happen. Hence they continue with their ordering of events to make this negative prediction come true. Only it becomes an entirely empty predicting because no action whatsoever can follow from it. These children must arrange objects in a certain ritualistic way. Unless they do, something terrible will happen.

Here we have a perversion of prediction since it should lead to action which should lead to events; except the prediction is that through one's action (the ritual) nothing will happen. It is the utmost defeatism about one's ability to manipulate the environment. Instead of my action producing events, all it can do is stop events from taking place. But if nothing happens, there is no life. And this is exactly the conviction of these children: that they have no life because they cannot give it any direction.

In a further stage of withdrawal, the ability to predict has also disappeared. Such children spend their days in many rituals; things have to be ordered just so, blocks have to be arranged in a certain order, puzzles put together in a certain way, songs repeated in a given order. But nothing follows from it, not even a prediction of what would happen if they did not perform these rituals. Years of treatment may pass before they regain the knowledge of which event they hoped to prevent from occurring through their compulsive ordering of bits of reality. Then it appears that behind each ordering was a striving for a prediction. If we succeed in freeing the child to take goal-directed action again, we can occasionally unearth the action of others they intended to prevent. It was in preparation for this that they once carefully assembled what they felt were important bits of knowledge and on that basis tried to predict which behavior of theirs would most likely prevent the bad consequences.

But there are those other children who withdraw even further and have no rituals, no ordering of objects. They have furthest withdrawn into nothingness. Examples of this utmost withdrawal are Marcia and Laurie, though in Laurie's case it is alleged that she once engaged in rituals.

All this is well known from the study of rituals and other compulsions in adults. I review it here because adult rituals are engaged in by persons who had previously developed rather complex personalities.

Studying them, and they have been adequately studied, does not help our understanding of how essential is this evolution—from a sensible ordering of events, to prediction, to goal-directed action—for the development of personality in the first place.

Piaget [1954] from his minute observation of very young children, arrives at conclusions that seem to parallel the constructions I present. He writes (italics mine):

Causality consists in an organization of the universe caused by the totality of relations established by *action* and then by representation between objects as well as between object and subject. Hence causality presupposes at all levels an *interaction* between the self and things, but [while] the radical egocentrism of the beginnings first leads the subject to attribute all external events to personal activity, the formation of a permanent universe subsequently enables the self to be located among things and to understand the totality of the sequences which it sees or in which it is engaged as cause or effect.

Now let us assume that in this first stage, where the subject "attributes all external events to personal activity," all these external events seem destructive to him, either because of their nature or because of the attitudes he fathoms behind them; that is, because of the emotions he senses in those who really cause these events to occur. How must such a person view his own actions? Doesn't it follow that if this is how he sees them, he will give up all activity since his own actions (he feels) are what cause all these terrible events? Because while the infant does not understand cause and effect, and hence does not know who (or what) causes what, he is responsive to the feelings that go with events.

The more he believes it is he who causes events that create such unpleasant feelings, the less he will act. Or even if events are not so destructive, or not destructive at all—what if the individual is prevented from acting and interacting with people or things? Then, too, according to Piaget, he cannot see causal relations. But in a world where no causality exists, no prediction is possible nor any planned action. If we cannot anticipate what the results of our actions will be, we are not in control of our fate. Then only two possible courses of action make sense: either to do nothing, since that at least saves us energy and disappointment; or to create a fantasy world in which we can imagine we are still in control of our fate.

Originally, the autistic child's doing nothing can have very different inner motivations, can be engaged in out of suicidal or self-protective intentions, can start as an utter giving in, or as extreme defiance. Unfortunately for those who use this defense, its nature is such that it debilitates the self till at one moment what was still utter defiance, may in the next moment turn out to be suicidal. Thus in a child's last-ditch efforts at assertion he defies his parents by doing nothing. But in doing so he gives up the very being he tried to protect. Or, to put it differently, the self he tried to protect by not acting becomes ever weaker, until it disintegrates through nonuse.

The self, as viewed here, is not an isolated entity. It is a totality of inner processes that develops slowly, but once developed cannot be stopped and started at will. If stopped too radically or for too long these processes deteriorate, and rebuilding them becomes more and more difficult.

Once the child has even stopped communicating with others, his self becomes impoverished, the more so the longer his mutism lasts, and the more so the more undeveloped his personality at the time of the onset of withdrawal.

It is true that learning can proceed without verbal communication or even the nonverbal communication of emotions, just as animals can learn in experimental settings. But for personality development some form of communication is required. While thought is a prejudging of the outcome of action with the smallest expenditure of energy, communication is a testing of the social outcome of our actions with the least danger to ourselves.

Communication with adults, who know so much more about the world, reduces the margin for error and improves the infant's ability to predict the outcome of his actions. Without language the intended message is more apt to be misunderstood. That is why the more complex parts of reality are best mastered through language, and why ego growth depends on correct concept formation based on language.

Of course, language, as Talleyrand remarked, can also be used to confuse others about our true intentions and feelings. Hence Bateson's [1956] "double-bind," so often observed in use by the parents of schizophrenics. If the spoken word communicates one thing, and the feeling behind it communicates another, then no clear message is received and the child cannot trust his ability to predict what will come of his actions.

Nevertheless, it is only when communication reaches the symbolic level of language that a self can become fully established with the "I" clearly separated from the "you." Only then can we validate experience enough so that intellectual learning can take place, as opposed to conditioning.

This means that language is tremendously useful not only for transmitting knowledge, but also for validating and making objective all that would otherwise remain a solipsistic way of perceiving the world. And even this is not reason enough for the human being to acquire language and keep using it, unless it serves him as an instrument for positive emotional contact with reality.

This does not mean that a parent's angry words will make a child give up language. Anger is an emotion, and usually a clear, unequivocal one. Verbal anger helps the child to judge correctly where he stands with his parents at the moment, and to plan his actions accordingly—to avoid, to object, to apologize. It is when language does not make any difference that it loses value; or if bad events follow, in spite of verbal protest. And even these are not always reason enough for language to die. The autistic child may still try to talk to himself or some imaginary person, or else to real people but in a private language they cannot understand. By such means he can still acquire the symbolic concepts, the ability to generalize from the particular, that alone permits reasoning to develop. But when he comes to believe that saying anything at all, even to himself or in private language, leads to mortal danger, then language is given up.

If this happens before he has fully learned to manipulate symbolic forms, before the age of three or four, then the child also fails to develop the higher intellectual processes. Since he cannot manipulate reality in fact or even in thought, he has nothing left to manipulate but his own body. Through what he does with his body or what goes on inside of it, he now funnels whatever efforts he makes to try to master reality if not also to fight it.

In extreme cases of mute autism it would be incorrect to say that the child returns through his mutism, as it were, to the position he was in before any interpersonal and intrapersonal development took place. Because the child may withdraw to a position of even less contact with the world than the newborn enjoys. Extremely autistic children do not react even to stimuli that all other human beings, including newborns, would react to with signs of pain. To all intents, they seem totally insensitive to pain.

§

The Extinction of Feeling

In the German concentration camps I witnessed with utter disbelief the nonreacting of certain prisoners to their most cruel experience. I did not know and would not have believed that I would observe similar behavior in the most benign of therapeutic environments, because of what children had experienced in the past.

Like others who have worked with autistic children, we were again and again confronted with a parallel blotting out of all pain.[1] At least

1. As Ribble [1945] remarks: "It appears from close observation that the first three months of life is a period in which the child is most vulnerable to severe physiological disturbances in response to anxiety. . . . It is an interesting fact that fear, as the direct appropriate response to a perceived external danger, is weakly expressed in children

it is difficult to imagine that anyone could stand the terrible pain some of these children must have felt if they were experiencing the pain as normal people do.

For example, a formerly mute autistic child who had recently acquired speech to the degree that she could fully understand, clearly respond, and express in complete sentences all she wished to say showed no pain reactions though she was obviously quite sick (high temperature, high white-blood count, etc.). Because, for a very short while, she had pulled up her leg in a way typical of children suffering from pain in the peritoneal cavity, we suspected appendicitis. So the persons she felt closest to questioned her about pain in this region, and she was also examined for this daily by staff physicians of the University's department of pediatrics, including professors. But she showed no tenderness to palpation when examined, nor any rebound tenderness.

Nevertheless, our suspicions remained. So in the course of the six days involved she was several times examined by specialists, including surgeons, in addition to several daily inspections by our nurse. Mainly because she still showed no pain reactions whatever, nor did she protect the area, the medical decision was that it was not appendicitis. To complicate matters, she also had a strep infection at the time, which might just have explained the fever and blood count. Finally she became comatose and was failing rapidly. As an emergency measure, an exploratory operation was performed, revealing a ruptured appendix, at least two days old.

From other autistic children we might have added many similar examples. I selected that of the ruptured appendix because it illustrates lack of normal reaction to visceral pain and because Mahler [1952] speaks of the "grossly inadequate peripheral-pain-sensitivity in these children" adding that "in contrast, proprioceptive stimuli, visceral pain, was keenly felt and reacted to." But my example (and there were others) suggests that the lack of normal cathexis is not restricted to the periphery. I believe the difference is due to the difference in autistic withdrawal. Mahler's patient was only three and a half years old, while autistic mutism in a twelve-year-old (the age of our patient) reflects much more far reaching alienation than in a much younger child.

Why these children are so unresponsive to physical pain is difficult to know. It is the more baffling because they seem to pay so little attention to the external world and to direct all their attention to themselves. Thus if the whole thing were to follow the laws of logic, they should be more

---

who have shown symptoms of anxiety tension in early babyhood. In somewhat the same way they are insensitive to pain that in the normal child would cause crying or other protest." Thus the unresponsiveness to pain of autistic children may be due to a very early acquaintance with deep anxiety.

sensitive to what comes from inside them, including pain, than are normal people. But actually the opposite is true. In a strange way they are just as alienated from the body and its normal signals as they are from the external world; witness the fact that their muscle coordination is poor, that they walk in strange ways and move so differently from normal children.

I believe what we have here is a concentration on their defensive system to the exclusion of all other stimuli, whether coming from inside or out. Or else all sensations are immediately worked into their defensive system and are therefore not perceived as originating, for example, in a broken toe or an infected appendix.

So they present another paradox. While many of these children, when they come to us, seem totally passive, inert, almost death-like, their resistance to the environment is the most powerful I have ever encountered. According to Selye's [1956] theory of the stress syndrome, for example, they should suffer from total exhaustion because their stress is unending. But this they do not. On the contrary, their defenses are powerfully backed up by energy. None of this energy is spent on assimilating or adapting to reality as we see it. In our terms they do little or nothing at all. Instead, all energy is funneled into the single defense: to blot out all stimuli, inner and outer, in order to avoid further pain or the impulse to act.

Even mutism in those autistic children who do not speak seems largely a defense against emotional pain or any further depletion of the self. As several once mute children told us, later on, they did not talk because it would have left their brain all empty.

In discussing language and the schizophrenic Bion [1955] remarks that "at the onset of the infantile depressive position, elements of verbal thought increase in intensity and depth. In consequence, the pains of psychic reality are exacerbated by it and the patient who regresses to the paranoid-schizoid position will, as he does so, turn destructively on his capacity for verbal thought as one of the elements which have led to pain."

Our experience has not led us to follow all the theoretical views of Melanie Klein [1932, 1950] in regard to the normalcy of the infantile-depressive, and particularly of the paranoid-schizophrenic, position. But we have little doubt that as speech develops in the child destined to become autistic, his psychic reality becomes much more painful and leads him to turn "destructively on his capacity for verbal thought."

Some do so to the degree of turning mute, while others only put a stop to spontaneous expression and resort to the repetition of songs or statements once heard, etc. In doing so they abstain from phrasing their own thoughts and express them only in the words of others.

A final paradox is that while autistic children do not seem to feel pain, their fear of it generates near-superhuman strength. I cite again the frail girl who did not react to the normally unbearable pain of being examined with a ruptured appendix. Later on though, when physically well, she had to be held by two adults when an injection became necessary. Thus external intrusion must seem vastly more dangerous to these children than anything that comes from within. This is further borne out by a type of behavior we have found in many—though not all—of our autistic children, namely their response to dentistry. And this, although we use only a dentist highly skilled and successful in treating even our most severely disturbed children.

Most of our autistic children have fought with inordinate strength, and with the violence of utter desperation even the gentlest of efforts to repair their teeth. Several of them showed no signs of discomfort though their teeth were rotting away, the nerves exposed. Though when questioned about it they gave no, or only the vaguest responses, and though they also understood that the dentist was there to relieve their pain, they so viciously fought off any intrusions in the mouth that they could not be treated. But I believe that had the children felt the pain enough, they would have fought the dentist less, despite the meaning to them of the oral intrusion.

In dental work, of course, the central issue is that something is done to the teeth, the organ of biting, and the child's attitudes are powerfully colored by his fear of what that something may be. From what we know of autistic children their main anxiety is probably that the dentist will destroy their teeth in retaliation for their wish to bite and devour. So it becomes understandable that these children will permit dental work only when they no longer fear the retaliation. And this again may be seen from the response of such children to dentistry.

As they begin to trust at least one person, they also begin to trust that he will not lend his hand to the destruction of teeth, that central organ of aggression and incorporation. (Later, they will also trust our explanations that dental care, though painful, is beneficial.) It is at this point that they begin to permit dental work, provided they can clutch the hand or arm of this one trusted person. Some, instead, will clutch and pull the hair of the trusted adult, holding onto his head during the time that things are being done to their own head. It is as if they can only suffer what seems like an aggressive intrusion if they themselves can be both active and aggressive while it happens. The being active, especially, prevents the experience of being orally overpowered from projecting them once more into autistic withdrawal. Thereafter the child also begins to cooperate with physician and dentist, and permits injections and similar procedures without fighting them. But it is also at this point of greater trust in some aspects of the world that the child develops a more normal sensitivity to pain.

Now the child not only begins to complain about pain, but usually feels it much more acutely than normal persons would. For example, some formerly autistic children would then complain about pain in a tooth long before X ray and careful inspection revealed any cavity. But then, a few months later, such a cavity would be found. This so surprised our dentist at first that when next such a child claimed pain in a tooth, he tried in all possible ways to detect a cavity. Again and again he was first skeptical and then baffled when in each case the child turned out to be right, though the most careful examination disclosed no damage at the early stage the child felt it.

The possibility exists, then, that these children are much more sensitive to pain of all kinds than are normal children, and hence have built up unusually strong defenses against it.

Or perhaps, in the desperate way some of these children first fight the dentist, and later on become overly sensitive to pain, lies a clue to their seeming insensitivity to pain of all kinds. Step by step they may have defensively withdrawn cathexis from the outer world and from all but the whole of their body: hence their unresponsiveness to what they see, hear, and feel. In a parallel process they concentrate all cathexis, all protection, on some last inner fortress, the very center of their life, as they feel it.

If this assumption is correct, and if the origin of infantile autism, the *Anlage* for it, has to do with very early, maybe the earliest experiences in life, then both damage around the oral experience, and totally repressed but extreme oral aggression are among the origins of this disturbance. Perhaps these children have some dim recognition that this is the place where the critical damage occurred. If so, isn't it possible that if the damage once inflicted in this area of bodily interaction with the world has by now spread to the totality of life, then the most important protective task is to guard it from any further damage? If the mouth (and teeth) can be protected, then at least no further damage to their central existence will occur. And if they carefully avoid any use of the teeth, as in biting or talking, then maybe there will be no more retaliation to fear. If so, then the more powerful the impulse to bite, the more they must guard against any doing at all with the teeth. This may be why they swallow food but do not chew it.

It would be nice if such speculation were supported by the mute autistic child's keeping his mouth shut for safety. But many of them habitually keep their lips slightly apart. This is perhaps because the lips are external, peripheral, compared to the interior—the gums that grasp and hold on to the nipple, the teeth that bite—and it is these above all that they seek to protect. In any case the protection seems to consist less in keeping the lips and teeth shut (except for the unexpected threat of the dentist) than in avoiding any doing with the mouth. And speaking too, is distinctly doing with the mouth. Of course the divestment of libidinal energy from the oral apparatus in other respects also works to keep the lips and teeth partly open. Like all central symptoms of emotional disturbance, this one too is overdetermined and has many sources and meanings, some of which will unfold in the case histories to come.

What probably heralds the extinction of all feeling, including pain, is an utter repression of hostility. At least this is suggested by what happens in reverse when the autistic child begins to emerge out of his autism. Marcia showed no violent aggression until she became interested in objects in the external world. In her first play (with sand), for example, she was still not reacting to the pain that getting sand in the eyes normally brings. But it was in the sandbox that she violently turned against us for the first time if we intruded on her privacy there. Similar slight intrusions had evoked no reaction before, because they probably did not come to awareness. Thus an unfreezing of hostility coincided with a first liminal interest in the world, and probably made possible the interest. This vague unfreezing of hostility—in which the world at large is no longer denied, though it is still seen mainly as threatening and destructive—is a long way off as yet from recognizing some specific target of one's aggression.

It seems reasonable to believe that the same holds true in normal development. While the infant reacts to discomfort with vague anger, he may (like Marcia) have to feel some attachment for a particular person before his anger has a focus. It seems that the world first comes to our attention as a vague entity that satisfies or frustrates. But while our feelings originate in specific events, they diffuse over our total experience of the world until such time as some of its positive features emerge as specific for us. Once this happens, then a like specificity can be granted the experience that provoked us to anger. So while our positive emotions organize the world of experience, they alone permit us to organize our hostility.

Such ideas are supported by our experience with other autistic children who begin to state their intense hostility only as they move from total nonaction, through a budding positive relation, to a more advanced insistence on sameness in the external environment. I call it more advanced because it entails the act of insistence, and because to make demands of the environment means that we grant its existence.

Others, too, have pointed out that the coming alive of autistic children begins with a freeing of hostility. I am tempted to add: because the repression of all or nearly all activity, and with it a total repression of hostility, led to autism. Rubinfine [1962] says of autistic children, "It is my argument that the . . . behavior of such atypical children in relation to human objects serves as a defense against awareness of these objects, thereby protecting both child and object from aggression." And he cites the behavior of one of his patients, because it was only as the patient's aggression became freed that others became alive to him. "At such times he is clearly angry at me, but also clearly, I exist."

§

Extreme Situations

Despite the incredible variety of symptoms among the several hundred schizophrenic children we have worked with over the years, they all shared one thing in common: an unremitting fear for their lives. This takes us, for the moment, beyond the narrower group of autistic children. The reason for this is my stated conviction [1956] that all psychotic children suffer from the experience of having been subject to extreme conditions of living, and that the severity of their disturbances is directly related to how early in life these conditions arose, for how long they obtained, and how severe was their impact on the child.

Studying the literature suggests that the same was true of the schizophrenic children others have described. Furer [1964], speaking of all types of psychotic children, writes that they suffer "from extreme panic and anxiety." And the more autistic the schizophrenic child, the more debilitating his symptoms, the greater is his mortal anxiety. Autistic children in particular not only fear constantly for their lives, they seem convinced that death is imminent; that possibly it can be postponed just for moments through their not taking cognizance of life.

Others who have studied autistic children psychoanalytically came to the same conclusions. During the year in which I presented this view, Rodrigué [1955] wrote: "I think the intensity of the autistic child's anxiety is similar to that to which imminent death gives rise."

Observing this mortal anxiety as it regularly underlies the symptomatology of schizophrenic and particularly of autistic children, I was for a time very much taken by Pious' [1949] views on the role of *mortido* in schizophrenia. Yet his views did not fully accord with our observations. Then, in my ruminations, checking ideas against observations, it occurred to me that once before I had not only witnessed but also partly described the whole gamut of autistic and schizophrenic reactions —not in children, but adults. More than that, I had known what particular conditions were producing this pathology in persons who, up to the time these conditions were imposed, had been just average normal people. And these reactions, though they differed from person to person, were all responses to one and the same psychological situation.

What characterized it most was its inescapability; its uncertain duration, but potentially for life; the fact that nothing about it was predictable; that one's very life was in jeopardy at every moment and that one could do nothing about it. This experience was so unique that I needed a new term, *extreme situation* to describe it. I refer to my discussions of the German concentration camps [1943, 1960] and of their radical effects on the personality of prisoners.

Since then a whole literature has been published, both on the effects on personality of being subject to extreme conditions, and on the simulation of isolated aspects of extreme conditions, particularly on what it does to a person to be deprived of appropriate stimulation. I refer here, for example, to experiments on sensory deprivation [1961]. One of the observations I discussed in this context was how different were men's responses to even most severe suffering than they were to any extreme experience. Suffering was dealt with by one's normal (or even neurotic) personality. Only the extreme experience led to radical changes in the personality structure.

On the other hand, just as the "institutional" setting was the same for all the children Spitz studied [1945, 1949], though not all of them became vegetating children, so the conditions in the concentration camp were more or less the same for all prisoners though not all men responded alike. One could observe in the camps virtually all types of schizophrenic adaptations and symptomatology—so much so that a description of prisoner behavior would amount to a catalogue of schizophrenic reactions.

For example, some prisoners responded with suicide or suicidal tendencies, including the inability to eat (which we may compare to infantile marasmus). Others developed catatonia; both a waxy flexibility—in which they responded to any demand of the SS guards as if they had no will of their own or had lost control of their bodies—and a total rigidity. Many went into melancholic depression, while others developed delusions of persecution far beyond any actual persecution they suffered. Gross distortion of reality, illusions, delusions, and ideas of reference were frequent, as was megalomania. Superego and ego controls broke down, resulting in delinquent and criminal actions but also in a regression to infantile behavior, including incontinence. Loss of memory was universal, as were extremely shallow, incongruous, and inappropriately exaggerated emotions.

True, the great differences in schizophrenic symptoms depended on the prisoners' personalities, life histories, socioeconomic background, and other significant factors. But that they developed schizophrenic reactions at all was the specific result of being forced to live in an extreme situation. This again, we may assume, they had in common with the babies Spitz studied.

Those, on the other hand, who remained convinced they could act in their own behalf and who did act, remained free, in the main, of severest pathology, though the actual dangers were no different for them. It hardly mattered how insignificant the advantage one gained for oneself or for others through one's action. Sometimes it was an extra morsel of food, a piece of paper to wrap around the body for extra warmth, a work task successfully avoided or completed. It did not matter as long as one could rightly feel that by taking action one had ever so little improved one's estate.

Thus what was startling about the experience in the camps was that though the overpowering conditions were the same for many prisoners, not all succumbed. Only those showed schizophrenic-like reactions who felt they were not only helpless to deal with the new situation, but that this was their inescapable fate. These deteriorated to near autistic behavior when the feeling of doom penetrated so deep that it brought the added conviction of imminent death. Such men were called "moslems" in the camps and other prisoners avoided them as if in fear of contagion.

The connotation was that they had resigned themselves to death unresisting, if this was the will of the SS (or of Allah). To the other prisoners, but also to the SS, this seemed a totally alien, "Eastern" acceptance of death, as opposed to the "normal" one of fighting and scheming to survive.

Moslems suffered not only from a total emotional depletion but also a physical one, and this added to their only remaining desire: to expend no energy on anything whatsoever. Although some autistic children (like Laurie) are anorexic, and others (like Joey) emaciated, there are others who are well nourished, even fat. Marcia, for example, despite her difficulties around intake and elimination, was of average weight when she came to us. By and large it is not a depletion of physical energy that accounts for autism in children. But the opposite is true of the once normal adult. For him, total exhaustion and near starvation have to be added to the psychological trauma to produce what seems to be parallel behavior.

For the rest, what was external reality for the prisoner is for the autistic child his inner reality. Each ends up, though for different reasons, with a parallel experience of the world. The autistic child—because inner and outer reality are not separated but are experienced as more or less the same—takes his inner experience for a true representation of the world. The moslem who let the SS get hold of him, not just physically but emotionally too, went on to internalize the SS attitude that he was less than a man, that he was not to act on his own, that he had no personal will. But having transformed his inner experience to accord with his outer reality he ended up, though for entirely different reasons, with a view of himself and the world very similar to that of the autistic child.

Rodrigué [1955], applying Melanie Klein's views on the early infantile experience, explains the autistic child's view of the world as follows:

These children deny the external world's existence because they have projected into it all (objects, feelings, situations) that is hateful and painful and frightening. The quantitative factor is extremely important and accounts for their extreme withdrawal: they seem to project and deny *en bloc* the whole of their aggressive selves. This massive disowning would explain, first, why their external object can suddenly turn into a fearful persecutor and secondly, why they are unaggressive to the point of even lacking self-preservation drives.

While this is an apt description of how such children seem to experience the world, I do not believe that the primary cause of infantile autism is the fear of a world made hateful by the child's projecting into it his own "aggressive self." Otherwise we could not explain why some children become autistic and others not, since at a certain age most children do project their aggressions.

I believe the initial cause of withdrawal is rather the child's correct interpretation of the negative emotions with which the most significant figures in his environment approach him. This, in turn, evokes rage in the child till he begins—as even mature persons do—to interpret the world in the image of his anger. All of us do that occasionally, and all children do it more than occasionally. The tragedy of children fated to become autistic is that such a view of the world happens to be correct for their world; and this at so early an age that they lack any other, more benign experience to counterbalance it. This fact is the cause of their adopting the autistic position, and not the projection of their aggressive self, though this later becomes part of it too.

While we can only reconstruct or speculate on how the autistic child experiences the world, I can be more definite about how the concentration-camp prisoner came to view the world he lived in. Though it was understood that SS and prisoners were mortal enemies, the prisoner was expected to think as his enemy thought, to see the world as his enemy saw it. The SS expected him to do only as told, never to form an opinion or to act on his own. The danger was not so much in his holding the wrong opinion as in having an opinion at all. Essentially, the prisoner was to efface himself as much as possible; that is he was not to be or have a self. Nevertheless, while seasoned prisoners made many Gestapo demands their own, they internalized only selectively, and never the demand that they should not live.

The prisoner was under specific orders not to observe, not to see, not to notice what went on around him, most of all what the SS guards were up to. Of course, the prisoner was also afraid *not* to see or know, because his life might have depended on an accurate perception of danger. The tragedy was that often the SS external command not to observe was reinforced by an identical command from the prisoner's ego because it was the only way he could manage not to react to atrocities happening in front of his eyes. Only by averting his gaze could he prevent himself from interfering—which would have cost him his life—or from detesting himself for not interfering.

Parallel to these observations, Goldfarb [1956] and others have stressed the diminished use of distance receptors, sight and hearing, by schizophrenic children who show no evidence of significant defect in visual or auditory acuity or threshold. He suggests that "the schizophrenic child can hear and see, but he does not look or listen."

Others have remarked on the averted gaze of autistic children, their looking vaguely in the distance without seeming to see, and their concentration on things close at hand where there is nothing to see but their own twiddling fingers.

Often if they glance right or left they only do it surreptitiously. The head does not follow the eye movement. This is essentially the same phenomenon as the prisoner's averted gaze, despite his warring impulse to carefully observe. Both behaviors result from the conviction that it is not safe to let others see one observing because one feels one is not supposed to. And indeed, since the prisoner was not supposed to observe he would look, if at all, surreptitiously, without moving his head.

In the prisoner, this was based on a correct evaluation of what the situation required. But the same cannot be said for his absence of muscle tonus. Moslems in particular, like many autistic children, did not walk but only shuffled, as if not willing or able to lift their feet up from solid ground; nor was there a smooth or alternate swinging of arm with contralateral leg. Despite this absence of smoothly articulated walk there was either a stiffness to the body or else a nonarticulated limpness, each one being just as characteristic of how one or another autistic child moves about.

Another important parallel is the disregard of reality and the withdrawal into fantasy life. Prisoners were inattentive to true causality in their lives and replaced it by delusional fantasy. Their nearly continuous daydreaming was a close parallel to the self-stimulation of autistic children, as in their repetitive twiddling. The purpose, in each case, was to blot out recognition of an immediate, threatening reality.

If another parallel were needed, the often remarked-upon autistic repetition of "empty" rote learning, lists of names or dates, and the like seems to include some of the same reasons why prisoners favored similar activities: to prove to themselves that they had not lost their minds, had retained memory and intelligence, though they could not use it to better their fate. And just as the mute autistic child has even given up trying, through such feats, to prove that his mind can still work, so did the moslems in the camps.

Again: in *The Informed Heart* I discussed the intense wish of the prisoners to have everything in the outside world stay unchanged, and their helpless rage if changes occurred. This parallels the autistic child's insistence on sameness, and seems to come from an identical feeling of helplessness about influencing the external world.

But perhaps the most important parallel is the feeling of hopelessness about things ever changing for the better, a total absence of hope that marked off the moslems from the rest of the prisoners.

Tracing the step-by-step deterioration of the concentration-camp prisoner, it appears that he first lost the ability to act in line with objective reality and withdrew into fantasy: first wish-fulfilling, then anxious, and finally rather vague daydreams. Then he lost self-respect, the feeling that he was indeed a person. Next came an inner curb on his perception of reality, and then even of his emotions, because both were too painful. Next he suppressed interest in emotional ties to his family, because those too were painfully upsetting. And finally came the true watershed between those prisoners apt to survive, and those apt to die: the death of all hope that things would ever improve.

With it came a withdrawal of all interest in the external world. The prisoner gave up seeing, hearing, reacting. When not only acting but even moving (the feet, the eyes) became severely restricted, the full range of characteristics was reached—or one might better say, the absence of characteristics—indicating "moslem" behavior with death imminent.

Here I wish to stress again the essential difference between the plight of these prisoners and the conditions that lead to autism and schizophrenia in children: namely that the child never had a chance to develop much of a personality. Entailed therefore are all the differences of intellectual maturity. Thus to develop childhood schizophrenia it is enough that the infant be convinced that his life is run by insensitive, irrational powers who have absolute control of his life and death. For the normal adult to suddenly develop schizophrenic-like reactions, this must actually be true, as it was in the camps.

The view is therefore proposed that infantile autism is a state of mind that develops in reaction to feeling oneself in an extreme situation, entirely without hope.

§

In Spontaneous Reaction

Turning to the origins of extreme situations in early childhood, it can be said that the mother's pathology is often severe, and in many cases her behavior toward her child offers a fascinating example of abnormal relations. But this proves neither that the mother creates the autistic process, nor that specifics of her pathology explain those of her child. Here it seems that the concentration on the mother or the mother-child relation stems again from an unrealistic ideal—that of the perfect infant-mother symbiosis, where the two form a blissful psychological monad. What is overlooked is that individuation, and with it stress and pain, begin at birth.

Fortunately, psychoanalysts are beginning to decry the haunting image of the rejecting mother. To quote Anna Freud [1954]:

A mother may be experienced as rejecting by the infant for a multitude of different reasons, connected with either her conscious or unconscious attitudes, her bodily or mental defects, her physical presence or absence, her unavoidable libidinal preoccupations, her aggressions, her anxieties, etc. The disappointments and frustrations which are inseparable from the mother-child relationship [must be] emphasized. The mother is merely the representative and symbol of inevitable frustration in the oral phase. To put the blame for the infantile neurosis on the mother's shortcomings in the oral phase is no more than a facile and misleading generalization. . . . The mother is not responsible for the child's neurosis, even if she causes "chaotic" development in some instances. By rejecting and seducing she can influence, distort and determine development, but she cannot produce either neurosis or psychosis. I believe we ought to view the influence of the mother in this respect against the background of the spontaneous developmental forces which are active in the child.

Sarvis and Garcia [1961], from a study of some eighty autistic children, arrived at notions similar to these and to ours, namely that it is not the maternal attitude that produces autism, but the child's spontaneous reaction to it. The authors feel that during the period of gradual differentiation from the mother (from six months to three years),

anything that happens to the child, whether from the inside or from the outside, is apt to impress the child as persecution by the mother. . . . Feeling the mother responsible for his difficulties, the child rejects the mother. We call this paranoid rejection the *autistic reaction*.

While we believe this reaction can appear soon after birth and not only as relatively late as six months, we agree with the authors that it develops into chronic autistic disease if the mother, in response, "seriously counterrejects or withdraws from the child." At the chronic autistic stage, they continue, "Evidences of his original negativism and paranoid attitudes remain, but the focus has shifted to compulsive, magical, autonomous efforts at mastery of the disturbance."

Thus the child's initial autistic reaction can be brought about by a variety of conditions, but whether this temporary reaction becomes a chronic disease depends on the environment's response. Nevertheless, both the original reaction and the later autistic behavior are spontaneous and autonomous responses on the part of the child.

On the basis of our experience we agree with these conclusions, but they fail to tell why the child resorts to autistic behavior as a consequence of feeling persecuted by the mother at a critical moment. Because no child can grow up without occasionally having similar feelings, even if one does not believe that all children go through a paranoid period. I believe instead that autism is the response to much more specific experiences than a feeling of being persecuted by the mother.

Again and again, in our work with schizophrenic children, we have found that their symptomatology was not alone a reaction to generalized attitudes of parents, such as rejection, neglect, or sudden changes in mood. In addition, some specific, and for each child different attitude or event had created in them the conviction that they were threatened by total destruction, had created the subjective feeling that they lived in an extreme situation.

Szurek [1956] and Szurek and Berlin [1956] have presented evidence for this contention. For virtually every example they mention our experience includes one or more parallel cases. For example, they report that "in one family it was the fact that the husband was not the father of the child, a fact known to both parents for nine years and never talked about."

We too have worked with an autistic child of whom this was true. In addition, we knew that both parents wished the child had never been born, and that he did not, by his continued existence, perpetuate their misery by reminding them of the lie they felt they were living. Mahler [1965], too, speaks of the mother of an autistic child as "warding off her own murderous impulses," to which is attributed the mother's behavior to her child. And Niederland [1965] reports on a schizophrenic boy who had been treated psychoanalytically off and on for some nine years, until at the age of about twenty-one the following story emerged:

They [his parents] told him that when he was less than a year old, they indeed had had to "thaw him out" of his urine, feces, and vomitus because "by mistake" they had left the window of his room half-open throughout a very cold winter night. They had ignored his cries during the night on the rec-

ommendation of their pediatrician. He developed pneumonia, was hospitalized, and remained an invalid for a long time.

But if childhood schizophrenia is an autonomous reaction, it can by
no means be identical with any external cause, nor even its necessary
result. Because if it were, no autonomy would be involved. Thus it
would be a serious error to assume that any parent wished to create
anything like autism in his child; quite the contrary.

The parents of autistic children simply lived their own lives, reacting
to its conditions out of their own psychological makeup. True they did
so with little regard for the nature of their child; but this they did not
know. What was spontaneous in the child was how he interpreted their
behavior and attitudes toward himself. And the less developed his grasp
of reality at the time, the less likelihood of any convictions he developed
corresponding with reality.

Ekstein and Wallerstein [1956], in discussing psychotic children,
remind us of the story of Hansel and Gretel as it illustrates how the
rejecting mother figure is transformed in the mind of the child. This
story, they note, "follows a regressive pathway . . . moving from the
suspiciousness of the children at the outset to the paranoid projection
of the devouring witch." In this, the authors anticipate the line of
reasoning in this volume. Going beyond their remarks, I would stress
that the figure of the destructive mother (the devouring witch) is the
creation of the child's imagination, though an imagining that has its
source in reality, namely the destructive intents of the mothering person.

Indeed the theme found in this and other fairy tales is still being
created—or I should better say, still haunts our children today. Like
Gretel, there is Martha, one of our schizophrenic girls who was convinced that her mother wanted to bake her in the oven and eat her.
This conviction she only revealed to her counselor after years of devoted care. But both the nightmarish anxiety and her autism were her
own creation: the nightmare being how she visualized and explained
to herself her mother's feelings about her; the autistic withdrawal being
her spontaneous defense against it.

How wide a gap may separate reality from the autistic child's interpretation or reaction is suggested by what actually prevailed in Martha's
home and conditioned the parents' behavior toward their child. Before
Martha was born, her mother had been depressive for years and also
subject to epileptic-like fainting spells. Nevertheless an older daughter
was born and developed normally.

The mother, who had great difficulty bearing children, then had a
miscarriage. There was abdominal surgery which, in its consequences,
endangered her life for a time, and she was told by her physician that

she could not have any more children. This aroused so much hatred against him that to prove him wrong, more than for any other reason, she got pregnant again, and gave birth to Martha. After the child was born the mother accused her pediatrician of being convinced that this child would not live no matter what the mother could do; a clear projection of her own feelings toward the child. The relation between mother and child was most difficult from the very beginning, so much so that eventually the father concluded he would have to choose between his wife and second daughter. If the two went on living together, he felt, one of them would have to go to a mental hospital.

Given this dilemma he decided, like the father in Hansel and Gretel, in favor of his wife. Still and all, though the mother felt that Martha was not destined to live, and though the father felt she was destroying the mother, nowhere did parental attitudes suggest the idea of baking the child in the oven to eat her, nor that she should live out her life as a nonspeaking autistic child.

Why and how, then, does such massive autistic withdrawal set in?

§

Dynamics of Autism

Seen from *outside* the person, all emotional disturbance is marked by some serious breakdown in communication with others.

Ordinarily, things do not happen with dramatic suddenness, neither the giving up of talking nor of the impulse to act. They happen rather in a slow, step-by-step process. In normal development the child begins to act as his mouth seeks the nipple, as he responds to auditory and visual stimuli, as he engages in visual pursuit. And communication begins as he nurses. Even in this earliest stage of acting and interacting which is hence the earliest stage of personality formation, things may go wrong.

The infant, because of pain or discomfort and the anxiety they cause, or because he misreads the mother's actions or feelings, or correctly assesses her negative feelings, may retreat from her and the world. The mother, for her part, either frustrated in her motherly feelings, or out of her own anxiety, may respond not with gentle pursuit, but with anger or injured indifference. This is apt to create new anxiety in the child, to which may now be added the feeling that the world (as represented by the mother) not only causes anxiety but is also angry or indifferent as the case may be.

Any such retreat from the world tends to weaken the baby's impulse to observe and to act on the environment, though without such an impulse personality will not develop. Retreat debilitates a young ego barely emerging from the undifferentiated stage, and leads to still further psychic imbalance.

How severe the imbalance will be depends on the nature and degree of the breakdown in communication with the outside. Those parts of reality that prove too disappointing or unresponsive will be defended against or replaced by imaginary ones that seem more satisfying; inner reactions that are too powerful will be repressed—all in efforts to retain some contact with the world and make at least some limited part of it secure. But when things go beyond this, when reality seems too destructive, then the person stops trying. Efforts to master some aspects of reality, and to come to terms with others through defense, are given up. Then the mental apparatus is made to serve only one goal: to protect sheer life by doing nothing about outside reality. All energy goes into protection and none is available for building personality. Behind it all lies the conviction that any being or doing would bring about some disastrous response.

The reasons why communication breaks down may be various, and take a wide range of forms. A person may not respond correctly because he misinterprets the signals he receives in terms of his anxiety or hostility; or he may read them only too correctly. He may need to send out confusing signals to "get back at others" or more likely, to avoid dangers he is sure would follow if others could know his true thoughts.

Yet whatever the initial cause, it is the degree and persistence of the persons's failure to send and receive messages correctly that accounts for the degree and persistence of his emotional disturbance. Conversely, when improved conditions or treatment enable the person to acquaint himself and others with his feelings and thoughts, and to correctly receive the communication of others, his disturbance is removed.

So much for what emotional disturbance looks like from the outside, as between persons.

Viewed from *inside* the person (or intrapersonally) however, this breakdown in communication is caused by overwhelming anxiety. The anxious person may seek minimal security by first reducing his contact with a world that makes him too anxious. In more severe cases he may later avoid such contact and lose all trust in his ability to deal with the world. If the retreat is not just temporary, he may be caught in a vicious circle where anxiety leads to retreat from reality, retreat to still greater anxiety, and in the end to more permanent withdrawal. Here it makes little difference whether the anxiety began because of real or imagined dangers in the world, or because of some inner psychic process. Inner hostility, for example, can arouse tremendous anxiety if we are convinced that giving vent to it will cause our destruction.

Still, as long as the person views his anxiety as caused by something on the outside, he remains in some distorted contact with reality. It matters little whether he is anxious about the hostile intentions of others or what they may do in response to his own hostile wishes. To the degree that he connects his anxiety or hostility to the external world he is in contact with it, though his view of it and responses to it are distorted. Depending thus on the degree of anxiety, and hence of distortion, it remains possible for him to view the source of his anxiety more or less correctly.

But if anxiety increases beyond a certain degree, if it overwhelms the organism and results in panic, then the contact with reality is lost. Whether anxiety reaches panic proportions depends on whether the person believes he can take action to reduce the dangers that caused it, and with it reduce the anxiety. Here again it makes little difference whether the external source of anxiety is in fact irreducible. What counts is whether the anxious person thinks so or not.

In panic anxiety, hostility is no longer felt as such. This makes matters so much worse, because in some fashion as long as we feel we are hostile to the world, we can see it as a reasonable consequence that the world will hit back. This, of course, makes us anxious. But while we are frightened, the world still makes sense. It is when we no longer recognize our hostility, and the world remains utterly frightening, that reality stops seeming reasonable. Living in such an unreasonable, unpredictable world, the best thing, the only protection, lies in doing nothing. If any action on our part is apt to bring about disaster, then not acting is the only safe course.

To protect such nonacting, the child's only safety lies in not being provoked into action. Any stimulus reaching him from the outside might provoke action, so he must make himself insensitive to whatever might reach him from the outside. And since inner hostility might also provoke him to act, he must make himself insensitive to what comes from within his own psyche.

This is autism as seen from inside the person.

§

Dialectics of Hope

To say that for survival one must take self-protective action is a truism. It is less obvious that taking action preserves our psychological integrity, while passivity destroys it. This is difficult to illustrate in the case of autistic children. Because of their immaturity and basic vulnerability their chances for taking action in their own behalf are severely limited, and their motivations grossly inarticulate, obscure.

Perhaps I can illustrate with the example of an exceedingly bright autistic boy (I.Q. well above 170). His father cared about him only as an intellect, the mother only as a soft animal to be cuddled. Unable to choose between them and develop accordingly, and lacking the strength to defy one or both of them enough to develop his own personality, his way out was to act in submission to both.

In order to remain the cuddly thing his mother wanted, he failed to develop his motor skills or to articulate his body. In submission to her he refrained from putting to use his developing physical maturity.

For the father, he developed his intellect; but since it could not interfere with his pleasing the mother, his intellectual activities had no substance, no "body," so far as his life or personality were concerned. He could not learn to differentiate right from left, or to read (because he could not know where that might eventually take him). Instead he applied his superior intelligence to issues totally unusable in understanding himself or his body, such as in learning how the solar system works.

In acting to please his parents he was, in a way, acting in his own behalf, but without any regard for his true personal interests. He took action, but without any concern for how destructive it was to himself. The result was that his own actions projected him ever deeper into autism, because with each act he removed himself further from contact with reality, and from mastery of his own body and life. Still, that he acted, and did not escape to the utter passivity of the mute autistic child, increased immeasurably his chances for complete recovery.

Thus as far as withdrawal from reality and the giving up of action are concerned, we may distinguish at least three, and possibly more, levels or stages, though they blend and overlap.

On the lowest rung of personal functioning stands the individual who has given up acting on his own, and does not react to his environment, who has *withdrawn all cathexis from all aspects of reality, inner and outer.* (Children who suffer from infantile marasmus, mute autistic children.)

Different from him is the individual who to some degree still acts, though he does not interact with his environment. He dares not act on his "natural" tendencies and interests, or the realities of the environment, but for all practical purposes is motivated only by anxiety. He has *withdrawn cathexis from the environment but not from his inner psychic processes though even those are undercathected.* (The talking autistic child who insists on sameness but still has angry, destructive outbursts.)

Then there is the individual who is locked in mortal struggle with an environment that seems both hostile and overpowering to him. Though he continues to act, he acts mainly in terms of his *inner psychic processes which he has overcathected*. His view of and contact with reality is distorted, his personality may be deeply scarred, but it has not disintegrated in toto nor in that most significant aspect: the ability to act. His actions are not effective in changing reality, because they are based only or mainly on his disorganized inner psychic processes, but they are intended to do so. (The schizophrenic child who often fights the world violently.)[2]

Often, though not always, and depending on the age and developmental stage at which massive autistic withdrawal sets in, this giving up of contact with the world proceeds in reverse order from what I list here as the three stages of alienation from inner and outer reality.

But why does a person withdraw so completely as to even abandon the self? That he abandons a frightening world we can understand. But why also this very inner self he set out to protect?

Two reasons have already been mentioned: namely, to keep stimuli from coming to awareness because they are too painful, and to avoid the temptation to act. But in consequence of these he pays less and less emotional attention to the world and his inner preoccupations loom larger and larger by comparison. Though he then pays them ever more attention, cathects them even more, they do not offer more satisfaction, but less. Because they cannot make up for what he misses when he breaks off emotional contact with reality. So this inner process that he hoped would make up for what he lacks, lets him down all the more as his reliance on it grows. That is why he eventually stops cathecting it too.

2. Some modern writers are beholden to this level of personality development as was the Marquis de Sade, for example, in a previous century. As he tried to act out his sexual fantasies in a world which therefore felt obliged to lock him up, so have mental patients always done. The difference is that the mental patient lacks enough control over his inner psychic processes to bring them sufficiently in order so that others can grasp them, or at least part of them. In a strange dialectic process some modern writers (Burroughs, for example) do not seem satisfied to live at the mercy of their untamed primary process thinking, but use drugs to create mental states akin to those of the schizophrenic. Their pride seems to derive from deliberately creating in themselves a state of mind which the mental patient cannot help living in. Having lost contact with reality, or at least the ability to act in accordance with its requirements, but not yet having "lost their mind," they try to lose it for periods of time by taking drugs. Their stance is that they do so because they reject a world that deserves rejection. Actually they find life wanting, and either they lack the courage to accept this as a temporary deficiency of personality that could and should be remedied, or else they lack the conviction that if this is a bad world it behooves one to improve it. This failure to act on the world or one's own personality, or both, they try to cover up by claiming it a virtue to escape into a drug-induced dream world. (I do not refer here to those who take drugs as part of a scientific inquiry, though their unconscious motivations for doing so are probably the same.)

And what at first seemed like a search for inner richness because the world was (or became) too devoid of satisfactions, turns to utter emptiness.

To view such eventual withdrawal too simply as escape from a threatening environment is to understand this process on much too rational a basis, as if it were a reasoned out, conscious decision. This is by no means the case, and to imply it does violence to how the human psyche functions. Actually the whole thing is more like a dialectic process. For each of us survival normally entails continuous struggle toward a synthesis of opposites. The autistic child seems to get stuck with the antithesis, never reaching the synthesis needed for successful survival.

Maybe I can illustrate again from the concentration camps. There the overriding thesis is mortal danger. And the first psychological re-action to danger is not to ignore it, but to pay it the minutest attention. That is, we devote to it the earliest, most primitive, but also the most crucial of all psychological powers: our attention.

So actually the concentration-camp prisoner at first pays inordinate attention to the SS guards (and to the prisoner-foreman, who was often the more immediate danger). So much so, day and night, that because the enemy is at all times overwhelmingly present in mind, he begins to seem so in reality too. And up to a point he really was, but by no means to the extent that the prisoner believed. This, then, is the antithesis: the reaction to the thesis of danger.

Those prisoners who did not become moslems moved from there to a viable synthesis. The enemy was paid a great deal of attention to, but not to the exclusion of self-preservative action—trying to find less dangerous or strenuous job assignments, making friends where one could, trying to move to a better barracks, or place to sleep; but also a lot of hoping and daydreaming about a better future to come, including the hope of revenge, and making plans toward this end. Those instead, who were destined to become moslems focused more attention than ever on the enemy to the exclusion of all else until soon nothing but the enemy seemed to exist. In turn this made everything destructive, because psychologically they were living in a world, inner and outer, where nothing existed but the unrelieved prospect of doom.

This then is the siuation when we make ourselves insensitive to all experience because it seems the only means to relief, but is not. We have, in fact become self-destructive because the psychological behavior we engaged in to survive—total concentration on the enemy—proved debilitating. This, psychologically, is what constitutes an extreme situa-tion: when we ourselves respond to an external danger—real or imagined —with inner maneuvers that actually debilitate us further.

Consciously or not, it is why, as mentioned before, many prisoners told themselves (and each other) that they had to do something every day, however insignificant, to better their lot; a precept that saved many lives. Not only because it proved, in the face of overwhelming danger, that one still had a hand in one's fate, but also because it forced one's attention toward something beside the unending peril of death.

It is more difficult to know what parallel process goes on in children suffering from infantile autism because for them all is played out in the emotional sphere, without clear recognition of why those they view as enemies are so bent on destruction. But consider, for example, the twiddling of autistic children (cf. pages 164–166) and how it represents their desperate efforts to reach the breast and satisfaction, though the twiddling never succeeds. Isn't it possible to see in this behavior the same total concentration of attention as in the moslem, until soon he was unable to think of anything else? And because his all pervasive thoughts of destruction were so painful, soon he was even incapable of thinking about that?

So too, perhaps, with autistic children, or if not all of them, then the twiddling ones. At first they may have concentrated all attention on the breast, hoping for the satisfactions it stood for. This concentration, unlike the prisoner's, was born initially out of desire, not fear, but a desire made all-consuming because of the fearful destruction looming everywhere. As more and more attention went to thoughts of the breast, all other activities fell away, at least psychologically, until there was nothing in life but frustration.

For such a concentration to occur, simple disappointment in the breast is not enough. As I have tried to suggest, the cause of childhood schizophrenia is the conviction that the environment is destructive in toto. It is what leads to the incredibly strong fixation on the breast as the only thing that offered satisfaction at one time, or at least some relief. And this impossible hope of getting everything from the breast cannot help adding to the child's desperation.

In response, he withdraws to an inner redoubt in an effort to survive within a totally frustrating environment. But no inner fortress has ever allowed for survival without help from the outside. The concentration-camp prisoner who did not get help from others, or could not use it, was doomed. This is why I have said that autism begins as a breakdown in communication.

The more communication is interfered with, the less contact there is with others and the more the person must fall back on his inner experience to interpret reality. As if this were not bad enough, the less contact with reality he has, the less he can test his inner experience against something permitting a balanced judgment about it. Hence the more this happens the more likely he is to interpret signals from the outside incorrectly, and those from the inside solipsistically. Where communication is given up altogether or if it was never established in the first place, the person has nothing but his inner experience to guide him, and he has nothing to go by in judging that.

On the face of it, this might suggest that the inner self would then develop more richly. But no assumption would be less correct. An inner life that is not validated against outer experiences and then organized through such validation, remains chaotic. If this is so, then the more attention we pay to the inner life alone, the greater its chaos.

The inner life, and with it personality, is not developed to gain greater richness of inner sensations or experience. Personality develops for only one reason: to deal with the external world and hopefully to be able to affect it. If personality cannot do this, no point in developing the inner structures for achieving such a goal. Just as language develops only if we wish to talk to someone or to understand what he is telling us, so personality develops only if we wish to do something with another human being, or to him, or for him.

This is equally true of how order is brought into the flight of images and ideas. We organize them into thoughts only if we intend to use them as a basis for action, or if we at least want to convey them to others so that they may share in our thoughts.

This is the secret of psychoanalytic technique. In order to convey the content of our "free associations" to the analyst we have to bring them to enough order so that we can express them in something like sentence form. Hence as we tell our free associations they are no longer free, but ordered. Mere exclamations can elicit from the analyst only sympathetic emotions or shrewd guesses on how the patient's thoughts could be ordered to "make sense." This may be necessary to get the analytic work started, and the analyst may be able to shape his patient's exclamations into sentences that express the flight of ideas behind the exclamation. But analytic material they become only as they are formed into sentences. And sentences are either actions or statements about actions.

If someone should object here that a sentence such as "This is blue grass" implies no action, my reply is that while it is not about an action, my saying it is. The intended action behind the utterance is to tell it to someone else. This may readily be seen from the small child's exclaiming "See!" which means one should look. And his somewhat later, more elaborate exclamation "A flower!" means exactly the same: that we should join him in his pleasure at seeing the flower.

Thus what are technically called free associations are no longer vague images or feelings, but ideas that have been ordered into thoughts and expressed in a form somehow implying an action. To produce them, to learn to express vague and chaotic ideas and feelings in a form implying action, even potential action, is curative. It directs the patient toward the goal of becoming active in his own behalf, though for some time his most important activity may, and often should consist of, the action of bringing order to his chaotic ideas and feelings.

Even the worst anxiety becomes more manageable if its seeming all pervasiveness can be captured and then limited by expression in discrete form: that somebody or something is threatening to do something to me. Because with a now more specific someone or something I can take specific protective measures in place of amorphous anxiety. That is why self-analysis will not achieve the same effect. In thinking about one's unconscious productions one is not forced to express them in sentences that can be understood by at least one other person. But without expressing our thoughts in sentence form they remain disorderly; often too they not only remain solipsistic but devoid of implied action.

All this applies particularly for the schizophrenic thought processes, most of all the autistic ones. The story is different for example, with the acting out person. His vague thoughts are action directed. Where the schizophrenic (and particularly the autistic) person suffers because his disorganized thoughts are not expressed in a form implying an action and hence cannot be scrutinized, the acting out person suffers because he can only act, but not think about action. In order to gain control of his acting out behavior he has to learn to state aloud his intended actions so that he can grasp their source and what is likely to come of them. In the last analysis both suffer the same deficiency though in widely different forms: neither one can really think about action.

What has been said about thought applies no less to feelings. Feelings, too, are separated out and refined only in hopes of telling them to someone who will respond to us with empathy. That is why autistic children neither smile nor cry. The not smiling could be explained by their unhappiness. The not crying is due to the fact that crying is meant to bring a comforting response; a real one if someone is there, or an imaginary one as in lonely crying.

If we in desperation feel sure that no one will respond to our crying, and if we cannot even conjure in imagination that someone would feel with us in our distress, then we do not cry. Crying, even more than smiling, is an expression of emotion that is intended to evoke a response. We may smile, for example, when feeling superior. That is, we may smile, and take ourselves for the responsive audience. This happens only very rarely in crying. Though occasionally someone may cry and take himself for his audience ("Look how great is my misery, or sensitivity, which makes me cry"), it is much more rare. That crying has little to do with the misery experienced could be seen in the concentration camps. Prisoners cried very rarely, and only when they felt sure of a receptive audience. Moslems never cried.

§
Decline of the Self

As experience with autistic children has taught us, and as reports on such children have suggested before, the more the person withdraws from reality into autism, the emptier, the more repetitious and stereotyped becomes his fantasy life, though this is all he has left: the vaguer then become even his sensations, the less content and structure has his self.

Among the reasons for this is that a self, if it is not to wither away, must forever be testing itself against the nonself in a process of active assertion. By self-assertion is not meant a rugged individualism nor an egocentric having one's way. Either of these might not be a testing of self against nonself, but a pushing away or a high-handed manipulation of the nonself. Testing implies both respect and consideration for what we test ourselves against. Otherwise it becomes not a test of self, but of something entirely different, perhaps of brute force.

As a matter of fact, what a person selects as a testing ground is most indicative of the nature and quality of the self. A passive yielding to certain experiences can be a much more subtle testing of the self against the nonself than meeting it aggressively. Success is then not a question of how unchanged the self emerges from the test nor how much it has bent the nonself to its will, but how enriched it became in the process.

Whatever the self tests itself against most constructively flows from whatever experience is crucial to us at the moment. Hence the infant's need to test himself against emotional acceptance by his parents, the child's need to test mind against body in his play, or himself against his playmates.

By the same token, if the nonself is not paid attention to (was never cathected, or became decathected) then it too becomes vague, non-differentiated. Richness of self and of nonself are achieved in a continuous, simultaneous process in which one enhances the other, though from our present stage of knowledge we cannot say what precedes what, or what is cause and what effect.

As the infant tries to grasp the variety and complexity of the world, as he looks at his hands and watches his fingers move in the outside world, he becomes aware that it is he, his internal will, that moves them. As he wishes to gain objects and goals, makes the effort and succeeds, his self grows. Since he can influence only his immediate environment, it is this he pays attention to. Distant events may startle him, but they do not really interest him. He concentrates on what he can feel through touch, smell, taste. Only as his personality develops, and his comprehension of the world, does he become interested in distant objects, problems, and finally in abstract thought.

The behavior of autistic children indicates a decline of self, or action, of interest in the outside world; or perhaps less a decline than a very early arrest. Like the baby, they are not usually interested in what goes on at any distance from them. If they are interested in anything, if they act on anything, it is their own body and a few objects that are handled over and over again in the same ritualistic fashion.

Fancy interpretative efforts sometimes succeed in ascribing deeply personal, specific meaning to these objects. True, they become invested with all that goes on repetitively in the child's mind, which is indeed all the meaning he can invest in anything. But these objects often function less as carriers of meaning than to ward off any challenge to action that might come from the world. The autistic child's concentration on the endlessly twiddled toy, on the over-and-over-again ritualistically put-together puzzle, his listening over and over again to the same record—above and beyond the meaning of such behavior—also serve to prevent stimuli from reaching him because they might tempt him to action.

Typically some of these children are very skillful at putting puzzles together but insist on working only with the blank sides. The emergence of a picture, were the puzzle put together with the picture side up, becomes too much of a change and hence a temptation to action since it shows they can produce something. Ending up with a blank, on the contrary, assures them that any effort to produce something new would be vain.

Similarly, these children are often very good at reproducing rhythms, and spend hours listening to the same rhythms over and over. It is the endless repetition of sameness that attracts them because it seems to assure them that nothing ever changes. In addition, the rhythm blots out any noise that might startle them and thus tempt them to action. Any discontinuity, or novelty, with its challenge to the self and to action, must be avoided at all cost.

Their vague, empty gaze at the far distance, nonfocussed and directed at nothing in particular, has the same purpose; not to see what goes on close at hand because that is what really interests them and is therefore what could invite them to act and hence to react. Both the external world inviting action, and the internal world that might react, are denied at the same time. The height of such deterioration of the self, the extreme forms of nonaction and of interest withdrawn from the world, these are reached when all communication is given up.

§

The Human Craving for Order

Many who have reflected on the autistic child's desire for sameness recognize that its purpose is to lessen anxiety. What is not stressed as much is that it stands for an ordering of things, an effort to establish laws by which things must happen.

With us, too, a scientific law signifies that, given the same conditions, the same events will take place. Thus the insistence on sameness is the autistic child's struggle to find a law giving permanence and order to his life. If the search for natural laws has a purpose, it is to predict events and master nature so as to make our lives more secure. Social law too, has no purpose except to safeguard our common existence. This—their intrinsic purpose—all our laws have in common with the laws the autistic child creates. He is firmly convinced that those he lives by are essential to his security. They must be observed or his life will fall apart, just as society would decay if no one accepted the law of the land. To prevent this, he must arrange toys in the same eternal order, repeat phrases in exactly the same way and with the same enunciation. What distinguishes his laws from ours is that his are nonadaptive and universal. One and the same law governs everything.

Erikson [1959] has described a disturbance occurring in adolescence which he calls "time diffusion." For time diffusion to afflict the growing youngster, things must have gone wrong in the very first crises of his life, because

the conception of temporal cycles and of time qualities is inherent in and develops from the first experience of mounting need tension, of delay of satisfaction, and final unification with the satisfying object. . . . Our most malignantly regressed young people are clearly possessed by general attitudes which represent something of mistrust of time as such: every delay appears to be a deceit, every plan a catastrophe, every potential provider a traitor. Therefore, time must be made to stand still, if necessary by the magic means of catatonic immobility—or by death.

If, in the early days of life, tension mounts and is not relieved by a "final unification with the satisfying object" (or what I prefer to view as satisfaction within a context of mutuality) there is impotent rage in which "anticipation and with it, future, is obliterated."

This description of what happens when the ego cannot support expectancy, fits the autistic child even more than the adolescent. Certainly all autistic children insist that time must stand still. This is why Joey could not let us speak of children or adults, or of people as being older or younger, for implied in these terms is a movement in time. The only ordering he permitted was by size, so he filled his world with persons big and small, not with children or adults. Time is the destroyer of sameness. If sameness is preserved, time must stop in its tracks. Therefore the autistic child's world consists only of space. Neither time nor causality exist there, because causality involves a sequence in time where events have to follow one another.[3]

Causality also implies that one event causes another, with a relation implied. But the autistic child is terrified by relations because they all seem destructive to him. In the autistic child's world the chain of events is not conditioned by the causality we know. But since one event does follow another, it must be because of some timeless cosmic law that ordains it. An eternal law. Things happen because they must, not because they are caused.

Time also implies hope. If things can be different, they may also be better. But hope too often disappointed projects us first into ungoverned rage, and in the end utter torpor. Therefore all disappointment must be prevented.

Without time there is no hope but also no disappointment nor the fear that things might even get worse. Hence the eternal repetition of sameness which rules out all hope that things will ever be different, but also all disappointment. Any change, even the slightest, might arouse hope, or the risk of worsened conditions, and must therefore be avoided at all costs. Hence infantile autism and the cosmic law. Once and for all, and absolutely, it ordains how things must be ordered. Sensible laws can be subject to sensible revision and hence permit hope to arise. Thus it must be an insensible law that never changes. And the essential content of this law is "you must never hope that anything can change."

Not all autistic children are like Laurie and Marcia and insist on eternal sameness in the environment. Others are like Joey, however repetitive their behavior and actions: in place of the autistic desire for sameness they look for some other ordering principle that is just as permanent and unchanging. Joey chose for this the absolute law of machines.

---

3. Some autistic children do speak of past events, but this is misleading, because to them such events are still in the present. One autistic boy spoke incessantly about rides he had taken through a tunnel with his mother; but though in our time years removed from the rides, in his experience he was still taking them all the time. So while he talked of "When I rode through the tunnel," as far as his experience was concerned he was still riding through it.

Each autistic child has his own way of dealing with his need to live outside of causality, because outside of time. Joey's solution was to turn the fact that machines were invented by men for their use, into the opposite: that men exist to be run by machines. To also master a world without time he avoided all mention of what pertained to its flow. Another autistic boy insisted that the sun did not set, but had to stay put in the sky. When the days grew longer he insisted they had to get shorter, and the other way around. Instead of abolishing time he tried to control it. other children insist they control the weather, often to camouflage the conviction that they thus control time.

How does the infant move from such a cosmic law to an understanding of the true relations between time, space and causality, and hence to the nature of social laws? Piaget has clarified how the normal child's thinking proceeds. What concerns me in this book is how the various steps in developing cognition are related to the child's vital experience with life. How does his experience with others affect his notions of the orderly functioning of his body, and through them his ideas about the natural order of things?

Autistic children do not recognize any order to the functioning of their bodies. To them, none of their bodily functions flow from the body and its needs. At best they are mechanical systems and follow some mechanical order.

But it is only by the way our body adapts to the varied conditions of the day, and our emotions to what unfolds in our human environment, that we come to understand causality with our deepest feelings; in our viscera, as it were. Somebody does something, and this makes us feel good or bad. Something goes in or comes out of our body, and the conditions surrounding it make us feel good or bad. As conditions differ, so does our sense of well-being—first the well-being of our body, and then the sense of well-being we get from being with others. All this makes up our primary experience of highly personalized causality. We learn that "this" causes "that." Onto it becomes grafted, or out of it develops, a much more stringent relation between cause and effect, a causality we no longer just "feel," but can also understand and put to use in our lives.

Part Two

THREE CASE HISTORIES

A Note on
Passionate Indifference

> . . . for it was not so much by the knowledge of
> words that I came to the understanding of things,
> as by my experience of things I was enabled to
> follow the meaning of words.   PLUTARCH

ACCORDING TO THE LITERATURE [Kanner, 1943, 1944] autistic
children do not relate to persons, though some of them relate to objects.
This book is predicated on the conviction that they do indeed relate to
persons, though no longer (if they ever did once) in a positive way. While
theirs is a strange way of relating, to say that they do not relate is to
take a strangely depleted view of human relations, or at least a pre-
Freudian image of the nature of human emotions.

Certainly, if we take relations to mean only positive attachments and
not also negative ones, then we can say with some justice that autistic
children do not relate. But since the advent of Freud it has become
difficult to think of emotions, most of all our feelings about others, as
anything but ambivalent.

At any given moment in time every human relation will comprise
some mixture of attachment and avoidance. This mixture we could place
at some point on a continuum that extends from the most intensely
positive to the most intensely negative attachment. The latter can sometimes look like total avoidance. But even extreme hate when we feel it

suggests an inner attitude of wishing to do something about the cause of our hate, which is not the same as avoidance.

Still, however extreme the position of severe hate on this continuum of ambivalence, there is one even farther out than a hate unrelieved by any love. (And beneath most hate is love, because we only hate if we care; otherwise we are simply indifferent.) The autistic child's total avoidance of relations with people is marked by an absence of visible hatred. It cannot then be inferred from his overt behavior, and bespeaks the depth of his disappointment in people. So much so, that he has given up all hope that through his actions he can satisfy his deepest desire: to be given to by people. In his case repression of the longing for related-ness is more total than in any more open or active show of hate. It is a repression of such depth that it has to be kept from ever coming to awareness by a total avoidance of all relatedness—which is certainly not a stance of indifference.

How can I be so sure that a relatedness of love and hate for other persons lies behind what others, who write of infantile autism, call an absence of relations? Simply because whenever we have penetrated behind it, we have found hatred, extreme and explosive. And behind the hatred was always the longing, eternally thwarted, but nevertheless not given up; a longing now deeply encapsulated in repression so as to keep it from coming to awareness in unbearable pain.

Others, too, have recognized that behind the autistic child's relation to objects that have to stay unchanged lies the wish for a relation to a person who will never change. As Rochlin [1953] points out, this desire for sameness extends to the autistic child himself and to everything within him. It is the ultimate statement that nothing more must be lost, because the autistic child is so depleted that any further loss would mean death.

Indeed, as discussed earlier, when the autistic child becomes convinced that change may be possible, when his emotions begin to thaw, what unfreezes first is blind hatred and rage. As likely as not he will direct these against the only available object, the self, in suicidal attempts. Thus autism is a position even more extreme than suicide; and suicide, or suicidal tendencies, are a first step toward once again becoming active.

If this is so, then infantile autism can indeed be viewed as a position coming as close to the extreme negative end of the continuum as is meet with survival. Suicide alone seems a more extreme position, but is not. Because suicide involves a goal-directed action that the autistic child seems even less capable of performing than the suicidal person. Infantile autism might be viewed as a position of despair where even the requisite energy to end it all is lacking, or else where all doing is avoided precisely to defend against a passive dying, as in death by marasmus, for example.

To relate, according to Webster, means "to connect or associate, as in thought or meaning; to show as having to do with." The word comes from the Latin *referro*, meaning "to carry back." And no term could more aptly describe the autistic child. His trouble is that more than any human being, he carries everything back to one, and only one set of experiences, to which he connects or associates all things.

I have spoken of how early infancy is so often described as a stage where the child lives in perfect positive attachment to the mother. I doubt that such flawless love is available to man, just because I accept Freud's view of the ambivalence in our feelings for others. But it is probably true that subtle emotional shadings are not apt to occur in early infancy, and that sudden swings from one extreme to the other are more typical of this age. So let us assume for a moment that the normal infant's positive attachment to his mother is more intense and complete than it will ever be to anyone else. Isn't it reasonable to assume that if he then becomes deeply disappointed in the attachment he may, given his immature judgment, come to avoid it as completely as he sought it before?

The extremes still touch each other, and in infancy most of all. If this is so, then infantile autism, far from being characterized by an absence of relatedness to persons, is marked by the child's relating everything back to what he experienced with one particular person, or set of persons.

The nature of this set of experiences, or the view of life derived from them, I have tried to suggest in the preceding chapters. If I introduce the next three chapters—the case histories—by discussing the autistic child's way of relating it is because we believe it is just this specific, most unusual, and idiosyncratic nature of his relatedness that must guide us in treatment.

Since the autistic child, in our opinion, lumps all relatedness together as destructive and inescapable, then our task is to help him recognize that other forms of relatedness exist. Because of the one single relation that propelled him out of a position of love and ambivalence with overwhelming force he became, so to say, glued to hate. It is our task to help him move from this position of extreme hate and dejection toward that human ambivalence in which normal relations exist.

From this it follows that I also disagree with those who say the autistic child does relate to objects (in contrast to persons) since the implication is that his relating to objects is positive. If it were, it would constitute a self-chosen positive attachment and this would soon permit the child to escape his exclusive relatedness to the one set of negative experiences. This is what Plutarch tried to tell us, and why I introduce the case histories with his words. When we can really encompass the meaning of things, it means we have successfully acted upon them. This is how thought is acquired and how we grasp our relatedness to things as opposed to feeling helplessly subject to them.

Since it is not objects but persons who seem to threaten the autistic child's existence, it is true that he is less fearful of things and might even act upon them. But he does not use them as they are meant to be used. And some mute autistic children, to protect themselves, have so completely withdrawn interest from the world that even objects are too scary to be paid attention to.

Or to put it differently: I am convinced that the autistic child's relation to those persons or experiences that projected him into autism is so total that no other relatedness, even to objects, is possible for him. I believe that even his dealing with objects takes place within the one context that pervades his existence to the exclusion of everything else. While I thus believe that autistic children relate to persons and also to objects—I believe they can only do so in highly idiosyncratic ways.

This does not mean that the ego is nonexistent in such children. Despite the fearful emptiness of their contact with people and things, intrapersonal developments have taken place, however deviately. The self is stunted, most unevenly developed, but still seems to function in some minimal way to protect them from further harm.

In addition, there are always some areas of living that are not totally riddled with anxiety and which remained fairly conflict-free so that the ego could and did meet its tasks. Some of these children are toilet-trained, dress themselves in some measure, feed themselves, though usually from only a very few selected foods.

Some of these tasks, though once learned to comply with a threatening environment, do not necessarily disintegrate when the child begins to withdraw. Unfortunately, this is not enough to make them tasks in which the self is engaged. Rather, they are performed like conditioned responses. The child responds when the conditioning stimulus is present, whether or not the response makes any sense in reality or to him. The original conditioning influence was usually a parental demand that was neither resisted nor made one's own. Once the demand is gone, such skills become slowly extinguished. Without any seeming involvement or sense of loss, the child then gives up what he has learned.

Again: because these skills were not learned for the comfort they offered, they had no positive meaning for the children. We found ourselves unable to preserve such abilities while changing their purpose from a negative one (warding off harm) to a positive one (making life more pleasurable). So under our care these children give up toilet training, for example, or dressing themselves, because those were too closely identified with compliance to some power that was hated and feared.

Only after a period of soiling or not dressing themselves do they relearn such a skill, but now within a more positive relationship and as part of a developing self—to gain a sense of well-being.

It seems that a learning experience without positive emotional connotations, one that began as a resented compromise or became part of it, cannot directly be made secure by just having a better experience. The self-alien experience has to leave the child's life, as it were, has to disappear in toto, before it can be built up from scratch in a positive way.

Since these children have stopped expecting any part of the environment to be need-satisfying, we have to provide for them an environment of potentially positive valence long before it wakens any positive interest. Only after they have been exposed to this for a long enough time do they begin to fathom that perhaps some other than the all-pervasive one they have known may be possible. Only then will they attend to reality, at least for moments, to recognize some of its aspects as having positive value. This makes the treatment of such children devastatingly slow.

For a long time they distrust that any doing or learning can serve any positive purpose. For each step in doing on their own—as opposed to an automatic performing—they have to make sure innumerable times that nothing is being forced on them, that it is they who want to eat, to move their bowels, to play or do anything, including talk.

That is why the first positive things they do are often the reverse of what they think we want them to do. It is also why they give up achievements like toilet training. But even to do that, to do anything on their own, they need encouragement from us—but not too much, or again they feel pushed. So in a strange process we have to encourage them to defy us, but to defy us because they want to and not because we encourage it. Only by defying us can they be sure they are something more than a subservience to the environment.

Our encouragement serves mainly to convince these children that they are neither alone nor in danger, in the struggle to find themselves. Even our pleasure at their contrariness—which comes easy because we are so happy that they do anything at all—has to be tempered, so that they do not feel committed to (or against) it on our account. Only after being contrary, and thus asserting their existence as self-determining human beings, can they begin to come to terms with the environment through some positive steps. And this effort, too, they have to protect as their own, by not beginning to "do" when we would like them to, but only in their own good time. They then dangle us endlessly, because only our patient waiting can convince them they are acting by their own wish, and are not being forced to by us. This, in fact, was a large part of Marcia's story.

Essentially, each of the three histories that follow is a description of the children's behavior, of the theoretical considerations that guided treatment efforts, and of what insights we gained. In one case our efforts were aborted. One, despite remarkable progress, was to a considerable degree a failure. The last one was a relative success.

Because children like Laurie and Marcia take important steps out of isolation before they achieve language in the sense of communication, we also decided to take moving pictures of some of them, provided it did not interfere with their current well-being or later progress. Nonverbal behavior is hard to describe in words. Even if we could do it well the reader would still have to trust our descriptions and interpretations. Moving pictures permit the viewer to form his own opinion. Thus far we have collected visual records of only a very few essentially mute autistic children.

The number of autistic children with whom we can work at any one time is relatively small because if we are to help them we can never have more than six to eight truly autistic children among our population of forty-five. Had we more, they would find themselves surrounded by essentially nonresponsive children, and have even less motive to come out of their isolation. In practice, we find that sometimes the presence of very active, even of acting out children—if the autistic child is well protected from harmful effects—can be very reassuring. They can see, for example, that a very assertive, even aggressive dealing with the problems of life does not lead to mishaps or to retaliation, but on the contrary, is welcomed by us.

For other reasons, too, we cannot afford to have too many autistic children at a time. Staff members could not maintain their positive attitude to these children if relentlessly exposed to rejection—or worse, to being treated as nonexistent—without letup. The other children, though quite disturbed, still respond more humanly to our efforts and offer needed relief. At the same time they present the autistic child with examples of relations that are there for him, if and when he can give up his total isolation.

Because the treatment of autism goes slowly, only little of an ego emerged in Laurie at the end of her one year with us. Still, she was in some fashion more obvious than other children we have worked with in how she went about taking some first crucial steps out of autism. Hers, therefore, is the first of the histories in this volume.

Laurie

Direct work with this child was carried out by several staff members, but principally by Wanda Weiss, Laurie's counselor, and Hazel Osborn, her teacher. To them belongs most of the credit for her progress under our care, and for the observational raw material on which this report is based.

L AURIE, A MUTE AUTISTIC GIRL, was admitted to the Orthogenic School at age seven. Shortly before admission she had been committed to a state mental institution. When we first saw her she was extremely emaciated, though exceptionally pretty and well groomed. Except for her severe anorexia she was completely inert, and had not spoken in more than four years.

§
Background and History

Laurie's mother, by her own account, had known little happiness in life. In her middle teens she found escape from home, particularly from an authoritarian and punitive father, by marrying a man considerably older than she was. The couple soon separated and some years later were divorced.

At about this latter time the mother seems to have suffered an emotional breakdown and for some time was under treatment for what she called a severe nervous condition. She then moved away from her home town.

Before she and her second husband met, each of them had known severe frustration in their separate love relations. They were aware of their difficulties with each other and decided not to have a child until they felt they could count on their marriage to last. Still, it was not long before Laurie was born, and some years later another daughter. Up to the time Laurie came to the Orthogenic School, the infant sister's development was proceeding fairly normally, though at our one encounter she seemed tense and compulsive.

According to what the mother told us (the father was not interested in giving us a history; he was "too busy") Laurie's pregnancy was planned because the mother wanted a girl. The contradiction between this statement and the one about planning to delay having children is one of many that characterized the mother's testimony and behavior. After Laurie was born the mother continued working, and from the time Laurie was six weeks old her entire care was handed over to a young nursemaid.

The mother saw no difference between her baby and normal children. Laurie soon hummed tunes, imitated entertainers she saw on TV, liked to play, loved to bathe at a nearby beach. The mother was well pleased with her plump healthy baby, who was pretty enough to win first prize in a baby beauty contest, which was very important to the mother.

Laurie allegedly began talking at fifteen months, saying words like: "no more," "hot," "pick up," "bye-bye," "water," "doggie." But she never addressed anyone by name, never said "mommy" or "daddy."

When Laurie was about two and a half, the young nursemaid left suddenly. She was replaced by an older woman who took care of Laurie until she was four years old. This woman, as well as other caretakers who followed her, never seemed of much importance to Laurie who, with the leaving of her original nursemaid, began to give up what she had learned.

Within a few days the mother noticed a great change in Laurie. She stopped saying the few words she had known and all talking was replaced by peculiar clucking sounds. One day, after repeatedly making what sounded to the mother like loud animal-like noises, the mother became very angry, spanked her, and told her to be still. Laurie then stopped talking and has not spoken since.

Soon Laurie gave up bowel control. A while later began an ever more severe withdrawal from the world, which by the age of six had reached such proportions that for long time periods she seemed blind, deaf, and unable to move on her own. Most of the time she spent her days motionless, staying wherever she was put, sitting in a chair, on the floor, or on the toilet, until bodily moved by someone to some other place. The small remainder of her days she spent in an empty turning of magazine pages without looking at them, or in tearing them into tiniest pieces.

The only activities Laurie engaged in spontaneously were destructive. She ripped buttons off her clothes, tore her sheets, ripped wallpaper off the walls. If she got hold of a piece of ribbon, she shredded it to a mass of fine fuzzy matter until it looked like a ball of absorbent cotton. Similarly she tore shag rugs to shreds, or her blankets. This is mentioned in contrast to an elaborate and complex tearing of paper that characterized her later months with us.

When spoken to, Laurie turned her face away. When annoyed or scolded, she simply stared at her hand or into empty space. As time passed, she withdrew more and more.

When Laurie was four, her pediatrician convinced the mother to have her examined by a competent team of psychiatrist and psychologist. On this first examination Laurie was described as a lovely child with long blond hair who sat quietly and made no response to the examiner's questions. When he stretched out his arms to her, she came to him immediately, her own arms outstretched, but with no facial expression of pleasure to go with the gesture. She let him carry her to his office, without any concern about leaving her mother, and during the hour with him showed no signs of anxiety at the separation.

Laurie's contact with the examiner was bland; she treated him as an object. At times she grinned a little, but not in response to any obvious outer stimuli. She proceeded to build with blocks in a perfectionist manner. Any effort on the part of the examiner to alter her arrangements upset her. With crayons she drew mostly squares, with some scribbling or "windows." If handed a half-finished square by the examiner, she finished it hastily, as if she could not tolerate open or incomplete figures. She never talked, never responded to any verbal request of any kind. She laughed in an odd manner at times, and now and then there was evidence of deep-seated agitation. When returning to the mother she seemed completely indifferent.

All medical and neurological examinations, including EEG, were negative. The diagnosis was infantile autism. The parents were warned that only residential psychiatric treatment offered chances of success and they were advised to seek treatment for Laurie, either at the Orthogenic School or some similar institution closer to home. This they did not do because, the mother said, "At about this time I had heard of a school for speech correction. I took Laurie there three times a week for two years." Then the parents felt defeated and gave up. At that time Laurie was about six.

During the first years after Laurie stopped talking she first screamed loudly and then cried more and more quietly. But even this stopped at about five. By then she had also stopped eating by herself and had become severely anorexic. She had to be fed, dressed, and undressed.

Occasionally Laurie had watched television; she had especially liked cartoons. During the last two years she deliberately turned her head away when she was put in front of the set. If the mother made a point of inviting her to look at it, she averted her head even more with signs of distress or annoyance.

She had once liked playing with pencil and paper, had copied drawings of dolls, cars, balls. This, too, ended when she was five, and after that she only fussed and twisted in her chair in angry rejection when her mother showed her a pencil, crayon, or paper. (This, too, is mentioned in view of the development of her crayoning with us.)

Even after Laurie became anorexic she had enjoyed Coca-Cola on warm days. But by the time she was six she refused to drink anything on her own, even coke. Once, to test her endurance or resistance and when she was quite dehydrated, the mother left a glass of coke where she was sitting. It was a very hot afternoon and Laurie's eyes lit up for a moment. The mother walked away, certain that Laurie would pick it up and drink it. But the glass stood untouched for more than an hour. When the mother did return, pick up the glass, and pour the liquid into her mouth, Laurie gulped it down in one swallow, without sign or sound.

Though the father spent long hours at his work and was rarely at home, both parents felt she had no love for them; that to her they were "just two people hanging around." She viewed them as objects, useful "to help her, dress her and undress her, spoon-feed her or hold her glass of milk for her." They were deeply hurt and resentful that she had never once called them "mommy" or "daddy" even while she was still talking.

After the birth of her baby sister, when Laurie was about six, her behavior became much aggravated. There was no more bizarre laughter, no more sounds, no destructive behavior. She spent her days sitting motionless in a chair or wherever she had been put. She still ate when spoon-fed, but by now extremely little and only very few foods. When the mother tried pressure by letting her go hungry and thirsty, she gave no sign; she sat and stared at her plate, meal after meal, without eating. She used her hands less and less in all respects.

When the mother had Laurie re-examined by the same team, they found her even more withdrawn, living even more than before in a world completely her own. The facial grimaces, smiles, the waving of hands she had shown at first examination, as if responding to some inner stimuli like hallucinations—these had all disappeared. There was now only blankness. She refused to draw or use pencils. Her autistic withdrawal was much more alarming and the recommendations were much as before.

On this second examination the mother, though quite controlled, even overcontrolled, appeared to defend herself against further defeat by having developed a hostile attitude toward Laurie.

It was after this second examination that the mother corresponded with us about admission to the Orthogenic School. During that time Laurie's behavior became worse, and weight loss due to anorexia aroused fear for her life, so she was committed to a state institution.

At commitment the mother's two concerns were that first, Laurie's long hair was not to be cut because the mother "just adored it"; and second, that Laurie should receive shock treatment.

When the mother informed us of this plan we told her we could not consider Laurie for enrollment if shock treatment was given, and our conditions were observed. So after a short stay at the state mental hospital we were able to accept Laurie at the School. This we did only after receiving written assurance from the mother, and the same orally from the father, that they would leave her with us until such time as we had either affected her rehabilitation or felt unable to help her any further. In entrusting Laurie to us the mother stipulated again that Laurie's hair was not to be cut. This we promised, and observed.

Laurie's mother impressed us as being a narcissistic person who was probably struggling to maintain a grip she held on reality with difficulty. She seemed to have withdrawn from the world to a large extent. The father seemed to have lost most of his interest in Laurie very early since he was convinced she had been irreversibly damaged at or before birth. He regarded her as a hopeless incurable, an act of fate which he accepted as his personal burden, despite the contrary judgment of several physicians and psychiatrists of his (or at least his wife's) choosing. This probably explains why he failed to participate in the various efforts at securing diagnosis, treatment or commitment for Laurie.

(In view of this attitude it should be said that the findings of the two psychiatric and psychological examinations of Laurie before she came to us were that she was definitely not feeble-minded or brain-damaged, but suffered from infantile autism. This diagnosis was confirmed by intensive examination at the University of Chicago, in which the Departments of Pediatrics, Neurology, and Psychiatry participated. During her year with us she was observed almost daily by our staff psychiatrist, herself on the University's faculty of Child Psychiatry. In prior years at the Mayo Clinic this psychiatrist had had wide experience in differential diagnosis between organic and functional childhood disturbances. Laurie was also observed almost daily by our several staff psychologists and by myself. In addition she was observed once a week by each of the School's two consulting psychiatrists (both of them child psychoanalysts). All concurred fully with the original diagnosis.

§
A Flicker of Will

What first impressed us about Laurie was that she seemed less of a self-contained, narcissistic, empty being, than did some autistic children we have known. On the contrary, behind the pretty, limp doll, behind her total lethargy we sensed, more clearly than we have with some other mute autistic children, a loneliness and desperation of which she gave no visible sign. To some of us she gave the feeling that deep within her lived a very old woman, mortally tired and frightened beyond endurance. More than any autistic children I have seen she shocked me by her resemblance to the "moslems" (pages 65–68) at whom one had to look twice to be sure there was still any life left. Her emaciation and limp inertia made the comparison all the sharper.

During her first days with us she remained extremely dehydrated. She ate and drank almost nothing, though she vomited frequently. As a matter of fact, the only time she showed signs of life were the moments when she was nauseated and vomited. It was as if all she could do was to give up, or out. But even then she passively allowed her vomit to run all over her face, hair, and clothes, as she lay without moving or any other reaction.

For months Laurie's mouth remained slightly open, her teeth and parched lips apart. Only weeks later, when she occasionally bit off pieces of cookies or candy, did we see her close her teeth; but even then it was only at the moment of biting. She ate only food she could swallow immediately, without chewing: soft food, one raisin at a time, or a tiny bit of cookie or candy. For these she did not need to close her mouth to chew. As soon as she had bitten something off, lips and teeth parted again, and her mouth stood half open as before.

At first we thought this mouth behavior went with the dehydration, but it did not change after she was drinking enough. We tried to wet her lips and also to oil them, to make her more comfortable. Her counselor rubbed her lips softly, and then gently put a finger in her mouth and on her tongue. (Laurie's main counselor, a young woman in her twenties, was a registered nurse by training who preferred to be a psychiatric child-care worker.) At first Laurie barely reacted, but later she seemed to like it, and for an instant she touched the finger with her tongue, may even have licked it for a moment. Then she seemed to want to have the whole thing repeated. But even then she never closed her mouth. Much as she seemed to like receiving the counselor's finger in her mouth, to enjoy touching it with her tongue, for the first four months she never closed her mouth on it or sucked it.

The way she kept her mouth half open, no matter what, and the way she reacted to our manipulation, gave the impression that her mouth was in some way a nonreacting part of her, or one hardly linked to other parts of her body. Her tongue, too, seemed unrelated to the rest of her person or even to the rest of her mouth.

But her mouth was not the only part of her body that seemed disconnected from the rest. As a matter of fact, to speak of "the rest of her body" gives an erroneous impression. There was no integrated body to Laurie, only an aggregate of separate parts that seemed to have nothing in common, not to belong together.

When we dressed her, undressed her, or touched her, she not only felt limp, but as though her hands, arms, and legs were disconnected from her and her consciousness. Each part of her body seemed an object apart from the others, and the various parts of her unrelated to each other because they did not function as a unit. When we washed her hands, even when she let her hand rest in ours—because at this early time she would not put it there herself—they felt ghostly, not like flesh-and-blood limbs.[1] Similarly, she made us feel she did not see us as whole persons, but was only aware of that part of us, a hand, a shoulder, an arm that did something for her or with her at the moment.

Even much later, when we did something she wanted us to, such as cutting a piece of string, she reacted only to our hand; there was sometimes anger or suspicion but no awareness of the rest of us, not to mention a look at either us or our faces. All there was of us, for her, was an isolated, disconnected hand cutting string.

Still, though she was utterly anorexic when she came to us, by the second day she began to eat and drink just a little when we hand-fed

1. When I first met her in her parents' home—where she had been brought for a visit from the state institution for me to see her and decide if I thought we could help her—then too, she had put her hand in mine. But this happened after I had made her an important offer. Before that I had sat with her for a very long time, first being with her quietly, then trying to make her more comfortable physically and emotionally, by chasing away flies, for example, which on this hot day had settled on her body, walked over her face, even her eyes, without her reacting in any way.

Then I had begun to talk to her softly, inviting her to come to live with us, far away from her home, telling her that I very much wanted her to do this and that we would help her have a better life for herself. After that had sunk in (or so I hoped), I suggested that we take a little walk, out of the scorching sun into a shaded area, and I stretched out my hand, inviting her to walk with me. After a considerable time she put her hand in my waiting one, got up, and walked beside me.

Her doing so probably happened because of my offer to take her away to something different, which seemed to extraordinarily activate whatever minimal energy she had for moving her body on her own. Once at the School, no such sudden new changes in outlook could be offered her and she would no longer put her hand in ours, at least not for the first few months she was with us. Later she did so freely and often, such as when going with us from one place to another.

her. We never tried to spoon-feed her. It seemed too mechanistic and distant a procedure to achieve our goal of bringing her slowly to life as a person. She soon liked it when we put raisins or crumbs of cookies in her mouth with our hands.

On her fifth night with us her counselor sat by her bed and, talking softly to her, put one raisin at a time in her mouth. Accidentally some dropped on the bed covers and Laurie picked one or two up and fed them to herself. It was the first time in several years she had put something in her mouth. As she did it, we heard a little laughing sound, the first noise she had made in as many years. For a month thereafter, putting raisins on her spread as she rested comfortably, and her picking them up and eating them, was her favorite game. We played it with her nightly for hours.

Within two weeks Laurie very occasionally and just for moments played as a one-and-a-half-year-old might. A week later she slapped the person who was devoting herself most intensely to her. Perhaps because there was no negative reaction to this feeble aggression, Laurie then put her arms around the counselor's neck, her legs around the adult's waist, and wanted to be carried. She laid her head on the counselor's shoulder with the back of her head against the neck. The counselor's sensation was that Laurie could better merge into the person caring for her if she did not see the person, or what either one was doing.

That evening she suddenly reached toward a cookie plate in front of her, picked up a cookie and ate it by herself. Some of the children were so surprised that one exclaimed, "I thought she didn't eat by herself." Five days later she ate a full meal: three bowls of spaghetti which we slowly fed to her. That day was also remarkable because she made more noises than ever before: clucking noises, some bizarre laughing, but also some truly baby-like throat sounds.

It seems worth mentioning that as Laurie became more active in feeding herself the same clucking noises reappeared which, some years earlier, had ended all speech because she felt she was being punished for making them. Perhaps the anorexia she showed—and the same holds for other autistic children we have worked with—was thus even further avoidance of any doing with the mouth. Perhaps also, the trauma she experienced when she made the clucking sounds was (or came to stand for) the original damage around the oral experience that made any doing with the mouth so strongly taboo.

In any case, late that same evening Laurie suddenly got out of bed, ran to the table in the middle of the room, took one bite out of a cookie that lay on a plate, and went back to bed. This sequence she repeated for almost half an hour. By then she had eaten all the cookies on the plate, some crackers, a few small pieces of chocolate, and a bowl of raisins. Delighted, her counselor got another piece of chocolate to feed her. But as she put it in Laurie's mouth, Laurie bit down hard on the finger and would not open her teeth (though her lips, as always, remained open) so that the counselor had to force the jaw open to get her finger out.

It may be that Laurie resented being hand-fed just when she had taken such a big step toward self-assertion by feeding herself. To this insult she responded with a hostile act (biting) in which the very organs that had just used autonomy (mouth and teeth) fought back. The counselor recognized that Laurie's reaction was appropriate, if painful, so she put another chocolate bar on Laurie's bed, close to her hand. Laurie tore at the paper, unwrapped the chocolate, the first time she had ever "fixed" any food for herself, and ate it. This was the beginning of a much more spontaneous, though still very hesitant, approach to eating.

Such moments of greater independence remained extremely rare. Mostly, Laurie was still either totally withdrawn or, when carried about or sitting in the counselor's lap, seemed to have melted in. She was like an inert part of the adult's body, not a child sitting on her lap. The rest of the time, Laurie's nonuse of her body and its inertness gave the impression that she had so withdrawn interest from the world that she could not (or would not) invest herself in those parts of her body that had any contact with the world. To what degree this extended even to her internal world we do not know.

The puppet-like way in which she let us lift an arm or a leg, for example, when we dressed or undressed her, suggests she had even distanced herself wholly from her body. Whatever happened to it did not happen. Nothing that touched it ever touched whatever comprised her inner being. This was not only true for the sense of touch and the moving of her body; the impression was particularly strong when, in addition to being mute, she also seemed blind and deaf; when sights and sounds brought no reaction, did not seem to penetrate.

§

The Slow Thaw

Still, a loosening up, an unfreezing was slowly taking place in Laurie, or at least in some of her bodily functions. During the years when she had so totally drawn away from the world, not even the most autonomic of her organs functioned properly. Or one might better say, their seeming nonfunctioning was quite appropriate to her state of near-suspended animation. This was also true of her elimination.

We were told that Laurie had moved her bowels only very rarely and that defecation had to be forced on her. We did not follow this course. So during the first month with us her stools were about nine days apart and stone-hard. In the following month they came more frequently: eight, seven, then six days apart, and gradually more often. By the end of the third month her bowel movements were only three days apart. Then for a couple of months she defecated two or three times a week, and after half a year with us it happened about daily. In a parallel process her stools, which at first were only marble-like pellets, became softer over the months and eventually, toward the end of her stay with us, acquired normal consistency.

Her growing autonomy in eating and eliminating was probably the result of our encouraging her to do so as she liked, little as she made use of her freedom. We did not put her on the toilet several times a day, as had been customary at home. We encouraged her to have bowel movements at random wherever she was: in bed, sitting on a chair, on a counselor's lap, or standing up.

Laurie was so unaware of what went on in her body that during the first months she gave no sign, either by gesture or expression, that she was eliminating. Often we only knew she had moved her bowels when we happened to discover a stool that had fallen from her underpants. In her third month with us she still showed no visible reaction when she defecated, but a while later she wriggled herself until the stool dropped out of her pants to the floor. When she thus began to be aware of them (and also showed that she was), it was first as a reaction to some foreign event—not of a process that had taken place in her body. In a further development, starting in her fourth month, she would occasionally, but not yet regularly, reach in and take the stool out with her hands. At about the same time she began again to build with blocks after a lapse of two and a half years.

By taking feces out of her pants she acquired some freedom in handling them, but not yet over their coming out of her body. This we concluded because her facial expression and her body still showed no sign of awareness, nor did she show reactions in any other way while she was moving her bowels; this, by contrast to the slight interest in handling her stools. And then a most interesting behavior began.

One day, shortly after moving her bowels some of these pellets dropped close to her block pile. She picked them up, held them in her hand and then dropped them, in exactly the same way she had been manipulating the blocks. This sequence she repeated many times. Then the play became a bit more complex as follows. First Laurie would build something out of blocks, then take it apart, then move her bowels. Then she would take pieces of feces in her hand and drop them, take some blocks in her hand and drop them. Then once again she would return to building with blocks, piecing them together.

We were greatly impressed when, after four days of this close sequence of block play and defecation, Laurie had a bowel movement and urinated at the same time. Up to then these two eliminative functions had been quite separated. (Her conscious discovery, or open show of awareness of urination, though simultaneous to these events, is discussed separately below.)

Even more important, it was after she had taken a block tower apart that for the first time, as she moved her bowels, she gave obvious signs of what was happening. Her face and her entire body showed she was straining to push out the feces. But as she did so her face and body also suggested how unfamiliar and engrossing an experience this was, after so many years of having defecated somehow. Then, having eliminated, she again took pieces of stool out of her pants, handled them, and so forth.

Step by step Laurie had progressed from "not knowing" she was defecating to at least knowing there was something foreign in her pants which she tried to get out by wiggling; to removing the feces by hand, to handling them as she handled her blocks, and finally to showing awareness of the act of elimination itself. Certainly the sequence suggests her developing awareness of a bodily function.

Perhaps too, there was parallel development around the earlier increase in frequency of stools. As she could do more with her body (defecate a bit more often) she also felt more (the pieces of fecal matter she handled). And as she did more and felt more, she knew more: she became aware of the process of defecation.

Her building up a tower of blocks, taking it apart, and then defecating, suggests something else too: a dealing with the problem of having or owning more (a tower, stools inside herself) and of having less (no more tower, stools leaving her body) plus the reassurance that she had not really lost anything (holding the expelled feces in her hands, rebuilding the tower again).

But even more was involved here: in a simultaneous process Laurie became able to do something with her body (strain to defecate) and to do something in the world (build with blocks). As the infant first becomes aware that he eats, quite a while before he is equally "aware" that he eliminates, so Laurie in recapturing her abilities to act and to know, first resumed being active around eating before resuming activity in other areas of doing (defecation, block play).

The conjunction of her playing with blocks and with feces may have had still another connotation. She knew that the blocks had been provided by us, and that the feces had not. Handling both of them thoughtfully may have helped her to understand more fully that it was she who had defecated, and most important of all that she had done a tangible thing. Whoever does, is a person. And with even this much doing, a first tentative and rudimentary feeling emerged of having a self, of being a person.

Beyond this, of course, other developments may have begun here, having to do with the problem of what is self and what is not. As she handled the pieces of fecal matter and thoughtfully dropped them, repeating the same motions with blocks, she seemed to be acting on the problem of how something that was once part of her self could suddenly become nonself. In addition to the question "was this really I who acted?" she seemed to be posing to herself the other question: "can something that was part of me become non-me, just as these wooden blocks are non-me?" This problem was much harder for Laurie than it might be for the normal infant.

But it was only after she had thus become active, self-determined and aware in her eliminating, that her stools came more often but also changed in consistency; grew messier. And as they did so, Laurie became more active and daring in handling her feces by smearing them over her body and hands.

By that time it seemed as if she were trying to take feces off, or out of, the various parts of her body: legs, arms, hands, wherever they had gotten smeared on her. Perhaps she was here exploring to see which part of her body, exactly, the feces came out of, to which part they belonged, which part of her body produced them, and whether we accepted that they were hers to do with as she liked.

In a strange way, a parallel process took place with her discovery of urination. According to her history, Laurie's urine training never broke down. When she came to us, we did not put her on the toilet during the day, as had happened several times daily, at home. Nevertheless, by her second day at the School, she had developed a rigid routine of urinating in the toilet twice a day. And this too seemed as nonexistent a psychological experience to Laurie as defecation. Now it is difficult to assume that an act that involves going to the toilet, pulling down pants, urinating, then getting off the toilet, etc., can remain unrecognized as such. But we cannot otherwise explain her later discovery of urination.

Whatever the case, Laurie had been urinating twice daily, first thing in the morning and last thing before bedtime, in a fashion we called compulsive to ourselves, because there was never any deviation from pattern. But when she began to explore where her stools came from, she also began to urinate more freely. For a time she still urinated twice daily in the toilet, but she also began to wet her pants in between, when she was sitting. And of this process too, she seemed as unaware as she then was of defecation.

A while later, as she became freer in handling her stools, she urinated not only as she sat, but also standing up, or in any position whatever. Then came a time when it was clear she felt she was urinating, as was evident from her startled, anxious, and fascinated response to what was happening. She now seemed to enjoy the feeling that it was she who urinated, as this became ever more an experience of her doing something. But the feeling so engrossed her that it seemed to leave no room for anything else. Her entire body became limp, and lost whatever little tonus it had. She even closed her eyes as if seeing would detract from the experience too much.

Finally came a time when she not only wanted to concentrate all her feelings on urination, but also wanted to see, to understand. The first time we observed this, it was reported as follows: "Laurie was wearing yellow panties, so it was easy to see that she began to urinate. For the first time she was very interested in watching what was happening. She pulled her dress back so that she could watch how her panties got darker yellow. Each time before, even when she began to concentrate on urinating, she behaved as if this was happening in some other part of the world, not to her. This time she seemed fascinated by it." Then for a time she urinated only on the floor, standing up, legs apart, as she bent over and watched in rapt attention how she urinated and made puddles on the floor.

The ability to explore this way was a sign of the inner freedom Laurie was gaining, of her awakening interest in herself, in what went on in her body, her self-assertion, and whatever added meaning her investigations may have had. With it came other signs of greater freedom and self-determination. Some of them were linked to her interest in elimination, such as her new ability to play with abandon in sand and mud, to get herself good and dirty.

Just as she had grown free of constipation when she could actively, even aggressively, deal with her stools, so she became free of anorexia the more she was able to eat actively, even to bite aggressively. Her eating grew more and more normal, if not for her age, at least for what is normal in a much younger child. She now loved to mess with her food, and that of her counselors and teacher as they ate together. But in doing so, her eating, as far as variety and quantity went, grew quite normal.

Interestingly enough, the first violently aggressive behavior (or what seemed so for poor, passive, ineffectual Laurie) began, in this once anorexic child, around eating. I have mentioned that once she slapped her counselor and once bit her counselor's finger. But these were discrete actions: a biting down, a single slap. Now we were all more than startled at the table one day when Laurie took first her spoon, then a knife, and finally a fork and one by one threw them with a bit of force over her shoulder to the floor. Then came the salt and pepper shakers which she hurled after them. As her counselor got up from the table to pick them up, Laurie too left her chair and very quickly walked out of the dining room, laughing. At the doorway, to emphasize her point, she took a plate from a dish cart and threw it to the floor. Then she left, looking pleased with herself.

With her greater freedom to be impulsive and to meet the world actively, Laurie came closer to language. Her throat noises increased in loudness, frequency, and variety of intonation. These sounds became much deeper, and we had a feeling that she was experimenting more with her voice all the time. Her sounds became more clearly pronounced, stopped being just noises, came closer to efforts at speech than anything we had heard from her yet. She also laughed more freely and easily, though it was never a loud or free laughter, just a little laugh. It only seemed so incredibly free by comparison.

Some of her teacher's observations indicate what she could do then, and how it struck us: "Laurie had taken a chair to my desk, was standing on it, reaching for my keys to open the cabinet where she had seen me get chalk. There are many ways in which she has lately shown this kind of increased independence. Although she had the ability to walk and the same measure of physical independence before, she didn't know it. Now I feel she knows it, and she walks and moves with pleasure, as well as sureness. Instead of waiting for me to take her coat off, she has several times this week taken it off herself and handed it to me.

Laurie also became more interested in her body; began to study her arms and hands. She would hold her arms up and carefully look at them, her gaze wandering up and down an arm, or pursuing it as she moved it up and down. We had the feeling that she was discovering her arms, or the connection between her arms and hands. This was entirely different from how we felt about her arm movements when they were vaguely, helplessly, and indifferently stretched out. The discovery of her arms and legs also led to mishaps. It came as a real shock to us when Laurie fell down. Up to then Laurie had never fallen or hurt herself. Now she occasionally fell and bruised her knees, like any normal child.

It was as if the unawareness of her body and its parts had given each limb an independent though "unconscious" existence of its own. This permitted the parts to perform somehow, but without central direction from Laurie's self. Now that she felt she could act, her body became her own as it were, and achieved greater unity. But then the long alienation from her body and its functioning, combined with the now conscious but awkward coordination of limbs, led to a more clumsy though more purposeful use of her body. Her limbs, now receiving central and goal-directed guidance from her mind, were unaccustomed to such direction. So they performed only clumsily, but at the same time entered Laurie's awareness.

§

What Is Me?

Returning to Laurie's central problem—first of becoming active, and second of gaining some awareness of the self—it might be repeated that this severely anorexic child first became active in connection with eating. But it was around elimination that she took her first important steps toward separating the self from the nonself.

As discussed in an earlier chapter, this sequence may relate to the difference between pushing out feces oneself as compared to being active around intake, where we are dependent on others for what we take in.

Here I might add another reason why elimination can serve as a quite decisive boundary between the self and the nonself. The normal infant, when he becomes aware of defecation—not as discomfort and then relief from an inner body tension, which comes much earlier, but as a process through which he expels matter from his body—is very interested in his feces. He handles them and smears with them as Laurie did. But this is normally very short-lived if the mother, through her negative reaction to the feces and his handling of them, clearly separates feces from child. Just as positive as her reactions are to him, so are they negative to his feces, or at least to his handling of them. This, in normal development, happens at about the time when the infant begins to view himself as someone of tremendous importance, mainly because he is that to his parents, especially his mother.

Since the developing self wishes to be and is of significance to the mother, it is fairly easy to separate this self from its product, which the mother declares to be undesirable. Thus the one experience (what is contained in me, my self, is desirable) and the other experience (what leaves my body and becomes nonself, is undesirable) forcefully enhance a positive self-feeling. It leads to the conviction: my self is desirable, the nonself is not.

But because something so close to the self as one's feces can be so undesirable, it becomes doubly important to delimit the self from the nonself. This importance of toilet training for forming a more clear-cut and positive image of the self has not been stressed as much as the child's difficulty in separating the self from the nonself around it.

If my speculation is valid, it would follow that overevaluation of the child and a clear rejection of his feces may be a temporary problem to the child; but it will help him develop a clear picture of the self, quite distinct from the nonself, and a self considered worthy of love. It also follows that if the child is not valued but rejected, and feces too are rejected, only more so, then since both are rejected, no clear separation between self and nonself will be established, at least not around this bodily function. On the contrary, without clear emotional distinction between the two, the deep rejection of the feces may extend to what they were so recently part of; may extend backward, as it were, to the child.

If all this is so, and it seems borne out by our experience, then parallel problems arise if the mothering person, or worse, if both parents, were so interested in the child's bowel movements and so little in the child, that to retain parental love, the child did not separate himself from his bowel movements but identified with them. As a result he felt himself to be "nothing but shit." Only in this case feces, or the feeling of being "shit," included strong positive connotations. While the child as a person is of little value to the parent, as the producer of feces he is at least quite important. The result of such a situation is a faulty personality development, but also the conviction that one is valued for something. Some such persons take great pride later on in their "shitty" personality.

Things are much more serious where the parents are not emotionally involved in the child's elimination, but for their own convenience make mechanical demands for regularity. I have discussed the effects on a child who must eliminate to please his parents, or follow their stringent demands. But we have come to be equally impressed by the strange effects on the child if he is toilet-trained by parents who are disinterested in him and his achievements, either in this or any other respect.

At the same time, it takes considerably more than simple indifference to so alienate a child from his bodily functions that they do not reach his awareness, as we see it in those autistic children under our care who only slowly, painfully, and with amazement begin to discover (or re-discover, as it were) feeling, eating, seeing, hearing, elimination. In regard to toilet training it takes, among other emotional attitudes on the part of the adult, disinterest or a total rejection of the child, combined with an insistence on mechanical obedience. Such a child comes to feel himself to be nothing but a feces-producing machine, as Joey's story will show.

Be this as it may, it certainly seemed true for Laurie: that because both she and her bowel movements met with overwhelming rejection or indifference, she could never clearly separate between body and its product. In her past, each rejection of her feces meant another experience that she should not be or do, an experience too painful to risk. Hence the severe not-doing in regard to elimination before she came to us. Hence also her ability to give up being constipated as she was made to feel more and more desired by us, and hence desirable.

We cannot be certain, but even her anorexia, another avoidance of doing, may have been aggravated by her experience around elimination. She was unwilling to take in from those who seemed like enemies to her. But as her constipation showed, she also wished not to give out. Not taking in made this easier.

We do not know how Laurie's nursemaid tried to train her, but a common method is to grab a child and put him on the potty as soon as he gives any sign of being about to defecate. If this happened with Laurie, then one source of her unawareness of defecation (and by extension also, of urination) may have been the wish not to show she was about to, or in the process of defecating, in order to avoid being coerced. But even if this was the case, being overpowered around elimination cannot be so far-reaching in consequence that a person becomes unaware of so vital a function of his body. Even Marcia, who was woefully overpowered in this area, did not lose awareness to that extent.

Like Laurie, several other of our autistic children suddenly discover late in life, that it is *they* who are urinating or defecating. Perhaps what then occurs is a first conscious correlation of the visual and auditive sensations of elimination with the kinesthetic, although the behavior of some of these children suggests that they were not even aware of any kinesthetic sensations before this. Which is striking because the infant's grimace shows that from a very early age he responds to the kinesthetic sensations of defecation whether aware of them or not.

If autistic children show no reaction whatsoever to defecation, we must assume that the process of alienation from their own feelings has reached such proportions that they do not even feel what goes on in their bodies. Such a notion is corroborated by their insensitivity to pain, as discussed in an earlier chapter.[2]

One is tempted to add: through a supreme act of her will, Laurie

2. Others have made similar observations. For example, Mahler, Furer, and Settlage [1959] comment: "These children are, more often than not, toilet trained at the age of normal children. This relative ease of toilet training seems to stem from two factors: One of these seems to be an insufficient erotization of the body surfaces and orifices; the second, the paradoxical situation that it is precisely the lack of emotional involvement which makes toilet training an uncharged conditioning process for these children. The autistic child neither eats nor defecates to please the parent, nor does he refuse food or withhold his stools to spite the mother. . . . Most autistic children have a relatively low cathexis of their body surface, which accounts for their grossly deficient pain sensitivity."

stopped herself from any feeling and doing. Possibly this would explain what may otherwise seem a contradiction in my discussion of infantile autism: that the autistic position, a supreme effort to safeguard one's existence, destroys selfhood. It would seem that libido is generated only if one means to expend it, and withers away if our decision is not to expend it at all.

At the School, Laurie began to feel just a bit that survival did not depend on not being or not doing. These, of course, were not thoughts, but mere feeling impressions. She no longer simply did not act, but occasionally acted, and this required a differentiating between when (and how) to act, and when not. Each acting on her own was another step toward self-determination. With spontaneous taking of action came the rudiments of a self; and with it a first interest in clearer differentiation between self and nonself.

The issue is important because of the underlying anxiety: if part of what was self (stools) can become nonself, then all of self may become nonself and disappear. The result of such reasoning—if the vague wondering of a small child can be called reasoning—is the fear, for example, that the whole child may go down the drain in the bathtub, or be flushed down the toilet. Moreover, how come that this very thing I created, this so important proof that I can do things, I am supposed to flush down the toilet?

These are some of the reasons why so many of our very disturbed children, even years after they have mastered the problem of elimination per se, still refuse to flush the toilet. Since we understand this, we are more than willing to flush it for them. But given the facts of sanitation we must nevertheless flush down the sewer this proof of their ability to do.

This I believe also explains why normal infants, when they become aware of defecation, try to hold on to their feces, which is often viewed as playing with stools; they do not want to let go at once of what was just part of the self. But the normal infant can and does learn to let go, because his self is well enough established by then: it is not shattered by the experience that a small part of what was self becomes nonself.

(How different was the experience of child and adult in a peasant society, even in the Western world, up to recently: then excrement was highly valued as fertilizer. It was not declared valueless right after the child was so praised for his production. Instead it was carefully collected and its value proved to the child as it helped to grow what he fed on the following year.)

Given the hazards or the alien nature of the nonself, one might ask: How is it that normal children do eat and eliminate? The answer, as suggested earlier in this book, is that much of their normal ability depends on the friendliness of the environment. But some is also due to the fact that the infant soon learns he is not at the mercy of the nonself. He can manipulate it, and when necessary, deal aggressively with it. An example of the aggressiveness is biting when he eats; of the manipulation, that his emotional reactions bring response from his parents.

Perhaps in this speculation lies the clue to why Laurie's ability to bite (her counselor's finger) stood at the very beginning of her efforts to develop a self, and preceded her separation of the self from the non-self (through elimination).

Nevertheless having to fathom, at the late age of eight, the difference between self and nonself in the context of stools leaving her body was a fearful task. That was why Laurie now studied and restudied how her bowel movements left her body, and again and again played it all out with blocks.

§

First Awareness of Others

In a parallel process, Laurie slowly became aware of the bodies of those who most intimately cared for her needs. We do not know the inner connection between the two processes: gaining awareness of the human body, first her own, and then of those who mothered her. But our observations leave little doubt that Laurie related more to her own body as she enjoyed greater contact with the body of her favorite counselor, and soon of her other caretakers too.

More and more often, and for lengthening periods of time, Laurie liked to be carried, but always in the same position: her body pressed against the adult's chest, her feet closed around the adult's waist, her head nestled against the adult's neck. Soon she began to like to sit on her counselor's lap, either in exactly the position described, or else with her back against the adult's chest, feet pulled up and hands curled around them, very much as in the fetal position.

Then she went further in "discovering" her counselor's body. One day, as the counselor lay stretched on her stomach reading the children a story, Laurie seated herself on the counselor's back. From then on Laurie could not get enough of a new game that began with the counselor lying stretched out on the floor and Laurie astride. Soon she preferred the counselor to be lying on her back while she herself just rested quietly for long stretches of time on her counselor's abdomen, curled up and very still. As she lay there in a fetal position, it gave the sensation of a baby curled up inside the uterus.

Again and again now, for weeks, she would pull at her counselor's shoulders, suggesting that she lie down on the floor. Then she became more active. After a period of quiet resting Laurie would not only sit or lie on her counselor's abdomen, but would bounce up and down astride her. After some time of this play, Laurie would stop, go to her bed, and either bang her head down on the pillow, or roll it from side to side for a considerable time. She seemed to be learning or re-learning head rolling as a result of becoming more aware of the mothering person's body.

Typically, this form of head rolling is found in blind children [Cutsforth, 1951; Lowenfeld, 1955] and is ascribed to their need for finding stimulation within bodily reach. Hence they turn to their own body as the source and object of stimulation. In seeing-children too, head rolling is viewed as the result of too little positive stimulation from the outside to which they respond with a concentrated search for self-stimulation. Thus what was startling in Laurie's behavior was that it followed her seeking and receiving bodily stimulation from another person. It suggests that the head-rolling child must have experienced the pleasure of stimulation in certain facial areas before he will seek to provide this for himself.

So long as Laurie's body was totally frozen, she made no effort to provide herself with self-stimulation. Or it seems that we provide ourselves with self-stimulation only after we have discovered it to be enjoyable through having received a modicum of it from others. These thoughts are in line with observations by Spitz [1962] who speaks of "the decisive role of mother-child relations in autoerotic activities." He states that "where the relation between mother and child was optimal" such play "was present in all cases" during the first year of life.

Head rolling is not limited to autistic children; many less severely disturbed children engage in it too. Watching them roll their heads back and forth on the pillow one cannot help thinking they are rooting for the nipple, at the same time stimulating that area of the face which in nursing is apt to touch the mother's body. If this is indeed what they do, it becomes understandable that Laurie began to roll her head on her pillow when for the first time (or for the first time again) her coming close to the body of another person, even a mothering person, was no longer something she was deathly afraid of.

Soon after this a new form of head turning appeared. It grew out of her seeking from her counselor's body still further satisfaction and closeness, in a way that included self-stimulation of her face and especially the area of the mouth. It began with Laurie coming up to her counselor from behind, to pat her on the buttocks. Pretty soon whenever her counselor was standing up, Laurie was tiptoeing up from the rear to pat her counselor's behind, and later running up to do it. Eventually it became much more strenuous as Laurie patted harder and harder. For a time she seemed to be constantly focused on the backsides of a few favorite caretakers, playing on their buttocks with both hands, patting, sometimes pushing so hard they found it difficult to keep their balance. When the counselor accepted this with pleasure and responded by reaching behind and gently patting Laurie on the back, Laurie broke into genuine laughter.

There were weeks of this play, the meaning of which we did not then understand but which made us happy because Laurie did it on her own. Then she began to repeat the behavior with her head, not her hands, turning her head back and forth on her counselor's behind. It seems that her earlier hand tapping was meant to test out how safe the approach was before risking exposure of the so much more vulnerable face and mouth. Again, as Laurie rolled her head back and forth, from ear to ear, and from buttock to buttock, it reminded us of an infant trying to nurse. At other times it seemed more as if she were trying to crawl into her counselor. She had learned only so recently that she could make something come out of the body at this place. Perhaps she was exploring to see if she could enter the body there too. But her way of doing so was typical of the fragmentation of her body and her experience. As she concentrated on what she experienced in the cheek and mouth area, there was no investment in, or participation by, any other part of her body. Her eyes remained closed, her arms and hands hung down limply, her whole body, except for the mouth and cheek was without tonus.

Once, as she was again patting and butting with her head, and was patted back by her counselor, Laurie circled around and gently patted the counselor's stomach with her hands. Her hands roved all about and then with her head she patted and turned on the counselor's stomach, laughing a good deal throughout.

The following day she experimented even more with touching the front of her counselor's body, exploring it, feeling the arms, and at last the breasts she had never touched before.

It was only after this ample and prolonged exploration of her counselor's body and after she had finally found the breast and dared to touch it that Laurie truly seemed to come alive. She became more aware of her own body, and able to use it. Now when she sat on her counselor's lap, it was no longer just a sitting on somebody, nor a mere melting in and disappearing, but as if Laurie sat with initiative. The adult felt more of the normal sensation of being with an infant; it seemed possible to try to play and communicate with Laurie.

At about this same time Laurie also began to hallucinate. This we concluded from the way she then looked up into space, preferably up to the ceiling, entirely preoccupied with something going on in her mind, and totally oblivious of what was going on around her. After such periods of hallucination, which were first very brief but increased in length and intensity with the passing of time, she would return to whatever she had been doing. At this point she seemed to have caught up with the state of functioning the psychiatrist ascribed to her at four, the state that was lost between then and her next examination at age six.

§

The Genesis of Play

Before her body began to come alive, Laurie had merely allowed herself to be dressed, but only as one would dress a mannequin or doll. Now she began to show playfulness around dressing. We also observed with delight that for the first time Laurie was focusing directly on her favorite counselor's face and eyes. Eventually she looked at her a good deal of the time.

Laurie had come to expect having her lips rubbed when we washed her, and at other times, too. Her always half-opened mouth was now ready to receive her counselor's finger as it entered her mouth, though she would never close her lips on this finger. Then, with her tongue, she pushed the finger over her teeth. Obviously despite her anxiety about intrusion she felt confident by then of her counselor's positive intention. Still, it all remained largely experimental in nature, an experience more interesting than pleasurable. She also let the counselor massage her gums; but about this she remained basically hesitant.

Finally she began to imitate her counselor. This she did after a long bath in which some relaxation along with pleasant skin sensations were enhanced by her counselor's stroking her and joining her in play with some toys. Laurie stood up in the tub and looked carefully at the adult; then she stepped out and sat on the edge beside her in exactly the same position. Noting the way her counselor's legs were crossed, Laurie crossed her own legs that way; observing how the adult had her arms folded, she folded her own the same way. Finally Laurie looked directly at the counselor and laughed. With great seriousness and distinct enjoyment she repeated the whole thing several times. It was as if she could begin to imitate her counselor after she had grown a bit more aware of her own body through the pleasant experience in the tub. With it she could also recognize the body of her counselor, and then could wish to undo the fact that they were two separate entities by making them alike.

Having recognized another body, and how to make hers more like it, she was ready for play. Because to play with someone means we must recognize a second person and that both of us can make ourselves enough like each other to engage in a common interaction. So from then on, at the end of her bath, Laurie wriggled about, twirled herself around, offered now an arm, now a leg, to be dried. This playfulness was radically new because until then she had just suffered herself to be dried, and to the counselor it felt as if she were drying wooden limbs.

Soon in other situations too, Laurie began to play more, though learning came slow. One day, for example, entirely on her own she suddenly went around the table on all fours, walking on hands and feet. We thought she might crawl but she didn't, though it was the closest she had come to it. Two weeks later she tried it again. First she carefully reached down to the floor with her hands and then, in a gliding movement down from her chair, got into crawling position. But she still walked on hands and feet. Finally, however, she lowered her whole body to the floor and crawled on hands and knees like an infant.

Learning in reverse sequence from what are the natural steps in development is painfully slow and complex. Ordinarily, the move from crawling to walking comes fairly easy to the infant. For Laurie, who could only walk limply, the task of learning to crawl was prodigious. It required the fairly smooth coordination that runs from the hand, through arm and body to leg. It was fraught with great anxiety, to be approached only with caution.

With her freer ways of being and moving came new developments in elimination which declared what was happening to Laurie to be exactly that: a gaining of freedom. Nor was development always or only toward higher achievements, maturity or socialization. Laurie, who had known how to walk, had to gain new freedom to be able to crawl. As described before, her new freedom in elimination went in both directions: toward higher socialization (eliminating in the toilet) and toward more primitive behavior (urinating on the floor). But the day came when for the first time Laurie went to the toilet on her own and had a bowel movement into the bowl.

One day at about this time, Laurie wet while sitting in her counselor's lap, something else she had never done before. When she realized that the counselor did not mind, was even pleased, it made her very happy. No laughter or pleasure had ever accompanied Laurie's wetting or soiling herself, but from then on she often wet on her counselors with obvious pleasure.

Handling and studying her stools had been more of a problem to be mastered than a source of pleasure. Wetting on her counselor was enjoyable because of the counselor's positive response. Pleasure in the functioning of her body had to be regained for each experience; separately, that is, for eating, crawling, urinating, and defecating.

Perhaps Laurie had to discover her counselor's existence as independent from hers (by exploring the counselor's body) before she could utilize the counselor's sharing in her enjoyment of bodily functions, and then imitate the counselor through body play (after the bath). Wetting on her counselor, urinating with and not just on the mothering figure, as it were, by getting both of them wet in a single process—perhaps this mutual enjoyment gave her the courage to act on her own; she then went to the toilet to defecate.

This more mature use of the toilet was only a transitory step, a demonstration that she could do it but not a habit as yet. The more normal behavior of infancy was being approached, but by no means achieved. It does not come naturally to move backward in time instead of forward, and never really parallels the normal forward movement.

§

Reconstructing Laurie's Development

At this point, Laurie's development may also be reviewed on the basis of what we know of her history, and with Erikson's theories [1950, 1956] on infantile development in mind. We may then speculate that in her anal development Laurie may never have reached either the retentive or eliminative modes. Or perhaps more likely, she gave both of them up after her nursemaid's leaving when she abandoned a reality that seemed too unresponsive.

When Laurie gave up trying to come to terms with her environment, elimination was forced on her. In reaction, she withdrew all cathexis from those body processes that involved interaction with the environment (intake and elimination); so much so that they may have seemed to stop functioning. She neither took in nor gave out (became anorexic and constipated). Whatever activity remained she expressed in her resistance to doing either. Only with opposition did she passively suffer (or lack the strength to fight off) a little food being put into her, and having her feces extracted. If this was so, then the first was not a true "taking in" and the latter was neither retention nor elimination: both were a defensive nonfunctioning. Her not defecating was then not due to a wish to retain, but rather to the fact that she had given up this bodily function. Perhaps then, as her stools came more often and lost their marble-like form and hardness, it was not a giving up of retention, but a slow return of this zone to its functioning.

Looking back on Laurie's early life, particularly her development up to her first caretaker's departure, it seems characterized on the negative side by stunted language development and the failure to recognize persons, as indicated by her naming only objects, never people. What took place between her and her nursemaid cannot have been satisfying, or she would have learned her name.

One might conclude that the nursemaid, while attending to some isolated aspects of Laurie's life, never treated her as an infant; that is, as a small and undeveloped, but nevertheless total human being. The maid may have been bent on pleasing her employers at the least emotional expense to herself. Or she may have trained Laurie to perform along lines most convenient for her or the parents or both: to be no trouble, to be regular in eating and elimination, to keep quietly occupied. This was probably brought about by discouraging all spontaneity in Laurie, a requisite step for getting something like a conditioning process going. Treated like an object, Laurie learned to name them, to make a few "conditioned" responses like "bye-bye." But never treated as a person, never permitted or encouraged to become one, she may never have learned to recognize persons; certainly she never learned to name them.

A comparison with the history of other autistic children we have known makes it possible to speculate further: namely, that the maid herself may never have behaved as a total person toward Laurie. Many mothers of autistic children fear to let themselves do this; others cannot, for one reason or another. Such a mother, sensing that she wishes her child were not there, is so afraid of her own inclinations that she inhibits all spontaneity in her dealing with the child, and all feelings about him. In her efforts to teach, she never relates to the whole child lest her own feelings intrude. She deals only with an isolated part of his body, or the isolated function she wishes to train.

Laurie may have been treated that way, but I doubt it. There is no reason to assume that the nursemaid had so deep an emotional investment in Laurie that she had to repress her emotions and thus treat her mechanically, as an object. More likely, being very young and probably full of interests and problems of her own, she was simply disinterested in a baby who was probably not too responsive to begin with. Lacking all emotional involvement in the infant or her housekeeping tasks, her only concern may have been that Laurie be as little bother as possible, whether in eating or elimination. Probably she was not even interested enough in Laurie to want her to perform in a hurry, or in any other particular way.

Thus what may have been most characteristic of the nursemaid's behavior toward Laurie was emotional indifference. Feeling no interest in Laurie, the maid felt no response to Laurie's feelings as the child went

about doing or not doing as told. And Laurie experienced no feeling
reaction to her doing or not doing. Except that this, the adult's disappointment in the infant's not doing, plus his efforts to lead the infant
toward activity, are as important for the infant's developing personality
as the feeling response to his doing. Lacking both, Laurie may have been
kept from all encounter with the other.

All of which could explain, in part, why Laurie failed to recognize
persons (including herself) or to communicate with others through
talking or gesture. Such a concentration on insignificant and isolated
parts appears in the mother's strong attachment to Laurie's long hair.
It may also have characterized the nursemaid who took care of her child.

If my reconstruction of Laurie's early experience should be correct,
it would explain the strange course of her development, and what happened at the departure of the maid. Contrary to what the mother believed—though the parents were not home a great deal during Laurie's
infancy—her development probably never did proceed along normal
lines.

What we, on first learning Laurie's history, had taken for a severe
reaction to separation from the maid, for deep mourning at the disap-
pearance of a beloved mothering person, may have been nothing of the
kind.

The nursemaid may have patiently trained Laurie to do a few "tricks"
that meant nothing to the child, tricks that were strictly related to this
trainer and had grown no roots in Laurie. As conditioned responses they
depended on the presence of the conditioning person. Mastery was of
no emotional significance to the maid and therefore had none for Laurie.
When the girl left, Laurie may have kept on more or less automatically,
as if she were still around. But when, after a few days, Laurie met such
different reactions to her "tricks" (the mother's anger and spanking,
where the maid may have been merely indifferent), Laurie simply
dropped them because they had not only stopped serving their purpose
but had unpleasant effects.

This reconstruction, as far as it goes, while convincing to us who
knew Laurie as well as anyone could know her, is still only partial and
incomplete. It disregards the innate potentialities of any human being.
It neglects the child's autonomous response to his environment, his wish
and ability to protect his life, no matter what the conditions. It overlooks, for example, what was positive: the fighting back that was part
of Laurie's doing nothing; the identification with a mother who seemed
empty to her, and with the nonresponse of both parents to their child,
as she saw it. These too, were part of Laurie's doing nothing. It neglects
Laurie's coloring and playing with blocks for some time after the maid
left. These suggest her spontaneous efforts at doing and developing,

efforts that only slowly disintegrated for want of reward, in a withdrawal that began in anger perhaps, and only later on turned to desperation.

Be this as it may, with the maid's leaving a retreat set in; in some areas a slow one, in others very fast. The retreat soon became total, so total that one can only wonder at this child's ability to make herself so deeply unresponsive. Speaking only of the oral apparatus, her not even "throwing up" when she vomited, but letting the vomit flow passively out of her mouth, shows how decathected was the eliminative mode of the oral zone. In our entire group of autistic children, including the mute ones, we have never had another child who showed no response to vomiting at all, neither physical nor emotional, not even a flicker of discomfort, anxiety, or disgust.

Her giving up of self-feeding shows that the oral zone became just as decathected in its active, incorporative mode. Laurie only passively ingested what was put in her mouth. She had even given up part of the very first mode, that of oral retention. It was impressive how she had given up closing her teeth and lips, a significant part of this mode. As described earlier, her parched lips stood open for months after she came to us; her teeth did not close, her mouth remained passively parted—most likely to prevent any biting or talking (see pages 60–62). Apart from this, the mouth, in its normal functions of incorporation and retention, seemed so little invested with energy that it could not exert any protective function of closure—except again in the case of intrusion (as when Laurie bit her counselor or when other such children fight the dentist).

To paraphrase the terms Erikson suggests, we might say that when she came to us, Laurie could do nothing, could not even receive; for the little food that entered her body had to be put into her. One is tempted to say that even her passivity had lost much of the investment of energy so needed for doing. In regard to the oral zone and mode, activity had never developed, or been given up long ago. At least there was no contribution from Laurie when she received something in her mouth. Her accepting raisins and later the counselor's finger in her mouth were her first steps in actively receiving. This, then, may have been when her passive receiving first became active intake.

If, on the other hand, Laurie should once have been fully active, then what happened after the maid's leaving was a withdrawal, in steps, to the prepersonal stage: she gave up talking, lost bowel control, gave up playing, and finally even moving, seeing and (one may assume) all human feelings.

We do not know the details of how her toilet training broke down. All we could gather was that soon after Laurie stopped talking, she gave up bowel control and then playing and motility, in that sequence. So it seems of interest that she became aware that it was *she* who eliminated (in contrast to the simple awareness of her stools, which came sooner) only after she had discovered and learned to enjoy the following: first, the body of the mothering person; second, her own body in interaction with this adult; and third, elimination brought into close personal contact (by wetting on her counselor).

As mentioned earlier, Laurie was still an autistic child even after gaining conscious awareness of her own elimination. She was still gaining or regaining mastery over isolated zone modalities, one at a time. She could not integrate them yet in concerted living. For example, when she could finally urinate actively, her eyes closed and her body lost all tonus. Her arms hung down passively at her sides following gravity, as if no muscles held her body together.

Thus when engaged with feeling and consciousness in the eliminative mode it seemed so intense an experience that it left no room or energy for anything else. No other modality was involved as she blotted out the locomotive and incorporative modes. While she had become active in urination, she had not become so as a person. Otherwise her other faculties (seeing, for example) would have taken part in the experience, as they did indeed later on.

Such a fragmentation we have also observed in reverse; that is, when the intention was that a stimulus should *not* come to awareness. Sometimes one of our autistic boys would suddenly assume a posture of absolute immobility, with fingertips to ear lobes, or with shoulder pressed to ear. We never saw this happen except when he was spoken to. It occurred several times, for example, when he was told that a staff member of significance to him was going on vacation. It also happened when he was told that the counselor who saw him in individual sessions was going to see another child in therapy too. The immobility seemed an attempt to avoid sensory stimulation; in these instances, an auditory stimulus that was specially meaningful to him.

But the point to be emphasized here was the total-body reaction to a stimulus, a reaction in which all sensory input was kept to a minimum, and motor activity ceased. That is, he was unable to respond appropriately or selectively to an auditory stimulus, by either hearing or not hearing. In order to keep from hearing, all sensation, including sensations derived from mobility, had to stop too.

Erikson [1950, 1956] makes the point that while one mode dominates in each stage of development, all zones and other modes remain present, and function as auxiliaries. This interplay of zones and modes was certainly absent in Laurie, and is absent in most of our autistic children.

Speaking of the very first developmental period, which sparks the whole process of personality growth, Erikson notes what must obtain for a healthy, well-rounded growth of the total personality: in the first incorporative stage, the predominant incorporative mode must become supported, step by step, by a clamping down of jaws and gums (second incorporative mode), spitting up and out (eliminative mode), closing of lips (retentive mode), and an "intrusive" (aggressive) tendency of the head and neck to assertively seek the desired goal.

When Laurie came to us all these supportive modes were absent. She did not use her head or neck to support her eating, did not bite or spit up, did not close her jaws or lips. Each of these modes Laurie had to gain or regain in a separate learning process. For example, she learned to seek a goal with her head and neck as she rolled her head on her counselor's body, and also rolled her head on the pillow. During her stay with us, only rarely did all modes support each other in a smoothly coordinated way. But before she left the School she had come close to achieving integration of the pertinent modes, and with it come extremely close to speech. At least the silent articulation shown in her mouth movements, and the increasing variety of noises she made, suggest this.

For nontalking autistic children such as Laurie, Erikson's analysis of intellectual functioning, as an example of a part function, is especially illuminating. He says:

We perceive an item of information; as we incorporate it, we apprehend that part of it which seems worth appropriating; by digesting it we try to comprehend it in our own way, assimilating it to other items of information; we retain parts of it and eliminate others; and we transmit it to another person in whom the appropriate digestion or insemination repeats itself.

Thus, for the development of speech as communication, an interplay of all modes is necessary. Since speech development, too, begins with incorporation (of information) an interplay of the various modes at the first and most primitive incorporative stage is a necessary precondition for speech.

But Erikson's analysis also enables us to view lack of speech as due to disappointment in its intended function; namely, lack of appropriate digestion by another person. Laurie, after the maid's leaving, may have tried to find out if she could begin life anew with her parents as she had once begun with the maid. So she went back to those clucking or nonarticulate sounds that begin preverbal interaction between parents and children, and which later develop into articulate speech. At this point her efforts were inhibited by her mother. But while this probably contributed to Laurie's lack of speech, her main difficulty in acquiring speech, in our opinion, was that she never fully integrated the various modes and never achieved a full functioning of her whole personality within even one zone or mode.

Laurie, who once had some speech and then gave up talking, shows a picture that is different from some other nontalking autistic children. Their failure to acquire speech seems due to a singular emphasis on the retentive mode of the first stage of development, to the exclusion of the incorporative, eliminative, and intrusive modes. For example, one seven-year-old nonspeaking girl, who like Laurie is said to have once spoken a few words, began to acquire speech with clucking sounds such as Laurie was said to have made. With our encouragement these sounds developed into an infantile ga-ga babbling with ever greater variety in intonation and feeling quality, until it approached true speech.

But the ability to talk does not lead to communication in these children. For that the oral apparatus must become fully integrated and secure in itself. Only then can it afford to put itself in the service of personal interaction. So this girl used speech for some time as signal and command ("No!" "Cut!" "Go!"). But when once again challenged to talk by the staff member closest to her she replied with a clear and decisive "Not yet!" And there it rested for a considerable time.

Marcia too, had been repeating a few words for a long time, after gaining full mastery of most oral modes. When she was ready to consider the possibility of talk in the sense of communication and her counselor encouraged her, she reacted with the very hesitant question: "Why you speak?" Even after speech was acquired, she needed to understand its value and meaning as an interpersonal phenomenon before she could master communication.

§

Collapse and Withdrawal

The foregoing theoretical digression was inserted here because at this point in Laurie's development a striking series of events took place which we still may not fully understand. Their outer and most distressing form was what seemed like a total collapse.

Once before we had seen a part collapse in Laurie, around Christmas time, when she had been at the School about three months. Of the staff members who worked most directly with her, two had already become specially important to her; first and foremost, one of her two counselors, and second, though to a much lesser degree, her teacher. At Christmas time her teacher took a week's vacation, which was hard on Laurie, and then her main counselor was absent for five days. During the last three of these days, sensing desertion, Laurie withdrew, became very quiet, ate and drank little, and again seemed to have lost all will to live.

During these days, and probably more during the last of them, she lost five pounds, an alarming weight loss in this basically very fragile child who was still more or less anorexic. But on the return of her counselor, she soon regained the weight and her behavior became as it was before the interlude. At that time, we viewed things rather favorably as an appropriate reaction to a desertion; a sign that some staff members had acquired meaning for Laurie which seemed to bode well for further building of her personality.

Still, after this dramatic withdrawal, Laurie's main counselor had worried, off and on, how she might ever take another vacation without risking grave consequences for Laurie and a burden of guilt in herself. When spring came, personal plans meant she might be leaving the School in the near future, and she was afraid her deep involvement with Laurie might prevent it. When the second, more radical collapse took place, we at first looked for its cause in the mothering person's contemplated desertion and resulting ambivalence. But in retrospect, it seems quite unlikely that ambivalence was the major factor in Laurie's collapse. Among our reasons is the fact that this particular ambivalence was present for some time before and afterward without its leading to far-reaching consequences; and this during periods in which Laurie made striking progress.

§

The Mother in Infantile Autism

Again I would like to digress, because the reason we began by ascribing Laurie's collapse to the ambivalence of the mothering persons seems of some theoretical importance. That is, so much is made in the literature of the attitudes of the mother as a causative factor in infantile autism.

Throughout this book I state my belief that the precipitating factor in infantile autism is the parent's wish that his child should not exist. While the same wish may not cause the same disturbance in other children, and while at some future time we may learn that some organic factor is a precondition of autism, the fact is that almost all organic conditions that have so far been linked to this disease are also present in nonautistic children.

This seems to me reason enough to seek in parental attitudes for the reason why organic involvement—if such a factor should turn out to be typical—leads to autism in only some children but not in others. The more so, since in all cases known to us that allowed us to assess parental attitudes with some degree of certainty, these conscious or unconscious attitudes were experienced by the child as the wish that he did not exist.

What I wish to emphasize is why the following discussion centers on ambivalent attitudes toward the autistic child. The reason is that ambivalence, in my opinion, is much too weak, much too everyday an occurrence, to explain infantile autism.

Speaking of the already autistic child, it seems impossible to care for him intimately, over years, without repeated periods of ambivalence, sometimes prolonged ones. The utter demandingness inherent in these children's disturbance, their needfulness of the mothering person, the rarity of positive responses—this and much more will generate ambivalence. At its core lies resentment of the degree to which they enslave, through negation and passivity; the frequent absence of clear positive responses even to the most devoted efforts, and hence doubts of whether the efforts are appropriate; the fear that one will have to thus serve them exclusively for years on end; and the guilt one feels about wishing to be free.

These and other factors create ambivalence even in staff members wanting most to help such a child, and who devote themselves beyond the call of duty. The ambivalence is usually stepped up when the child withdraws, because the withdrawal, when serious, seems to put in question all prior achievement; creates the hurt that great efforts have been in vain; arouses the fear that one may have made mistakes, may have failed the child. There is also the anxiety that the whole ordeal of having gotten the child this far will have to be repeated. Thus the rise of ambivalence, or its aggravation, is often what follows the autistic child's withdrawal and not what caused it.

The action of an infant or a young child directed to his mother, and the mother's reaction to it, are often so instantaneous that one is hard put to get a correct picture of their time sequence. What was consequence can easily be mistaken for cause. Also, the mother's reaction may come to awareness much sooner than the child's action. If the child's emotional action gives the mother only a liminal cue, the mother's awareness of her own reaction may come first, and the liminal cue come to attention only later, if at all. The same is true of the autistic child's relations with his caretaker since the autistic child, like the infant, often gives only liminal cues.

We can now posit the following sequence of events: a liminal action of the autistic child—and most of their actions are liminal or subliminal—evokes ambivalence, or a negative response in the caretaker. To this the child responds with massive withdrawal.

Confronted with such obvious and threatening behavior, the caretaker ponders why the child withdrew. All she remembers or is aware of, is her own ambivalence or negativism. Out of her own guilt she takes this to be the cause of the child's withdrawal, or it is taken to be its cause when she reports on her self-observed ambivalence. The child's withdrawal is then viewed as the consequence of the caretaker's feelings, when actually these feelings may not have been the cause, but the effect of the child's earlier liminal or subliminal withdrawal. But since only one set of causes is recognized, we grasp at it for a ready explanation of a behavior (total withdrawal) that threatens us while it remains unexplained.

I think parallel phenomena may explain maternal attitudes described in the literature. Maternal feelings, indifferent, negative, or ambivalent, are then made to explain infantile autism, while in my opinion only the extreme of negative feelings in the parents can set the autistic process in motion.

Laurie's collapse, a total withdrawal from the world, provides an instructive illustration of this error. Because we too, influenced by the literature, looked first to the emotional attitudes of the mothering person for an explanation. Looking for it there, true, we found it. Her counselor was aware of great ambivalence toward Laurie at the time, and had she not been it would have made little difference. It was quite apparent to other staff members concerned with Laurie.

So for a time we felt strongly that we knew what had probably caused the collapse. But from the vantage point of time—this was written nearly a decade after the event, and after the most careful review of the material—we could see that the mothering counselor's ambivalent reaction to Laurie was her instantaneous response of deep disappointment to Laurie's withdrawal, as it barely began to reveal itself.

As far as we can determine, all that happened was that Laurie walked backward into the dormitory when returning from the classroom with her teacher. This liminal sign was consciously recorded by the counselor because it was unusual behavior for Laurie; but she failed to recognize its unconscious meaning for Laurie, and what it may have expressed of her inner feelings. In any case, the counselor unconsciously recognized it as withdrawal reaction, which it was, and viewed it as rejection, which it was not.

Having invested so heavily in Laurie's progress, the anxiety aroused was so great that the counselor became acutely ambivalent in her attachment to Laurie. This ambivalence was experienced consciously as already described: in thinking again about plans for leaving the School, of how Laurie's needs made that impossible, and so on.

For the rest of that day, and particularly on the following two days when Laurie withdrew even more into a death-like state of anorexia, the counselor's guilt over her recognized ambivalences rose to ever higher pitch. It became dominant in our anxious speculations about what brought on the collapse, and what needed to be done to bring Laurie out of it. What appeared to us then as the essential cause of the collapse, the counselor's ambivalence, we now see as perhaps a minor contributing factor to the initial withdrawal, and as a continuing factor once withdrawal set in.

The different reaction, by us and the counselor, to Laurie's withdrawal and anorexia at Christmas time, when compared to what happened in spring, sheds further light on how ambivalence may aggravate withdrawal. At Christmas we viewed Laurie's withdrawal as a sign of her deepening attachment to the same counselor, which pleased and reassured us. Hence the counselor could immediately bring to bear upon Laurie all her old positive feelings, and those additional new ones that came from viewing the withdrawal as token of her success in reaching the child. As a result, the withdrawal was soon reversed.

In spring, on the other hand, Laurie's withdrawal came when the counselor was more ambivalent in her feelings, for all the reasons described. Given this ambivalence Laurie's behavior aroused guilt, anxiety, and resentment in the counselor. From this she could draw no narcissistic satisfaction, nor any additional strength for resolving her ambivalence. On the contrary, it brought an onslaught of negative feelings that could only be stemmed and reversed by deliberate effort.

If this, our experience, is accepted as applicable to the relations between infants and mothers—which it may or may not be, or only with modification—what is then central for the child's fate is whether a spontaneous withdrawal is met with a positive, ambivalent, or negative response. But while the mothering person's attitudes to the child's withdrawal are thus crucial, we must not therefore assume that they caused it. And, even a negative response will not lead to infantile autism unless it is so extreme as to lead to the child's permanent conviction that he should not be.

Animal trainers have told me how comparatively easy it is to work with large feline animals, because they show typical prodromal behavior before attacking: they withdraw a few inches. Whether this incipient, often just liminal behavior will lead to a vicious attack or be passed over without incident depends entirely on the trainer's response. If he responds in one way he may be attacked, even destroyed; at least his relation to the animal will suffer severe damage. If he reacts another way, nothing untoward will happen.

It would seem erroneous here to blame the animal's behavior on the trainer's response, though it would be easy to see that the trainer's fear is what preceded the animal's attack. But it was not the trainer's fearfulness that provoked the attack, as is often thought. On the contrary, the sudden fear is an appropriate (if unfortunate) response to the animal's prodromal behavior. Since the liminal moving backward of the animal is undramatic and easily overlooked (like Laurie's walking backward into the dormitory) while the trainer's fear and the animal's subsequent attack are very dramatic, the mistake is often made of ascribing the animal's assault to the trainer's fear. And the explanation is accurate as far as it goes, only it does not go far enough to correctly explain the whole sequence of events. It overlooks the one action that touched it all off.

Does this, then, leave us with the question of what comes first, the chicken or the egg? I doubt it. All children are born with differential sensitivities and react differently to their environment. All soon show some positive and some negative responses. There is no child, at any age level, who does not sometimes react negatively to his parents, withdraw from them. Most parents learn to know the prodromal reactions of their children, and most parents learn to respond to them—consciously, and more often unconsciously—in ways that reverse or at least neutralize the child's negative responses and encourage his positive ones.

Thus in infancy all depends on the response of the infant's caretaker to his positive and negative reactions. (One need hardly add that the caretaker's reactions will be shaped by her own personality and history.) Because even the infant's positive reactions can be misread as intended rejection. If the child's intentions are read correctly from his often only liminal action, the caretaker will respond appropriately. If they are misread—because of the caretaker's bondage to her own needs and desires—the child's development will be interfered with.

Thus in the realm of interaction it really matters little who makes the first move, who begins the interaction, or even the nature of the action. What counts is whether the action is interpreted correctly and meets an appropriate response.

Does it follow from all this, that the attitude of the mothering person is immaterial to the autistic child? Certainly not. But while Laurie's counselor was ambivalent about her relations to Laurie, and the demands it implied, she was never ambivalent about her desire to see Laurie become active. On the contrary, at the heart of her ambivalence was the fear that for Laurie's sake she would have to remain at the School years longer than she planned, so that every step forward by Laurie evoked pleasure and lessened the ambivalence. Moreover, this ambivalence was conscious, not repressed or denied.

§
Collapse and Rebirth

Now then, if the counselor's ambivalence did not cause Laurie's collapse, but was only an added factor, what did cause it?

We shall never be certain. But in retrospect we think that Laurie may have reached a point in her development where she felt that satisfactions were available to her, both within herself and in the world. Starved for them, she may have reached out for much more than she was ready to handle. But having done so, she may have been overwhelmed by feelings she could not integrate because she was so unprepared for them. All of which could have frightened her deeply.

In the week preceding her collapse Laurie had begun to masturbate in earnest. When she came to us, she never masturbated at all. She was a model of propriety, immaculate and perfectly groomed, totally inactive and hence modest. Interestingly enough, her masturbation, according to what the mother told us, stopped as suddenly as her talking: "I caught her masturbating once or twice. I slapped her hand," and so ended the masturbation. After a few months with us she began on rare occasions to touch her genitals, but it was surreptitious, a bare experimental touch and no more. In this one week, however, she had played with them actively and persistently.

Prior to that her legs were always closed in a way that seemed decorous, though it was probably another way of exposing herself as little as possible, another protection of her body. Now she would lie on her bed in the evening or during the day, legs wide apart, rubbing her genitals actively and using her fingers to feel around inside them. After a week of this greater awareness of one of her body openings, she made much freer use of the organ most severly inhibited, her mouth.

The day before the breakdown, she finally closed her lips together and also played a good deal with tongue and lips, licking the lips or just touching them with her tongue. This we had never seen her do before, certainly not persistently. Her lips had always been parted and her tongue had usually stayed in her mouth behind her teeth. If she played with her tongue, it was only against the rear of her teeth and the roof of her mouth, never farther out. That evening the play became intensified, with a repeated playful wetting of her lips or the tongue moving across them.

That evening too, for the first time, she reached out for her counselor's hand and rubbed it across her own lips. After a while of this, Laurie rubbed her lips with her own hand, as she had first done with her tongue and then with her counselor's hand. Later while lying back comfortably, Laurie played with her hair as she had often done before, running her hand through it, or taking several strands of it to play with. Then she suddenly reached over, took the counselor's hair, and played with it much the same way. All her exploring of the counselor's body had never before extended to face and hair. On the following day Laurie collapsed, stopped eating and drinking, closed her eyes and kept them shut.

Our first interpretation (other than the counselor's ambivalence) was based on her new and greater courage in touching and feeling her own body during the past few days, most of all on the preceding evening. This, combined with her radically changed masturbatory behavior and much freer mouth activities, suggested that she may have wanted to feel even more; that by closing her eyes and thus shutting out the world, she hoped to feel touch more deeply, both contact with the mothering person's body and the touch of her own. (Despite her closed eyes she walked about without hesitation or mishap.)

But by nightfall she withdrew to her bed and shut all of us out. Then we became concerned, a concern that increased in the following days as Laurie gave up all bodily functions within her control. Her eyes remained closed, she did not move, neither ate nor eliminated and seemed not to hear.

Hard as it is for us now to understand why we were so blind to the obvious signs Laurie gave us, the fact is that we disregarded the one dramatic move it all began with: that Laurie, on returning from class had turned to look back at her teacher as she walked backward toward her counselor in the dormitory. (It should be noted here that "class" meant the hours spent with her teacher in what, to all intents, was a prenursery school setting geared entirely to the therapeutic needs of the children, with a psychoanalytically trained professor of group work functioning as the "teacher.")

Possibly the walking backward was a wish to prolong contact with her teacher from whom she would now be separated till the following day. Perhaps she wished to avoid facing her counselor who she feared might be viewing the new relation to the teacher as betrayal. If so, Laurie was indicating her ambivalence about leaving one person who had just begun to be important to her too, and about rejoining the other who was still the most important person in her world—or one might better say, the only one there was, up to now.

Had we understood this then, as a question—"Is it all right to be interested in more than one person? Is it acceptable, is it safe, for me to be interested in both my counselor and my teacher?"—had we realized that just as she was so much more active in approaching her own body, she had also become active in her interest in the world, our reaction would have been entirely different, and the course of the next days' events might have been radically altered. After all, her counselor had wooed her long before Laurie had felt any positive interest, when it was still very much a one-way affair. Her teacher had tried also to reach her but only succeeded much later. By that time Laurie had become much more active and was probably aware that she, too, was moving out to this new person; that it was not just the other person's doing. This may have roused her anxiety about how her counselor would react to such independence.

All this happened at the beginning of our concentration on autistic children, at a time when we knew far less about them than we do now, and were much more subject to prevailing notions about autistic children being passive, unable to relate. We thus made the mistake of viewing Laurie's behavior as being caused by the adult's behavior toward her, instead of viewing it as her taking her affairs in her own hands.

Here, then, is another example of the self-validating nature of preconceived notions. We viewed her walking backward not as a positive step but a negative one; not as a walk toward the world, but as turning her back on the world. That is, we viewed infantile autism not as positive efforts by the child on his own but (because lacking in empathy) as entirely negative. And from this erroneous notion came our response. Had we interpreted correctly, her counselor would have been delighted. If Laurie was now reaching out to her teacher then the counselor had less need to worry about the dangers of her possible leaving. And Laurie, encouraged by this positive response to her widening interests, would not have needed to collapse.

But when her reaching out to others was interpreted as withdrawal and met with worry and ambivalence, then her worst suspicions were confirmed: nobody wanted her to have a life of her own, not even we at the School. And she returned to the autistic position.

We were so worried at first lest we add to her discomfort by changing the accustomed pattern of her life that we tried to keep on with old routines as much as her condition permitted. But by the third day it seemed clear this would not do. We then radically changed our attitude of trying to go on with life as usual and decided that her favorite counselor should attend her continuously with the most infantile care. So for the next days her counselor held and cuddled her for most of the day and much of the night. At first Laurie resentfully withdrew, but after several hours she began to accept it. Thirty-six hours after we began this virtually continuous cuddling, lap holding, soft patting, stroking, and talking to her, Laurie emptied her bladder, the first of her voluntary body functions to resume working.

The next day we put her in a large doll buggy, nothing else being available at the moment. We had first asked if she would like this and by way of response, or for reasons of her own, she cooperated through her movements (raising her arms to be picked up, for example) as we lifted her into the buggy. There she remained for a considerable time as we wheeled her about and she seemed to enjoy it. That being a Sunday, we had to wait a day to get a real baby buggy. The next day we secured one and we told her it was now hers.

In this larger buggy she no longer just sat but tried curling up, which was not easy, considering her size. Later that day she began to take small amounts of liquid. For the next few days, and much of the nights too, she was either being wheeled about in the buggy, or being held, cuddled, or rocked.

It was while being rolled in the buggy, exactly a week after closing her eyes, that Laurie opened them again; at first only for moments at a time as she lay back, looking up at the ceiling, blinking her eyes open and shut as a baby might on wakening.

That morning she took a decisive step toward coming back to life as her counselor talked to her, telling her that life wasn't as bad as she thought, that things would get better, that if she didn't want to look at anything now it was all right, but when she wanted to, she could look again. Laurie made no response but she looked more pleased all that morning, and even smiled a little. Shortly thereafter, we took her to breakfast, and she ate her first bit of solid food since the episode began.

We also let her begin to spend part of her days with her teacher again. Though her eyes were closed, she found her way about on her own, carefully avoiding chairs and other obstacles, even things that were not always in the same place. In class she kept her eyes open for quite a solid stretch as she stood drawing at the blackboard. This, her drawing lines, squares, and circles very intensely with chalk, marked her full return to life. The next day we felt she was resuming her normal behavior, and her eyes remained open for most of the day.

Two days later the whole episode was over. Laurie was back, or so it seemed, where she had left off before it all began. Her return to the world, and the feeling it gave us, are best conveyed through her teacher's report at the end of the day on which Laurie came "all the way back."

"The last two days were two of the most generally happy and easy days for me and the children. There was tremendous relief, plus happiness, when Laurie opened her eyes, and at the same time was so much more filled with life than she had ever been in the past. In fact, my association off and on during these two days was: when the little girl

woke up from her sleep, she seemed to be greatly refreshed." This observation was made long before we were aware of Laurie's coming new
achievements.

Laurie was not simply back where she had, as it were, left off living,
because her period of total withdrawal marked the end of one development and the beginning of another.

Years later we also understood what had baffled us for so long: why
she opened her eyes for short moments with her counselor, who had
seen her through the whole trying period, but kept them open for a solid
stretch while in class with her teacher. But it was the counselor's reaction to her walking backwards that had reduced her to desperation, not
the teacher's. That is why she returned fully to life with her teacher,
and why it was in class that she first showed she had come back "greatly
refreshed." Her new lease on life, however tenuous, was predicated on
the belief that relating did not mean a life restricted to one person only.

We may never know for sure what restored Laurie to life or led her
to make a real new beginning. But we cannot exclude the possibility
that with so many new experiences she may simply have needed total
rest from all physiological functions and psychological experiences.

She had taken great strides forward. But maybe, because of deficiencies in her earliest development, she took them too fast, on too weak
a foundation. Or one might better say, a Laurie who found her emotions
suddenly overextended had to radically retrench.[3]

By walking backwards she may have expressed her overriding need
of the moment: to go back; to have a "moratorium." This she needed
in order to regroup her new acquisitions in a way that had space for
more than a single exclusive relation. Or perhaps more correctly, she
felt a need to give up an organization that was predicated on only one
relation, and to build up from scratch a way of life that had space for
several relations. For this she might use the same tools she had so recently acquired, most of all the feeling acquaintance with her body
and its functions. But they had first to be wholly disassembled and
reassembled in new combinations.

3. Discussion of this point was sparked by exchanges with Dr. Peter Wolff after
his reading of an early form of Laurie's history. I am much indebted to him for
these and many other helpful suggestions, and particularly for his generosity in
explaining his thoughts by means of a personal experience, "At the present time I
don't have the courage to take cello lessons. I squeeze by if my quartet partners
have tolerance enough. By teaching myself I'm sure that I have learned many things
wrong, and every cello teacher I have approached so far has been very enthusiastic
about telling me that the only way they could teach me would be if I started from
scratch. I would suggest that only after reaching a certain level of proficiency could
I give up what I learned so badly. Similarly Laurie, perhaps, had to have acquired
a certain stable pattern of walking, or general balance in other areas of spatial control, before she could explore a new way of approaching that space."

If all this is so, then Laurie's withdrawal this time was not the anxious not-being with which she came to us, or did not remain so. With our help it soon turned into something new and positive, an effort toward a new start at the very beginning of personality development. This happened when, of the several things we offered her, she selectively responded to being put in the buggy. Thus she chose to return to a state of babyhood that allowed her to respond positively to being cuddled and rocked, to enjoy being wheeled about. Maybe the continuous infantile care she then received was enough to replenish her emotionally.

During the preceding months Laurie had acquired some feeling knowledge of her body, had learned that it works and can do things. So when she came out of her withdrawal, what she did was entirely different from what had characterized her development during her first months with us. From now on she did original things that expressed what she wished to be dealing with. No part of it was just a taking or a copying of what we offered. It was autonomous new invention; her own way, not ours, of struggling toward becoming a person.

It was as if Laurie had returned with a new attitude to the world. If we were to put it in words (which would take us outside of Laurie's way of experiencing things) she might have been saying, "I tried to be myself by following my counselor's leads but that didn't work. If I ever try again, it will be on my terms, not hers."

On this process of establishing a positive self Laurie now embarked with determination. It occupied her till the day before she left us, during most of the time when her mind was active. But although far more active than before, most of the time she was still doing nothing.

§
Self-assertion

This original and purposeful new doing consisted of three related activities: (1) tearing of paper into long strips, (2) coloring, and (3) creating boundaries. Each one of these appeared separately, but then merged with the others as when, for example, Laurie first colored a sheet of paper, then tore it into one long strip, and then used the strip to create a boundary dividing her very own world from the rest of the universe. From her history we know she had once colored, and had also torn things into tiniest shreds. But the coloring and tearing that now appeared were entirely different in nature.

Each of the three activities began with a specific event. Laurie began to color paper after she had begun to use finger paint, and she began to finger paint only after she had done it with saliva. Any activity had at first, and for some time, to be intensely and immediately personal. Only by using part of her body (saliva) to wet the paper could she finger paint. Her feeling of self was much enhanced if her body, so to say, had a part in the creation, whether the materials of creation were feces or paint. If her saliva went into it, the picture was so much more hers. Only when she had thus experienced these paintings as her very own doings, did she later add crayons to her tools.

It seems then, that mastery in the outside world begins when an extension of the body (the body ego) seeks to encompass, to manipulate, or modify this outer world. Smearing, painting with feces or saliva, is using something that comes from the body to modify something on the outside which thus becomes our doing and hence our possession.

A highly personal extension of the body, a merging of body and external things, stands at the beginning of an important recognition: that this world, though not ours, is ours to try to change as we wish, is to that degree here to be made our own. Only when we feel we can do that does the world not seem alien. Because we have the experience that we, with our body (and later with our minds) can do things to the world. If we do, then it carries the impress of our will, becomes ours, because we made it.

Most remarkable was Laurie's tearing. Out of a regular 8½ by 11-inch sheet of paper she would create a single long strip by tearing concentrically from the outer edge until reaching the center—and this without looking as she tore. In this way she managed to turn such a page into a continuous strip eighteen feet or longer, while staring at the ceiling all the while. With her self-created strips, she then set down boundaries between her very own world (what she was or did, and what belonged to her) and the rest of the world.

It began one day just after she had defecated and had again, or so it seemed, carefully explored the problem of how something that had just been part of her could become nonself. Leaving this problem, she took one of her wooden pull-toys and tied its string to a balloon she had. Then she used the balloon string to tie both to some other toys, finally using the strings of other pull-toys to tie all of them together.

That her first string was attached to a balloon may have been significant. A ball or balloon, to such children, often stands for the breast. The balloon hovers tantalizingly over the child's head, as the breast seems to remain tempting but unavailable to these eternally frustrated children.

As for the pull-toy she used, it was connected with feces, because it was this toy, a wagon containing blocks, that she had used in her first simultaneous play with feces and toys. So maybe she was thus tying together what she wished most not to lose: the breast and the contents of her body.

Perhaps by tying the balloon to her toys she was making sure that these, her possessions, her stake in this world, would not be flushed down the sewer, nor escape into the sky (as the breast disappears upwards, when withdrawn). Perhaps the mother's breast is the child's first "possession." But for Laurie the breast seemed unreachable as an emotional experience. Now too, she experienced that her stools were escaping her. So she may have decided that this time she would make sure that the balloon representing the breast would not vanish. But she may also have expressed how much all objects were still tied, for her, to the very first object, the breast.

Eventually she became dissatisfied with this way of tying together all that was hers, perhaps because the strings did not make things sufficiently her own. So one day, and again just after defecation and a preoccupied handling of her feces, Laurie tore a sheet of paper into a single long strip, as described. That the tearing, going round and round the sheet as she tore, was an essential element of her activity, was suggested by the fact that she never cut paper that way. By this time she was cutting quite readily with scissors. But with scissors she would merely cut off piece after piece of the paper, usually triangles, and just let them drop to the floor.

The first use she made of her self-created strip was again, to link together what was most important to her. She used it to connect her buggy to her bed. Next what she had thus linked together became a boundary that separated her very own world from the rest of the room. Inside the area thus created were Laurie and all her favorite possessions, closely bound; no child or adult was permitted to enter. So precarious still was her possession of a world of her own that any intrusion destroyed it, threatened her independent existence.

Within a few days the tearing of strips and creating of boundaries became independent of defecation, just as in the tying of strings. From then on daily, and for hours, she worked with utter abandon and intensity, tearing paper sheets into single continuous strips. These she used for laying new boundaries, but always in such a way that she remained inside the area marked off by these self-created borders.

A short time later she made the boundary strips even more her own by coloring them before tearing. She engaged in either activity with incredible concentration and absorption, usually actively hallucinating as she did so. She would, for example, crayon for an hour and a quarter with greatest absorption and without stopping or tiring.

Still later the tearing and laying of boundaries, and the crayoning of paper became separated, acquired independent importance, and developed along different lines, though in a definitely parallel process. Only for the sake of presentation are they separately discussed. But in doing so, it must be kept in mind that the growing complexity of each of them was an expression of the same inner developments that gave them unity: Laurie's efforts to master inner pressures were given symbolic expression in creations that could also help her to master significant aspects of the external world. Exactly as psychoanalytic theory has it, an ego began to develop as it took up the simultaneous struggle of its two functions: to master inner pressures and external reality.

The first new element that entered her tearing gave some further indication of why she seemed to have no use for the world: because its very center was not for her. Laurie began to tear off and drop, as if by chance, the end of the long paper strip she had made; the piece that had once been the center of the sheet. Nor was this accidental, since she did it each time. Later she progressed to throwing the piece away deliberately, an expression of disgust on her face. In the final stage of this evolution she tore out the center of the paper at the very start, threw it away, again with an expression of disgust, and only then began tearing toward the now vacant center. It was impressive to see how skillfully she tore out the exact center, with seemingly no effort, and how her tearing always ended exactly there.

It was at this point that she stopped using plain white paper, and first made it her own symbolic universe by coloring it over with crayons. At first Laurie colored both sides of the sheets a uniform black, though all colors were available to her and she saw other children using them (Figures 1 and 2).

Next came a coloring in which the nearly black hues were not made with black chalk or crayons, but by heavily covering the paper with many layers of various colors of chalk. These colors she carefully selected from the box of chalks and crayons, which were now very important to her. The end result was still black or a very dark gray.

Perhaps to make this paper her very own, Laurie had to color it a "body" color, the dark color of her feces which was the first thing she recognized as both her own, and something of hers that existed outside in the world. The later mixing of many colors that ended in the same blackish hue might then have paralleled the foods of many colors that go into producing the single-colored stool. But these remain speculations, since without Laurie's telling us we cannot be sure whether such was the meaning of her coloring.

Then, one day after she had entirely blackened one side, she was satisfied to leave the other a light gray. Later she was satisfied with a light gray on both sides, and finally she colored the paper in bright

FIGURE 1. A 9 by 11-inch sheet torn by Laurie into a single long strip after she had first colored it black and torn out its center. The strip has been folded back to show how she fashioned it out of one sheet of paper.

FIGURE 2. The same strip folded out, with a yardstick placed above the right half to show that the strip is some twenty feet long. At center, is another strip folded back to its original sheet form.

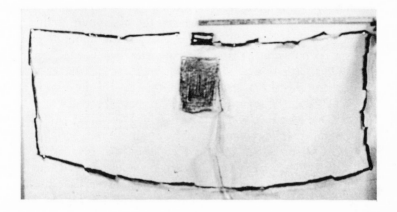

hues of red, green, violet, or any other color before she tore it. Her life had become "colorful."

Biting the counselor's finger, exploring with her stools—these were certainly autonomous activities, as was Laurie's masturbation, and her messing with food. Still, these activities pertained to her body, were directly tied to the sensory experience. Her tearing of paper into strips and then laying them as boundaries between the self and nonself—these were her first spontaneous, deliberate activities and most important, they were symbolic. It was an activity for which she had no example. It was truly her invention; self-created from external material to master inner pressures. Nothing we or the other children did or thought could have suggested such an activity, as may have been the case with masturbation or her playing with feces. No one at the School ever did such a thing, neither child nor adult.

But while her methods were unique, her needs were not. There were several other children in whom we were able to follow quite intensive efforts at creating boundaries in the outside world. Those who are more advanced do so with materials such as paper chains or string. Those more arrested use only their own body, most often through an idiosyncratic manner of walking. One boy, for example, walked or ran in a shuffling-hopping gait. He took only very short steps, sliding his feet along the floor in such a manner that contact with the floor was maintained at all times. Inspection of his shoes revealed none of the usual scuff-marks on the heel or the toe, worn spots being evident only on the soles.

This unbroken maintenance of contact with a surface is an important preliminary to true boundary behavior. It could also be seen in the boy's preferred way of walking stairs. He would place one foot on the step above him and then bring the other foot to that step before approaching the next higher one. After many hours of patient instruction and encouragement from his counselor he "learned" or rather dared to walk up (or down) stairs in the more usual manner of using alternate feet for the alternate stairs. But this he did only with a trusted adult. When alone he reverted to his old pattern for years.

This child's "boundary behavior" included also his walking (or running-shuffling) from wall to wall at the periphery of any semi-enclosed space, whether in the dormitory, gymnasium or playground. Out-of-doors, when permitted to do so, he walked only along the curb next to the street, close enough to touch the parked cars. In this way he avoided the sidewalk itself which had no vertical boundary. When he first came to the School, at age seven, he would only move if he were close enough to a vertical surface to touch it. His daring to walk at the curb marked a considerable freeing of anxieties about moving around.

§

The Empty Center

At this point we may try to view Laurie's tearing behavior from the perspective of her central symptomatology: her inability to take in (and hence to give out) or to relate to the world. If we then consider how eating begins in life, if we think of her raptured hallucinating as she tore around and around the paper, if we consider how she fingered it without looking, only gazing upward, perhaps it is not too farfetched to interpret the tearing as one way of approaching the very center of her disturbance. The primal source of food, or relating, and at the same time the most important nonself, is the mother's breast, something the infant gazes up at, and which he fingers without looking.

Just as the infant gropes for the breast or the bottle to find the nourishing nipple, so Laurie, in her hallucinations, may have been groping for, working her fingers toward, the center that gives life. As the infant looks up at the mother's breast and face, so Laurie looked up in her hallucinations as she fingered the paper, clutched at it, and tore. Just as the infant fingers the breast, tries to hold on to it, so she fingered and tried to hold on to the paper.

In tearing the long strip she also provided herself with a tactile sensation similar to what the infant may experience as he fingers the mother's breast, face, or body. The two fingers that tore were in rubbing contact with the fingers of the hand that held the rest of the paper; the fingers of both hands moving, they touched each other as they worked along the edge of the paper. Except that the paper did not gratify her longing; the life-giving center gave no life, nor did it offer itself freely to her frantic search. When she finally got there, it held nothing but disappointment. So in symbolic action she destroyed what she could not have. She tore away, as it were, the wall that kept her from getting at the satisfactions of life.

Thus her tearing may also stand for her anger, frustration, and hostility at hopes forever disappointed. She acted out both her desire to get at the life-giving center, and her anger that it was so hard to get at; that when she got there it was empty for her. All the longing went into her intense efforts to get at the center; all her anger and frustration into her tearing off and throwing away the end piece when she finally reached it.

To again put Laurie's behavior into words, she seemed to be playing

out her image of how the world looked to her: A wall of unresponsiveness had shut her off from life and its satisfactions. This indifferent
mother, who cared only about her own needs, who had kept Laurie
from getting at life, who had not offered her the breast or any substitute, was recreated in a blank sheet of paper. The unresponsiveness
that had stood between Laurie and the core of her life, she now tore and
made into a wall that shut her off from the rest of the world. Just as
she had felt walled in for so long, she now walled us all out. That she
could actively do this herself meant she was no longer a passive object
to be pushed about by external forces; it signified great progress toward
self-determination. But she still ended up shut off from the world.

The next big step would have been to free herself of her bondage
to this elusive, always frustrating core of life. But this step Laurie
could not quite take yet. She approached it by angrily doing away with
the frustrating center when she reached it, by tearing it off in disgust.
In a further step, she anticipated, sooner than wait to be disappointed
at the end of her striving. She tore the center out first, before she began
to tear strips for her boundaries. Her adoption of color, at the same
point, was a further step toward an active expression of feelings, desires and also independence. The white blankness may have been what
she saw as an empty blankness in her mother; the black, as suggested,
may have symbolized that she now gave it content of her own.

Being able to express in symbol what preoccupies one's mind is a
crucial step in the development of personality. To be able to do it in
elaborate ways that suggest some grasp of geometric principles (tearing a rectangle of paper into an unbroken strip several yards long)
indicates both determination and intellectual skill. Using the object thus
created to mark off one's world is another big step in self-assertion and
personal development. But one of the most critical functions of the
mind is prediction: the ability to anticipate the future. It alone permits
successful planning, and then action based on those plans.

Laurie took these steps toward becoming a person and taking her life
in her hands when she no longer waited passively for disappointment to
come at the end of her search, but anticipated it actively. It was as if
she had decided she could now have her own life, independent of the
frustrating mother, if she could give her up by deliberate decision. So
she gave up both the overriding passive wish for the good mother (the
"good" breast) and her hatred and fear of the bad mother who stifled
all her active desires (the "bad" breast).

Now, as Laurie began to do and to be—to move out of her autism—
it was as if she began to understand the dilemma she had been caught

in. Wanting totally opposite things, both of them equally and over-whelmingly, she could neither affirm nor negate, and could hence intend nothing. Now that she finally began to affirm (her area, her possessions) she also began to negate (discard bad things). From now on she might perhaps even try to master what had been bad in the past and live freed of it, by her own efforts. When this point was reached, the full spectrum of color entered her world.

§

The Verge of Speech

In a next stage of development Laurie's tearing became much more complex; again beginning with white paper and later on sheets she had colored herself. It is only with hesitation that I interpret her next typical design. It consisted of a double row of interlocking "teeth," made by first tearing out a center line on the page, and then tearing in a back-and-forth direction on either side of the line (Figure 3). The possibility exists that after she had torn out and thrown away the unpalatable cen-ter, she created a mouth full of teeth with which to meet the world more aggressively, in a more grown-up way. Maybe she created two sets of teeth because there are two breasts; who can say?

This, like all other interpretations of Laurie's behavior, is highly speculative. Unfortunately, she did not remain with us long enough to acquire speech, which alone could have told us, later on, what her thoughts were as she colored and tore.

But our speculations do not rest on single pieces of evidence, such as the tearing thus far described. By the time Laurie began to tear the centers out first, she had reached a higher degree of freedom and self-determination, because she also began to make boundaries other than those she created with her paper strips. The same need or idea she could now express in a variety of situations and with various materials. That is, she had learned to generalize. She built boundaries by means of elaborate designs which had to meet rigid specifications. She used sand, for example, to make designs on the ledge of the sandbox which in this way became her domain.

The suggestion may seem fanciful that she possessed, or had acquired, rather complex geometrical concepts which she now set to use. It may therefore be added that out of such unsuitable matter as tanbark she created a row of fifty near-perfect sine curves on a seventy-foot long ledge separating one of our play yards from a sidewalk. More astonishing, she solved with great skill the difficult problem of rounding

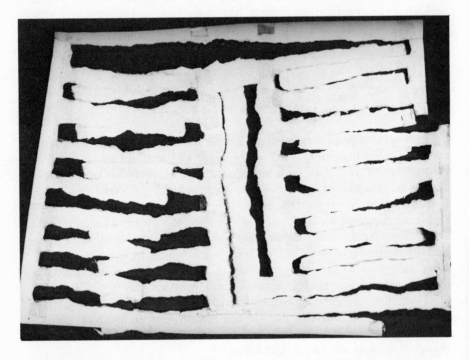

Figure 3. A sheet of paper with the center strip first torn out by Laurie, and then each half of the paper torn into two rows of interlocking teeth. (The tear on the right border was not in the original, but was made when we stretched it for mounting, before photographing.)

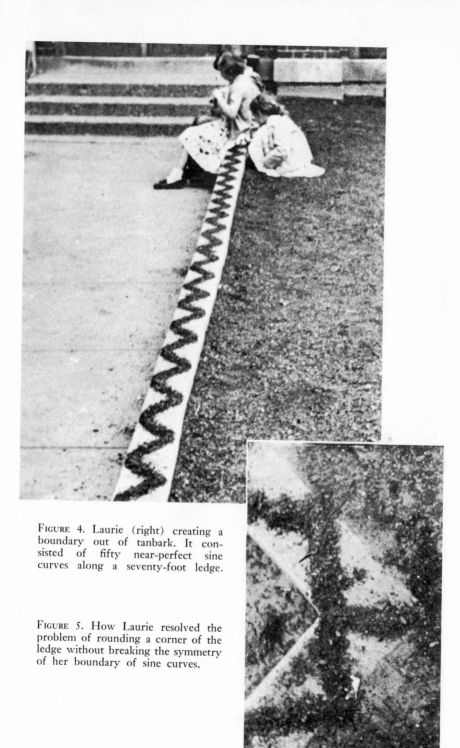

FIGURE 4. Laurie (right) creating a boundary out of tanbark. It consisted of fifty near-perfect sine curves along a seventy-foot ledge.

FIGURE 5. How Laurie resolved the problem of rounding a corner of the ledge without breaking the symmetry of her boundary of sine curves.

a corner of the ledge without breaking her continuous design. Invariably she remained inside these boundaries; they always separated her private world from the rest (Figures 4 and 5).

Again, if the link we suggest between the tearing and her early feeding should seem farfetched, I might mention the way she began, about this time, to eat chocolate bars. She did not tear out the center of the bars (maybe because they were good tasting?), but with her teeth she worked around the bar exactly as she tore around the edges of the paper: by taking small bites along one side, then turning it ninety degrees to continue biting tiny bits off the next side. In this fashion she would circle a chocolate bar five times or more before she had eaten it all.

Whether or not these interpretations of Laurie's behavior are correct, there is no doubt that she acted out of one all-pervasive underlying motive, because her coloring underwent a development that closely paralleled that of her tearing, and her nibbling around the sides of chocolate bars.[4]

When Laurie first began to tear out the center of the page, there appeared a definite design in her coloring. First the solid black receded somewhat to cover only about two-thirds of the page. Then only a corner, about an eighth of the page, was colored in heavy black; the rest she divided into four rectangles roughly equal in size. She managed to link the dark area in the corner with the center of the paper by drawing a heavy black line between the two.

This was followed by another design in which the rectangles were gray but outlined in black, with black lines emanating from the center. Still later, some of the lines emanating from the dark corner became colorful: green, red and blue.

The darker square corner area Laurie drew first, and spent much time in elaborating. The lines emanating from it she added fast and furtively in the very last seconds, and then she was through with that side of the paper (Figure 6).

Speculating again, it is possible that these designs—first all in black, then with only a corner in black, then in gray with a heavy black border —represented again the idiosyncratic way in which things had to be her very own by being black, and then only partly black, so that ever larger areas were left free to exist independent from her.

If her preoccupation, as we assume, was with the bad mother (the "bad breast") then she may have tried to master this by reducing it first from all the world (the whole paper) to just a small area; and

---

4. Long before these interpretations were arrived at, staff members spontaneously connected her tearing and coloring with eating. For example, they reported in terms of how "hungry" Laurie was for crayoning, how "starved" she was for coloring.

FIGURE 6. Crayon drawing showing the dark core area from which at first only black rays emanated. In later forms, this design also gave off colorful rays.

FIGURE 7. Drawing with two centers, probably symbolic of (or representing) both breasts.

then by refusing to see it as all black but only gray. Finally, she may have begun to hope that something positive could come from it all, despite the darkness of the core. Perhaps that was why she so fast and furtively drew the colorful lines emanating from it. Perhaps as she reduced it in space and importance, it slowly became possible to accept the bad in the world, or the "bad breast," since she could now exist independent of it.

In a still further development, Laurie made new designs full of color. These were characterized by a heavy center area in hues of pink or red, with many other colors faintly superimposed and covering the rest of the paper. This center became a deeper and deeper red, the color of strong emotions. The center, which in her tearing was torn out and thrown away, was here accentuated as most meaningful and full of color. In a next step she made diagonal lines in the corners so that finally an elliptical area surrounded the red center, giving it still greater prominence.

Laurie may now have been having fantasies about the wonderful good life, the "good breast." If so, it was a wish she felt could not come true, because she returned again to dark centers, though they were no longer black. Instead, she again used a heavy mixture of red, blue, green, and brown to create her dark area, while the rest of the paper, the rest of the world, as it were, remained colorful. In the very last stage of this series of drawings, two such centers appeared (Figure 7). Possibly Laurie was here expressing her realization that there is not one but two breasts from which nourishment and life may be given as she may have created two sets of teeth for the same reason.

What Laurie had done with the dark, chiefly red-colored areas, she later repeated in white. This began about a month before she left. One day she sat on her desk for about an hour and a half in deep absorption, looking at some of the old style coloring she had done. Then in quick succession she colored three pieces of paper in deep reddish hues. But though she went over each of them many times, with several layers of color, each sheet had a single round white area spared out within the red, a white "hole." These white areas were much more prominent than any of the holes she had made, either in her tearing or drawings (Figure 8).

Either because she had exhausted herself in this achievement, or because it freed her of her anorexia, or for still other reasons, that noon she ate six bowls of vegetable soup and some large servings of blueberry cottage pudding desert, an unusual amount for any child and an unheard-of quantity for Laurie.

This style of drawing, a heavy overlaying of red and orange with one center area left white, culminated in an added white area, so that two circular white areas were then spared out amid the heavy red background (Figure 9).

The very last of Laurie's "art" products suggest a combination of her coloring and tearing, as well as a combination of her efforts to free herself of the frustrating life-giving center that for so long had seemed a barren hole. This she did by accentuating the hole. Her drawings consisted of heavy red stripes, alternating with white or faintly rose colored stripes. But after finishing such designs, she would fold the paper in two (sometimes in four), tear out a ragged hole, and then reopen the paper. What resulted was a large area filled with alternating red and rose stripes in which appeared two gaping holes, two empty centers in an otherwise colorful world.

These drawings with holes torn out of them ended the development of her crayoning. But there was one more thing she did before she left us. One day she got hold of a paper loop. It seemed to fascinate her and she skillfully tore it in half lengthwise, so that she then had two loops. These she then twiddled on her fingers, looking at them intently as if puzzling deeply about their meaning. As we watched her do this, several of us felt immediately, and independent of each other, that she was lost in thought over the difference between the good and bad breast. This, of course, was our speculation, but what else could we do but speculate in dealing with such a child; and at least our speculation was based on having been concentrated on Laurie and her behavior for many months, often all day long and through much of the nights.

While these developments were taking place, she was making louder and more differentiated noises. Her mouth and lips began to form words; but, alas! she never got to the point where she voiced them loud enough for us to be sure she had said them.

Our frankly speculative interpretation of Laurie's behavior is that she had been caught eternally between her overwhelming desire for the good breast (the good mother) and her despair because, in spite of all her efforts there seemed nothing there for her, not even a "bad breast," but just an empty nothing. Not being able to affirm or negate, she became inert and remained so. This conflict kept her from moving out into the world. Any move out to reach the good mother just brought her closer to the dangers of nothingness. In this predicament she knew only one defense—to do nothing at all by not acting, by not even eating.

With us she began slowly to act and to be. In her tearing and drawing, she tried symbolically to visualize, to understand, to act out and resolve this dilemma, and in so doing developed something of a self. Certainly

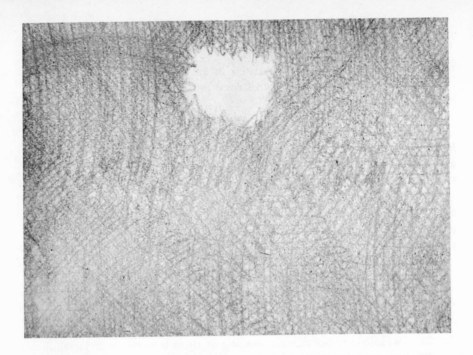

FIGURE 8. Drawing probably symbolic of the "white" breast—that is, the good one.

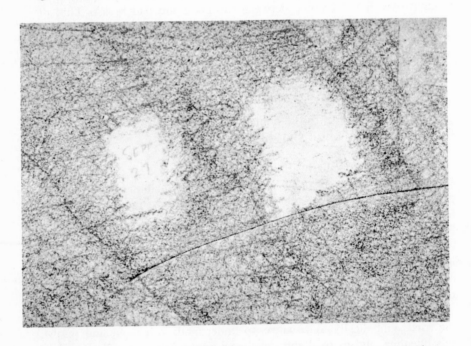

FIGURE 9. The same idea expressed through two white "holes," probably symbolic of two "white" breasts.

she moved out from her vegetative existence toward a life that for brief but ever longer stretches was busy and active, assertive. To be able to express her needs and feelings symbolically, through literally thousands of drawings and repetitious creating of boundaries, was a tremendous step toward assertion. Through them she created her own life sphere and tried to deal with her overwhelming problems in wholly self-devised ways.

Unfortunately, it belonged to the inner logic of this case that at this point the parents who had been kept informed of her progress all along, decided to withdraw their child.

On the day before her first year with us would have ended, the parents came to the School, having informed us beforehand that they wanted a short visit with her. They took her with them to spend the night, but called the next day to tell us of their decision to withdraw their child. They had planned, they said, to do this several months earlier but had not been able to come to Chicago till now. They had no answer to my question of why they had announced this as a visit. They both said, but the mother in particular insisted, that Laurie belonged to her, that she could not live without her. They set a time later in the day at which to come and pick up her belongings.

On first seeing Laurie the preceding day, and again during the phone conversation, both parents were full of praise for what they called her "unexpected" and "remarkable" progress during the year with us. They were particularly impressed that she was no longer constipated, was fully toilet-trained, ate so much better, and was much more independent.

In the meantime we had arranged for our two psychiatrists, who had followed Laurie's progress, to consult with the parents. Neither parent wished to talk with them, but finally agreed to, out of respect, as they put it, for the good work we had done with their child. Though they said again that they recognized Laurie's progress, both parents listened impassively, the father without interest, to what we (the psychiatrists and I) had to say.

One of our psychiatrists summed up her impression of the interview by saying that throughout our talk with the parents, she felt they were so unwilling to listen to what we said that they probably did not hear us. We offered to keep Laurie at a fee agreeable to the parents but this was of no interest to them. I suggested they might call in a psychiatrist of their own choosing for further consultation. This did not interest them either. Whatever we said seemed to bore them. My belief is that this went deeper than mere disinterest. Both parents had reached the end of their rope with Laurie. For years she had caused them to feel totally defeated as parents and by now they could afford to feel no more. Least could they afford to hope once more since they were convinced that to hope meant only to be the deeper disappointed later on.

In reply to all arguments the father insisted that Laurie was his daughter and "the burden" he had to carry; the mother, that Laurie belonged to her and that therefore they had decided she would have to leave the School.

When I reminded them of our agreement—that if we accepted Laurie she would be allowed to stay with us for as long as we felt was required —the father said, "I agreed because I was convinced you wouldn't keep her and that she's hopeless. Since she's made such progress . . ." and there he stopped.

I persuaded the parents to permit Laurie to see once more the children and staff she had lived with for a year, to at least let them tell her good-bye. When I took Laurie back to her dormitory, she eagerly ran with me to return to her teacher, her counselors and the children. But a few minutes later, when I told her that she had to leave the School, and when the children and staff had said good-bye to her, she collapsed into the total nothingness in which she came to us. She could not, or would not, walk out of the School. Her father had to pick her up and carry her out to his car, as he would a lifeless package.

About a year later we learned that shortly after her withdrawal Laurie was committed to a state hospital for mentally defective children. There I visited her a couple of years later and found her pretty much as she was when I first met her: extremely emaciated, responding to no one and nothing.

I sat with her for a while and told her how terribly distressed we all of us still were that she had left us; that our greatest wish was that she could have stayed. She turned her head, looking into my face with eyes that suggested some understanding, and laid her hand on my knee. In much the same way she had put her hand in mine at our first meeting when I told her I wanted her to come and live with us. Responding to her gesture as I understood it I told her that much as I would like to, I had no power to take her out of the state hospital. She slowly withdrew her hand, and though I stayed for another while there was no more flicker of response or recognition.

Despite the distressing end of Laurie's stay with us, her development, even during the one year, has many implications for our understanding of infantile autism and early ego development. Beyond this, her story proves what a potential for inner richness and complex structures of mind can lie buried behind the autistic child's not doing or being. Of these, the signs may be only liminal or subliminal; hard to recognize and even harder to understand. But despite the difficulties, let us never hold in low opinion, nor underestimate the power of determination, nor desert those who, on weighing the question "to be or not to be," elect not to be. They do so only until such time as we have helped them find the courage to be.

Marcia

For life I had never cared greatly
As worth a man's while; . . .

In earliest years—why I know not—
I viewed it askance;
Conditions of doubt,
Conditions that leaked slowly out,
May haply have bent me to stand and to show not
Much zest for its dance.

With symphonies soft and sweet color
It courted me then,
Till evasions seemed wrong,
Till evasions gave in to its song,
And I warmed, until living aloofly loomed duller
Than life among men.   THOMAS HARDY

*To Karen Carlson Zelan and Inge Fleischmann Fowlie belongs the
major credit for Marcia's progress in rehabilitation, and for the observations on which this report is based. The many other staff members who contributed include Margaret Fuller, Shelton Key, Hazel
Osborn, and Fae Lohn Tyroler.*

MARCIA did not come to the Orthogenic School until she was almost eleven years old and on the verge of puberty. When we first knew
her she was not only mute and autistic but did not even respond to
objects. She reacted only to her own body.

Her solipsism became apparent when she did begin to talk, for even
then she did not speak in any organized language. What seemed like a

stream of silent associations was from time to time interrupted by single words, most of them with private meanings, and all pronounced in highly unusual, idiosyncratic ways. For some time, to make any sense of what she said, we had only our empathy to guide us and this, despite our best efforts, often led to misunderstandings.

It is hoped that these fragments of her history will show how the growth of a self and of personal relations develop in a parallel process, and how both precede language. In addition, they may show how closely linked are all three to the higher mental functions.

At first meeting, we found Marcia very appealing. This was probably a factor in our decision to accept her, despite our serious doubts about admitting children of such extreme pathology when we start our work so late in their lives.[1]

In spite of her remarkable progress we doubt if she will ever be able to live entirely on her own in society. Still on the basis of our experience with others like her, we feel there was a fair chance that she could have done so one day had she come to us three or four years sooner.

Before Marcia, we had restored some children like her to full functioning in society, but they had come to us when they were only eight years or younger. A few others had been accepted at age nine or ten, with results not nearly so favorable, but in each case, special circumstances had been present, such as shock treatment (Anna, see pages 374–377) or a long period of institutionalization with only limited, custodial care (Andy, see pages 379–381). In line with our goals, it seemed important that we also make an effort to help children who were physically just as mature, but where no prior bad experience with treatment would impede our therapeutic efforts.

Hence another important reason for our decision to accept Marcia was her age. Puberty is an important watershed in the process of maturation. Among the many unsolved problems alluded to at the start of this book was the question: to what degree is personality development

1. Early in her stay, we began to record her nonverbal behavior on film. As a result we can demonstrate some of the steps in her rehabilitation, at least those we could photograph, and the extent of what can be achieved by our treatment methods. The film also suggests how much remained of the initial disturbance after five years of work, which is where the film ends.

We were able to produce the film thanks to grants from the Ford Foundation, and Child, Inc. The early parts of it were photographed by K. Karpuszko, with the help of I. Yahalom; the later parts by C. Sharp, with the help of M. Carey and others. That the project was possible at all we owe to the special efforts of those working most closely with Marcia, foremost among them Karen Carlson Zelan.

We are also grateful to Marcia's parents for their splendid cooperation all through her stay with us, and for their permission to publish this report and to show the film for scientific purposes.

based on physical maturation and to what degree on emotional experiences and the social relations they generate? While maturation depends on a more-or-less fixed biological time clock, we do not know for sure which steps in personality development require which particular levels of physical maturity.

Consider dependence, for example. The human infant is utterly dependent on his social environment for survival. Therefore it is hard to know if dependence, and the emotional experience that goes with it, are necessary for personality growth. If they are not, then psychological development should be able, in theory, to proceed even without them.

But what if it should turn out that, despite physical maturity, certain steps in personality growth require that state of relative psychological dependence that is characteristic of infancy? If so, then we have gained support for the notion that some steps in early ego development will not take place unless emotional dependence and the satisfaction of dependent strivings create the proper setting for it; and this holds irrespective of whether or not the dependent care is imperative for survival.

Nor does even this tell us if personality development must occur step after step, as in the very young child. If physical maturity were present, could they occur all at once, or in some other sequence? Laurie did not remain with us long enough to trace this sequence of steps very far. The account of Marcia's stay with us was selected to follow next, because it takes us much further in this sequence.

Since hers is a story of only limited treatment success, I might mention here what will be spelled out again in later chapters: that while we cannot be sure that endowment plays no part in the development of autism, or what exactly are the consequences of the very early experience, the fact that we have reversed the autistic process in many cases certainly suggests that endowment does not preclude rehabilitation. The children's own accounts suggest that whatever the role of endowment, they themselves feel they withdrew from reality because it seemed to threaten their physical and psychic existence. So the first question to be explored here is: What made Marcia so convinced of the all destructive nature of everything in the external world?

§

Marcia's History

As with all autistic children, the origin of Marcia's troubles preceded her birth. Her mother, who was born and raised in England, had a difficult childhood. She was the oldest child and as her father died when she was eleven she assumed family responsibility early. In adolescence she felt a great deal of resentment at being a girl, growing into a woman. As she put it, "The whole idea was horrible."

In school she did well, became a nurse and enjoyed her profession. After the start of World War II, she fell in love and married, but within months her young husband was killed in action and the tragedy brought on severe depression. Eventually she joined the services herself, as a nurse. While on war duty she met Marcia's father, and after a short and indifferent courtship they were married. She felt respect rather than love for him, since her emotional attachment was still to her first husband. But she hoped the new marriage would help her forget, and relieve her depression.

Marcia's father was the youngest child in a large family and described himself as just a farm boy, born of poor parents, in a small town. Where Marcia's mother had been the mainstay of her family, Marcia's father was the unneeded child in his own. He felt teased without mercy, both by his parents and older siblings, a teasing he dreaded acutely. His mother was very domineering and tightly controlled all the children, most of all her youngest son. In this respect his wife reminded him of his mother.

In school the father did well. He left college in his last year to enlist, advanced rapidly, served with courage and distinction, and left the service with considerable rank. During the war, the girl he hoped to marry suddenly broke their engagement, so he too wanted to marry to escape loneliness. In addition, he was subject to anxiety attacks. These grew more and more severe in the last years of the war, though they never interfered with his duties and remained restricted to his private relations. He hoped these attacks would subside once he had a home and a permanent companion. He married while still in service and was demobilized when his wife became pregnant.

The father's emotional difficulties were by then of long standing. The most annoying symptoms were what he called his attacks of blushing and anxiety, both of which made him want to avoid being with people.[2] After marriage, and the return to civilian life, his difficulties grew. He recalls having to leave work suddenly to return to his apartment where he sat crying, realizing that he was falling to pieces. As he described it, "a terrific fear built up and it boils over inside of me and I couldn't control it, so I had a complete breakdown." This happened

2. He did not reveal to us what emotions caused his blushing or were hidden behind it. But in view of Marcia's fear of her father, it should be mentioned that Feldman [1962], who studied pathological blushing, speaks of its main cause as the inhibition of strong aggressive drives. Afflicted persons "think that their aggression could drive them to killing."

when his wife was in her fifth month of pregnancy. He then sought and received psychiatric care for several years.

In talking about his emotional difficulties he repeatedly spoke of how they "popped out," and always connected them in his mind with his wife's pregnancy. Though he did not want a child, he felt swayed by his wife and reluctantly agreed to their having one. Inwardly he was afraid "it might cut into my territory." He realized that his wife, though she wanted a child, had grown insecure in herself as soon as she knew she was pregnant. Her growing insecurity and her withdrawal from him during pregnancy confirmed his worst fears about losing out to the baby, and he "broke." This, of course, made the mother feel desperate about herself and the child's future.

When Marcia was born the father was still very disturbed, but had improved enough to resume work. To him, Marcia was simply "an ugly little baby." She was "really of no interest to me. I felt she was my wife's child." Children, particularly babies, had never appealed to him. He had only one interest in them: he who hated being teased, loved to tease small children: "I like to get babies mad."

Marcia's mother, on the other hand, states that she was very happy at becoming pregnant. The feeling changed radically when her husband's breakdown came in her fifth month, though she felt renewed hope as he slowly improved. Despite their financial worries, because so often the husband could not work, and despite their concern for his mental health, the mother recalls Marcia's development as proceeding normally during the first year and a half.

When Marcia was eighteen months old, and while the father was still in therapy, his condition took a turn for the worse and he had another severe relapse. This time the mother felt trapped in her marriage, resented husband and child, thought of leaving them both, and would have done so except for Marcia. Because she felt responsible for the child she could not bring herself to act on her real inclination: to live her own life, and leave the two of them behind to fend for themselves. Finally, both to earn enough to keep the family going and to forget it all, she went back to nursing. Although they were close to several hospitals, she chose to work in a setting that matched her own feelings of hopelessness: a hospital dealing mainly with terminal cases. The infant's total care was left to miscellaneous baby sitters, some of whom seemed to inspire Marcia with great fear. What little the mother did do for Marcia "I did in a hurry. I'm a bossy person."

When Marcia was two, the parents had to move for financial reasons. The mother felt estranged and resentful in her new surroundings, and from then on hated everything about her life, deeply rejecting both husband and child. "We were all utterly miserable." Marcia's reaction to all this was to withdraw and give up saying the few childish words she had learned to say, though for some time there was one exception. When the mother was openly angry at her, Marcia could say a few words clearly and lucidly. Thus when the signals were invested with feeling and the feelings were definitely directed to her, even in anger, she would take this for evidence of some emotional interest. Therefore she would still say a few words in response, reacting to a clear signal from the outside with one of her own, though her response was not a true communication. As if to make it obvious that she could talk but did not wish to, she would say a new word now and then, quite correctly, and never repeat it again.

From what the parents said, and from the impression we got from them and from Marcia, it seems reasonable to speculate that much of the time both parents wished that Marcia should not be. But their reasons were not the same. The father wanted her out of the way so that he could have more of the mother; the mother wanted her out of the way so that she could be free of them both. Thus while the parents' reasons differed about why they wished Marcia gone, the signals she received were clear enough; that both wished her gone. To this, the desire of both parents, Marcia acceded by living a life of nonexistence.

The father she simply feared. Maybe it was in defense against his teasing that she first closed her ears, and then turned her back to him. Her relation to the mother was more complex. To her Marcia felt beholden for the care she did get. This care Marcia accepted resentfully, and only in small part. One is tempted to say that Marcia kept on living because to her it seemed the worst revenge she could take on her parents.

More likely she did nothing because it seemed safest since any action led only to further pain and disappointment. Beyond that, there were neither challenges nor rewards for any doing, so that doing nothing was also simplest. Perhaps she also feared that any action on her part might provoke one or both of her parents to make real their wish to be rid of her. The more the mother rejected Marcia and the sicker Marcia got, the more guilty the mother felt. Out of guilt she then did things that added confusion to Marcia's conviction that she should not be. This confusion about what went on around her emotionally may have been further motive for her total withdrawal.

Such was the emotional climate when toilet training began, so it was a big problem from the start. Marcia stopped moving her bowels on her own soon after her mother began to train her at age two. It was not simply an infant's unwillingness to give up what had once been inside of her. It became symbolic of the central conflict between Marcia and the world, as embodied for her in the mother. This we learned only much later; also that the determination not to talk was part of a broader decision to protect herself by not giving out with anything, by holding on to her thoughts and feelings no less than to the contents of her bowels. Only the latter could be forced out of her, and this the parents proceeded to do, particularly the mother. Marcia could not prevent having her feces forced out of her, but she was even more stubborn about not "giving out" with any words.

Various methods were tried to make her eliminate. When she was about two and a half, constipation was so bad that from then on weekly enemas were forced on her, with the exception of a few intermittent periods when daily laxatives were used. The enemas she fought violently, and as she grew stronger the father had to hold her down. This he did by lying down on the bed with her, face to face, holding her fast against his body while the mother-nurse administered the enema.

It was Marcia's first intimate bodily contact with a father who had otherwise hardly ever held the child or played with her, all of which highly eroticized the procedure. Much as she dreaded the enemas, they excited her. This, we believe, came to symbolize her central conflict. It made it ever more impossible for her to move at all and forced her even further into autistic withdrawal. The event she dreaded most—because her own body was made to violate her desire to hold on and was made to give out—was also what produced greatest sexual excitement. Moreover, the persons who thus excited her were seen as mortal enemies, while she was wholly dependent on them.

If what we dread most is also, in a way, the only excitement we experience, then we can no longer trust our own judgment or desires. Worse, if what we most fear having happen to our body, if what intrusively penetrates it also gives us, for moments, our only bodily pleasure, then we cannot even trust the body and its signals.

If the close bodily contact the small child normally loves and reaches out for turns out to be painful, then he concludes he must shun what he seeks, and disbelieve that anything good can come from his body or his seeking. And if, in addition, the persons who provide greatest sexual excitement are those who seem intent on disemboweling him, then he further disbelieves that anything good can come from other persons. Because as soon as they excite him they destroy him. So Marcia could not even trust herself or her desires, because the wish for sexual excitement made her want what was utterly destructive. Unable to trust herself or her parents, her solution was to end all commerce between them, even to denying their existence.

I might mention here that Pavenstedt [1956] reports on a boy whose speech temporarily "dropped out completely" at twenty-one months when for a few weeks he "was put through a ritual every evening before supper: the father at first held him down with his legs over his head while the mother gave him enemas or suppositories." Though the procedure was dropped after a few weeks, it was not until several months later, and after he had been encouraged to be more independent in other areas too that he "recommenced speaking, however his words were at first much less distinct than they had been [but] his withholding of feces for three or four days at a time . . . has persisted till now" that is, up to the age of twelve.

Marcia, from the age of three on, stopped even looking at the world or at people, and closed her ears (and even her nostrils) with her fingers —no longer just to her father, but to one and all. Otherwise she either did nothing, or else rocked or tapped her chin with her fingers or small objects.

When she turned four and still would not talk or do anything on her own, she was taken to a local child-guidance clinic and received treatment for the next two years. It is claimed she made some progress there, though she was neither talking nor did she otherwise leave her autistic isolation. By this time the father had improved enough to decide to move back to the area he was born in. When the child was seven years old they could no longer keep her at home and she was placed in a custodial type of school where again she did nothing. Psychiatric examination showed her to be clearly schizophrenic. Various other examinations led to diagnoses running all the way from infantile autism to brain damage or feeble-mindedness. Examination at the University of Chicago showed no neurological signs.

(I should add here, because it has bearing on Marcia's later treatment, that about three years after she came to us, a sibling was born. Once she was living at the School, and particularly since she began to make progress, both parents felt relieved of tremendous guilt feelings. Slowly they were able to make a better go of life. They came to feel that despite their separate difficulties they were as well matched as they might have been with any other partners. With the new lease on life they then found in each other, they were adjusting much better and were encouraged to re-establish a family by having another child. This child developed normally.)

§

Early Days at the School

Marcia came to the Orthogenic School at the age of ten years, nine months. As had been true of her now for many years, she spent all her days in mute, angry, and frightened withdrawal. She sat on her bed for hours in a strange yoga position, her feet crossed under her, either motionless or excitedly rocking up and down. In this sitting position her rectum was certainly protected from intrusion; but in the rocking up and down she may have been trying to recreate the exciting anal stimulation of the enemas. At such times she was certainly concentrating on some inner sensations. Outwardly there was a strong, rhythmic change from quiet to highly aspirated breathing.

At first what little speech she had consisted of very rare, simple, highly selective and only whispered echolalia. For example, when we asked her if she wanted some candy, she would merely echo "can-dy." She would say "no" but never "yes." During those first weeks she said only two one-syllable words on her own: "no" and "bread" (when she wanted food); she also said "hurt" once (when constipated) and "close door" once (when angered at our efforts to reach her). After a few months she began ever so slowly to add to her speech a very few whispered demands (or commands). For the first years all her bits of talk consisted only of signals like these for things she wanted—all of it couched in short, single words, further broken up into parts and separated by long pauses.

Getting her dressed required infinite patience because her choices came only after endless rejection of what pieces of clothing we offered. Dressing her was further complicated because she would let no one touch her. But since buttons and zippers were too difficult, she eventually commanded us to "fasten," though as always, in a whisper.

It was not our language she used, but a private one of her own. This "fasten" was enunciated "fas . . . EN," the first syllable hardly audible, the second heavily stressed, in a whisper. Despite the whispering, each syllable was like a short burst of air or of flatus. Only the tiniest amount of something was emitted from her body; then the mouth closed until a second bit of sound was unwillingly and anxiously emitted to complete the signal of what she wanted. Months later, when breathing out heavily, she once in a long while voiced syllables that sounded like "udder." Over time, this changed slowly to "mud-der," again pronounced so idiosyncratically as to be a word out of a private language.

Other autistic children have similar difficulties with language. Some, like Marcia, speak only in a whisper and enunciate very indistinctly, put the accent on a different syllable than is customary, slur their letters. Others, when they begin to speak in more than monosyllables, run the words of a short sentence so much together that the entire sentence is pronounced as one word. This makes it extremely difficult, often impossible, to disentangle the words and hence to understand what was said. Again others speak overclearly but with such a nonusual emphasis that they too, turn each word into a symbol of their private preoccupations.

All words in fact have private meanings to them that tally only in part and by chance with the meanings we attach to them.

In addition, words carry magic power for these children—things may or may not happen, depending on whether they say certain things. Most of all, through their use of language, they show that words are very much their private property, and are not used for the purpose of communicating and relating.

Like many of these children, one girl was incredibly preoccupied with weather. She studied it with intense fascination and for a long time it was the only thing she would talk about. Only years later, when she was well on the way to complete recovery, did she let us know that among a variety of reasons for her monomanic interest in weather was the fact that contained (for her) in this word was: "we/eat/her." This was a child whose wish to devour was so strong that she had defended herself against it by an anorexia that required her to be hospitalized several times before coming to the School. Convinced that her mother (and later all of us) intended to devour her, she felt it imperative to pay minutest attention to this "we/eat/her." There was only one way to prevent such an ever present danger and that was to know everything about it. She had to watch and take note of anything even vaguely related to this "we/eat/her," in constant dread of which all her life was swept up.

This girl had never given up talking, though it was a long time before she communicated with us. But she, at least, had known something of what was behind her fixation and her deathly anxiety about a word. Very often, however, the very private meanings words bear in the minds of autistic children are so highly overdetermined that in the end the child himself no longer knows what exactly they stand for. Marcia's udder-mudder may serve as an example. When she first said "ud-der," we thought it related to nursing and hence to the mother. The connection seemed confirmed when it changed to "mud-der." But with her slurred pronunciation the word could equally well have been taken for "mother" or "murder." Had this been so for Marcia, the contradictory meaning of something that can stand either for a life-giving person or a killing one shows how talking, in the sense of communication, becomes near impossible.

Talking certainly evoked panic anxiety in Marcia. Each time she spoke it meant that her anxiety at not getting what she wanted had won out over the anxiety that stopped her from talking. As our efforts to reach her began to penetrate and brought an occasional wish to respond, she bit her lips as if in a frozen fury. She seemed forcefully preventing herself from saying something, biting hard on the lower lip as if to more securely close a mouth that some opposing tendency was pushing open to talk. The exception was her warding-off "no" which she also said only rarely, but with less extreme resistance.

As before, she continued to turn her back to the world and other people, particularly to adults. She also continued, for long stretches of time, to press shut her ears, and sometimes her nostrils. When her forefingers were stopping up her ears, the little fingers would close up the nostrils.

Any body contact was angrily rejected, even a touching, or a holding of hands. She walked as if in a dream. Whenever she moved she seemed wholly alienated from her body as if she neither knew it existed nor what it could do. Her movements were few and even those were rigidly frozen, with a single exception.

§
Twiddling

Inactive as she was Marcia had nevertheless, and long before she came to us, developed a twiddling behavior, a rapid shaking of one or two of her fingers. Often the twiddling was self-hypnotic. So was her staring at shiny, light-reflecting objects (such as a metal box) or most often at the ceiling with its light fixtures. Looking up at the ceiling she seemed to have particularly frightening hallucinations. Occasionally she put her hand flat to her face or nose. Perhaps she did this to make sure where her body ended, since in hallucinating she may have felt it extended to the images she projected on the ceiling. Or perhaps she did it to form a protective screen between her and a world she only dimly perceived, or what she hallucinated as being out there. Much later when she hallucinated this way she said, "See mom," and pleaded desperately, "Take mom away."

Marcia's twiddling was not only self-hypnotic but also a discharge behavior, as if it were a compromise between the most primitive reactions of the animal or human being when confronted with imminent danger: to freeze or take flight. If anxiety mounts and neither device seems successful then a compromise ensues, a frantic and aimless running back and forth. Marcia's body, frozen in total immobility, seemed to represent the first fright reaction. But the extremely rapid, back-and-forth shaking of her fingers might be likened to the desperate, purposeless, back-and-forth running of the cornered animal who cannot or dares not take flight.

For Marcia, twiddling her fingers in front of her face represented the sum total of the world and all experience for her. As we learned later, her eternal twiddling expressed her wish for oral and tactile (kinesthetic) stimulation, and her dread of giving in to any oral desire; because for anything to enter one of her bodily openings seemed much too dangerous to her. Hence she twiddled only against her chin, not her mouth. It provided her favorite self-stimulation—as she told us later, it "feels good"—and also gave magic protection against any stimuli that might come from the outside.

In many ways such twiddling at the age of puberty duplicates and validates Hoffer's observations that the "hand and mouth convey the primal sensation of self." And on this, the earliest level of ego development, Marcia remained pegged emotionally, though she had progressed beyond it in isolated achievements like dressing herself.

Hoffer [1949] following Lewin [1946] and others, relates that oral eroticism and skin sensitivity are merged in such behavior with tactile and kinesthetic sensations. The hand, instead of being the organ that grasps, remains chiefly an organ that is sucked to relieve tension. Only Marcia did not find such relief. Far from being the hand that grasps the breast, and thus supports the grasping mouth in its sucking, this hand was not even sucked as a substitute breast to relieve tension. And while it did come to stand for the breast, it was a breast Marcia reached for but that nevertheless remained inaccessible. She shook or twiddled only the forefinger, supported often by the third finger; but though she was constantly moving the finger or fingers toward her mouth, they never touched it, much less entered the oral cavity.

Linn [1955] has postulated a primordial face-hand-breast cluster in which

even casual observation of feeding infants will impress us with the active role that the hand plays during the sucking process. The hand clings to the breast almost as strongly as the lip clings to the nipple. In artificial feeding the infant clings with equal strength to a bit of blanket or to the finger of the mother if permitted to do so. In short, at this early stage grasping is intimately associated with sucking.

If so, he adds,

then we must extend the psychoanalytic theory to read that in this primitive state of awareness face, breast, and hand are all fused into a single homogenous primordial cluster. When the breast is withdrawn, continuity of the cluster is maintained by substituting the hand for the absent breast.

From our observations of Marcia's twiddling and the changes it underwent during her stay with us we feel this symptom has little to do with grasping, but relates mainly to sucking. We base this not only on

Marcia's case, but on those of several other autistic children who had difficulties with sucking, and in whom a parallel form of twiddling behavior was closely related to hallucinations projected against the ceiling.[3]

There seems little doubt that Marcia's twiddling had to do with loss not only of the mother but of reality itself. Certainly it was most frantic whenever she was most out of contact and in deep distress, seeking some discharge for it, if one can say this of a child who was never really in contact. If the breast was beyond reach, and if the hand (according to Linn) was substituted for the breast, then the twiddling is indeed understandable as an alternate movement of the "breast" toward the mouth and a withdrawal away from it to avoid the disappointment of not being able to grasp it, hold on to it, and suck. Thus twiddling seems the opposite of thumb (or finger) sucking. Far from satisfying the desire to suck, it symbolizes the desire for and total absence of this pleasure.

The connection between twiddling, sucking, and the overwhelming ambivalence surrounding it, could also be seen in the boy described by Pavenstedt [1956] above. Pavenstedt relates that

Much of the time he moved in little volleys on his toes. He shook one hand or both, twirling them in rotary motion. Thumbsucking . . . was actively interfered with by strapping his hands at eleven months and putting him into metal cuffs at thirteen months. At eighteen months, when the mother put bitter fluids on his hands and slapped him hard, he finally abandoned it. The mother is almost certain that his hand waving, which was still present at age ten, had begun then.

For Marcia it took years before she could let the twiddled finger touch her mouth, only quickly to move away. When she first came she dared not touch even the region of her mouth. She simply twiddled away from her body or only toward her lower chin. Anything that might enter the body, even her own finger, created too much anxiety. It was a signal of new freedom when she later began to twiddle more toward her body, and finally toward the area of her mouth.

In her twiddling and chin tapping with its high speed back-and-forth movement, every move out into the world (the outward movement of the fingers) was immediately denied or undone by a move inward, away from the world, toward her body. And both occurred in such continuous succession that all perception, decision, and action were effectively

3. Eisenbud too [1965] discusses "the role played by displacements and projections of oral longings, aggression and guilt onto the hand." He speaks of a "hand-breast complex" which, "as a dynamic and symptomalogical pattern [is] related to object loss" because of "the inborn connection between grasping and sucking in the early nursing situation. . . . Grasping is especially strong at the time of maximum hunger. . . . All movements are part of a total pattern of the infant's behavior aimed at securing the gratifying object at the time of greatest need."

shaken off too. For a long time she was thus moving inward and outward at the same time. What she actually experienced was that any move toward the world ended up in nothing but an inner kinesthetic stimulation of hand and fingers, later in skin stimulation of the chin-mouth area—but without sucking.

In any case, twiddling, with rare exceptions, was the only spontaneous activity that had positive meaning for Marcia. At least it provided discharge and some bodily stimulation. (Other spontaneous acts such as the closing of ears or nose were warding-off actions, to avoid painful experiences.) Autistic as it was, she at least seemed alive as she twiddled, or more so than in her mechanical, up-and-down rocking while in yoga position.

In the sphere of motor behavior, autistic disorders defy description in classical neurologic terms. Though they vary greatly from child to child, they are remarkably consistent, persistent and unique to the individual child. Thus "twiddling" too is individually unique. One child uses mainly a unique finger movement. Another child flexes and extends the wrist as well as the fingers. A third child may twiddle in a rotary finger movement with alternating pronation and supination of the forearm, with fixation of the shoulder, elbow, wrist, metacarpal, metacarpal-phalangeal, and interphalangeal joints.

Nearly all autistic children tap and twiddle with their fingers, but each does it in his own way. Many will use an object, in addition. The choice of twiddling object too, is unique and has personal meaning. One child utilizes a rigid object of particular shape, like a pencil. Another child uses a floppy piece of cloth, or a sock. A third child rotates a ring-shaped object about the end of her finger, as Laurie may have been about to do. A fourth youngster prefers a cloth or leather strap. A fifth will "juggle" small objects in a characteristic manner.

Twiddling as a symptom (to which should probably be added rocking, head rolling, and head banging) is highly overdetermined, has many roots and serves many purposes. Among its uses, we have little doubt that it creates a "dream screen" on which the child projects his own private reality. For example, while autistic children show an apparent inattentiveness to sensory stimuli from the outside, some actually achieve the inattention by the excessive, unvaried self-stimulation that arises from their strange motor behavior. In this way outer stimuli are blotted out by and "lost" in the sensations the child stirs in himself. His own behavior converts his state of "wakefulness" into an overwhelming attentiveness to himself, and effectively obliterates his perception of reality.

The twiddled fingers, as they move in front of the face, have the effect of blurring the vision of reality. The result is that whatever the twiddling child sees, he sees as if through a self-created screen. Reality, if seen at all, flickers by in a discontinuous manner, but a discontinuity that the child himself creates. Watching his eyes, as he stares at his twiddling fingers, suggests that he is peering, so to say, through a filmy veil he has superimposed on what is actually there. On this "veil" he seems to project his vague and essentially empty (because unvarying) daydreams and semihallucinations. In lieu of an unbearable reality he creates a private one whose visual appearance he controls through the speed of his twiddling. To some degree it is thus an effort to reshape reality and make it bearable.

By the same token, it seems likely that twiddling serves to reshape the reality of the child's own body, and who controls it. Clearly twiddling is not a diffuse activity but has a special relation to one object in particular: the child hits *himself*, twiddles against *his* chin, pushes against *his* face, displaces *himself* through space, moves *his* fingers in front of *his* eyes, shakes *his* arms, and so forth. In some vague form this allows him the pretense of a megalomanic self-sufficiency of the body and its organs. Through the twiddling part-object (shreds of paper, a rattle, or straps) he tries not only to gain additional body organs but ones that he controls.

Whether or not an external object is used as part of the twiddling procedure, the emphasis is always on action; on influencing, manipulating the whole world. And this, by his own actions, the child has narrowed down to the twiddling arena. Since he controls the twiddling, it permits him to hallucinate absolute mastery over both the external world and his own body—though my separating the two goes far beyond the autistic child's intellectual grasp of any reality. It is why I began by saying that for Marcia, when she twiddled her fingers in front of her face, this was the sum total of the world and all experience for her.

As long as these efforts remain fixed at the twiddle stage, it leads only to another experience of debilitation, namely of not being able to influence reality. The breast is never reached, the mouth remains empty and the longing unsatisfied. Nevertheless it is important not to interfere with the child's twiddling, since it represents his maximum ability for dealing with reality. On the contrary, we have to help him improve on it, as we later encourage him to twiddle with real objects.

Perhaps a word more here, about our attitude toward the autistic child's symptoms. With whatever symptom a child comes to us, and some are not easy to accept, we try to communicate our respect for the means he has worked out for dealing with his inner pressures and the impact of the world.

Marcia's twiddling, rocking in yoga position, her closing her ears with her fingers, and her constipation were all fairly silent, unobtrusive symptoms, and easy to accept. One boy presently with us has the more annoying symptom of jumping and loudly clapping his hands, a rather ennervating behavior when practiced throughout the day and much of the night. At home his parents had tried hard to make him give up this symptom because to them it seemed to advertise his "craziness." We not only encouraged him but occasionally joined him in his clapping.

Strange as these symptoms may be, and however ineffectual, they still represent the child's greatest spontaneous achievement. Marcia's highest ego achievement on coming to us was the twiddling that effectively warded off an intrusive and frightening world while satisfying some hallucinated desires. It was by no means easy to twiddle her fingers as she did. Despite our efforts to copy it in order to better understand it, none of our staff could ever twiddle as fast as she could, not to speak of keeping it up as long as she did, because our wrists gave out after a few minutes. Since the child's symptoms are his highest accomplishment, higher forms of achievement must derive from them, as indeed happened with Marcia.

Most important: if we do not respect this, the child's greatest effort, if we encourage him, for example, to drop it, then we cannot convey our respect for the child himself either. We simply validate the only convictions he has: that we think him nothing, and that his spontaneous efforts to gain relief and even some mastery of his tensions are disparaged by us. Worse, it gives him the feeling that we ignore his communication—and all symptomatic behavior contains a communication—and wish him to communicate on our terms since we are unwilling to do so on his.

Perhaps an example may illustrate further, though the symptom involved does not happen to be twiddling. Marcia, in her first days with us, ate no regular meals but restricted her intake to candy. More specifically, she could not eat at the table because her forefingers were plugging up her ears, and her little fingers were plugging up her nostrils. She had therefore no way to get food from her plate to her mouth. To say to such a child something like "It's O.K. to unplug your ears and nose," falls woefully short. It tells her we do not understand that it certainly is not "O.K." to unplug her ears and nose, because if it were O.K. she would unplug them herself.

Similarly, to offer to feed her or actually do so will not convince her that we understand her plight, because if she could trust anyone to feed her, she would hardly need to plug herself up. Our solution was to offer to plug the ears for her; then she could have some fingers free to eat with. Hearing our offer, Marcia promptly plugged her nose with her forefingers and with her other fingers brought food to her mouth by bending as close to the plate as she could—a performance that astonished both the other children and all adults present. Thereafter she ate at meals, with our help in the plugging, until she no longer needed to shut out the world to that extent.

Why, one may ask, did this work when other procedures either had no effect or increased her withdrawal? Firstly, we think, because the offer to help with the plugging recognized and gave credit for her having some very important reason to hold back from the world. Secondly, it recognized that while she wished to remain plugged up, she may also have wished to eat. That is, she may have been in conflict. Our offer showed that we recognized her dilemma, and wanted to help her satisfy both needs without her having to give something up. This, we felt, was crucial for a child who had repeatedly been made to give up what she wanted to hold on to.

After about half a year with us the connection between intake and twiddling became quite clear when Marcia used her two twiddle fingers, and only them, to bring food to her mouth. First she dipped these two fingers into a sugar bowl and then put them to her mouth to lick the sugar off. She liked even better to lick salt from her fingers and hand. There was no sucking, nor did her lips touch the fingers. The mouth remained partly open as the tongue licked the sugar or salt away. The lips stayed just as open when she ate with utensils. This she did by vaguely and mechanically putting a spoon filled with food into her open mouth, dropping the food in without the lips ever touching it. Eating as she did was an incredibly slow, mechanical procedure, as if she was neither aware of what went on, nor that she ate. Only when the two sugary fingers came close enough to her mouth to be licked did she seem a bit more cognizant of what was happening.

§

Beginnings of Self-Assertion

From the moment Marcia came we were convinced that if we were to force her to do anything, to give anything up, we could never help her out of her isolation. Nothing seemed more important than her acquiring the feeling that she was at least in charge of her own body. So from the beginning we assured her that we would not force her to move her bowels, that at the School she would never be given enemas, or any laxatives, and that in regard to elimination she could do as she wished. During her first two weeks with us, therefore, she did not move her bowels. We made no efforts to induce defecation nor did we tell her she should, but we did ask her how she felt about it. Finally, though not in answer to our question, she whispered "hurt."

In those first years with us Marcia never spoke to us; the few things she said, she made it clear, were not directed to anyone. If she said anything at all, she spoke to empty space. Still when we spoke to her she evidently heard a voice coming from somewhere; an intrusion she shut out by closing her ears. For a long time she understood as little of what we said as we did of her words or behavior. Most of what she heard was an irritating noise, not only because it intruded, but even more perhaps, because it made demands on her to understand. Only on rare occasions did she seem to vaguely grasp what we said. This was when the content of our words and their emotional intent were closely attuned to what was going on inside her. Since nothing on the outside was recognized as existing, nothing coming from the outside made sense unless the two happened to coincide.

This is not as odd as it seems. The same is probably true for the infant —that he understands the mother's message only when it tallies closely with his inner experience. The rest of what she says may be vaguely pleasurable because of its feeling tone, but the meaning escapes him unless more or less the same meaning is already present in him. What is crucial here is that most of what he hears must at first be present in him and only later can be more or less so. Because on this, his growing ability to respond even when "less so," is built up the continuous enrichment of his inner world. With it he is more and more able to send and receive messages of greater complexity. But at first, and for some time, the difference between message and inner experience must be small, or the message is not received. If too many messages intrude, and thus threaten the integration of the inner world, all messages may be blotted out.[4]

All of which suggests that Marcia could respond only to those messages of ours that told her what she was inwardly quite familiar with. It was not (as the reactions of schizophrenics sometimes suggest) that our behavior showed that we "understood" her; this presupposes a distinction between one who understands and one who is understood. This distinction was beyond Marcia at the time. Her existence was either supported or interfered with, that was all. If interfered with, the mes-

4. In later life, larger differences between inner and outer world can be mastered, though never without limit. This is why one's age mates, or the persons one grew up with, make better "sense" to us throughout life, than those whose pattern of life is more alien. Interactions with the former require less adjustments of one's own inner experience and hence threaten our integration less. It is also why new acquaintance with different social groups, or cultures, is so challenging and enriching, provided one's inner experience is wide enough, and one's security great enough, to adjust to the challenge instead of being overpowered by it.

sage was blocked out; if supported, the message was allowed to come to awareness.

Hence it was critical for her that a set of inner experiences that had formerly been interfered with seemed suddenly to find support; when she not only heard an inner voice telling her she should defecate only as she wished or not at all, but an outer voice saying the same. This voice from the outside told her repeatedly, in a nondemanding, non-threatening, sympathetic tone, that she did not have to defecate in the toilet but could do it wherever and whenever it was easiest for her. She then began to soil for about a month.

Marcia's experience around soiling must also have freed her in other respects because she changed her way of closing her ears with her fingers. Up to then it had happened when just about any word or noise reached her. From then on it became slowly more selective. When the message was in tune with her inner life, and later when it was merely neutral, she at least let it in as something heard. But for years she continued to put her fingers in her ears at sudden loud noises, or at words that were angry-toned, annoyed, or exasperated.

In her third month Marcia toilet-trained herself spontaneously by defecating daily in the tub while she was having her bath.[5] Apparently it took a pleasurable experience that extended over her entire body—the warm temperature, pleasant skin and kinesthetic sensations, to which were added gentle stroking when she allowed it, and our talking and trying to play with her in the tub—to enable her sphincter to relax. She could surrender her stools to the gentle medium that enveloped her body because at this moment the confines of her body extended to the water so that her stools were not entirely lost. Soon she also handled and played with her feces in the tub.

Perhaps our pleasure at this restriction of her soiling to a single place also encouraged the play and further localized defecation to the bath-tub. This continued for several months and then diminished. After about a year and again in her own good time—though we occasionally made tentative suggestions—she began to eliminate in the toilet. There, as she sat for literally hours, she began to make her first spontaneous, jabbering noises—as opposed to the few, single-word, whispered demands—finally breaking the near-silence she had maintained consistently up to then.

5. That a bath can have such a relaxing effect is possible only if the child understands that its essential purpose is the pleasant sensations it provides. This can happen only if it is not conceived of by the child as a way of cleaning his "dirty" body. A ministration that begins by being critical of the body is not likely to create sensations of bodily well-being, or will detract from it to some degree. Hence we do all we can to free the playing in a warm bath from the connotation that its purpose is to get the child "clean," and try to make it as pleasant, unhurried, and playful an experience as we can.

Bladder training seemed to have been no problem either before or after coming to the School. But after a year and a half with us she began to cling, not to urination, but to the urine itself. By pressing her thighs tightly together, she formed a puddle of urine in which she would play for quite a stretch. After that she would let it fall into the toilet by separating her legs.

As she held on to her urine and played in it with her fingers, she gave up bladder training because it, too, had been imposed on her. Only after many months did she stop clinging to and playing with her urine, and again train herself on her own.

As far as we can make out, Marcia's first positive response to our efforts came when we encouraged her to soil. The next time was when we offered her something to grasp while she twiddled, that is when we deliberately introduced a transitional object in her life. What we gave her were two separate straps, and she soon preferred these by far to twiddling only her fingers, or with the two ends of a belt, as she had occasionally done on her own. Much as she liked the straps, however, she did not want to receive them; this would have meant having to recognize the giver or the giving. She wanted the straps to just be there, laid out for her on a table, ready for use when she entered a room. It soon became very important to her that these two straps of material were laid out for her. It was one of the first objects she took the trouble to look for as a thing of specific interest to her.

What Marcia had first done with part of her body was now extended to these external objects that permitted greater variety and elaboration of this self-stimulating activity. Later she would twiddle the straps with only one hand, leaving the other hand free to do something else if she wished, whereas twiddling her fingers or even the ends of a belt had kept both her hands occupied.

Once the straps became habit she slowly elaborated the twiddling: first from an up-and-down to a sideways movement; then from an outward to an inward twiddling; and finally to a chin-tapping.

Whereas stools had been part of her body and became external objects she handled, these straps had originally been external objects which, when twiddled, became part of her body. External and internal world were not separated yet, but for some few isolated objects a transition was being made.

Over time, both the straps and their use had some of the qualities of all the seven stages of development ascribed by Winnicott [1953] to transitional objects; among them that they stood for the breast. However, as twiddled objects the straps failed to give the security that an object, firmly held on to, can offer. Being devoid of what is gratifying in the transitional object, they contained largely those features referring to the desire, and none to the satisfaction. Hence they only parallel the qualities Winnicott lists. But as far as their history is concerned, the parallel is complete. To illustrate, I will mention only the last three of Winnicot's special qualities.

In the *fifth* stage the object "must seem . . . to move, or to have a texture, or to do something that seems to show it has vitality or reality of its own." Such a reality Marcia's twiddle object did not acquire for her for another two years.

In its *sixth* stage of development the transitory object "comes from without from our point of·view, but not so from the point of view of the baby. Neither does it come from within; it is not a hallucination." Except that when Marcia reached this point in her relation to the twiddle object she had been with us nearly three years and was no longer a baby but close to fourteen.

The final dissolution of the transitory objects in its *seventh* and last stage of development is described as follows:

Its fate is to be gradually allowed to be decathected, so that in the course of years it becomes not so much forgotten as relegated to limbo. . . . It loses meaning, and this is because the transitional phenomena have become diffused, have become spread out over the whole intermediate territory between "inner psychic reality" and "the external world as perceived by two persons in common."

This stage Marcia reached only after more than four years at the School.

As far as eating was concerned, Marcia was at first highly selective in the foods she would eat. She did not like to drink, would not touch milk, and took only water. Months later she made a slip and whispered, "want milk," but quickly corrected herself and for once demanded loudly and angrily, "wat-er!" She ate only a very few starchy solid foods. She ate them laboriously and with excruciating slowness, but only after she had twiddled above the dish with her hands (and later the straps) for a considerable time. Even this did not make the food safe enough to touch her lips. Any lip or mouth sensations seemed to terrify her. She made an effort to bypass the mouth by trying to put water in her ears and nose instead.

Her lack of interest in anything going on around her was quite obvious, or perhaps it was an unwillingness to let herself, or anyone else, see her interested or responsive. If we seemed too interested in what she was doing, she stopped.

Interestingly enough, our filming of her was not viewed by her as an interest, at least not for a long time. Though we began to take pictures of her some three months after she came, she showed no awareness of the process for two years. Since she seemed to have no more negative reaction to this than to anything else, we continued with the filming.

After about seven months, her favorite activity was sitting in the sandbox and giving herself what we called a sand bath. Her position in the sandbox, her pouring of sand over herself, were exactly like the way she sat in the tub and poured the water (often also the feces in it) over herself. Those of us who had seen her in the tub could not doubt that she had transferred her play from tub to sandbox. But in this sand play, more than in the tub, two activities merged and led to enriched play and exploring. In the tub she played with water and her stools; she did not twiddle them. In the sand play her handling of a solid substance merged with the twiddling and tapping movements.

Whatever Marcia did, she did slowly, purposefully, and did it over and over. So now she spent hours in the sandbox, twiddling the sand with both hands, or holding it in one hand while the other twiddled on it. Later out of this twiddle motion developed a true tapping of the sand. Later still she pushed it around, held it in her hands, rubbed it against her face, poured it over her head.

Each sequence in sand play began with an autistic twiddling of her fingers to make the sand safe, or her own. But with her greater freedom of hand movement, she now twiddled her fingers in the sand instead of in the air in front of her face, and this permitted her to see better what she did. Slowly it changed to really feeling the sand, taking note of its texture, exploring it. And every motion needed to handle and explore grew out of the one set of motions she knew: the autistic finger shaking and twiddling.

Marcia, who still allowed no one to touch her, made use of sand to provide herself with skin sensations that she seemed to find fascinating. Sand was one of the first objects she somehow recognized as belonging to the outer world, and also experienced as pleasurable. (Feces, which she handled earlier, are also an external object after leaving the body. But this is so only in adult experience which has clearly established what is self and what is not. For the young child they stand in an intermediate position.) That may be why sand so aroused her curiosity that her exploring of objects began there. Certainly she seemed to study it, as if wondering as hard as she was able.

But however enjoyable the play, even with sand she could only sustain contact for very short periods. When even this limited emotional experience got too much for her, she immediately withdrew to twiddling for whatever relief, discharge, or security it gave her. After thus returning to complete autism, she would venture forth again and go back to her play.

Sand baths nevertheless remained an autistic experience, since she allowed no one to join her in the sandbox. If a child or adult crossed the border she immediately withdrew into total isolation. Only slowly, over the months, did her play grow less formless until finally she hugged the sand against her body, or juggled it like a toy.

It was not just the outer world and people to which Marcia was still wholly insensitive. Many of the most autonomic, involuntary, and spontaneous body reactions to outer stimuli were also lacking. When she rubbed sand against her face, or poured it over her head, sand got in her eyes, nose or mouth without visible reaction; her eyes did not blink or close, she did not sneeze, she did not wipe the sand away. It was impossible to wash it from her eyes because she allowed no one to touch her. At any movement to help her, this totally withdrawn, and up to then inert child now lunged out furiously; she would grab at our throats or make as though to strangle us. Certainly, in her case, aggressive self-defense far preceded any development toward human relations.

Still, before a year with us had passed, her body began to unfreeze a bit. With encouragement she tried new movements like jumping and hopping, though for a long time they were very awkward. She no longer sat only in a yoga position. When sitting, her feet did not drop down naturally yet, but once in a while she extended them rigidly, straight down.

As we had done with the straps, we placed a ball with her in the sandbox to see if we could induce her to twiddle it.

Unlike other autistic children, she did not suck on the ball—probably because she sucked nothing at this time. But of all the toys we offered her, this one that was breast-like in form was the very first she accepted. Some three years later she loved to lie on her bed, with a huge, lightweight ball or balloon resting on her mouth and face, so that it blotted out the whole world. Even then her lips did not react but remained in their usual half-open position as she looked up at the huge sphere for hours, contentedly, without moving.[6]

So the first two objects she accepted and enjoyed were sand (closely related, psychologically, to feces) and a ball (closely related, psychologically, to the breast). Certainly the ball, as she twiddled it against her mouth and chin, stimulated the same facial area that would have been stimulated in sucking from the breast.

6. Eisenbud [1965] in a paper mentioned earlier, describes the importance of the perfect sphere for one of his adult patients, and how it stood for the breast. He also discusses at length what he calls "hand-breast" objects which, according to him, were held in the hand as symbolic representations of the breast. One of them, which he describes and reproduces photographically, is exactly "the size and shape of a human nipple and surrounding areola." But though he discusses a series of archeological and artistic hand-breast objects, he fails to mention that one can hardly walk down the street without seeing some child fondly handling a ball, the perfect sphere and an object often made of what was once skin.

Only much later, after she had been twiddling the ball this way for quite a long time, did she also learn to push it a bit, though for another and much longer time she would not catch it as it fell.

Eventually a few other objects caught her eye, moving or at least movable objects. One day the motion of the seesaw roused her fleeting and surreptitious interest. To show open interest was probably still too scary. Walking by the seesaw she pushed it down as if by chance, and then continued to walk past it as if nothing had happened. The most she dared do was glance backwards to see what had come of her action. On seeing that the seesaw did not stay put but righted itself, and on hearing the noise it made in doing so, she became very frightened and anxiously put her hand over her rectum, as if to protect it from this thing that could act on its own.

§
Relating

For years, Marcia's only means of asserting independence had been to deny all validity to the external world through autistic withdrawal. But this not talking, this limiting of spontaneous language to "no," this doing nothing and giving nothing (no words, no stools) did not lead to an emergence of a self. For that was needed some active recognition of the outer world.

Theoretically, the basis for the experience of a self is its delimitation against the nonself, since as long as no outside exists then no self exists either. But in practice, the self begins to emerge to the degree that it begins to act on the nonself. Stated theoretically, it sounds circular: the self emerges as it acts on a nonself, but how can a self act if it has not emerged yet?

The solution to this riddle is that action requires no awareness, but having acted brings first awareness. Action, then, creates the separation of self and nonself out of primordial chaos. More correctly it should be said that action creates a cleavage between what acts and what is acted upon, a separation between what (through action) becomes a self, and what (through being acted upon) becomes its object. And the separation is made the more secure, the more tangible the advantages that accrue to the self from having acted on the object.

Marcia's first positive assertion has been described. It came when she used our assurance that as far as soiling was concerned she could safely have an independent will. This, more than anything else perhaps, gave her the courage to do something about the outside world. Her stools were the logical first object to investigate because produced by her, hence more her, and "safer" than other objects.

Another reason was that investigating stools no longer seemed to threaten destruction or desertion. Our pleasure, first at her defecating on her own and second, that she did it in the bathtub helped her feel that stools were an object we approved of. Thus they were safe internally (they came from her body) and externally (because of our pleasure).

From this basis of safety Marcia's play with her feces in the bathtub enabled her to begin to wonder if something could and did exist in the outer world. As formulated in theory and discussed at length in earlier chapters, this experience of having pushed out a substance that was once part of our body and then becomes part of the external world forms the necessary link between the two. It permits us a first vague recognition of both the self and the nonself, and the distinction between them. So next Marcia provided herself with skin stimulation coming from the nonself (sand), just as skin stimulation is one of the infant's earliest experiences. With even so minimal an interest in something on the outside, with even so minimal a wish to go ahead on her own, it seems that enough of a self was established to ready Marcia for some beginning interest in other persons.

In her case, it was not any interest in the mothering person as a person, even less any relating to her, that led to the recognition of an outside, and set going the development of a self. On the contrary, it was the development of a rudimentary self, and a beginning interest in the world, that made possible some interest in at least isolated aspects of this person who took care of her so well. Just as the small infant recognizes the mothering person's voice before others, so Marcia now gave a slight movement of her head toward the voice of her counselors when she heard them in the small crowd of children and staff at the School. True, the infant probably scans the mother's face sooner than he reacts to her voice. But this face is for some time part of the nursing experience and as such is experienced as part of him, not separate, to a degree that is probably not true for the mother's voice. Unlike the infant, Marcia showed no pleasure or any reaction to her counselor's voice when the two were alone.[7]

From an interest in the world, her next step was to seek something from it. Once Marcia began to recognize the existence of an outside, she seemed to want it to recognize hers. She was not ready to take part in this world yet, though the wish to take part is the basis of human relations. But she was ready for it to be part of a single significant experience of hers, or to provide it for her.

7. At this stage in her life Marcia's two counselors, Inge Fleischmann Fowlie and Karen Carlson Zelan, were equally important to her. Only gradually, during the following year did Karen become the central person in Marcia's life, though Inge never ceased being very important to her too.

When Marcia had been with us a little short of a year, she began to play a game, her only one—a game of being chased. For some time she played it only with Inge; then with Karen or Inge; and for the next two years with nobody else. "Chase!" was one of the first things she articulated clearly enough to be heard, though still in a whisper. There was nothing mutual about this game; she never ran after any one of us. There was no participation on her part since we had to bend to her inflexible rules. But at least she needed us to play it. None of us had achieved any independent existence; there was no persistence of object or person as yet. The game, her contact with the chasing person, stopped immediately when she lost us out of sight (as Piaget has noted of objects during the early exploratory age).

Nor could Marcia take the initiative of seeking us out. The game did not begin until chance brought us into her field of vision; only then could she invite us to chase her. Yet whoever chased her had to keep a careful distance because she could not bear any physical closeness. It would not only have killed her enjoyment, but the game itself. Likewise for years if we wanted her to have anything to do with us, we had to pursue her both emotionally and physically, always keeping our distance.

In time, during these chasing games her bodily movements became freer. She no longer shuffled her feet but ran. Apart from this game she still dragged her feet and would not lift them off the ground. Much later, and for a long time only when inviting us to chase her, she used a personal pronoun for the first time. Then she did not always whisper, but sometimes said loudly, "*You* chase!"

The "you" in this request was not yet a differentiation between an "I" that wished to be chased and a "you" that would chase her. It referred to both, as an undifferentiated entity. The separation of two partners involved in a unified activity came only much later when again, around the chasing game, we saw her first tentative efforts to distinguish herself from the adult. Then she whispered, "Chase—me—catch" and then more loudly, "—YOU." If she was to gain some cognizance of another person (catch you), this person had to actively pursue her—but only as she wanted it, and from a distance.

Thus a communal "you," comprising her and the other, had to be accepted as existing before the "me" could be separated out. The singular "you" was not accepted until Marcia had established with certainty through thousands of repetitions of the game that never again would anyone get hold of her and overpower the now barely emerging "me." Hence the chasing could never result in being caught.

It seems reasonable to assume that at one time, and to a minimal degree, Marcia had achieved some awareness of the nonself though essentially of its dangerous propensities alone. Because if she had never had any dim recognition of the nonself, why would she try so assiduously to deny its existence by turning her back on it, also closing her ears and her nostrils? But such a denial of the nonself, including the "you," with necessity extends backward, as it were, to obliterate the "me."

This is the difference between the assumed "happy" feeling of omnipotence in the infant—if he has such feelings—and the autistic child's terrified withdrawal from the world and himself. If the infant's union with the world amounts to a fantastic sense of well-being it depends on his being comfortable, since it breaks down the moment he is not.

When the infant is unhappy, his desperate wail suggests that from feeling he is all he is projected into the misery of nothingness. The autistic position might be described as a terrified feeling that all (oneself included) is worse than nothing, and this not just sometimes but always. If the infant views whatever interests him in the mother, most of all the nursing breast, as being part of him, such unity needs no name. Any name would posit the existence of other things, named differently. And if the breast is sometimes his and sometimes not, it still does not mean he and it are two different things. It means only that without it he is not complete. Such completeness as might be expressed by the "us" precedes any separation of the "us" into "you" and "me."

Thus the "you" children use when the self first begins to develop really signifies an "us." But unlike the "us" they acquire much later, it does not consist of a "you" and "I," but an inseparable unit. Only from this unit can the "you" and "me" be separated out. If my speculation is valid then any retreat from the finally singular "you" must lead to an extinction of the "me." Therefore this "you" must be regained before the same can be achieved for the "me."

The infant who begins to relate is much too immature to invent so complex a game for acting out what is needed to establish true relations. But Marcia could, being so much older, with body and mind so much more developed. And since her disappointment was so deep, from when she first had tried as an infant to relate, she needed to play out relating for a long time before again hoping it was possible for her. So she played that we tried to get close to her and pursued her. And this pursuit enabled her to get hold of our existence. The distance she forced us to keep seemed designed to reverse her old experience: to prove that others can exist without being overpowering.

With such tenuous and rare reaching out appeared her first active and persistent emotional response to an external world. She began to have violent temper tantrums several times a day in which she screamed piercingly. Now that we began to exist, she dared to show how deeply she felt. But the feelings themselves were still much too chaotic to be felt by her in any specific way, such as being angry at a particular person, or about a specific event. They were simply disorganized feelings of anger now breaking through the wall that had so far dammed up all feelings. Though we existed enough for her to vent her feelings on, we did not exist enough to relieve her distress. She went into open fury when we tried.

The violent anger that now began to appear had been her reaction to being destructively overpowered. If, as she felt, her entire experience with others meant being aggressed against, how could she now believe that others would approach her with different intent?

But with even this little freeing of emotions—little because most of the time she still retired to her nothingness—it became easier to have her repeat single words in echolalia. Occasionally she would also whisper words of her own creation, carefully broken into syllables and with deep personal and anxious meaning. This was in stark contrast to the loud, inarticulate screaming and pounding of her temper tantrums. Yet it was the beginning of communication, since she was giving us information instead of just signals of what she wanted. She would say, "Typewriter broken," or "Fire engine, bang, bang;" first spoken indications of her preoccupation with damage and destruction. But she was also telling us that a device for sending messages (the typewriter) had been destroyed by the all-consuming "fire" of her emotions.

At about this time, we felt that her counselor, in addition to the time spent with her daily, both alone and with the group, might now work with Marcia in regular individual sessions.[8] Soon afterward she hailed one of these play sessions by singing quietly, "Hi ho, hi ho, it's off to work we go." Personal pronouns were still not available to her except through a memorized song, or in the chasing game. Yet through her choice of songs she could now express quite complex emotions. After hearing a record of "My Fair Lady" (which the staff had also acted out for the children) she singled out one of its songs and sang it repeatedly: "Why can't the English teach their children how to speak?" (her mother was English). On learning that her favorite counselor was going on vacation she sang, "From this valley they say you are going."

Singing, repeating the words of others—this seemed less dangerous than saying things on her own. Spontaneous talk was still restricted to echolalia, or at best to completing a sentence, as when we told her "We're going to the . . ." and she might say "store." Either way, someone else had to assume the real commitment for what was said. But she

8. Not to give the erroneous impression that counselors work all the time, I might mention that each counselor works an average of four and a half shifts a week, of about eight hours each. But since most of them live at the School which is an integrated unit of several connected buildings, and have their meals in the common dining room, children and staff also see each other at meal times and on many other occasions. Counselors also drop in on their children during their time off, rather repeatedly when they work with such a difficult child as Marcia.

learned to say a few words of neutral meaning to her. She would name colors in picture books and count up to five. Personal names she steadfastly refused to say, or any personal pronouns referring to herself—always excepting the chasing game and songs.

Shortly after the chasing game was fully established, Marcia's sand play and twiddling finally developed into true play as she used a toy (her ball) for the first time in a more or less appropriate manner. Having begun by touching, patting, and twiddling it, and then to throwing it a bit, she moved eventually to bouncing it.

This ball was also the first object she twiddled in an exploratory movement against the area of chin and mouth. Possibly more important was what she did with her mouth. With straps, sand and ball she had simply stimulated this area of her face, and only in the context of hallucinations. Now for the first time it was part of a true exploring. As she felt the roundness of the ball she opened her mouth wide and round as if trying to form a circle with it. Through mouth movements she seemed to be trying to comprehend an object outside of her body; such as here, and for the first time, the form and properties of the ball.

From then on the mouth area became progressively more invested with interest, and all important learning or other efforts at mastery were first preceded or accompanied by mouth innervations. She also began to move her tongue around in her mouth. It was as if she could better comprehend what she did if she also did it with her mouth. Or maybe it was her primitive way of making any new thing her own by experiencing the thing with her body. Perhaps the mouth was chosen because it is the prime incorporative organ.

In any case, the new use of her mouth made her try to understand its functions in herself and others. She watched her counselor's mouth and with encouragement put her fingers inside it, felt the counselor's teeth and then her own, as if exploring and comparing. Out of all this came a gradual ability and tendency to form the mouth into configurations that expressed what went on in her mind, or at least how she felt about it.

Other interests arose. After twiddling with straps became fully secure she developed a spontaneous interest in other objects that might serve the same purpose. She began to observe blades of grass before plucking them to twiddle with. After fifteen months at the School she could follow simple directions when they fitted her dominant interests, such as stringing beads into a chain which became another twiddling object.

This was not simply a learning task mastered, or an external object (straps, sand, a ball) used for idiosyncratic purposes. For the first time she was fitting separate pieces that were useless to her in themselves into a more complex whole that could serve her purposes better. She could simply have twiddled with the string alone. By stringing it with beads, she indicated what she had learned: that in addition to accepting or rejecting reality there was a third possibility: to actually change it into something better.

This was different from twiddling a ball we had put in her hands. There she merely followed through on what we initiated for our reasons. Even in the chasing game, if we could not run after her she was helpless to make the experience come about. But in stringing beads, she herself initiated the action and followed through to completion. More, it was an action where she complied with social custom: stringing beads is something other children do. So here an ego was truly at work, since she fitted pieces of reality together to create a more complex form, did so in ways that are socially approved and expected, and used the product to satisfy instinctual desires.

All postulated ego functions were present: manipulation of external reality (stringing beads) in socially approved form (through typical child play) and in the service of instinctual tendencies (the twiddling, in its emotional meaning to her).

Soon after Marcia felt safe about handling a ball, she very tentatively began to play with stuffed animals for seconds, very much as if they too were balls. Later she explored to see if they had any body openings, and where they might be.

After having twiddled the ball in isolation, and after stringing beads in the presence of other children, it became possible to engage her in activities that paralleled what other children did. This was a tremendous step forward from the chasing where others had to do as she wished. Even so it had to be an activity that was built around a juggling or twiddling movement, such as the shaking of bells in rhythm with other children. As with all complicated efforts, mouth movements accompanied her twiddling of bells in a common rhythm with others, reflecting the inner experience that went with it. Still, her capacity for parallel activities was very limited and she soon withdrew to twiddling the ball by herself.

By this time the rest of her body, too, began to reflect her state of mind. Her way of sitting would now indicate the degree of her contact with reality. When paying attention to the world she began to sit in a normal though rigid position. When she withdrew, she also returned to the old yoga stance.

§
Symbolic Expression

Slowly there also came parallel improvements in symbolic behavior, including speech. Just as she had helped herself to a better twiddling object (ball, chain of beads), so in individual sessions she could better ask for help, though not in her own words but only through the song, "Help me, help me." She began to use words signifying emotion, but only angry ones, as when she said, "Mad!" Her expression as she said it left little doubt that she understood its meaning.

Having learned that she could manipulate pieces of reality to serve her most personal needs, and having learned to express some emotions in words, Marcia seemed ready for a significant task: to symbolically express and master her inner stresses, as opposed to repression or discharge, or trying to satisfy them in part through her twiddling.

In analysis the adult patient must either silently experience or, preferably, say aloud what goes on in his mind. He must voice his associations, fantasies, desires, and dreams, including the emotions that well up in him, and his bodily sensations, in order to ask himself, and get the therapist's help in asking: "Why do I have them? What do they mean?" Through such questioning and the light it brings, he arrives at understanding—though both the ideas and emotions he comes to recognize have been in him all along.

True, understanding alone will not cure him. Emotional difficulties are not cured until we begin to act on them in appropriate ways. This can happen, for example, because one has had what Alexander and French [1946] call the corrective emotional experience, or because of a process and experience which in psychoanalysis is called "working through." Still to understand, for example, what it is one is afraid of, is often a big step in resolving emotional problems.

In much the same way, it seems that mute children like Marcia have to play things out in symbolic representation, since they cannot hear themselves say what they feel.

Or, to put it differently: since they are deathly afraid of what would happen if they were to say aloud what preys on their mind, they cannot ask themselves the questions adult patients might put into words or else wonder about in silent thought. Instead, they ask their questions through what they do in silent play. They ask it over and over, by playing out the same sequence thousands of times, until they find the answer, or until their play affords them the experience of having worked through the problem that oppressed them. Nor can they express in words the solution when they find it. But the observer can read it in how the play sequence is modified by the child.

When Marcia was able to pose to herself inner, nonverbal questions, to express them symbolically, and to look for answers, she used an element she had never lost contact with but which suddenly took on new interest. Water, because of her particular history, had been linked in her mind with her central problem: What went in and out of her body, and what had this done to her? Though we knew little of all this at the time, we were pleased to see water play added to her extremely limited range.

When she began to explore in her counselor's mouth and her own, we felt the time had come to offer her a baby bottle. But though we repeated the offer from time to time, she remained totally indifferent, until about eighteen months after coming to the School. One day at this time, she angrily grabbed for the bottle, filled it with milk as she had seen us do, dumped the milk out, and filled the bottle with water. She did not want the bottle to drink from but to fill up with water, again and again, and to dump the water on the floor. Only years later did we understand what this meant. As she had been flooded by the enemas, by water coming out of an "enema bottle," so she now flooded us.

For a long time no new developments took place—except that our floors got more thoroughly flooded—until we felt it was time to limit and structure this pouring of water, because eternal repetition did not seem to be leading anywhere. And while the suggestion was ours, she signified that she was ready. The bucket was her own choice from among the various alternatives we offered for bringing more structure to her game.

Marcia now elaborated her play by making use of a squeeze bottle (actually a catsup bottle) where the water did not simply spill out but had to be squeezed out by force through a protrusion. Again and again she played at squeezing water out of this bottle into a bucket. Just as she had explored what sand felt like and what you could do with it, so she now explored water—but with a marked difference, and progress.

This was no simple letting of water run over her hand. She seemed to be testing it as she squeezed it out, just as a mother might test the temperature of milk coming out of a baby bottle. Her play also demanded more complex manipulation of objects: the cap had to be unscrewed before filling the bottle, and screwed back before she could squeeze water out of it again. Her tenseness in squeezing the bottle was obvious, not only in her face but throughout her body; even her legs and feet became extremely rigid. By contrast her whole body, including her legs, was more relaxed when pouring water from bucket to bottle. The two operations seemed to have very different emotional meanings for her.

A most remarkable consequence was that as she became able to play out in symbol what preoccupied her emotions, when she became able to squeeze and to pour of her own volition, she also became openly sensitive to what intruded into her body or got squirted in. Marcia, who had shown no reaction to getting sand in her eyes, now had a perfectly normal, autonomic, immediate reaction—though still enacted in very slow motion—when water squirted in her eyes during her play. Her eyes closed, and she wiped them.

And still no interest in persons was evident. Even her favorite counselor was just a convenience, no more important or remarkable than any other physical convenience. She was not a person, but a something to which a hand was attached. The hand conveniently lifted objects that had dropped to the floor and thus saved her the trouble of picking things up. Yet she could be made interested in learning tasks and achievements which, to the best of our knowledge, had no direct link to inner needs. She learned to build with blocks, to pile them into a tower and was pleased when she could build one up high.

This suggests that if one form of play becomes emotionally significant, the importance of play itself can be transferred to other forms. Out of Marcia's new block play, which had little emotional significance beyond the chance to achieve, and our delighted praise, still other play activities developed.

As always with Marcia, there were parallel developments around the mouth. There was less chin-tapping and more play with lips and mouth. She added vegetables and fruit to her diet, though she still ate mainly starchy foods.

Exploring further in her counselor's mouth, she sought to learn where sounds come from. For the first time she said the letter "L" after carefully feeling in the counselor's mouth to see what the tongue did in making this sound; because the "L," more than other sounds, involves tongue movement. Though she was now saying more, she still seemed to treat each syllable, or very short words, as separate entities, as a substance of her body that she wished to retain. Though there was more language, there was no growth in communication but only in enunciation.

Once in a while she now spoke above a whisper and enunciated her single words so that we could better understand them. But her world was still depersonalized, since she could not or would not call anyone by name or use personal pronouns correctly.

On the other hand, she could now manipulate some objects and do more with what belonged to the world of the nonself. But before using them she still had to make them safe or part of the self by twiddling them near her chin, either above or around or against it. This was clear indication that she could not really grasp the existence of the two worlds yet, of their independence and relatedness. Still, the twiddling became freer. She now twiddled in a variety of ways and with all fingers, not just the two forefingers.

Eventually, doing with things extended to doing with people. Marcia progressed from parallel play to a play that required interaction. And the first and only play for a long time in which we could interest her was playing with a ball. This, again, like the infant, she could do only with the mothering persons. She could not or would not play ball except with her two counselors. And again, there was a long time of twiddling before she could enjoy pushing the ball feebly away when it was rolled to her gently, and later tossed.

Her anxiety in all this, and her hesitation, showed how fearful she was about any active manipulation of objects, and about personal interactions. She was still so alienated from her body and its normal movements that she never seemed quite sure which movement might be effective in dealing with problems such as pushing back a ball. Or maybe she was so beholden to her twiddling movements that only they or their outgrowth were available to her. So for a long time she remained unable to really catch the ball or throw it back. But a movement that developed out of her twiddling motions eventually enabled her to push it back quite well.

Again there was further progress in speech. She no longer talked as if she were addressing the air. Just as she had learned to use objects but not yet people, so she began to talk first to objects. Since there were now objects she could control, it was safe to talk to them; they would not retaliate.

People she did not trust in their reactions, so she would not talk to them. When asked to whom or to what she was talking, she would name the object—not the person—she was talking to. Since the object she liked best to hold in her hands was a ball, she would say she was talking to the ball. Despite our prodding she would not entertain the idea that she might be speaking to a person. But as she had begun to be active and to act, she added verbs to her language. Now, on a walk to the lake shore she would say, "Girl goes to beach." She began to discriminate between big and little, but again only around objects that had special meaning to her and which she had therefore learned to use and was thoroughly familiar with. So she would say, "This is big ball. This is little ball."[9] Along with this she began to count objects spontaneously.

After about twenty months, interactions began to blend slowly into dependency, at least between Marcia and Karen who was now the fa-

9. This again, on the printed page, is grossly misleading, because her pronunciation of these simple sentences was so idiosyncratic as to make them sound like a totally foreign language.

vorite of her two counselors. It was a being dependent because of the way she needed Karen and viewed her as part of her world. It was not relatedness yet, not to speak of a true personal relation between them, because there was still no give-and-take, only a take, with no interest in her counselors as persons. Much as she now needed them, particularly Karen, Marcia could not afford to acknowledge even that. We could see this in her pretended lack of interest, in her deliberate turning away from the counselor, and in the way she behaved as if responding only to inner stimuli. But we surmised some first relatedness when her motivations tallied ever so rarely with what her counselor expected or wished her to do. This was true only within the narrowest limits, and if we waited with endless patience, never prodding her. Then, hours later, Marcia might do something vaguely resembling our suggestion.

Eventually she permitted some bodily contact and later, at rare moments, even sought it out. She began to hug her counselors in a way that was affectionate and hostile at the same time; as if affection were possible only if she could also defend herself against it. Or, perhaps more correctly, since she had deeply repressed both the desire for affection and her anger at the world, once the one appeared the other had to come too. Once the sluice gates that dammed up her emotions were opened in the smallest degree, they could not release only the single emotion, but had to let them all out in their admixture of opposites. Yet if the counselor's pleasure at being with her ever brought a spontaneous hug, Marcia withdrew.

In this connection Federn's thoughts on anxiety are of interest. He wrote: "The ego faces danger and feels either courage or rage, or readiness to fight. If the urge to fight is stopped, the emotion of dread follows. The ego senses or remembers its weakness and flees. Then when the flight is hindered, a feeling of terror results—it is a feeling of nearness to death" [Glauber, 1963]. As Marcia overcame her "feeling of nearness to death," she took flight (in her chasing game). But in our pursuit of her, the fear of separation that underlies anxiety (according to Freud) was negated.

When she no longer had to flee, that is, when she had overcome her feeling of a death-like weakness of her ego, she regained the courage to feel and show rage, though it did not appear in full form until later. At the same time she gained the strength to show positive feelings—that is, to undo the separation anxiety and the anxiety about being destroyed, which together had set the process of autism going.

With even this minimal freeing of her emotions, Marcia became much more openly hostile. Her dislike of a rival named Mary she could now express through the song, "Bloody Mary." Destructive and aggressive words appeared in her speech. She would say "rip" (about her clothes);

"spank," and "hair-wash." (Before she came to us there was considerable to-do about her hair, which she seems to have disliked intensely.)

One of the first uses she made of her freedom at the School was to prevent any touching of her hair, and for nearly two years we left it pretty much alone. Now that she could express her anger and anxiety about hairwashing, she was willing to let us take care of it. But as she felt freer to be hostile she was also freer to say "yes" and a while later could name one of her most tabooed actions by saying "chew." That done, she began to make sucking and nursing movements with her mouth before eating, though she still would not suck or chew.

At about this time, her twiddling took on one more dimension and we began to understand better what her different ways of twiddling seemed to mean. When she shook her fingers sideways, which was new, it was as if she were warding off. Twiddling outward continued to stand for eliminating something out of her system; while in tapping against her chin or the mouth-nose area she seemed to be taking something in, though the twiddling itself retained its antithetical meaning.

§

Extending the Self

It was while hugging Karen one day that Marcia addressed her for the first time by name. Soon she began using both names, Karen and Marcia, but refused to differentiate between them. Both of them were either Karen or Marcia. In merging the two into one, she used the pronoun "us" for the first time when referring to the unit. So her self—or perhaps more correctly, whatever stood in the place where her self would later be—became extended to include the person who most devotedly took care of her.

Whatever achieved importance in this outside world she tried to possess, to make her own. And once again, these efforts evolved out of what had originally served the two opposite aims: to possess and blot out. To make this other person her own she must be made to participate in what Marcia was most herself at: the person too had to twiddle. Holding the counselor's hand or arm just below the wrist, Marcia shook it so fast as to make the hand and its fingers twiddle and shake as her own did when she twiddled. Having made safe, and perhaps her own, first Karen's arms and later Inge's (her two "mothers"), she moved first to accept being held, hugged and carried in their arms, and then to love it.

Marcia was not ready to face the world, but she took more of it into her self. With objects she had done this before. Even as early as her first play, sand became for the moment part of Marcia's self-system. What was new was that she now accepted a person into her self, and that she *knew* that her self now included both Karen and Marcia. Hers was not yet an independent self that could relate to a nonself; but as a more extended self it contained clear elements of a personal nature. Once she was no longer alone in the world she no longer needed to keep its messages from reaching her. The stopping up of her ears became rare, and in a few months disappeared altogether.

Along with progress toward relating, Marcia's play, beginning again with ball play, became freer and more complex, though it retained all its tapping, patting, and twiddling qualities. She could now bounce a ball quite effectively. Her play expanded from the making of towers by merely piling blocks on top of one another, to building things like "houses." She began to look at things in her surroundings. And when next we took pictures of her she walked up close to the lens and for the first time took a good look at the camera.

Extending the self to take in something from the outside, this is radically different from narrowing the self to the smallest possible space because the less self there is, the less there is to be hurt. Marcia had tried to have as little self as possible by keeping anything from intruding, either feelings or sounds. She tried to do it by sitting all hunched up in a yoga position. Now that she could take in a little, could extend her self, she began also to take a role, to play a part, without fearing to lose her new self because there was so little of it.

After two years, Marcia's existing and acting side by side with others enabled her to join in ball play and take the appropriate role in rather complicated games. For example, she could play in a relay race where each child had to push the ball with a broom to the end of our gymnasium and bring it back the same way. She was not ready for free play with others, for catching and throwing a ball in a give-and-take, a free-flowing back-and-forth interaction. But she could and did play a solitary role in a context that also involved others.

More important, she had learned to learn, though not much at first. Marcia became better able to deal with symbolic representation. Holding in all her anger seemed to have kept her not only from talking and from seeing the world around her, but even from thinking about it. Now she could be induced to draw. As usual she pretended total disinterest at first while paying closest attention, as if to learn from a position of safety if this was dangerous or not. Before she could use crayons she had to get to know them by rubbing them between her hands until she got a tactile cognizance of their nature. Then she had to make them safe or her own by tapping them against her chin. She began with mere scribbling but soon learned to draw some forms. And again, any learning she acquired had to come through her body.

She could comprehend a form only when comprehension came first through her body or its movements. She learned to understand the difference between a square and a circle by first having Karen move her finger around their perimeters, and then by repeating the movements on her own as she recreated their forms with her mouth. She recreated the two forms (one is tempted to say internalized them) by opening her mouth wide to grasp the roundness of the circle, and by closing it rigidly to comprehend the straight lines, or perhaps the angularity of the square.

Rather than offering our own interpretation of this behavior, I prefer to quote Piaget who made a parallel observation. According to him, such an understanding of spatial phenomena through an active participation by the mouth is part of normal child development. Usually it occurs during the last stage of sensorimotor development, the stage in which the child first becomes capable of representation and symbolic adaptations, that is of true thought. This permits him to correctly infer a cause if only its effect is given, and to foresee an effect, given the cause. It is the precondition for responding to the world not just emotionally but intellectually too.

The example Piaget uses [1952] is that of hiding an object in front of Lucienne (sixteen months old); he hides a chain in a matchbox which he leaves open just a bit, the slit being three millimeters wide.

A pause follows during which Lucienne manifests a very curious reaction, bearing witness not only to the fact that she tries to think out the situation and to represent to herself through mental combination the operations to be performed, but also the role played by imitation in the genesis of representations. Lucienne mimics the widening of the slit.

She looks at the slit with great attention: then, several times in succession, she opens and shuts her mouth, at first slightly, then wider and wider! Apparently Lucienne understands the existence of a cavity subjacent to the slit and wishes to enlarge that cavity. The attempt at representation which she thus furnishes is expressed plastically, that is to say, due to the inability to think out the situation in words or clear visual images she uses a simple motor indication as "signifier," or symbol. . . . Lucienne, by opening her mouth thus expresses, or even reflects her desire to enlarge the opening of the box.

Soon after this phase of plastic reflection, Lucienne unhesitatingly puts her finger in the slit and, instead of trying as before to reach the chain, she pulls so as to enlarge the opening. She succeeds and grasps the chain.

Thus Piaget on plastic reflection in the very young child.

But since Marcia was not sixteen months but over twelve years old, once she had internalized and fully grasped circles and squares, she could immediately move on to draw their forms. In less than six months she elaborated her at first vague circles to making a human face, then to ever plainer human forms, and soon afterward drew a complete and well-organized human figure. Here her development was much faster than for the normal child—only the normal child can do all this at a much earlier age.

Having achieved a mental image of one person, Karen, she could represent persons in symbolic form by drawing them. The faces she drew were those of significant persons. (One of them she suggested was a portrait of me, others of three faces in her family.) In retrospect, her development from the drawing of a round face to that of a human figure seems affected also by her notions of fecal birth. That may be why she had to build the human figure out of elliptical "droppings." She could still master reality best where it lent itself to elaboration within her all-consuming preoccupations.

Like other children suffering from similar difficulties, Marcia seemed to have an easier time learning numbers and number concepts than in comprehending sentences or thoughts. Once she had grasped the concepts of bigger and smaller, she learned with relative ease to count and manipulate simple number concepts.

Perhaps the reason is that to such children numbers and their use do not seem to commit them. To say a sentence means exactly that—to say something. And to say something is to act, it implies some commitment about the world or oneself: one affirms or denies. To count or not to count the number of objects seems much less of a personal commitment. Therefore they seem more ready to learn abstract things such as numbers. In a way, counting for them is like taking part in a game, and most of the early table games children play are, after all, simple counting games.

For example, Marcia had a clear recognition of form boards with one to ten holes. She would begin by taking out the correct number of cubes before putting them into the holes. Spontaneously she would always begin with the highest number, ten, and work backward, selecting the one with nine holes after that, and so forth. Taking away, making things less, she could still do much better than adding. The board with only one hole she hesitated to finish. On her own she would count from the highest to the lowest numbers. Counting forward from one to ten, or higher, she did only with resistance and to do it she needed our help. It was as if she knew that to grow, to increase, she needed our support.[10]

10. That she could only count backwards on her own suggests that she certainly manipulated symbolic numbers in line with her inner needs. Did she know that she had to go backward, had to regain what are normally the earliest experiences, to acquire a more normal personality? The speculation is not as far-fetched as it might

After twenty-seven months with us, Marcia took a major step forward in playing out her inner problems. This she did through her water play, which had since grown quite complex. We now began to understand its meaning a little better. At this time she always used three objects: a bucket, a glass, and a bottle. Her number concepts had definitely gone beyond mere counting or enumeration. So the concept of Three stood for something very concrete: the members of her family. The bottle she named the "lady" bottle: it was so shaped that with some imagination one could see it as having breasts. (Originally its label showed the picture of a woman.) The pouring back and forth followed one rigid rule: whenever she poured from the bucket she sat down; whenever she poured from the other two she stood up.

Our interpretation was that she was here exploring with containers, representing her family, the problem of who received what, in which way, and from whom; but she also seemed to explore what was done, by whom, and to whom. Clearly the lady bottle stood for the mother (as probably the squeeze bottle did in her earlier play with water) and the bucket was again Marcia.

Some of the pouring of water from bottle to bucket suggests that she was again recreating events out of infancy, such as being fed, having enemas forced in, testing the temperature of the milk or the enema water as a nurse might before giving it to a child. About the standing and sitting we can only speculate. Perhaps her standing up when she poured from the bottle and glass represented how her parents had towered above her; the sitting down as she poured from the wide-open bucket might have then reflected her own helpless passivity. But these remain speculations.

As she poured water from one container to another, thousands of times over months, inner developments took place that eventually freed her to talk with her counselor during her water play, mainly about scary experiences. Intermittently she would look up at the ceiling, hallucinating. When first asked what she saw there she said (in the reply mentioned earlier), "See mom" and "Take mom away." Later she elaborated

---

seem. Nearly all schizophrenic children with whom we work understand the meaning of age as represented by birthdays. But though eventually they enjoy the presents and festivities, they still have a great aversion to getting older. Many of them insist that their age is much lower. Either they do not wish to face their inability to meet age appropriate tasks, or they are expressing the wish that they were younger and could better receive and enjoy infantile satisfactions.

In the context of numbers, I might add that on the most primitive level numbers relate only to that which concerns the person most immediately. *One* might be oneself or a parent, *Two,* some other significant person, etc. Numbers to Marcia, at this point, seemed to represent her own age. In a subsequent development, numbers for her also represented significant persons. *One* then meant herself; *Two* her counselor or her mother depending on the context; and *Three* either her father, the three members of her family, or her family in general.

that "Mommy's on the ceiling" and said "eat grandma." Still later she indicated that in part of the water play she was acting out "Mommy feeds baby."

Alternate images of a devouring and food-giving mother seemed to form the content of her hallucinations. And as usual, these images were projected upward. At least once at this time she could tell us that twiddling was closely related to the mother. Asked why she shook her fingers she answered: "Mommy."

Talking, for her, was still linked to the forced giving up of stools. She now established the connection by inhaling with a characteristic deep sound immediately before defecating, and we heard exactly the same deep pained breathing before any talk, another indication of the close connection between speech and anal experiences.

How intricately speech and elimination had become connected—or how little she could separate them—was further suggested by the fact that for nearly four years she could not talk to us if she was sitting down. It was as if she had to free her anus before she could give out from either anus or mouth because the two were so intermixed. Words too seemed to have bodily meaning to her, possibly akin to pieces of feces. Because if she wanted to address us, she had to walk up close to the person she was talking to, as if to bring him the words. Certainly the syllables of each word were ejected from her mouth as if they were small pieces of stool, leaving her body one at a time.

Physical presence was so important to her that it took more than five years before she could answer or talk to a person she could not see or who was not in the room. Only then, for example, could she carry on a conversation from one room to the next through an open doorway, or at least answer a question this way.

Returning from such later developments, it was after some thirty months with us that her greater courage in looking at reality developed into tentative efforts to explore it. This she could do only when actively supported by her counselor. While a few months earlier she had, for the first time, openly looked at the camera, she now dared with Karen's help to explore and name it, saying "Camera!"

When frightened she now rushed to her counselor for security and comfort, after which she could go on exploring. This was no longer a short hug, as much feared as desired. She who for so long had avoided and resented all bodily contact now clung to her counselor for hours each day, and the clinging was no longer hostile or ambivalent but affectionate. There came a new interest in her counselor's face, her behavior and attitudes—in short, of Karen as a person—all of which Marcia now observed with great interest. With that, she finally learned to use all pronouns correctly, and though she was not consistent about it, she used them correctly much of the time.

There were, however, two exceptions. Firstly, to use the "I" remained difficult. Our impression was that this was due in part to her lack of true comprehension of the concept, because she still lacked enough feeling of self. Instead of "I" she often used "you," though she used the "you" correctly when speaking of others. Her avoidance of "I" was also due in part to her not wishing (or being unable) to commit herself.

The other exception happened only around Karen. Marcia still used the same pronoun for herself and Karen, thus preserving a symbiotic image of the two as one, though she could and did view herself as separate from persons other than Karen.

In the presence of Karen, in talking about their unity, in using their names interchangeably, the wish for symbiosis persisted. Marcia's self had so little boundary that if Karen was present it simply extended itself to encompass them both. Since her access to reality came only through this one of her counselors, much of the time spent apart from Karen was still filled by an empty, anxious escape from reality, taken up by unvaried daydreams or hallucinations.

But just imagining Karen's presence no longer sufficed. Marcia could simply do so much more, feel so much more intensely and pleasurably, could *be* so much more, that the imagined presence lost out by comparison. It forced her to recognize that Karen had a life of her own, independent of Marcia, though she could not yet feel that she (Marcia) had a life independent of Karen. So now she wanted to know ahead of time when Karen would be with her, and when not.

This was no mere difference between vague comfort or discomfort any more, depending on the vagaries of Karen's presence or absence. Now that Marcia could extend herself and merge with the counselor in her presence, it gave her a distinct sense of well-being, of being alive. Karen's presence and absence now made a great deal of difference in what had once been an unbroken, unspecific stream of things to be endured, if they could not be excluded from awareness. Time had entered her life as an experience and a concept, and there was a future in her life: when Karen would return. Time was now broken into an orderly sequence of events; the presence or absence of Karen gave emotional rhythm to Marcia's days. But only when this was fully established did the organization of time slowly extend to the rest of her life too. Then the presence and absence of Inge and to some smaller extent of her teachers and me became very important as well.

This rhythm of time she wanted to learn to understand, because then she would be able to predict when Karen would be with her, and when Inge; when Karen would be with her alone, and when with her and other children. So Marcia developed a concept of time, learned to name the days of the week, and on leave-taking might say, "Good-bye. See you Friday."

As people in her present world became real and she looked forward to seeing them in the future she also acquired a more definite sense of what had happened in the past. At least she began to speak by name of some figures in her past, such as "Aunt Jenny."

Unfortunately when I say that Marcia began to recognize some isolated events out of her past, it does not mean they were past for her. Past experience still dominated her present life too much for her to be able to believe that anything could be over and done with. That an experience is truly behind us requires the feeling that important past events can no longer shape the present for us. Since this was certainly not true for Marcia, nothing was ever truly past for her. Hence the phenomenal memory of such children.

If one wished to clarify through opposite concepts, one might say that the neurotic tries to assign his experiences to the past and believes he is through with them, when in fact they or their derivatives still dominate his present very much. But to the schizophrenic these past experiences are still truly present. Thus Marcia believed that the invasion of her body remained an ever-present threat to be defended against. To separate past and present, and hence to have a future, depends on a sense of time. And this, at least in rudiments, Marcia began to acquire.

We do not know if there was any connection between this new sense of specificity in time, and her being able to talk and worry about specific bodily functions, where before she seemed to have only total reactions to both. Probably both were the consequence of her growing relation to Karen, because of which Marcia was becoming a person whose body had specific functions.

She began to speak of these functions, and confided secrets like the belief that she was "sick" when she menstruated. (Later we learned she believed she was sick when she urinated, too.) What she called being "sick" she connected with her mother, saying, "Baby is sick to her mommy." Thus she indicated her feeling that as a baby her mother had made her "sick" by forcing body content out of her as in the enemas, just as she still felt she was "sick" when she urinated or menstruated. But being "sick" also meant emotionally sick; meant her difficulties in living. In reply to questions of why she was living at the Orthogenic School, or why she could not do things like other children her age, she said it was because of being "sick." At the same time she also became openly curious about the difference between boys and girls.

With her recognition of bodily functions and her consciously connecting them with being "sick," came one of two major setbacks in our work with her: this first one was a delayed reaction to the onset of menstruation. Marcia began to menstruate about seven months after coming to the School, when she was still totally alienated from her bodily functions. Even of menstruation she took no cognizance at all, neither of the onset of her menses nor their recurrent appearance. This changed only when Karen achieved great emotional importance.

Through the intense unity she now felt with Karen she became somehow aware that she was female, like her counselor. The awareness was sharpened by her recent realization that boys are different from girls, and that she was a girl. It was then that she entered a depressive phase lasting several months. Underlying it was less her resentment at being a girl, and not a boy, than her feelings that Karen, the first person she had ever trusted, had tricked her. It was her identifying with Karen that had made her a girl and forced her to menstruate like Karen.

Once more it seemed that a predominant anxiety had been borne out in fact: any move she made into the world, any coming close to another, gave them the power to inflict gross damage to her body. Worse, it made something flow out of her body as in the enemas. So she withdrew from this person who had become a part of herself, and withdrew from herself too and from whatever outside contact she had established. The external signs were the old ones: she became severely constipated and gave up most of the few things she had learned to do.

In a slow process extending over many months, we discussed with Marcia her conviction that Karen had inflicted menstruation on her, until she was able to resume progress in relating. But for several more years each menstrual period was still accompanied by a short-lived depression and constipation of as much as several days' duration. Sometimes she came out of it on her own. At other times we had to talk briefly again of her conviction that her counselors inflicted menstruation because they made her want to do things in the world, including being a girl. Whether this was needed or not, and how much of it, depended on how good her contact with reality was at the onset of menstruation, and how positive her relations with her counselors at the time.

In any case, a relation had certainly been formed, and when Marcia came out of this first prolonged depression about menstruation her body movements became much freer. Perhaps in working through the depression she had also worked through something about the spontaneous functioning of her body. Since the working through took place with her counselors, her new bodily freedom appeared at first only with them. Within a few months she could run more freely and catch and throw the ball like a normal child, but only with her own counselors.

It was about this time that she told us she had been shaking and twid-dling her fingers to make herself "feel better." Except that by now it was not autistic twiddling that made her feel better, but the relation to her counselor. From using the counselor as a convenience, to letting her do things for Marcia, to doing things parallel with her, Marcia had moved into a symbiotic relation which at last showed some features of a per-sonal relation. This Marcia realized and at first said that "talking is playing"; that is, she could now deal with what troubled her not just by twiddling or playing, but also by talking. She then firmly stated the value: "Talking is good."

She could also tell us more about the connection in her mind between defecation and the giving out of words. Again it was first while sitting on the toilet, but later in other situations too, that she told us how words go down the toilet. Having come to understand that talking is good, she could show that her relations to words and feces were sometimes friendlier now. Once in a while she said a warm "bye-bye" to her bowel move-ments as they were flushed down the toilet. Later she extended this to "bye-bye B.M." and again later, reassured herself that it would happen again by adding, "see you tomorrow," the identical reassurance she gave herself when her counselors left her at night. But it was still an ambivalent attitude, more often negative than positive, because most of the time she did not want to give up or let go. She still would not flush the toilet though she now let her counselor flush it in her presence. She also told us it was "wrong" to defecate.

§

Early Identity

While still largely beholden to old anxieties, Marcia had a dawning recognition that relating can have positive value. Once the child has separated a rudimentary self out of a vague totality, the next important step toward recognizing *what* he is (though maybe not yet *who* he is) lies in differentiating between child and adult, and in recognizing that he is a child. Still another big step is to recognize the nature of one's sex, which helps the child toward realizing *who* he is.

Differences in size, as between child and adult, carry the implication that to be smaller is to be less, and thus helps to determine what one is not. For similar reasons defecation (and to some degree urination) lends itself to delimiting the self from the nonself by finding out what one is not. But even under the best of circumstances, it tells us only that the self can eliminate something that thus becomes nonself; it cannot suggest what that self is.

In Marcia's case, little selfhood could be gained by differentiating between child and adult. Partly because of the symbiotic relation to Karen, the differentiation between the two was largely denied in Marcia's mind. Also by now she was actually the size of a short alult (which Karen is), while menstruation proved she was one, physiologically.

Matters were naturally different in regard to sex. And sex differences, by contrast, tell not only what one is not (as one is not one's own feces), but also what one is. So as Marcia's interests awoke, she began to be interested in the differences between boys and girls, at first in a negative way, by denying them. In her single-word language she first asked what are girls, and what are boys. But though fascinated by the difference, the main purpose of her questions was to insist on their sameness.

In echolalia she would repeat that boys "are different" from girls, but could not take it any further. When asked what boys have, she would say "feet," "finger," etc., naming only body parts common to both sexes. When questioned more specifically, she would insist that both have vaginas. There was no indication that she wanted to be a boy; the symbiotic relation to her female counselor would alone have mitigated against such a wish. That is, she gave lip service to the idea that the sexes were different and that she was a girl. But emotionally and intellectually she insisted that the difference had no specific content, certainly not a bodily one. To accept the nature of the sexual difference would have brought her up too sharply against the problem of who and what she was, and this problem had to be avoided as too complex and too threatening.

So Marcia's beginning interest in the existence of two sexes, her recognition that she was a girl plus her denial of what made her a girl, added up to a conflict of wishes: that she should be a girl (like Karen); but that no difference should exist between boys and girls. When she could recognize that it is hard to accept things as different when no characterizing difference exists, she entered the realm of logical thinking. So while she continued to deny that sexual differences exist, she could no longer avoid the question of why boys and girls were different. As she began to wonder about this *why*, she took her first step toward recognizing causal relations.

Typically her approach to causality cropped up around speech, her severest inhibiting symptom. One day, Marcia and Karen were talking and Marcia seemed to want to know something about her counselor. As always, she was encouraged to find out in any way she could, and this time her reaction was, "Why you talk?" It was the first time she had ever asked "why" or shown an interest in the reasons for someone's behavior.

Once she had raised this all important question she could soon report spontaneously, without being questioned, about important events in her life. Because of her teacher's illness one day, Marcia was temporarily moved to another classroom. On meeting her counselor after school she immediately told her, "Miss Lukes (her teacher) all gone. Jack all gone. Jeanie all gone (two of her classmates who were temporarily moved to a different classroom)." That the three of them were "all gone" showed that though she now took cognizance of real events, she still functioned on the all or nothing principle. Nothing and nobody continued to exist when out of sight, except what directly pertained to herself, as did Karen.

Within a few more months, toward the end of her third year at the School, she really explored objects of neutral meaning to her. What she had tentatively learned with adult help she now mastered alone without the presence of her counselor. But she still needed to get to "know" something with her body, by doing something to or with it, before she could grasp it intellectually. Thus she had to pour back and forth to understand what went in and out. In her case mastery through manipulation certainly preceded understanding.

The way she learned to play on the seesaw was typical. In this, as in other learning experiences, she seemed to have to repeat the developmental sequence that comes naturally to the infant. First she lay on the seesaw quietly, though it was very difficult to keep her balance in that position; then she sat on it to keep it in balance. In doing so, she really tamed this object that seemed to have a will of its own, that was not like other toys which stay put, but which righted itself. Finally she learned to walk on it upright. After thus mastering its movement, she proceeded to study how it worked. She began by exploring each end, touching it first with her chin. Then she manipulated and came to understand it through hand movements taken directly from the old twiddling and tapping. Having made it all safe, she went on to investigate the center and finally teetered on it.

When Marcia now set out to learn something new, such as walking an inclined plane, she showed great persistence. And though she reverted to her tapping and twiddling when anxious, she soon returned to the work she had set for herself. After any such effort to do things as they ought to be done, or as we wanted her to do them, she had to assert her independence by running away. But since she still liked to be chased, it was now possible to bring her back.

Only after having mastered the seesaw and understood its movements all by herself did she go on to something more dangerous: learning to interact with another person. This was much more difficult, and a much greater achievement, than learning to master an object. So the teetering back and forth in rhythm with another person was a milestone.

Once Marcia could do it, she greatly enjoyed teetering, though for some time only with her counselors. Next she used it to act out aggression in socially acceptable form. Playing on it with her counselor, she enjoyed dropping her abruptly to the ground. But any such act aroused immediate anxiety. With it came arm- and hand-shaking, flight, and the need to be "chased," that is, to be lovingly pursued and brought back. Nor did she trust our good will enough yet to persist.

Soon Marcia could take part in more complicated interactional play, as in a game with two balls and two children. For a while this happened only when her counselor played beside her, but later even when her counselor was not in the game. More important, she could continue the interaction even when small anxieties intruded. Formerly when anything went wrong, as when she dropped a ball, she became so discouraged with herself that she immediately withdrew. She would twiddle helplessly or angrily run off. Now she stayed; and when she failed to catch a ball she picked it up and continued the game. If things got too confused for her, which happened easily, she would clap her hands or in some abortive way deal with her tension, a far cry from her earlier response.

When Marcia had thus become a somebody because she could do things in the world—and much more important, with others—she stopped insisting that her name and her counselor's were identical. She was no longer limited to doing things only by being Karen, or part of her. But it did not come easy to differentiate herself as a person. She accepted her name as her own, but did not yet recognize her own self as an "I." When her counselor tried to tell her "You are you and I am me," her eyes filled with tears, and she tried to deny it by stating, "You is you is me is me!" But the tearfulness showed that she no longer believed in the symbiosis. She now knew it was only a wish on her part. And when Karen told her this was what she wanted to believe but it was not so, she agreed "That is right!" Much as she feared independence, her self was well developed enough to assert that she was a being in her own right.

Her speech still consisted mainly of repeating single words in echolalia-like fashion—but with some words of her own added. Still, the repetitions were more selective and she was more proficient at changing pronouns to their appropriate form. If we told her, "It's your mouth you are talking with," she would now repeat "my mouth." Before this, if she repeated at all, she would simply have said, "your mouth."

She had learned to recognize feelings, but not yet as her own. Feelings originated in the outside, or in that more alien part of the symbiotic totality she lived in. She would occasionally say "angry" when she was angry, but she might also say, "Karen angry." When she cried she might say, "Karen crying." It was never "Karen cries" (with a singular verb) because this could have meant that another person was crying. She always selected plural verb forms as if she and Karen were a plurality of one.

The first time she recognized a feeling as truly hers and not Karen's, was when she could locate a specific, narrowly circumscribed example of it in her body. She said, "hurt," and when questioned, pointed to a tooth that was aching. (The "hurt" she had said at the beginning of her stay with us was very different, a kind of cosmic "hurt." It referred to a state of the world—hers, the only one she knew. But it did not refer to any specific place in her body.)

General feelings of anger and frustration were not yet felt as such, nor as residing in her. The outbursts of temper tantrums she had had for some time were discharge phenomena, or attacks on others, but not from a self that knew itself to be angry or frustrated. Feeling her anger as such would have engulfed her still too precarious personality; it could withstand the invasion of a toothache, but not being flooded altogether by anger or aggression. Still, her greater ability to project feelings enabled her to be openly aggressive from time to time instead of just passively defiant as in her extreme procrastination. She could also be aggressive toward her counselors, however tamely. That there were no bad effects reassured her and she became more openly aggressive in other ways.

As she directed her anger against external objects she let us know more about its content, including what she hallucinated as she stared at the ceiling. It began with her aggressively jumping for our circular ceiling fixtures in actual attempts to pull them down. "Jump to lights" and "break lights" was her favorite activity for some time. After hundreds of repetitions, and the experience that we not only accepted such destructive behavior but approved of her acting in line with her feelings, she was willing to tell us why she wanted to tear the fixtures down. "Baby needs breakfast," she said, in answer to our questions, as if this explained everything. And indeed it did when she eventually and from then on consistently said "Break breast" for "breakfast."[11]

It seems that Marcia had to leave the symbiotic position somewhat before she could show aggression toward the person who had formerly been part of herself. (Her furious lunging at us in earlier days was not directed against another person; it was a diffuse lashing out in self-defense and a far cry from her present small acts of aggression.)

Had she imagined up to this point, that the breast was part of her too? And if so, how could she vent her anger against it without also destroy-

---

11. Break breast is probably an idea more readily available to a baby fed from a breakable bottle than to one nursed from the breast.

ing part of herself? Be this as it may, it seems worth noting that with the separating of Marcia from her counselor, with her ability to turn aggression against her, she could also try to break a symbol for the breast. That these fixtures and light bulbs stood for the original source of her fury became still more certain a few months later when in a quite different context we asked her why she was so angry and she would answer, "Mad at light bulb."

Her selection of our light fixtures for this acting out is by no means unique. Quite a few of our children equate ceiling light fixtures with breasts, particularly when the light bulbs are plainly visible or the fixtures circular. (Many of them, incidentally, have the same response to car headlights.) Several explanations are possible, only two of which seem to fit most cases we observe. The first is that the nursing infant looks up from below to the mother's breast, or else to her face and the bottle. Looking up that way makes the ceiling part of his total visual experience, and one part of it may come to stand for the other—the ceiling (or ceiling light) for the breast, face or bottle—since all is projected against the ceiling while he nurses. As a matter of fact this may apply more to the bottle-fed baby than to the breast-fed baby, whose head is more apt to turn inward toward the breast than upward toward a bottle.

But the round, illuminating fixtures may simply stand for the breast. This second explanation has to do with the experience of children who were felt as an imposition by the mother. Their mothers rushed through the necessary procedures unwillingly and with speed. They wanted the baby to sleep as long and often as possible, often darkening the room for that reason. When eventually they came to feed the infant, the turning on of lights or the opening of the curtains was a signal that food had come at last. In such cases a kind of conditioned response can be established between light and food. Certainly Marcia's "Baby needs breakfast" as she jumped at the lights suggested her wanting them to come down and feed her. Or else she wished to destroy them for not doing so. Her desire for these light fixtures suggests her desperate oral cravings, while her "break breast" reflects her anger at being frustrated.

Here, as in the autistic child's hallucinating while staring at the ceiling, the causative factors seem the exasperated waiting, followed by the disappointment that even while being fed they miss appropriate emotions in the mother. And some autistic children were fed with the bottle propped up; even more reason for them to gaze upward to find the person behind the feeding.

Indeed, I believe this is exactly what these children hallucinate: the person behind the feeding, the person whom they never reached emotionally and whom they both search for, and wish to get rid of.

Our acceptance of Marcia's anger at mothers, plus our willingness to sacrifice our fixtures, enabled her to do more than be helplessly angry. The expression and acceptance of anger in symbolic form (through talk, play, dolls, and the like) may be adequate in the treatment of neurotic children. But for formerly autistic children, even our making it clear that it is all right to be angry at some distant object or person and to act it out symbolically, or only in the treatment room that remains isolated from the rest of their lives—this is simply not enough.

They do not fear destruction because of their hostile wishes toward particular persons. They fear destruction pure and simple, by everyone. After all, since it is not us they would like to destroy, for example, but their mother, why would we retaliate? But we are still part of a world they believe to be uniformly destructive. And if they were to act out hostilely against us, we would destroy them. So until they can direct their aggressions against us they find little security in our verbal assurance that we will not retaliate.

But if they begin to attack us, or objects they believe are very important to us, and we stay accepting as before, then they eventually begin to believe we were not just talking acceptance of anger, but really meant it. Of this Marcia had to make sure before each jump at the fixtures, and then again after the jumping, irrespective of whether she succeeded in tearing them down. (Fortunately, the part of the fixture she could reach and pull down was lightweight metal, so that nothing happened even when it fell.) Before starting her running jump she went to her counselor for a hug, clung to her as if to make sure she was still intact and full of affection for Marcia, and returned for the same after jumping.

What we have to convey to these children is that we find both their anger and destructiveness justified and acceptable to us, because they are valid expressions of their feelings. Only then do they begin to believe that their feelings are really important to us, even more so than our valued possessions. Once they know this, their destructiveness subsides almost immediately because they were not really interested in destroying, but in testing us out.[12]

Our acceptance of Marcia in whatever she did enabled her to discharge the anger. But that she had more of a self enabled her to inflict

---

12. Actually, the damage Marcia did in pulling down the fixtures was fairly inexpensive to repair. Her flooding of our floors over months was much more costly, though our acceptance of the damage had no meaning to her. At that time she was much too involved in herself to feel any interest in our intentions or reactions beyond whether they threatened her or not. Still, had we been more interested in preserving our floors, or in saving ourselves hours of mopping, she would have known where she stood with us and would never have gone on to show us the content of her anger.

on others what they had inflicted on her; because to do this required a pretty clear distinction not only between the self and the nonself, but between the self and other persons.

It was about this time that she played hundreds of times at what she called "tea party." It consisted, after compulsive preparations, of forced feedings of her doll and of giving it enemas. A favorite teddy bear, representing the father who once gave her such a toy, was always made to sit close by watching, but otherwise doing nothing. Clearly, he was the father who looked on as the infant was violently intruded upon by rectum and mouth.

Eventually she told us that in this play she was both suffering child and retribution. Just as she had merged with her counselor, had been Karen and Marcia at the same time, so she was now mother and child at the same time, and so was the doll. At one moment, or probably in the same moment, hard as it is to comprehend, Marcia was Marcia herself, forcing food and enemas on her mother (the doll). And at the same time Marcia was the doll, suffering all that Marcia (as her mother) inflicted on the doll.

This game, more than any others, was no longer marked by anxiety and hesitation. Even in her jumping at the lights, hesitation and getting ready took up most of the time, whereas the jumping itself was done in a hurry. In this play there was no anxious hesitation, but compulsive and purposeful action. The cups out of which she poured water into both ends of the doll had to be set up just so. She left the table and went to fill each cup separately in the bathroom, one at a time. And for the first time a very specific ritual emerged, consisting of a double step that separated one living space from the other. Typically, her ritual separated the bathroom from the dormitory. Though seemingly absorbed in other things, it was always right on the threshold that she took the double step. The bathroom, with its dangerous purpose of elimination, had to be clearly marked off by symbolic separation from the safer world of the dormitory. Then the dormitory could stay free of contamination.

Marcia's growing courage extended from a more active dealing with her old inner pressures to becoming more active and self-assertive in reality. For a long time she had passively accepted our taking of movies; later she had looked at the camera and again later explored it and named it. Now at last she had an appropriate reaction and wanted to destroy the camera that intruded on her privacy. "Take camera away," she said, and since we did not comply fast enough, she went further.

This time she did not, as in other tense situations, resort to short-lived abortive twiddling, but folded her hands as if in prayer. (Did she pray that her daring would have no bad consequences?) After which she went up to the camera and said clearly, "Break camera."[13] From then on we never filmed without asking her permission. Sometimes she said it was all right; other times it was not and then no pictures were taken.

§

The "I" Appears

After three years with us, Marcia was becoming more of a person, more aggressive, more interested in the world around her. Most of her time, however, was still spent in withdrawn isolation. There she concentrated on her inner bodily sensations and on vague hallucinations and daydreams of more or less limited and stereotyped content, as her comments revealed when we questioned her and she was willing to answer. It was part of her becoming a person that she developed a few specific symptoms for dealing with specific anxieties (the double step, folding her hands as in prayer) as compared with a lifetime of preventing destruction through the single nonspecific symptom of autism.

Most important of all, she was more of a human being because some people had become significant to her as persons instead of mere caretakers. Up to now she had never reacted when a counselor told her she was going to be absent. At most she would respond with her usual "See you Tuesday" or whatever the next day was, though the counselor had said she would be gone a few weeks. Marcia simply denied their absence and relied on her ability to hallucinate their presence. Now she would scream whole days because her counselor had gone on vacation, or was planning to. Before this when one of her counselors or teachers returned from an absence of some duration she ignored them, or behaved as if she had seen them only yesterday. Now, when her counselor returned from a month's vacation she was full of angry tears at first sight of her, but soon laughed with her and for the next few days smiled and waved whenever she saw her.

Having and showing the normal feelings of a child toward the persons who cared for her well, including sorrow at their absence, she seemed ready to experience what normally happens at the very beginning of personality development: an activation of the oral apparatus, and the enjoyment of licking and drinking, though not yet of sucking itself.

This new experience she provided for herself spontaneously. From time to time, as noted, we had offered her baby bottles and other suitable

---

13. Since she did so after we had photographed the play of forced feedings and enemas, there may have been some connection. Perhaps the big, protruding tubular lens reminded her more of the hard protruding piece that was inserted in her body during enemas.

objects for sucking. She had always rejected them. Milk she still would not touch and other liquids she drank with little pleasure. But one day she discovered a liquid food not contaminated by anything in the past. On a trip to a local store she spied a honey jar shaped in the form of a teddy bear; perhaps this helped since the teddy bear had always stood for the less intrusive father.

Honey was an acceptable liquid because it was not one the mother had ever tried to force, and she now licked it and drank it for hours with delight and abandon. Many of her once frozen mouth and tongue movements were freed in the process; she licked the bottle freely, putting her tongue deep within it. Drinking this way she was in good contact; it was not an isolating activity, but a relating and very gratifying one. Her once rigid hand and finger movements were freed too as she contentedly fingered the bottle. Wherever she went, she carried the honey-bear bottle with her, as a small child might carry his nursing bottle.

A minor but important consequence was that she began to like some solid foods, though there was still no enjoyment of eating, that is of the biting or chewing involved. But she, who had always been the last to finish eating, was now one of the first to be through at the dinner table. Part of the reason was that while she now liked some foods but not the eating of them, she stopped trying to put off the eating and instead tried to get it over with as fast as possible.

With her new involvement in drinking and licking came ideas about oral incorporation of the mother. No longer did Marcia want only to break the bad breast, but to eat up the good breast. As she told her counselor, what she was thinking about was "eat you up." With it came a wish to possess this good mother. As she contentedly licked from the honey bottle, holding on to her counselor all the while, she spoke of "my Karen" and "your own Karen." This was quite different from the earlier relation where both of them had been experienced as one big vague unit, or the later symbiotic one. What now emerged was not symbiosis, but a wish to possess.

Such a wish did not yet imply any recognition of selfhood. That would have precluded the wish to possess others, which is always the consequence of a feeling of incompleteness. But it did imply awareness of the independent existence of the other—an apartness one wishes to undo just because one is painfully aware of it. It was also why she craved greater closeness to this person whom she no longer felt she possessed, or was one with.

Although Marcia had mentioned enemas before and had acted them out hundreds of times, it was only after she had mastered them in part through re-enactment that she could verbally connect them with her mother. This she did through a contamination of the two words, speaking often now of "enemommas." Her neologism suggests that both the mother and what she had inflicted on Marcia had become a single emotional experience. This is why Marcia had found it so nearly impossible to master. When she tried to master the trauma of the enema, the experience of the mother had intruded because the two were so hopelessly linked. This made it impossible for Marcia to free herself of enemas and constipation because it also meant giving up the mother, and all the hoped-for satisfactions the mother still stood for. And if she tried to come to grips with the emotional experience of the mother, the traumatic experience of the enema intruded and made that equally impossible.

Finally she hit on the double step as a symbolic way to separate the place that stood for the forced elimination from her living quarters where she played out forced elimination on others. By doing so, she also separated the living room where she could live her own life (could even eat when she wished) from the place of elimination. More important, it was a symbolic separation of passive suffering from active mastery.

Two other experiences were essential in Marcia's overcoming the past. First and foremost, one person had become separated from the function she performed. Karen had become a person in her own right, and emerged from her caretaking function. Through her, action and person became separated, unlike the mother who was inseparable from what she did to Marcia. Secondly, Marcia had separated an enjoyable experience (licking honey) from those who provided it. So first the person had emerged from behind her actions, and then a gratifying experience became separated from the person. With person and experience now distinct, some order could begin to be brought into the external world and its mastery attempted.

So at this point came markedly new achievements. As Marcia spoke, even in isolated words, of her ambivalence about the breast she wanted so badly, but also wanted to break and destroy, she took her first steps toward freeing herself from the pervasive ambivalence that had always stymied her.

It then became clearer what Marcia's predicament had been. Feeding and enemas had become so unified an experience in her mind that it blocked any ability to act or be. Feeding, enemas, and the mother had all been the same. Things were poured into her, only to be extracted out of her. Liquids were either poured into her mouth, or forced into her rectum. So what was mouth, and what anus? What served which function?

She could form no personality because her parents' rejection made it hopeless to interact with the world, or too dangerous, and hence unwise. This left her thrown back on her own resources—that is, her body. But the enemas made her disoriented about even this last remaining thing that was hers. Literally uncertain as to which end was up or what organ served which purpose, which part of the body took in, and which eliminated, she was left in control over neither.[14]

Worse, none of these organs were given freedom to act on their own. They were acted upon by insensitive, overpowering forces, and at least one of them contrary to its natural function. The rectum, which should eliminate, was also made to take in. All that remained possible was to protect whatever little body and body functions she could still call her own by holding on for dear life, by giving out with nothing, neither with words nor with stools, and by avoiding any taking things in, be it food or affection.

Small step after step, each one endlessly repeated before proceeding —from pouring water between bucket and bottle, to repeating the process with bottle, glass, and bucket, to her endless pouring of water into the doll's mouth and rectum—Marcia learned to actively master some of these experiences. Mouth and rectum were finally separated. And with the ability to enjoy taking in (honey bear) Marcia became ready for true speech. It finally enabled her to grasp intellectually what she had acted out with just an emotional grasp of what was involved. With speech she could also grasp it all by means of concepts.

In direct consequence of her relation to Karen and some first understanding of intake and elimination, she felt herself to be a person. The concept of an "I" became fully developed, though not taken for granted for some time. For example, she would say "I" and "I'm" excitedly and often during the day now, as if to reassert to herself her new-won identity.

As with all autistic children Marcia's difficulties with pronouns had to do with her struggle to separate herself as a person from her world.

14. It does not take such an extreme history as Marcia's to throw a child into utter confusion about his body, and with it his very self. It has been our experience with many severely disturbed children that for parallel reasons an emesis has a temporarily shattering effect. The child's sense of his body is shaken by the experience that the organ that should take in has eliminated out. Since the feeling of self is built up from the experience of having an orderly body, the experience of an emesis shakes the child's very trust in himself.

Conversely, our severely disturbed children find it most reassuring when we can demonstrate that their bodies are functioning appropriately and well. A simple experience—of which we have to provide many and varied ones—may illustrate. These children are amazed to find that they will swallow some liquid, or a morsel of food, even when they are held upside down. It then turns out that many of them, if they have ever given it thought, were convinced that food went down their throats not because their bodies were functioning, but because everything falls down; because of gravity, as we would say, though these children may or may not be familiar with the term.

To say, for example, "This is my ball," presupposes a clear understanding of person and object, with the object standing in a particular relation to the person. Since everything that pertained to Marcia's world was Marcia, once the "I" was established she would say, "I am the ball." But somehow she knew she was not the ball. So when questioned, and dimly sensing a difference she couldn't quite grasp, she would quickly assert, "I am not the ball."

Since at one moment she *was* the ball (because it was part of her world) and at the next moment not, this failed to solve the problem of whose ball it was. Worse, it left her totally confused about who or what she was.

In effect, Marcia could not claim a possession without falsifying her identity. I have spoken of how the infant, as he becomes aware of his feces, is confused because at one moment they are part of his body and at the next moment are not. In Marcia's experience this was doubly complicated by the enemas. Her difficulties show the tremendous task a human being encounters when at the late age of fourteen she begins to try to understand herself as a person, and her relations to the objects in her environment.

Marcia became especially confused around any incorporation of objects. For example, when she had eaten something at Stineway's drugstore, and was willing to tell us about it, she would quickly add, "I am not Stineway's." The problem was that as soon as she had taken something in, she *became* it; and since she had eaten at Stineway's she was afraid she had become Stineway's drugstore.

The more fully she recognized her independent existence, the more she had to recognize her counselor's. The more Karen became fully a person, the stronger became Marcia's reactions to any temporary absence of her counselor. Now she cried at the briefest separation, as when leaving for class in the morning. Yet with greater trust in our intentions, Marcia, who had always violently resisted any intrusion in her mouth, finally let our dentist work on her teeth. This was true, of course, only in her counselor's presence and with her counselor's renewed assurance in her ears.

She used adjectives and adverbs more freely. The honey she licked became "sticky honey." With the "I" and "me" fully acquired, correctly used, and clearly separated from the "you," "we," and "us," she began to use the names of other staff members and children correctly. Her emotions too, became freer. She was able to cry or scream when she was angry, and to sing and talk when she was happy. When deeply involved (but only with Karen) the whole range of emotions was theoretically available to her, though in fact the occurrence was still rare. She could even, at times, take a look at herself. Then she called herself a "brat," or a "stubborn girl."

At about this stage in her development Marcia's brother was born and this brought on a second major setback in her progress. We did not tell her of the pregnancy, but informed her at once of the birth. All very distressing situations weakened her still tenuous selfhood, seeming to prove how inadequate the self was to protect her. Her ego boundaries were at all times still shaky. Now they gave way, and to survive at all she withdrew from reality to a vague inner self, trying to merge again with her favorite counselor. But to do so meant that everything threatening originated with her counselor. So Marcia immediately blamed her for the birth of the baby.

Still, it indicates the progress she had made that she did not freeze in her emotions. Though she projected the baby on her counselor, she had an immediate and appropriate emotional reaction: she cried profusely. While insisting it was Karen's fault that the baby was born, she clung to her frantically for support. But it was some time before she could accept that the baby brother was not Karen's doing but her parents'.

§

Working Through

When spring came and Marcia had been with us about three and a half years, her body movements were so released, and her security in the world so grown, that she not only ran freely and chased her counselors (which began some months earlier), but let other children chase her. More important, she began to chase them back. She took part in dancing, and could take her turn in rather complicated games such as "Duck, Duck, Goose" with the help of other children. Their willingness to allow for her slowness, and their help when she wavered about what to do next, was another measure of how far Marcia had come in joining human company. While she was still loathe to interact, they had left her alone and kept their distance.

When Marcia was ready to take the next step in separating squirting bottles from squirting enemas, she again provided herself with the play material to do so. That same spring she found in the dime store a set containing a baby doll, a baby bottle, and a water bag (which she soon called the "enema bottle"). Now again, she played out hundreds of times with baby, bottle, and enema bag what she had played out less clearly in her last water play. For some time the main issue was to force liquid into the doll and to have the doll expel it.

At first she used the baby bottle and "enema bottle" interchangeably. But slowly she distinguished between them. The baby bottle became separated from the enema bottle as the one most connected with being fed, since she twiddled it against her mouth and chin area and took meticulous care in filling and preparing it. In later stages she fed only with the baby bottle and came closer and closer to sucking from it. The temptation was great, but she never went further than a twiddling that brought the nipple ever closer to her mouth.

At last the old tapping and twiddling movements became clearly connected with both baby and bottle because eventually she twiddled the baby doll, too, against her mouth, expressing still more clearly how these twiddling movements stood for both nursing and baby. She would touch and tap the doll's cheek and chin with the baby bottle before forcing the nipple in its mouth. But for Marcia herself there was still only the craving and the fear, so that the nipple did not enter her own mouth.

This play was accompanied not only by mouth movements but by talking to herself. Old compulsive rituals disappeared; she no longer separated the bathroom from the living room with a double step, but walked freely between them. By the same token she played freely with the doll in the dormitory and bathroom alike.

As with each of her efforts to master inner experience, Marcia drew courage from close body contact with favorite adults. She reached out to them now and invited it. From a touching and holding on to part of the body, and later a hugging, there developed over the next few months a seeking of contact involving greater parts of her own and the caretakers' bodies. This was more than a temporary hugging or a jumping on them. She enjoyed truly relaxed, prolonged rest as she lay curled in her counselor's lap.

In Marcia's first water play of more or less simple pouring, the two experiences of liquids entering by mouth and by rectum had been merged and contaminated with each other. In the play with cup and doll, pouring water into mouth and rectum were clearly separate as acts, but not as emotional experiences: both alike were aggressively forced on the doll. Though the two body openings became separated, what it felt like to take things in through one or the other was not distinguished. It was not until she licked from the honey bear that Marcia gained for herself a clear emotional conception of what it meant to take in with pleasure. While this helped greatly in viewing the world as more satisfying, at least around feeding, it remained disconnected from the old central experience of the enemas. When she tried to go further as in the last play described, it all became one big, hostile experience again.

Marcia had to leave this form of re-enactment, had to forego play with water, to securely establish the separation of pleasant intake, from intrusion. And this again she did on her own.

One day in a toy store she spotted a new plaything—a popgun that shot out a ball that was attached by a string. What caught her interest most was that from this gun she could expel something that did *not* get lost; it was always there at the end of the string. She could always retrieve it, and start all over again. For the first time Marcia could experience letting go and holding on at the same time.

At about this time she became fascinated by another toy she discovered on her own. It was a little doll that held a maraca in each hand and shook both of its hands. She quickly removed one maraca, so that one doll hand shook a stick with the same twiddling movements as her own. The other hand continued to shake the maraca, which not only looked like a breast but was conceived as such by Marcia. Here then was another combination of a twiddling movement by one hand and the shaking of a breast-like form with the other. Her mouth movements as she played with it by the hour further suggested its deep oral meaning for her.

Through the two games (with popgun and twiddle doll) Marcia was able to separate between her desires for passive incorporation and aggressive destruction. This division proved a crucial step in her developing relations. Marcia, though she related to Karen, did not yet relate to persons. She was too tied to Karen, and Karen was too all-important for others to be truly experienced as separate persons. Now that hostility and pleasurable intake were separated both as acts and emotions, she could also distinguish between persons.

With Karen, she now carried the twiddle doll wherever she went. With Inge, she invariably carried the popgun. People and play experiences each had their unique meaning for her now.

A while later Marcia no longer needed to keep activities separate in order to keep people separate. With either counselor she could play games in which she was fed, games in which she let go, and games she used either aggressively or for reaching out. She could experience pleasure and anger with both of them and not lose the realization that each was a different person, though closely related to herself. Her world was no longer a symbiotic one, but populated by different persons.

Marcia had occasionally been interested in looking at books but had shown no desire to learn to read, nor had we been able to induce it. Now she was ready, and in a short time learned to read first her name, then by her own choice, "ball," the name of the first toy she really used, and next, three sentences built around her name. Here too, in order not to push her, or evoke her usual stubborn resistance, we asked what she wanted to learn to read and then printed what she dictated, as follows: "Marcia goes to school;" "Marcia goes to the store;" and "Marcia goes to dinner." Each was a main daily event. But this may have been less important than the fact that each told about something she did on her own.

Not only had Marcia learned to assert her feelings, but also to satisfy them. She finally began to masturbate. Interestingly enough she began in the bathtub, one of the earliest situations with us in which she had experienced both comfort and independence.

Her life was gaining added dimensions. She could talk of her anxieties about her caretakers' comings and goings. Where she had once screamed when told that one of them would take a vacation, she now pondered and worried on her own that "Karen might go away." It was the first time she had voiced any thoughts of the future, or used the subjunctive with all it implied. She began to have a future, though in terms of her outlook on life all she could do about it was worry and expect the worst.

She could use the correct pronouns in rather difficult sentence structures, such as when she was asked, "Are you attached to me?" and would answer, "I am attached to you." Since our question acknowledged her need to remain attached, her thought was freed enough to recognize that the question involved two separate people.

How well she could express herself depended largely on how great her involvement. For example, when trying to play with a yo-yo it fell to the floor and she struggled with saying, "Goes in the floor," recognizing that "in" was not the right word. But she could think of nothing else to say. Things were different when her feelings were involved, as in playing with a toy she called the "long thing"; then she could play on words ingeniously. If she could not manipulate the toy well enough to make it do as she wished, she called her "long thing" the "wrong thing."

§

Exploring "Why"

Moral evaluations began to appear in her speech. Things and people were either "good" or "bad," and soon persons acquired more distinctive features. They were no longer just jealous or angry, but were jealous of particular persons, or angry about particular events. She had since recognized that she was stubborn, but now she knew it "has something to do with mother." Later she elaborated that because her mother was so stubborn, she became doubly so. But she also began to decide what she felt made for good mothers and to distinguish between good and bad ones. Good mothers, she said, "hope things" (that is, create hope in the child of better things to come); bad mothers "go away" (not only leave the child but project him into loneliness and despair). And at this point the existence of her baby brother, who seemed to have lost all meaning for her, suddenly hit with renewed impact.

It happened about seven months after the baby's birth and temporarily brought another angry withdrawal. But this time she could clearly state the reason: out of spontaneous realization, she felt that her brother would be all right because her parents had a better life now. On occasion she tried for an easy way out, saying he would be all right because he was a boy. She also overestimated his achievements. She assumed he was already talking, and could do many other things she had barely, and only recently, mastered. We assured her he could not, and that she still had a chance to stay ahead of him.

She then told us she was "mad at mommy-daddy," merging them in quite a different way than she used to. During her first years with us the all-overpowerful mother stood for herself and both parents. Her use of the teddy bear who watched the enemas being given to the doll was the first use of a symbol representing the father alone. But "mother" still stood for both parents as a unit. So in her "mommy-daddy" she was actually separating them more, because she recognized that the unit had two separate parts.

Again the enemas were the reason: though they by no means accounted for her autism, they had come to stand for all the bad experiences whose totality alone can explain the depth of her disturbance.[15] It was true that when administering the enemas, her parents did different things. But in the way she experienced their intentions and behavior, they were a single blurred unit. And to this unit she had surrendered, in despair and full of hatred, the contents of her body.

One day after she had said again she was "mad at mommy-daddy," she went on as if in explanation, "Mad because they are happy." Then it emerged that she felt they could be happy because she was no longer there to wreck their lives; and with it came a semiconscious awareness that she had deliberately tried to do so. We could now raise the question of why she had wanted to wreck their lives. And her answer was, "Because mommy-daddy make you sick."

Even now, in dealing with deep emotional problems, Marcia could not use the "I" for herself, but only the "you," another sidelight on

15. That is why, when I speak at various places of Marcia's predicament, or her crucial problems, etc., it must always be understood as what was superimposed on her original autism; that is, on her reaction to the parents' unconscious wish at the time that she should not exist. Without this, no doubt, even her most traumatic experiences, such as the enemas, would have interfered less radically with her development.

the personal pronoun in relation to the development of a self. That is, Marcia could still not speak of herself as "I" unless the feeling tone was distinctly positive and implied her being active. When it was negative, whether hostile or anxious, and particularly when the situation was one implying passive suffering, she protected herself by the old self-alienation, as now expressed by regarding herself from the outside, in the second person, as "you." She also continued to refer to what her parents did to her as "make you sick," not only using the second person, but linking to a common source both a physical disturbance (constipation, or the watery enema stools that she may have viewed as diarrhea) and her emotional disturbance.

About her parents she could do no more for the present than be helplessly angry. But about her brother she began to understand her feelings a little better. This she accomplished in play by doing away with him. Interestingly enough, she did it by drowning. As she felt she had been assaulted with liquids, so she now destroyed her brother again and again. Usually she did it by drowning a baby doll that she said was her brother, in a toy bathtub, in sinks, or in similar containers.

After she had thus dealt with him in accordance with her feelings, she could accept his existence in reality. This she did about a month later by creating out of candy beads some human figures. There were always four now: herself, her parents and the baby. These persons, who had so far been represented only by what they did to her—forcing liquid into or out of her—now achieved human form as well as independent existence. Though she made herself much bigger than the others, the most important in her family, she was only one among four.

Now in exploring her feelings around the enemas she could recognize that not all of them had been unpleasant. She continued to say with deep feeling that enemas "felt worse," but with some hesitation sometimes added, "warm" or "felt good." She began to recognize her ambivalence around this single experience that had been both destructive and exciting.

She gained more courage about elimination and could finally flush the toilet after defecating. Eventually, in answer to our questions, she told us that every flushing of the toilet had meant receiving an enema outside of her body, in which the water carried her feces away.

A while later she could tell us about the connection between defecation and talking, and how she had given up talking because of her experience around toilet training. In a relaxed and responsive mood, as Marcia sat in Karen's lap, Karen tried to get her to jabber by doing it herself. But Marcia refused to talk freely. Finally her counselor invited her to jabber, too. To this she unexpectedly replied, "dirty." Asked who was dirty, she answered, "Karen dirty with shit."

It seemed quite clear that to Marcia the counselor's talking had been shit. When asked whether she felt Karen was full of shit for talking so freely, Marcia said, "yes." So Karen tried to explain the difference between talking and elimination, and after she thought she had made her point, concluded, "Either talking is like shitting, or it isn't," to which Marcia replied with deep conviction, "Is like shitting."

In many ways, given Marcia's experience, such a view of talking is readily understandable. Both body openings had been made to serve the same function, and the emotional impact of giving out from the rectum was so much more powerful that it imposed itself on what it felt like to give out through any bodily opening. Up to this time we had viewed her reluctance to talk as an indication of her basic negativism: her mistrust of those she might speak to, what the consequence might be if she said something, and most of all her over-all wish not to let go, not to give out. We had been unaware that to her, words as such were the same as feces.

At the same time one cannot help but be impressed with Freud's wisdom and ingenious selection of technical terms. It is so much easier for the therapist to deal in his mind and feelings with what are called anal experiences, and to talk about them, than it is to deal with what is called shit. It is so much easier to participate in games with objects or materials symbolic of feces—such as fingerpaint, plasticine, mud— than to deal with stools in and out of the toilet bowl. But with Marcia— as with other autistic and schizophrenic children—we could not afford the luxury of sublimation as by using the terms anal, or anality, because it would have gotten us exactly nowhere. We had to accept her shit as such and with pleasure, or she would never have given up her constipation and toilet trained herself.[16]

16. As to how the staff member manages to do this, I felt that Karen should answer for herself and the following was written some two years after her leaving the School: "You ask how come, for example, we could encourage Marcia to soil, given our middle class antiseptic training? For one thing, the idea of her not ever defecating scared the living daylights out of me. I found myself with a child in my care who just wasn't shitting. After a week or so of this, I was going around saying to any and everyone on the staff who would listen, 'I don't care *where* she goes, just so she goes!' Her behavior told me flatly: 'Either you adults let me run my own bodily functions or I simply won't function.' My middle class notions (only defecate in the toilet!) quickly vanished, and this change in my attitude no doubt made a difference. After weeks of this she finally began to defecate in the bathtub. I was overjoyed, not to speak of my tremendous relief. At the time, I myself marveled at my ability to 'take' her behavior with equanimity; not only did I take it, I welcomed it. Shitting in the tub and soiling her pants was just better than not shitting at all. With my visions of attendant physical complications, soiling was just better than my fantasies.

"I suppose my own involvement went even deeper. But I found that with a little encouragement my attitude toward such matters underwent a rapid about-face, and

A few weeks later Marcia told us that "Words go down the drain," and in many other ways let us know that her difficulty with talking had come from how strongly she had identified these words that people tried to drag out of her with the feces they had actually dragged out. Another day she told us spontaneously, in respect to her being constipated: "I not talk." Not only were words like feces to her, but stools were also like words.

Some months later, on the fourth anniversary of her coming to the School, she said again that enemas take things away. But this time when asked who was taking things away from her, she did not just say "mommy" as so often before, but added, "Mommy takes kind of shit away." So this time it was more than feces that were dragged out of her. We could now ask what kind of shit was taken away by the enemas and she replied in clear distinct tones, "Marcia!" Finally she had recognized where, how, and why she had lost what by that time may have been the roots of her selfhood, and why whatever was left of it had become identified with feces. Forced to defecate when and how her mother wished, her reaction was to lose all desire to talk or relate, and with it she had lost her feeling of self.

Having recognized what she felt her mother had done to her, she could also recognize how important this mother had been. Talking about her life at the School, and how her interests had grown, the counselor spoke of how Marcia had first become interested in water play. Marcia corrected her, saying, "sand." The counselor praised her for being right, and agreed that Marcia's interest in things had indeed begun with sand play. Again Marcia corrected her, saying dreamily, "mommy." Finally she had unearthed her earliest interest, but one that seemed so frustrating to her that it became her reason for losing all interest in the world.

Having viewed elimination a bit more realistically, its pressure on her oral apparatus was reduced and she could more fully enjoy the pleasures of the mouth. Feeding her doll then became more important than giving it enemas, or forcing water into its mouth. As she truly fed the doll, she finally dared to put her finger in her own mouth. For some time she could only do this very tentatively and with anxiety, but finally with some pleasure. It was not her thumb she used, but her twiddle finger. But a finger that can be held in the mouth need no longer move to and from the mouth in endless indecision, and at this point the twiddling and chin-tapping disappeared almost entirely.

I was not only able to tolerate so-called uncivilized behavior but it eventually began to make sense to me: not just in terms of the psychotic child's needs, but also in terms of rapidly evolving new attitudes of my own."

From playing parallel to other children, to taking a role in their play, to playing active games with them, Marcia had progressed after four years to talking with them and interacting on her own. Of course this made them take a far greater interest in her. Some children really tried to befriend her, because they felt her responsive to their efforts. Her behavior and play were no longer so strange to them, and they could now understand her emotions and what she was acting out. To these they responded with empathy and tried to help her find better ways for dealing with her problems.

Typically our children do this most readily when in some fashion the problem is also their own. One girl who had been abandoned at birth, and during her first years of life had suffered from marasmus, was particularly upset by the way Marcia fed her baby dolls. She had objected before but Marcia had paid no attention. Now that Marcia was a bit more like other children the girl tried again to reach out. She told Marcia that that was certainly no way to treat a baby. What was new was that Marcia permitted the girl to show her how a baby doll should be held and cared for, listened attentively to the other child's explanations, and tried to follow her suggestions.

She lessened her distance from us too, and we came to understand more fully why the chasing game had been so important. Because what she wanted now was to be chased by us before she defecated; she not only let us, but wanted us to grab and hold her—which in the initial game was so strictly avoided. Early in the chasing game she had re-created the exciting situation where her mother tried to get hold of her to give her the enemas; except that with us it was Marcia who won out. We were never permitted to come close to her, not to speak of touching her.

Three years later, in a very different chasing game, she provided herself with the excitement that had preceded the enemas, including her now being grabbed and held by her counselors. But being hugged, in this game, took a new form. She wanted to be held from behind, pressing her back against the front of her counselor's body, with her counselor's arms holding Marcia around her middle. Thus she offered the rectum she had always protected, to convince herself it was not only safe now to expose it to a mothering person, but that the counselor's body, like a shield, would protect it from intrusion. After which she liked to go to the toilet on her own and there freely and pleasurably eliminate. This was so important to her that for months she would defecate only after her "game" of reassurance.

Intellectual progress followed, though much slower than with the freeing of emotions. After Marcia had been reading simple sentences for a few months, she learned to print. This, too, she learned by using a material closely related to feces, namely plasticine. And the first words she printed were the same as the first ones she learned to read: her own name, and the word "ball."

By the time she had been with us four and a half years she had mastered all preprimers. Reading and printing were not easy for her. But she concentrated on both tasks, worked hard at trying to understand, and was obviously thinking of what she was doing, not escaping into hallucinations. When she achieved well her whole face radiated pleasure. She felt she had become a real schoolgirl. She made further progress in understanding her own disturbance, and in expressing her hope of getting well.

But often she was still quite discouraged about herself and told us she was not sure if she wanted to become a smart girl or preferred to remain a stubborn, withholding one. She clearly distinguished between a Marcia who "stays crazy" and a "sensible Marcia" who "can write 'girl'." She could differentiate herself from other children. When she was asked why she was not a playing or a talking Marcia but a stubborn one, she answered, "Marcia is a stubborn girl; Jean (one of her rivals) is a playing girl; Ellen (another girl in her group) is a talking girl."

While these traits were by no means the ones most unique in the other two girls, they were the ones that, to Marcia, distinguished them most from herself. Much as they became unique persons because they did things peculiar to them, so was Marcia unique by being stubborn. Implicitly she recognized that being stubborn was part of her effort to be a distinct person.

During her fifth year Marcia really worked hard at how to make a better life for herself. She realized that "Getting better makes you worse" (that is, makes you feel worse), and when asked what gets worse, she answered, "Marcia."

When we asked more specifically, "Don't you feel better if you talk about what's scary?" she answered, "More scary." And, in fact, as Marcia came further into the world, she felt more acutely her inadequacies, her anger, and most of all her unhappiness.

She recognized that her real strength lay in her way of resisting, which she called doing nothing. "Marcia is a strong girl," she said, and when asked, "Strong to do what?" she said, "Strong to do nothing." When asked what she was so afraid she might do that it was better to do nothing, she answered, "Bad stuff." So her doing nothing was predicated on two different anxieties, one about doing and the other about feeling. If she did anything at all she would do very bad things. And if she let herself feel, she would feel terrible about herself.

§
More Working Through

For over four years Marcia had been surrounded only by persons who tried to make life as pleasant as possible for her; nobody had forced his will on her. Why did life continue to be so bad for her that every little gain had to be fought for, against excruciating resistance?

One day her counselor said, "Listen, Marcia. Either the Orthogenic School is good for you, or it isn't." "School is good," she answered. So the counselor asked, "Well, if you're in what you think is a good place, why not act sensible?" To which came the startling reply, "Not the first place." For Marcia it was all the past living she had done before she came to us, that made it impossible for her to really feel good about anything, including life at the School. So the problem she now set out to tackle was why.

It soon became clear from isolated types of behavior that Marcia was making renewed efforts to reach beyond the experience of the enemas and somehow loosen their deadening grip on her life. In order to get at traumatizations that must have preceded her anal traumata she seemed to have to master the anal ones first. And this she had been trying to do for years. But it seemed as if every effort to reach beyond them was blocked.

Anal material, because of how it had attached itself to oral phenomena, obtruded on all that had to do with feeding, with the mouth, with talking and the earliest relations to the mother. Each time she tried to recapture those earlier relations and experiences, thoughts of the mother seemed to make her so angry about the anal experiences that she had to stop and deal with them again, never getting to what lay behind them.

Again she selected her own object for acting it all out. It was a cup, red on the outside, white inside. Red, we knew by now, stood for the enemas, given from a red water bag. When she now began to re-enact enemas again with doll and cup, and did it incessantly for weeks, we could not help feeling, "Not again!" But from long experience we had learned that she knew what she was doing and that no progress would come unless we followed her lead; so good sense won out over temporary exhaustion.

Eventually we were rewarded. In the past, each time we had tried to talk with her about feeding experiences she had introduced the enema experience. Now began tentative efforts to do it the other way around.

The white inside of the cup represented the breast. Just as the enemas had superimposed themselves on the feeding experience and were all one could see from the outside, so this cup was entirely red from the outside. But within this cloaking experience was hidden and contained those still earlier ones; the disappointment in her mother and in life, as represented by the inner white of the cup.

As so often before, she had to act out a problem before she could understand its meaning: so now she had to violently attack what stood for the mother before she could understand the nature of her anger. For this she selected a play doll that became "mommy" and this doll she banged around, then beat up, and finally tore its head off, saying over and over how good it felt to bang mommy around.

Repeatedly her aggressions were interrupted by denial and guilty anxiety. Each time after mistreating the mother, she called the baby doll a bad baby, and said the mother was a good mother. When asked what was wrong with the baby, Marcia said, "Her mouth." And when asked what was the matter with the baby's mouth, she said, "Drinking up a bottle." Once more came the old confusion: having a bad mouth must have been the reason for both—for why she was fed so unpleasantly, and why things were forced into her mouth and her rectum. But it was also a bad mouth because it had wished to devour not only the milk but the whole breast ("drinking up a bottle").

We had known all along that for some reason her mouth and any doing with it was taboo, and how difficult was every experience around her rectum. But now she could tell how she felt that both these body openings were bad, and could finally recognize and say that of the two, the anus was not as bad as the mouth. Only with this realization could Marcia, who had so angrily acted out the enemas, *say* how much she had resented them. So taboo were words, so much more dangerous were words than deeds—or any doing with the mouth than all other doings.

Now as she acted out the enemas with the dolls she would also scream, "*Don't like enema!*" over and over and over, with intense emotion.[17] But when exhausted by this verbal assault against enemas, she would suddenly say, "Give me a bottle."

From the very beginning Marcia had always kept us waiting interminably, for everything. Now she spoke about it as she complained that bad mothers (the play dolls) were mean. Asked how they were mean, she said about twenty times, "Wait, wait, wait, wait, . . ." At first we didn't quite know what to do with this important information. But then, in response to the question, "Didn't they feed you right? Is that why they were mean?" she repeated many more times, and with violent anger, "Wait, wait, wait. . . ." So behind the resentment of forced feed-

---

17. It was the first time that she was free enough in the use of language to use a contraction like "don't," but for some time to come this usage appeared only when strong emotions were involved. Otherwise language did not flow freely enough for such liberties.

ings and enemas stood the deeper and earlier resentment about the mother's having kept her waiting for any ministration, and above all in the anxious waiting to be fed.

We do not know if the mother really kept her waiting, and if so, how much of it was because of the miserable situation that prevailed at this point in Marcia's infancy. What counts is that for Marcia the waiting was a devastating experience.

Nor is the wish to devour the breast so unusual; likely as not it is universal at a certain age. Every infant feels some separation anxiety, feels the wait is too long. He wishes to devour the breast because then he will have an unending supply of milk and will never again have to go hungry, have to wait. What makes the difference is the mother's reaction, her feelings when she finally reappears. It is her pleasure in offering the milk that reassures him the wait was just as hateful to the mother; that the pleasure both experience now, means that separations will always end in a happy reunion. And only the happy ending wipes the experience clean of anxiety.

What is the difference, then, between separation anxiety—which seems to be man's basic anxiety, and which only later comes to be felt as a fear of destruction—and the anxiety that leads to autistic withdrawal? I believe it is the infant's correct reading of the mother's emotions when she reappears: that the reunion is unwelcome to her; that she would rather it did not happen again. This is when separation anxiety turns to the certainty that one's nonexistence is wished for. With it, every separation becomes an experience of possible desertion and hence annihilation, a fate that only desperate efforts may possibly ward off.

Residues of this ancient anxiety still forced Marcia to distance herself from the original anger and its source. Hence much of the time she put all the blame on the milk. It was all the milk's fault that she was kept waiting so long to be fed; it was also the milk's fault that she was fed in such painful, unpleasant ways. Her dumping of milk and water as she had flooded our rooms long ago had been many things, but among them, her revenge on the milk.

Depersonalization had always been her blanket defense. If nothing worse than milk threatens one's life, one is reasonably safe as compared with believing one's mother is bent on one's destruction. Except that depersonalization did not stop with the mother, but extended to Marcia. Because if an infant's caretaker is not perceived as a human being, then neither can the infant grow to be one.

We already knew from Marcia that her twiddling and chin-tapping were related to sucking. Now, when we asked what she would like to suck, she said, "Inge"; and when asked where, she said the counselor's mouth. That anything good could come from a breast she still could not believe, but she was ready to be fed mouth to mouth. Unexpectedly, she added that to drink milk is "bad stuff." A toy dog was then accused of drinking milk and was viciously beaten on its mouth, after which came the revelation that chin-tapping had also stood for an abortive slapping of the mouth for its wishing to drink milk—or so it seemed at first.

Within a few weeks it was more than the wish to drink milk that the mouth deserved to be slapped for; it was also the powerful desire to bite. Against this she had long defended herself by not closing lips or teeth when she ate. Instead, food was put in her mouth in such a way that all biting was avoided.

Biting, according to Marcia, was "bad stuff." And what was the bad stuff she was so afraid she might do? "Eat Inge," she replied. Then, as if to justify such a desire, she added spontaneously, "Inge eats Marcia." We asked her, "When does that happen?" and her answer was, "bad." That is, when she felt bad, or did bad things (when she wanted to bite, to devour) then she felt she would be devoured in retaliation. For this reason she had had to put terribly strong restraints on herself to keep from doing what she wanted so much to do, namely to devour the mothering person.

It was not sucking alone that she wanted. When we told her she could suck candy or gum she rejected the notion as silly. "What so great about sucking candy?" she asked with disdain. It wasn't just sucking she was after; she wanted to have the breast, and she wanted to bite it. Some recognition of this desire began when she returned for a short time to shaking her finger in the old ways, not against the region of her mouth but near her counselor's breasts. When asked, "Why do you want to bite my breast?" Marcia's answer was, "All the time!" Meaning her desire was less to bite it, than to possess it. Just as she had *all the time* been preoccupied with what others had done to her (forced feeding, enemas), she herself had *all the time* been preoccupied with what she had wanted to have and possess. And if she could not have this, then she longed to bite and devour—in order to have and possess.

When asked why she was still hanging on to her preoccupation with enemas, she said, "For good stuff," meaning that she was trying to salvage something good from her bad experiences. When we told her it is most difficult to make good stuff out of bad stuff, but that she could look about in the world to find good stuff for herself, she for once happily agreed; she would give up thoughts about enemas for more enjoyable activities, like sucking honey. Unfortunately these were more often statements of intention than a true state of affairs.

In all her emotional world, in the totality of her experience, in her longing for "good stuff," she had encountered only people who seemed bent on her destruction. So she felt driven to destroy them lest they do it to her. All doing, hers and theirs, was nothing but a terrifying round of mutual destruction. No wonder the only solution she could hit on was a total not doing.

Still, she began to try to sort out which things were really bad. All of them had to do with feeding, since they were "bottle," "mommy," and "mouth." Then she said decisively that it was mommy's feeding the baby that was so bad. Breasts remained taboo as a topic. When referred to, Marcia responded with a barrage of private language we could not decipher. But though senseless to us it must have freed something in her, because for the first time when asked what was in the breast she replied, "Milk in it."

She then made herself a breast out of pink-colored clay, put salt on it and licked it off. For years she had poured salt on the flat of her hand and licked it off. (Thus in twiddling the hand she had expressed the wish for and fear of the breast while in the licking of salt and other food from the hand it had stood for the feeding breast.) Now at last she could give up feeding from a part of her body that represented the breast to feed from a symbolic one.

§

The Self Regained

Slowly she began to feel it was not both the baby and the mother who were bad; that the baby might have been good and only the mother bad. Next she began to accept that there might even be good mothers, and this good mother she tried to find in her favorite counselor.

In school she wrote the following story on her own and saved it for her counselor to see:

> Marcia saw Karen in the playyard.
> Karen likes Marcia. Marcia runs
> to Karen.

But when her counselor said, "Karen likes Marcia and Marcia likes . . . ," the answer was "Marcia." So basically she remained caught in her egocentricity, though she was aware of it. Because when asked what the greatest problem was she said, "people."

And only now did she more clearly see the origin of the chin tapping. When asked why she did it she said, "Because of sucking." She was finally ready to enjoy a pacifier and later to suck from baby bottles.

Here, as in many other situations when she took a step toward providing herself with much-desired satisfactions, she had to make

sure it was now she who was in command; that it was an active reaching out and not a passive receiving. So repeatedly she had her counselor
fill the baby bottle only to dump out its contents and refill the bottle
herself. After that she would twiddle the bottle by its nipple, much as
she had twiddled her hands, straps, and later other objects. Finally
she dripped the content of the bottle on her counselor's hands because
hands, as we now knew, had also stood for the breast.

This her counselor understood; also that Marcia probably wanted
to drip milk on her counselor's breast but was too afraid to. So the
counselor took the initiative and did it herself, saying that she knew
Marcia wanted to feed from her breast; that unfortunately she had
no milk there for her, and hence like all children whose mothers
cannot nurse their babies from the breast, she would have to make
do with a bottle. With such encouragement Marcia took the bottle her
counselor had offered her for sucking and in a determined move put it
in her counselor's mouth. When this was accepted with pleasure and
her counselor had drunk some, Marcia relaxed. But there were many
repetitions before she was satisfied with her active role in nursing.
Only then did she at last take the bottle from her counselor and
enjoy sucking from it while the counselor held it for her.

Here, too, it was a long time before she would drink from a bottle
containing milk. At first she spilled the milk out of the bottle onto the
floor, in a final repetition of her earliest water play of dumping water
on our floors. Then she was willing to suck fruit juice from a bottle,
and later water, until finally she could enjoy sucking milk, the first
food.

Having gained mastery of her earliest experience in life, and enjoyed it, she tried to become ever more herself. The most she had been
willing to admit up to now was that she was Marcia and that Karen
was Marcia, too. Now she could say what she had never compre-
hended before, when she told Karen firmly, "You are not Marcia."
The nonself was recognized as such. This nonself could now be dealt
with by appropriate emotions. When Karen told her she would be
taking a vacation, Marcia told her forcefully, and again and again,
"Go to hell!"

She became sensitive to the feelings of others. A little girl in her
group (Jean, the "playing girl"), was upset by Inge's vacation and was
making marbles appear and disappear with great anger. Marcia observed
this intently, and so was asked, "Why do you think she's doing that?"
and Marcia replied, "Inge go away." It was the first time she felt enough
interest in others to understand their emotions and actions. Of course,
the feelings were close to her own, since she too felt keenly the absence
of a counselor.

Toward the end of Marcia's fourth year, Karen got married and moved out of the School to live in her own home. Marcia was annoyed at Karen's husband because of the unacceptable idea that she would have to share Karen with him. But since there were few occasions when she saw him, including the wedding in which she participated, he did not trouble her much. Fortunately for her state of mind, though unfortunately for her grip on reality, what did not happen right in front of her eyes made little impression. Karen's husband and married life were largely invisible to Marcia, by design. And since Karen took care of her as before, the marriage had less impact than we feared. But probably our fears were fed by our wish to believe that distant events made a deeper impression on Marcia than they did.

Her jealousy of Karen's husband began around eating. Marcia was jealous of "Karen baking in the kitchen," that is, of Karen's feeding her husband in addition to Marcia. Actually, Marcia's interest in the husband was just a step toward exploring the depth where she had buried her image of that other man, her father, who had robbed her of her mother.

In play she acted out those early days when she felt so totally neglected that she withdrew. Moreover, during the time she felt that her mother gave her nothing, she had had to watch her taking care of the father. In play she ordered her counselor to act out how daddy was sick, and was put to bed. Then mommy came in to take care of him and fed him orange juice. When we asked her, "What about Marcia?" she put the baby doll in a chair and rocked it so violently that it fell out of the chair to lie helpless and neglected on the floor. In play she showed how her rocking had been an act of desperation, an effort to get something for herself as she was forced to stand by and watch her father receive what she wanted.

Then she acted out a fight between the mother and father. This, she said, made both daddy and Marcia sick, and then "Got mad at daddy." When asked what else happened, she said, "Marcia get sick." She was telling here about the connection between her father's sickness and her own.

Having acted out her father's illness, Marcia returned again to the intense anger at her mother. But this time she tried to go beyond a mere expressing of anger and for the first time took steps to get rid of it.

Through symbolic play she tried to do this by eliminating the mother out of her. The dolly that was Marcia had for years been fed and made to eliminate. Now in repeated games she was also made to vomit. True, Marcia had shaken water out of the dolly's mouth before, but this time it was clearly an acting out of emesis. Marcia herself called it vomit as she viciously pushed the dolly's stomach in until it spit up a stream of water, three or four inches in the air. When we asked, "What's the

matter with her?" Marcia replied, "She got a vomit." "How come?"
we asked, and Marcia told us she was, "Throwing up mommy." We
told her that was extremely interesting, but why was dolly throwing up
mommy? And Marcia said, "Cause she is a bad mommy." Later, as if to
explain, she added, "Marcia is a bad mommy."

And this in a way summarized what she was trying to understand,
to act out, and master: that the "bad" mother had taken possession of
her to such a degree that she had taken over all her inner functions as
she had taken "possession" of her elimination; that it was the bad mother
within who gave all the trouble, and whom she now tried to vomit out.

But expelling her from the mouth was not enough. She had to be
eliminated from all parts of Marcia's body, since she had taken possession of them all. So in a next step she said and acted out, "Marcia shitting
mommy." How did mother get into this part of her body, we asked,
and her answer was, "Shitting for mommy." Having been forced to take
in and eliminate as the mother required, she had lost all control of her
body and personality. Her total self had been replaced by the mother
who regulated the functions of her body and its inner workings. But
since she hated the mother for it, she could make no use of what had
taken inner and outer possession of herself.

This was no introject. Had Marcia introjected or incorporated her
mother, it would have been an act of volition and would not have shattered her self. Her tragedy was exactly that the mother was neither acceptable as an introject (because she wished Marcia out of the way),
nor did Marcia have the ability to introject her (because by regulating
Marcia's function, she permitted Marcia no action on her own). Hence
the bad mother, the bad object, was not incorporated but simply took
possession of Marcia. To do anything at all would have meant adding
to the power of the invader, so she did nothing at all.

Only now, after five years of struggle, could Marcia act on this.
Through all of her body openings, from all parts of her body, she got
rid of what had possessed her for so long. Having thrown it out should
have allowed her to build up a real self at last. But for the moment it
left her empty. Because the steps toward the building of a self that I
have just finished detailing were unfortunately no more than that: steps
toward a goal that was still out of reach.

§

Concluding Remarks

What, then, are significant steps in the personality development of
an autistic child under residential treatment? It has long been assumed

that the infant's relation to another, to the mothering person, must stand at the very beginning of human development. But our experience with Marcia, and with other autistic children, fails to show this is necessarily so.

Concerned caretakers the child does need for coming out of autistic withdrawal. To do that, to begin to do anything on his own, he needs at least one person who wishes to relate to him most positively. His needs must be met, his desires must be recognized, respected, and as far as possible satisfied. But even if we do all that and much more, such as providing comfort, stimulation, concern for him, and our company, what first emerges is a rudimentary self, not a relation to others.

In the normal course of events, that part of reality which first interests the infant is his mother. This tends to obscure the fact that it is not any relation to her but his own actions and her appropriate responses that spark an interest. It takes at least this interest in reality, plus the experience that one can do something about one's life, to set going the development of a self.

In Marcia's case this development of selfness came from her own body (elimination), and from the twiddling which to her was an extension of her body. One of the first steps she took in asserting her existence was her soiling. This was no present she gave us, anxious as she was, nor a step toward relating—but a stubborn, defiant self-assertion. Next, out of her autistic twiddling developed her first efforts to get something from an external reality (sand) when, to the kinesthetic sensation of shaking, were added new tactile sensations from the outside.

Each new achievement in mastery developed out of, and just a tiny step away from, the autistic position, while any frustration led to immediate retreat. Thus the self began with Marcia's recognition and active use of isolated aspects of reality. Yet to speak of a self is to conceptualize a state of being that preceded the ability to form concepts. It would be more correct to say that Marcia, who had been an autistic something, now became a somebody as she devised things to do on her own volition.

Only then did other beings enter her world. Characteristically this happened in a game combining flight with the search for a relation. In her simple chasing game, the adult had to pursue Marcia without catching her. There was no mutuality involved, and typically for autism, the little language Marcia had at this stage was not yet communication, but echolalia.

From this point on, as was probably true of what went on before, instead of finding a neat sequence of developmental steps we found quite the opposite: a simultaneous moving out in various, even contradictory directions.

There was the move toward positive object relations coupled with a mastery of the outer world. But along with it came aggression and symptom formation. When I say symptom formation I do not wish to imply that autistic isolation cannot also be viewed as a symptom. But it is such an all-encompassing one that I am reluctant to call it so. The symptoms I refer to deal with fairly discrete aspects of mastery or defense, ones she developed for dealing with particular problems, not with life as a whole.

It was only after Marcia began to try to solve problems that some real interest in another being emerged, and with it aggression and the ability for symbolic representation; that is, for true thought. It seems that once the individual begins to feel an interest in the world, he also grows attached to one or more persons because people stand out clearest from all that is not self. But then he begins to take further note of the world by turning his aggression against it. Or maybe it is all far more primitive. Maybe it is only after he can feel any attachment that he can feel any frustration coming from it, and hence become angry and destructive. Only as a human being persistently seeks the autistic child with his positive emotions does the child become interested in the external world. But once he does so, he is also open to frustration, whether from objects or human relations.

Again: it was only after Marcia had learned what it feels like to cling, to hold on to and manipulate a favorite person, that her pleasure led to further development of a self. Because at first she tried to retain the new pleasure without giving up her old isolation. Symbiotically she tried to merge with her counselor, to deny their separate existence. It was the very failure of her effort that enabled her to recognize reality; to see that the mothering figure was an entity, and she herself a separate person in her own right.

Thus personality development seems a dialectic process. As the human being reaches toward individuation, opposite tendencies emerge. Only as we give up some of our interest in ourselves and become interested in others does our own self develop in depth. As we begin to love some persons we start to be jealous, and hate others. It is only as the human being reaches toward greater comprehension of others that he becomes more of an individual himself.

By the time Marcia had reached this stage of development she was fifteen and a half years old. She had regained the full range of emotions, and formed a relationship of deepest emotional meaning. But her intellectual abilities were woefully inadequate for the richness of content she was now ready for emotionally. Her reading comprehension was barely that of a fourth grader, and a not very keen fourth grader. While it continued to grow, it was a very slow growth.

To have reached this level should have been heartening since Marcia had only begun at the preprimer level some three years before. But exactly because of the great emotional strides she had taken, she was terribly disappointed when her intellectual advances did not keep pace. Here her story resembles that of some of our other mute autistic children, whereas matters are very different for those who talk. While it seems possible to restore the mute autistic child to full emotional life, to make available to him his full libidinal energy, the same is not true for his grip on reality, for his ego.

At the start of this chapter I spoke of the biological time clock that seems to govern our physical maturation. I can now state that there seems to be no such time clock for the development of our emotions, but that there is one for the intellectual development that is based on those emotions. If the requisite emotional experiences are not available to the child before puberty sets in—that is, at the time when it is necessary for the unfolding of his full intellectual (or ego) development, then the ego remains stunted, even though he may catch up in emotional development later on. Or so it seems, until such time as we learn better how to circumvent this difficulty in treating autistic children.

Thus, unfortunately for Marcia, once the emotional potential for gaining a self was acquired, once she had assembled all important pieces toward the building of one and had readied herself by freeing the self from the nonself, it was too late. She could no longer change this potential into fact.

My purpose in telling her story was to show how the separation from the nonself led to the emergence of a self, and there it must end for the moment.

How well would Marcia hold on to those gains she had made? We cannot be certain, but there were straws in the wind.

Inge, the first person who became important to Marcia at the School —who helped most in her first steps toward unfreezing and with whom she played the first chasing game—married and left the School some five years after Marcia came to us. Karen, who was Marcia's mainstay in life, left two years later. In both cases, but more so of course after Karen's leaving, Marcia went into mourning for a time. We feared she might lose much of all she had gained, when Karen left, but such was not the case. While she was depressed for some three months, and came out of the depression by being quite aggressive, even assaultive, it ended very soon. She emerged after some six months with hardly any loss and resumed her making of small gains. This gave us hope that if we were to close our work with her, she would be able to make the transition to living with her parents without serious loss in her development. By this time her parents had become very different people, deeply concerned for her and ready to offer her the sheltered life she needed.

Our hopes for her, for the results of our work, may have been unrealistically high. It seems cruel that what we could do for only slightly younger children we could not do for her. But at least she had reached a stage where a sheltered life outside of an institution was a real possibility, and her parents were ready to provide it.

Marcia could perform simple tasks, could take care of herself and be useful in the home. She took good care of her clothes, her possessions, loved to work in the kitchen and the dining room. Most of all, this once totally frozen, nonreacting girl was now alive, full of feelings, and the appropriate ones. In Hardy's sense we had courted her when she had not cared greatly for life,

> . . . till evasions seemed wrong,
> Till evasions gave in to its song . . .
> Until living aloofly loomed duller
> Than life among men.

Joey

My joy, my grief, my hope, my love,
Did all within this circle move.
A narrow compass.   EDMUND WALLER

*During his years at the School, Joey was cared for by his devoted
counselors and teacher, Fae Lohn Tyroler, Louis Harper, and Barbara
Beachy, in about that order of importance. Chiefly to them, but also
to many other staff members, belongs the credit for his improvement
and for the observations on which this report is based.*

THE VERY FIRST DESCRIPTION of an autistic child tells how, in his
second year of life, "he developed a mania for spinning blocks and pans
and other round objects," and how later on he so disliked tricycles and
similar wheeled vehicles that he seemed to "have almost a horror" of
them [Kanner, 1943]. Since then the fascination with things that turn
about themselves has become one of the characteristics that permit us
to diagnose infantile autism. This circle in which the children endlessly
turn is the smallest and worst of all possible worlds. But at least it rotates around them, is their own. Moving beyond it, even on a tricycle,
is to court destruction.

Unlike Laurie and Marcia, Joey was a talking autistic child. That is,
he had speech, though he did not communicate. While both girls had
to learn how to strive for some autonomy, Joey had never wholly given
up the struggle. Since the world he found did not grant him even a small
measure of autonomy, he created a separate, unique world of his own.

If the world of human warmth was closed to him so that to feel was to be hurt, he would create one where feelings had no place. But since things do happen, it had to be a world where they can happen without feelings being involved. It had to be a world of machines.

Elsewhere [1960] I have discussed the fact that while all psychoses are due to conflict within the person, his specific delusions will reflect the hopes and anxieties of the society he lives in. Comparing modern delusions with those of the Middle Ages, for example, I suggested that even Lucifer was viewed as a person, though a distorted one. What is entirely new in the machine age is that often neither savior nor destroyer is cast in man's image any more. The typical modern delusion is of being run by an influencing machine.

Just as the angels and saints of a deeply religious age help us to fathom what were man's greatest hopes at that time, and the devils what he trembled at most, so man's delusions in a machine world seem to be tokens of both our hopes and our fears of what machines may do for us, or to us. In this sense Joey's story might also be viewed as a cautionary tale.

When we first met Joey he looked very small and fragile for his nine and a half years. He seemed all eyes in a painfully thin body, dark sorrowful eyes looking vacantly at nothing. If he did anything at all, he seemed to function by remote control—a "mechanical man," run by machines that were both created by him and beyond his control.

A human body that operates like a machine, and a machine that performs human functions—each of these is uncanny, the more so if the body we observe is a child's. This is specially eerie because a child seems closer to nature than adults, because childhood implies a process of unfolding, of natural growth, all of which is negated by mechanical behavior. And Joey was a child devoid of all that we see as essentially human and childish, as if he did not move arms or legs but had extensors that were shifted by gears. Nor was his the behavior of a decorticated, vegetating animal; on the contrary. Behind everything he did one felt tension and purpose but also a complexity beyond his grasp. Only these did not come through to us as human tensions and complexities. They were more like the tension we sense in a highly charged wire, or a steel cable strained to the breaking point.

In most ways Joey was typically autistic. But while he showed all the behavior we ascribe to that disturbance, even a complete catalogue of his symptoms would fall short of the true picture. Discussions of autistic children in the literature take as their point of departure comparisons with normal, or abnormal, *human* beings. But to do justice to Joey as he was when he came to us, and remained in his central features for the next couple of years, I would have to compare him simultaneously with a most inept infant and a complex machine. Often it took a conscious act of will to make ourselves perceive him as a child. Unless we held him in the focus of our attention, he escaped into nothingness. In the same way we are blind to pieces of machinery around the house unless we are using them and they whirl. This boy-machine was only with us when working; it had no existence when at rest. Though just an instant ago not "there," in the next Joey seemed a machine, the wheels busily cranking and turning, and as such held us rapt, whether we liked it or not.

Yet Joey was not so perpetually "nonexistent" as some of our extremely withdrawn or mute autistic children, nor as subhuman as other autistic youngsters who, because of their ferocity and wildness, have been likened to animals and called feral children. His was not a reduced human existence, nor an animal-like one. He was "real," all right, but his reality was that of machines.

There were the moments, for example, when a long span of nonexistence would be interrupted by the machine starting up, getting into ever higher gear, until its climax was reached in a shattering "explosion." This happened many times a day, ending with Joey's suddenly hurling a radio tube or light bulb that would splinter and burst with a crash. He had a remarkable ability to get hold of tubes or unscrew light bulbs before we knew what was happening. If one of these was not around then a bottle would do, or any object that was easily shattered.

Once the time had arrived to explode the world, this child who lived in utter stillness, mute and unmoving, would suddenly go beserk, running wildly and screaming, "Crash! Crash!" or "Explosion!" as he tossed a bulb or a motor. As soon as the thrown object had broken and the noise died away, Joey died with it. Without any transition he was back in his seeming nonexistence. Once the machine had exploded, no movement was left, no life, nothing at all.

During Joey's first weeks with us we watched absorbedly for example, as he entered the dining room. Laying down an imaginary wire he connected himself with his source of electrical energy. Then he strung the wire from an imaginary outlet to the dining room table to insulate himself, and then plugged himself in. (He had tried to use real wire, but this we could not allow; putting wire into real outlets endangered him, and the rest of us were apt to fall over the wires crossing the floor.) These imaginary electrical connections he had to establish before he could eat, because only the current ran his ingestive apparatus. He performed the ritual with such skill that one had to look twice to be sure there was neither wire nor outlet nor plug. His pantomime was so skilled, and his concentration so contagious, that those who watched him seemed to suspend their own existence and become observers of another reality.

Similar wires had to be laid down before he could sleep, play, read, and so forth.

Just as the infant has to make contact with his mother to be able to nurse, so Joey had to connect with electricity, had to plug himself in, before he could function. Electricity that seems to flow through the wire, he made run through his body. It connected him to a power source larger than his own, much as the child in his mother's arms becomes part of a larger circle, becomes connected to a larger source of energy.

Just as none of us wishes to come between nursing mother and child, is hesitant to break into their life sustaining circle, so children and staff took spontaneous care not to step on Joey's imaginary wires lest they interrupt the current and stop his being.

Even maids at the School, long inured to the many strange ways of our children made an exception for him, impressed by the appeal of his infantile fragility. His paper-thin body, with the ribs showing through and the lost, hungry look on the face, was strangely at odds with a megalomanic grandeur that he based on the power of machines. Occasionally some part of the complex apparatus fell down that Joey had fixed to his bed, making it a car-machine that would run him (or "live him") while he slept. This breathing machine he ingeniously created out of masking tape, cardboard, pieces of wire, and other odds and ends. Usually our maids, as they clean, will pick up such things and put them on a table for the children to find. But to Joey's machine, they carefully restored parts that had fallen because "Joey has to have his carburetor to breathe" (Figures 10–11).[1] It was a car-machine that powered him, and a "carburetor" that enabled him to breathe. In the same way they would carefully preserve for him the exhaust pipes through which he exhaled, or the motors that ran his digestion.

The children whose presence he lived in—because he could hardly be said to live *with* them—were protective, too. Though not always so cooperative, they moved carefully around Joey's things. Spontaneously they made room for his apparatus, even later when he had reduced it to a bare piece of cardboard. "Move over," they would say, "can't you see you're pushing Joey's transistor?" And they made way for a transistor Joey had fashioned out of empty space.

Here, then, was a robot, but a helpless one; because behind it all we sensed a total desperation. Yet often Joey's behavior not only froze our ability to react to him in a therapeutic but even in an ordinary way. It

1. Maybe a measure of our awe, and our rejection of the uncanny, shows up in our failure to take pictures of the most elaborate devices Joey created for running his body and mind. Only after this phase was in decline did we have sense enough to photograph them. Unfortunately they show the machinery that ran him at night in the very reduced form it had taken after a year and a half at the School.

FIGURE 10. Joey's car machine which powered him, including (at the foot of the bed) the carburetor that permitted him to breathe, and the motor that ran his body.

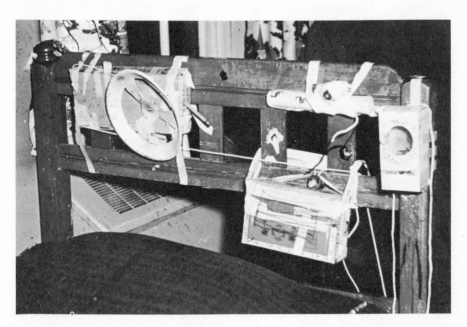

FIGURE 11. Closeup of the headboard of Joey's bed showing the wheel (left), the battery (lower center) that powered the speaker (right), and other parts of the machinery that ran him during his sleep. The "speaker" not only enabled Joey to talk but also to hear.

was as if in watching him and emotionally trying to join him in his mechanical world we lost some of our humanity ourselves; we could not even be companions for him in his autistic world.

That a schizophrenic child, particularly an autistic one, can create a vacuum around him, can wholly isolate himself in his delusions or empty preoccupations, is so well documented that alone it is hardly worth mention. But Joey had the added ability to hold the fascinated attention of those who watched him in his vacuum, to seduce them into believing him a machine.

Perhaps we acted in self-defense against so uncanny and dehumanizing an experience, and because even our best efforts to relate to him shattered on his machine-like existence. But all those who tried to befriend him, including his parents, ended up by providing this mechanical boy with the tubes and motors he seemed to need for his very existence and to crave more than human affection.

In retrospect it is easy to see what was so upsetting to us who tried to come close to him. All of us have feelings about how powerful our machines have become: in this nuclear age we have reason to fear that our own creations may destroy us. In Joey it was so blatant that this had already happened. Joey had lost command of himself to machines; he was living proof that our fears were not groundless. This is why, however strange his talk, his behavior, and later his drawings, they cannot compare in shock quality with what we experienced in his presence. It is why his delusions had an impact which we, accustomed to living with autistic children, had experienced with no other child. I cannot recreate it in writing. The best I can do is to say that watching him interfered to a serious degree with our ability to experience and relate to him as human beings.

Often the fascination was morbid, instead of the vital one so needed to reach him. It also belonged to the tantalizing question of what was the purpose of this machine, because it posed the unspoken anxiety of our age: do machines still serve our human purposes, or are they cranking away by now without purpose? Even more unnerving: are they working away for their own ends which we no longer know or control?

§

Early History

The conditions of life that made Joey decide to be a mechanical contrivance instead of a person began before he was born. At birth, his mother "thought of him as a thing rather than a person." But even before that he made little impression. "I never knew I was pregnant," she said, meaning that consciously the pregnancy did not alter her life. His birth, too, "did not make any difference."

Each parent had entered marriage on the rebound, in the wake of a frustrated love affair. In the mother's case, she had loved a man who had only recently died in air combat (World War II). Each parent had suffered deeply from strong emotional attachment to a friend they had lost, and each decided that a reasoned choice would now help. Though less exciting, it was less painful and hence safer to risk.

Both parents had had difficulties in growing up. The mother's adolescence had been stormy. At one time she refused to go to school, had no friends, and lived in trepidation of fainting spells. Her mother took her to a psychiatrist and though the girl discontinued treatment she was able to return to high school where she did well in her final years.

Joey's father too, had difficulties in high school, where he often skipped school. But once away from home in boarding school he did well, as he did later in college, in the army, and still later in his professional life.

What the young couple wanted most out of marriage was forgetting their private, unshared hurt. They were not able as yet to give each other true comfort so they tried to distract themselves from past unhappiness and from the hardships of a wartime existence by a hectic social life. The mother's pregnancy was not allowed to interfere. Delivery was easy, and motherhood itself made little difference, since Joey "was a good baby." Or more correctly, the mother did not let it make an impression on her.

Neither parent was psychologically ready or prepared for a child. But neither were many other parents, particularly in some of the army-post marriages, of which this was one. Fortunately, most parents begin to change as soon as the baby is born. But not in Joey's case. On the contrary, while the mother had, in a way, enjoyed the thought of becoming a mother, of having a baby who would make her less lonely, once the child was born she was terrified of the new responsibility. Frozen by the anxiety that she would make a poor kind of mother, she wanted nothing to do with the infant. In self-defense her emotional investment went into binding this anxiety. What she then told us should be viewed not as indifference to her baby but as what it cost her to maintain herself in a crisis.

In the hospital, after Joey's birth, she did not want to see him. "I did not want to nurse him. I had no feeling of actual dislike—I simply didn't want to take care of him," not out of neglect, but because she felt he was more than she could manage. Thus he was received in this world with neither love nor rejection nor ambivalence. Out of sheer anxiety he was simply and completely ignored.

In the hospital Joey did well, but once at home things changed. For the first three months of his life he "cried most of the time." He was a colicky baby, kept on a rigid four-hour feeding schedule, not touched unless necessary, not cuddled or played with. While he was strong and healthy at birth, he soon became a violent head-banger, swinging his head rhythmically back and forth, and from side to side.

At this point the father was transferred to another post and the mother moved in with another army wife. Anxieties and tensions continued to mount, partly due to the parents' relations to each other, and partly because of the war. The mother became physically exhausted and preoccupied with herself, leaving Joey alone in his crib or a playpen most of the time. After a few months she rejoined her husband, but there was no relief from inner tensions or the uncertainties of the war. This, and the mother's poor health (she said she had been "walking around with pneumonia for some time") made for what the parents described as "the most difficult time for both of us." Often the father's irritability was discharged against the infant; his crying at night was met in a punitive way. Then the father left for overseas duty.

After his departure the mother took Joey, now a year and a half old, to live with her in her parents' home. On arrival, the grandparents noted a marked and ominous change in the boy. They were concerned with his remote behavior, which compared unfavorably with an earlier responsiveness to them. He was entirely preoccupied with machinery, most of all an electric fan that his parents gave him at age one. This he could take apart and put together again with surprising deftness. His interest was explained by the fact that he had often been taken to the airport when his father was coming from or going on assignments and that these trips had a great deal of meaning for him. His interest in electric fans had first been aroused at the airport. The bizarreness of the toy and of such a focus of interest failed to startle the parents for years to come, as did the more obvious danger sign that Joey's speech was directed only to himself.

Given the parent's defensive distance from Joey, from each other and from life, we cannot wonder that little could be brought to light about his early years. But we learned something of how his originally normal language became autistic.

Living in such an emotional vacuum, Joey's language, step by step, became abstract, depersonalized, detached. He lost the ability to use personal pronouns correctly, later lost the use of them entirely. Certainly his case shows it is not inability but choice that leads such children to develop their autistic language. Since Goldstein [1959] and others have viewed infantile autism as an inability to engage in abstract thought, one example to the contrary should be cited from Joey's language development, though it happened in the idiosyncratic way that is typical of autism.

While at first Joey named foods correctly, calling them "butter," "sugar," "water," and so forth, he later gave this up. Instead he subsumed particular foods into new groupings but in doing so deprived them of their nutritive character. He then called sugar "sand," butter "grease," water "liquid," and so on. Physical quality took the place of nutritive quality because he was fed only physical substances and not also emotions. Thus he deprived food of taste and smell, and these qualities he replaced by the way they feel to the touch. Clearly he had the ability to engage in abstract thinking. It is also clear that in his transposing of names, as much as in the giving up of pronouns, the autistic child creates a language to fit his emotional experience of the world—which is an intellectual achievement. Far from not knowing how to use language correctly, there is a spontaneous decision to create a language that will match how *he* experiences things—and things only, not people.

When Joey was brought to the School, we talked at length with both parents. What impressed us about the mother, in addition to her "fey" quality and deep insecurity, was her marked indifference as she talked about Joey, her inability to see him as a person in his own right. This seemed more remarkable than any actual mistakes she made in handling him. Certainly he was left to cry for hours when hungry, because she fed him on a rigid schedule; he was also toilet-trained with great strictness so that he would give no trouble. But these things happen to many children who do not become autistic or remain so.

In the mother's recollections Joey was fused at one moment with one event or person, then with something or somebody else. She never knew if it was Joey or some other person who had done a particular thing. About other people and events she spoke with animation and clarity. But when the conversation turned to Joey, she immediately became impersonal, detached, and was soon unable to keep her mind on him, switching to other topics. When she told us about his birth and infancy, it was as if she were talking about some vague acquaintance, some person or event she had heard about and noted without interest. Soon her thoughts wandered away to other people, or herself. It seemed that Joey simply never got through to his mother.

True, by the time we talked with her, she had already told Joey's history to teachers, psychiatrists, and social workers. With repetition, much of the flavor of immediate experience would certainly have gotten lost. Yet the qualities we observed as she talked of him were the same that others reported about her years earlier, when Joey was four. At that time he was referred to a child-guidance clinic by a nursery school teacher who recognized that he needed psychiatric care because of his total isolation and obsessive interest in a single activity—twiddling. The clinic recognized Joey as an autistic child and he and his parents were accepted for treatment.

Psychotherapy helped the mother to realize how much she initially felt "trapped" in her marriage; how for years she had only thought she loved her husband while all her deeper feelings had lain dormant. She had been terrified at the mere thought of "letting go" of the rigid control she kept on her emotions. She felt numb, while "putting on an act" with other people. Often her thoughts turned to her former sweetheart and his death. Then she had anxiety attacks in which she felt she was coming "unglued" and was terrified of becoming "a mental patient." She sought forgetfulness in alcohol but neither became intoxicated nor found relief. During her years of therapy, and particularly after she was relieved of Joey's care because he lived with us, the mother recovered fully. The marriage became a good one and the parents raised two normal children, a sister six years younger than Joey and a brother thirteen years younger.

The father needed much less therapy. The changes it brought about in him, combined with the mother's improvement, were enough for both parents to achieve a good marital and life adjustment.

§

Outpatient Treatment

When Joey was four he entered a nursery school for emotionally disturbed children conducted by a University Child Guidance Clinic. There he also received individual psychotherapy. During his three years at the Clinic Joey made some progress though without ever freeing himself of his autistic attitudes.[2] Some of the observations made there should be recounted.

Joey was described as small for his age, a frail, ethereal looking boy with a faraway look. Most striking was his detached smile, directed at no one and unaffected by friendly overtures or any efforts at evoking a response. He paid no attention to his mother or to anyone else, moved about swiftly, and looked constantly at his hands which he gyrated like a propeller. He immediately discovered an electric fan and neither the children's efforts to draw him into their play, nor anything else, diverted him from the fan for a moment. When prevented from concentrating

2. A master's thesis written by his therapist, M. Monk, describes events of these years in detail.

on that, he "breezed" through the spacious school grounds, gyrating his hand in front of his face while making continuous noises like an electric fan (or propeller). He was then not only the powerful propeller but also the aircraft it drove.

His term of therapy there was characterized by how repetitive his activities, how narrow his interest, and that he restricted it to things rather than people. His intense and obsessive preoccupation with fans ruled out all contact with reality. Nothing claimed his attention except what could instantly become a gyrating propeller, such as a shovel, a leaf, a spoon, or a stick. No encouragement could motivate him, for example, to use the gyrated shovel for digging, not to speak of playing with toys. Whenever he spotted a real fan or motor, not even his imaginary "propellers" could divert his attention. He could not be kept away from them, plugged and unplugged them, carefully examined the slowing down or quickening movement of the blades. He imitated with almost mechanical precision the variations in sound that accompanied various speeds. His grasp of the mechanics involved would have been remarkable in a much older child. He used such precise terms as "blade of a propeller," "fan belt," "spinner" (of a washing machine), and "governor" (on a record player).

When not preoccupied with imitating motors—or to put it as he experienced it, when *he* was not a whirling motor—he was often so frustrated that he went to pieces. Then he would throw dishes, pull down shelves to make them "crash bang," or turn his violence against himself.

His total lack of responsiveness to anything alive and his fascination with things mechanical formed a dramatic contrast. What is normally taken for granted in any therapeutic relation—that the therapist is there for the child—presented in this case a near hopeless problem. His orbit was so solitary that it seemed impossible to meet him as he circled on it, oblivious to all. Still, his therapist's skill and persistence over the years eventually brought her to his awareness. Later he even responded to her a little and added a few things to his severely limited repertoire of interests and activities.

While he never came out of his autism, he began after a while to use personal pronouns in reverse, as do most autistic children. He referred to himself as "you" and to the adult he was speaking to as "I." A year later he called his therapist by name, though still not addressing her as "you" but saying, "Want Miss M. to swing you."

Such talking in reverse, or in opposites, is not easy for a small child to do and further demonstrates his capacity for logic. It is not easy to talk consistently in opposites, to do quite well in getting across what is wanted, and never once make the "mistake" of using pronouns correctly. Shortly before his treatment there ended he was able to use the "I" correctly, and to name some of the children in addition to his therapist. But he never used names or personal pronouns in direct address, only in the indirect third person, when referring to them.

Despite such progress Joey never played with other children. Only during the last year, when he was six, was he at least aware of them enough to express extraordinary hostility, or to forecast their coming doom.

Unfortunately, he had then reached the age limit of the Clinic nursery school and much of his progress was lost during the following two years which he spent at a rigid denominational boarding school. There he gave up using personal pronouns, and referring to anyone by name. His world which had begun to be humanized in the therapeutic setting of the nursery school became entirely depersonalized again. Clearly the nonuse of personal pronouns, or what Kanner terms pronominal reversal, has nothing to do with innate disabilities, but with how the child experiences the world and himself within it. Things went from bad to worse until eventually Joey stopped talking to anyone except his mother, and then only in a whisper. Subject to the repressive system of the boarding school, he worked out new and very crippling compulsive defenses, which he called his "preventions." It was at this point that the machines expressing his fears and desires took over.

Since human beings had failed him, machines were now his protectors ("preventions") and controllers. Since human beings did not "feed" his emotions, electricity would have to do it. Since he felt excluded from the circle of humanity, he plugged himself into another circle that nourished—the electrical circuit. Under no circumstances, now, could he eat unless in touch with the table. He had to sit on a piece of paper, pressed against the table, and his clothing had to be covered with napkins. Otherwise, he later told us, he was not insulated and the electric current would leave him. That is, if the life-giving circuit was broken and no energy flowed into his body, how could he eat? He could not drink except through elaborate piping systems built of straws. Liquids had to be pumped into him (or so he felt). Therefore he could not let himself suck. These and other debilitating preventions controlled and interfered with all areas of living.

His condition worsened so that he could not be kept in the boarding school and had to wait at home until he could come to the Orthogenic School.

Even in his now severely limited talk, deterioration set in. First he began to avoid saying "Mommy" or "Daddy" but would spell them out, telling his mother, for example, to "tell D-a-d-d-y that. . . ." Later, he would merely tell his mother to "ask 'him' if. . . ."

By talking only to his mother and in a whisper, he had tried to force her to pay close attention to him; but it did not bring the closeness he craved. Things got so bad during the final three months that he made a serious attempt at suicide. Being home all day where he could see his baby sister getting all the things he yearned for, drove the cycle of his desire and his anger to the breaking point. Life itself became unbearable, and flooded by destructive rage he tried to get rid of it. Once more he learned that to feel is to be destroyed; that only if he were totally un-feeling could he survive. Since he would still have to act, he had to be sure it was an unfeeling thing that took action, a machine. And as such he came to live with us at the School.

§

Rotating Blades

The airport origin of Joey's interest in fans and the fact that rotating blades were prime in his obsession with things mechanical suggest the extreme importance of his visits to the airport. This raises an interesting psychological problem. If attachment to his father gave propellers their exclusive importance, how could this obsession kill all interest in people, including his father? Also, obsessions defend the person against deep anxiety. The more sweeping the obsession the greater, we can assume, the anxiety it binds. Thus, despite the propellers' and the airport's direct link with the father, we cannot believe it was the father as a person who caused Joey's obsession.

While his initial experiences must have had to do with persons, they must have been so agonizing that to survive them at all he had to deper-sonalize them; only in this form did they seem open to mastery. Of course they are not, because the farther we remove ourselves from an experience, the less we can understand it or master it. But how is an infant to know that, when so many adults do not? Joey's emotional experiences must have been devastating, and he could do nothing about them. In some way, perhaps by chance association in time or space, ro-tating objects (propellers, fans) became connected with these experi-ences and came to stand in their place. This can easily happen when the child is very young; when he is not able yet to separate the essential from the accidental in what to him is a total experience; and when he has strong emotional reasons for taking the insignificant part for the whole.

A fan was something Joey could take apart. He could put it together again. He understood it. He was not as helpless about that part of the experience as he was about the experience in toto. If the fan could stand for the total experience, if machines could be as totally important as his parents, could even stand for his parents, maybe he could understand and master the experience itself.

What I have tried to describe here deductively can only have been vague and amorphous thoughts overwhelmed by feelings in a child of one year or one and a half. But they may have driven him more powerfully than any reasoning might. Because reasoning presupposes much experience; hence it can never engross our whole life. Strong emotional reactions in early life can do that because they do not compete in their impact with all other experience. If Joey's reactions at the airport were those I suggest, it might explain what set him to translating his experiences with people into those related to machines. As to what, in his experience with human beings, was so painful and threatening, we can only speculate.

Perhaps take-offs and landings aroused strong feelings in the mother, some belonging to the death of the man she had so deeply loved, others to her anxiety about the father's arrivals and departures. In any case, these machines could stir emotions in the mother that Joey had no power to evoke. If he had their power or magic maybe he too could arouse his mother's feelings. Here, then, was an infant, not attached in mutuality to any person, craving response to his existence, and exposed to thundering noises, vibrations, and the deafening air blasts of propellers which at one time (on departure) caused deep anxiety, at another (arrival) great joy. They could do what he could not.

The emotions these blades could create—rotating or at standstill—were at once mysterious, overpowering, and contradictory. The noise of the air blast literally shook him up, as the emotions he directed at his parents should have shaken them but failed to do. At one time these propellers created anxiety, at another relief. If one and the same thing has the power to project us into great joy or deepest despair and if, because of the parents' detachment toward Joey, nothing else does, then this infernal machine is indeed what regulates human emotion. Hence the fascination with rotating blades, the need to understand them and perhaps in this way to acquire their power (the holding on, taking apart, and putting together of the fan). When all this failed to bring the relief that only an adult's love can give the small child, Joey may have sought control of these machines through a psychological maneuver known as identification with the aggressor. And aggressors these explosive noises were, since they reached deep into Joey's inner life where they shook him with the violence of his contradictory feelings.

The explosive noises of the airplane engine may have been the prototype of the violent "explosions" that so characterized Joey's first years with us. The depressive withdrawal that immediately followed any "explosion" suggests how great the "explosive" tension that preceded the noises at take-off or landing, and how it left him disappointed and empty once the airplane had taken off or landed and the hoped for emotional response did not come. In his parents, too, emotions may have been building up to high pitch until the moment of departure—and in the mother up to the moment of arrival. Perhaps it was her feeling of emptiness, once the excitement was over, that gave Joey the pattern of build-up and sudden letdown that he later reproduced in his "explosions."

Did the father's final departure for overseas duty put an end to the only situation that offered Joey at least the tangible involvement with reality he knew at the airport? Or had each successive arrival or departure been a trauma reinforcing the one before? Or perhaps the airplane propellers that initiated flight came to stand for an end to tension and human rejection. Were they symbols of escape from the suffering in all human relations and reality itself? All these are possible clues for explaining Joey's fascination with fans and electrical energy (which starts up propellers).

It all happened too early, during the first eighteen months of life and before emotional experience can be put into words, for any closer decoding of the messages in Joey's behavior. But we can be sure that even all the excitement of the airport, the sudden roar of the planes and the stillness that followed, could only exert their deep impact on an otherwise vacuous life; such events could only take on their excessive emotional meaning in an otherwise torpid existence. Only by comparison with the "unreality" of his parents could machines become more important than people.

Joey attached himself to machines because they offered the more significant experience. Though dangerous, they were at least tangible. More important for his efforts to gain autonomy, they were predictable: they started up with a roar, and when they stopped, all the roaring stopped too. At least they were tangible compared with the "fey" quality of his mother and her aloofness from Joey. Even when he invested himself in a fan, this message, too, was not received because of the parents' disinterest; just as little mutuality developed around it as around anything else. Since the mother offered no fertile soil for any tentacles of response to take hold, perhaps they attached themselves to things strongly invested with feeling by those around him, such as airplanes.

Given the infant's startle reaction to loud noises—which in the case of airplanes would drown out every other experience—perhaps the motors and their explosive noise came to stand for all complex feelings, and the fan blades for their symbols. Added to this, Joey had heard from an early age on about the dangers of flying, which made these machines seem to hold the power of life and death. (Hence the exclamation "Crash! Crash!" that accompanied his "explosions" and referred both to his crashing of light bulbs and the crash of a plane.)

Joey's experiences at the airport, and all others connected with them, may explain his selection of a fan and of explosive, electrical motors as a way of conveying the central need of his life: to be able to reach out to others with a request that they listen to and understand his needs. This above all is where he needed help.

Obviously the airport experience alone is not enough to explain Joey's fascination with rotating machines. As suggested earlier, a preoccupation with rotating objects is typical for many autistic children but not all of them were given fans or taken to airports. Circling objects must have a deeper meaning. They must be particularly suitable for expressing something that typifies the disturbance in general. I believe it to be that they circle around and around, never reaching a goal.

Rather than speculate further I prefer to rely on Joey's comments to us on a visit some years after he left us. At that time he told us what we had only guessed up to then: that for him the very shape of these rotating objects suggested the circle he was helplessly caught in. They represented the vicious circle of longing and fear, of wanting so much from others and of being mortally afraid to let his longing be known, either to them or himself.

There was something else that belonged to the vicious circle Joey moved in: a great anger. Had he permitted himself to feel his anger it would have flooded him, perhaps beyond repair. Had he vented his anger against those who aroused it, he feared they might have hit back or deserted him, and he would have perished.

I have said before that I believe all childhood psychoses, but particularly infantile autism, can be traced to the child's conviction that his life is in mortal danger. Short of this conviction one simply does not erect such wholly debilitating defenses. As long as there is hope for a life, one does not shut it out altogether. Only when life itself is in question does withdrawing from the world seem the necessary price of sheer survival. As long as an animal hopes that fight or flight will save him he does not play 'possum.

If one wished to extrapolate from Joey to other autistic children who use rotating objects to state where they most need our help, one might say that to them the turning objects represent a vicious circle that goes from longing to fear to anger to despair, and comes full circle again when the longing has started up anew.

The child longs for mutuality. He wants to be part of a circle consisting of him and his parents, preferably with him as the center around which their lives revolve. This the autistic child states in his back-and-forth rocking and his circling. But the more desperately he longs for mutuality the more his anger mounts that it never comes. This anger must be contained, or it might destroy him. So, in a vicious circle, he endlessly turns to longing again and thence to anger, until exhausted, he surrenders all hope and no longer rotates anything. The back-and-forth twiddling of Marcia, and the tearing round and round of Laurie, represent the same desire for and fear of the breast; they are thus more primitive precursors of the rotation of objects. But they represent the same desire for and fear of mutuality.

This may explain the meaning Joey found in rotating objects, particularly fans. Or as a recent report tells us, one autistic boy's "interest centered around wheels and windmills" and he was "preoccupied with the spinning of round objects. . . . His mother explained this as 'turning himself on and off like a machine'" [Alpert and Pfeiffer, 1964]. But while many other autistic children are fascinated by rotation and things mechanical, they are not reported as needing to plug themselves in, nor do they believe they run only on electrical current. So while electricity runs rotating machines and may be part-explanation for Joey's convictions, it cannot be the whole story. While the electrical circuit is indeed a circle, the meaning of electricity in his case must have been overdetermined.

Electricity provides us with warmth and light, both of tremendous importance for our well-being and survival. As we learned later, these were very important in Joey's reliance on electrical power, though not of central importance. But electricity is also power. So if electricity also powered emotions, powered the vicious circle of longing and anger, and if this circle was all there was to Joey's life, then it did indeed power his life. And if it did all that, couldn't it also provide what he so deeply needed, what for want of a better name I might call sustenance through love? If electricity provided so much that we normally look to from a mother, why not expect all the rest from it too? Then, to "plug himself in" was to connect himself to the flow that sustains life.

That these speculations have some validity we learned from many things Joey told us after we had known him more than a year and a half. By this time he was constructing his own machines instead of relying on commercial equipment, though it led to moments of desperation if things did not work. Thus he told us one day that his machine was not working because a fuse had burnt out. This meant the current was broken and power had stopped coming through on the wires. His counselor offered to help repair it and then added spontaneously, "Do you want to take some candy or gum till it starts up again?" Joey's response showed that he felt she had just said something sensible and meaningful. Because he reached over, took some candy, and then glanced at the machine saying, "Now the wires are okay." Being fed with love, the vital energy flowed in. He was connected again.

Joey's "preventions" show that he went much further than either

Laurie or Marcia in building up an inner world of specific anxieties and complex defenses against them. His personality was far more differentiated than theirs. And while he did not really communicate with others, he had perfect command of language, knew even difficult technical terms and understood their meaning. For all these reasons, rehabilitation for him could not consist of a single main stream, flowing out of his autism toward human relations and the growth of a richer personality.

At one time, one aspect of his private ideas stood in the center of his slowly joining a world common to him and to us. At another time an entirely different one took its place. None of these efforts proceeded smoothly or in any logical order. Certainly they did not come in any orderly time sequence, of taking up one problematic issue, resolving it, and then turning to the next. Therefore to present his story as it proceeded in time would have made confusing reading.

Instead, a number of main threads in his development are taken up, one at a time, and followed through for varying stretches of time. This means that the reader may learn of a "prevention" Joey was able to give up, only pages later to read about Joey in a different context, but a point in time where this defense was still in full force. It means that the reader will have to rely on his own empathy with Joey to relate to each other the lines of development I describe here in relative isolation. Most of all, he will have to reconstruct in his mind how the care Joey received, and the trust it engendered, kept the whole growth process going.

I chose such a course because I felt that more could be learned from the three histories I selected for presentation if each one stressed what was peculiarly instructive about the development of that child. Thus in "Marcia," for example, I felt there was most to be learned from a chronological account in which the interplay of experience and achievement, of treatment and progress, was made as evident as possible. To repeat that for Joey seemed of less value than to concentrate on the deciphering of one autistic system to the point where its analog in familiar human needs could be recognized, in order then to be satisfied.

§

First Days at the School

Joey arrived at the Orthogenic School with his host of preventions full blown. All those attachments that belong normally to human beings (in a child's case, most of all to his parents) Joey had invested in machines. As soon as he entered our doors, violent explosions took place— of tubes and emotions. But when the time came for his parents to leave, he gave no sign of feeling. For about his first year with us his face wore an expression of total blankness, except for the moments of extreme involvement and violence during "explosions."

A first fleeting crack in the armor came on his third day, when we gave him a teddy bear. Taken by surprise he showed a momentary delight. But our hopes of pleasing him with other presents turned out to be empty. He was on guard now, and for months nothing we tried brought another positive emotion. Maybe his pleasure in the teddy bear faded so quickly because he knew he could never hold on to it without giving up some of the tubes and the heavy motor he carried. We tried, as a compromise, to have the counselor carry the motor while he carried the teddy bear in one hand and the tubes in the other. But by the time he had shifted things around he was back to a total absence of emotions and had lost interest in the toy.

During those first months we tried hard to reduce the frequency and violence of his "explosions" and his aggression toward other children. We tried to direct them against us, hoping at least for an aggressive relation to us which we could then change to a more positive one. Mostly he tried to throw things at other children. Though it showed some kind of interest in them, we had to stop it for their protection.

We tried to find ways for him to act up in ways less dangerous and exhausting. But his preoccupation with machinery made it very hard to reach him on purely practical grounds. If he wanted to do something with a counselor, such as play with a toy that vaguely caught his attention, he could not do so because first he had to turn off the machinery in a complicated process. By the time he had filled all the requirements of his preventions, he had also lost interest. When offered a toy, he would say in the most languid tones, "To play with this would be perfectly delightful," but he could not touch the toy because his motors and tubes left him without a hand free. Thus, even our offering to play with him was only an added frustration.

All our play equipment he "transformed" into threatening, destructive machinery. Our swings, for example, were wrecking machines. There, or on the jungle gym, he spent hours making noises like machines, and if one didn't look one would have thought a machine was ticking away close at hand. How dangerous these machines were could be guessed from the names he gave them, such as "skull cracker."

Many colors were dangerous and rendered things taboo because they endangered life, either his life or others': "Some colors turn off the current; no one can touch them, because no one can live without the current." Or, "This color is almost black; it will explode the dormitory."

His depersonalization was reflected not so much in an absence of personal pronouns or names, as in their being too dangerous to use. To mention names, or to say certain words, he admitted months later, was very dangerous. Whatever name we tried to call him by, his own or some affectionate term, evoked immediate terror; that, or if anyone wrote him a message addressed with his name. Personal pronouns he would not use. As mentioned before, he had twice given up the use of the "I"—once, before he entered the nursery school, and again during his stay at boarding school. If one has twice struggled to see oneself as a person and had to give up, it does not come easy to try again. But not feeling himself a distinct person, no one else seemed a distinct person either.

He never referred to anyone by name; others were simply "that person"; later, with some differentiation, "the small person" or "the big person." In his nonpersonal world things happened, and people were described or ordered, according to size.

At first he let nobody join him in anything; later the best we could expect, and only when he felt somewhat good about himself and us, was an oblique suggestion that one of us should care for, or serve his machines. Eventually, but very rarely, this included himself. He would then tell the air, making sure he spoke to no one in particular even if only one other person were present: "The person should go away," or "The big person should tell the small person not to touch the tubes." It infuriated him to hear anyone use the word "grown-up" not to mention "adult," instead of the only safe term, "big person." Later, when in much better contact, he told us never to say "grown-up" or he would stop talking to us altogether. Similarly, he was unable to give its true name to anything he felt strongly about.

In class he would do no reading for more than two years unless he could skip the word "father" when it occurred on the page. For other dangerous words he used neologisms that he changed constantly if he thought we had caught on to their meaning. When I speak of Joey's reading, the impression might be that he took up a book like any other child. But this was not so. There was nothing he could do unless powered by machines. Before beginning to read, even before he could sit down, he had to connect up his desk to a source of energy. Then he had to plug himself in, plug his book or pencils into the desk, and then tune himself in.

Often he complained that "not enough power was coming in," as if to express that while physically all was well, not enough emotional energy was coming in from us to risk the dangers of reading. If things were not just right, he became terribly angry at himself, would try to jab a pencil in his hand. For the first two years he would only read a word or two at a time. Eventually he would read a phrase, then stop for a while as if collecting enough energy for the next one. Nothing ever flowed smoothly.

Objects, on the other hand, particularly controlling parts of machinery such as motors or tubes, had a life of their own, had names that did not change, had even feelings. Later on he began to warn us about impending explosions so that we could act to relieve his anger or distress, either by comforting him or by removing the light bulb before he threw it; then he might say, "That light bulb is going to have a temper tantrum." This was not simply a reversal between people and things to avoid punishment for his own behavior. It was the logical consequence of his being dead, and of tubes and machines having the full life that had died within him.[3] Having feelings, these tubes also suffered. They "bled" when they were hurt, and sometimes got sick. The reversal between him and objects was persistent. This remained true for Joey even at a much later time when he began to think that maybe some other persons had feelings. As he then put it: "There are live people and then there are people who need tubes."

It was not that Joey did not know a great deal about living things. He knew more about physiology than most children his age. But it was a physiology he ascribed to objects, endowed by him with life. One example from a later time may illustrate. Joey had been playing with a little bottle he misplaced and was now hunting for frantically in the school room. Eventually his teacher unearthed the bottle from beneath a wooden block on the table. As soon as Joey saw it he took the offending block and hurled it across the room.

For months now, day after day and many times a day, Joey had been creating his own frustrations this way. And each time, when his teacher tried to resolve the predicaments he got himself into, Joey responded by throwing things around, or else himself. This time, however, the teacher was out of patience and picked up the block saying, "Look! This block cannot move. If you put it down on the table it cannot get up and walk away; it cannot hide something under it. This is one of the blocks you were playing with." Joey looked at him in amazement—because of the unexpected demand that he should see things our way. Still, because of the many times his teacher had accepted Joey's view of things, had helped him straighten things out as Joey felt they

---

3. The difference between infantile autism and other severe types of primary behavior disorders of childhood may be illustrated by a comparison between Joey, with his mechanical world void of human beings, and Harry, a boy who might have been classified as schizophrenic because of the severity of his paranoia and delusions. Even at his most delusional Harry (whose story I presented in 1949 and 1955) never doubted that the world was populated by human beings, though he could not reach them because they were all wearing masks that he could not remove.

should be, he was inclined now to stop and consider. At least his teacher's remark made him wonder for a moment, while he studied the block intently. Then he said with conviction, "It *can* move. The nerve impulses cause the muscle to move."

But there were also contradictions in Joey's system. While motors and tubes could thus feel and act, they were at other moments so much better off than man because they had no feelings and could not be hurt. Later, as Joey became more human it did not make his tubes less alive; it just meant he could better control them. They were then in pain because he had punished them for not taking care of him well. As he told us: "I used to break my tubes when I got mad. I let them lie on the floor, hurt them, stepped on them, made them bleed. I let them bleed all day."

Not only colors but many routine noises were dangerous since they amplified his tubes and made them "crimp at the end"; that is, made things explode. Most of our efforts to talk to him were sounds of this kind and for much of the first weeks he neutralized our voices with "Bam!", his most frequent reaction when spoken to. Unless he neutralized what we said there would be an explosion. This, however, was when we spoke to him. Things were different when talk originated with him. Then he was not mute, was often even voluble. Only his talk was entirely in the service of his defenses. Most of it was thrown out to the empty air, delusional remarks having to do with motors and tubes, neologisms or exclamations such as "Explode!"

At other times there was a pseudo-logic to his talk, as when he claimed that the wooden block had nerve impulses that caused its muscles to move. But for the most part he spoke so much in opposites, in private allusions, and with such erratic word order and usage that for a long time we could make little sense of what he said.

It was quite clear from the beginning that Joey's talking in opposites had purpose. Through it he asserted autonomy and was able to bind his anxiety about threatening things he felt he could not control. As long as his statements were as cryptic as the assertion that "Circles are straight. They are a straight line," it was hard to know what it was that he wished he could change or control. Later, when we understood how much he dreamed of a mutuality that seemed forever out of reach, even this statement began to make sense. If all circles are straight, then nobody was enjoying what he missed so much; it was not his personal fate, but a fact of cosmic law.

By contrast, we understood much sooner why he said things like, "You can't let me draw" as he sat there drawing away, or told us "Be quiet!" when we were both being silent. He was providing for himself the experience that on his own he could violate our orders.

If he continued to draw then his statement proved his drawing an autonomous act. And if we stopped him, it still did not threaten his autonomy; we were only stopping him as he told us to do. This was very important. Because short of his explosions, and the passive resistance of not giving out and not relating, Joey was for the most part excessively meek and compliant. This was not true where his preventions were involved, or when his motors gave him superhuman strength. But neither did that alter his weakness because the strength was not his but the machine's. To himself Joey was always debilitated, helpless. Hence the need and value of autonomy through talking in opposites.

Another advantage of talking in opposites is that one can talk of what is most on one's mind without saying what it is. One is then spared the disappointment of never getting what one craves most of all. Later, for example, when he had come to trust us quite a bit, he said, "Parents should be mean to children. If I were a parent I would kill my children. You shouldn't like me. You should do things to hurt me. You should beat me and be mean. You shouldn't do things I don't want you to do." By this last statement he meant that we should not treat him with tender care. By talking in opposites he could ask for what he wanted most without the risk of falling apart if he did not get it.

One of the first things Joey liked at the School was being bathed, though for a long time this too was a mechanical procedure. In the tub he rocked hard, back and forth, with the regularity of an engine and without emotion, flooding the bathroom. If he stopped rocking, he did that too, like a machine. Suddenly there was no movement at all, except for the water rushing past his rigid body. Whether rocking or absolutely still, his face showed no expression. Only once, after months of being carried to bed from his bath, did we catch a slight puzzled pleasure on his face and he said, in a very low voice, "They even carry you to your bed here." This was the first time we heard him use a personal pronoun.

§
A Curb on Tubes

It was around eating that we first interfered with the acting out of Joey's preventions, perhaps because we dimly felt that problems of intake at that time were less central to him. After a few weeks we got so tired of his bringing big motors, tubes, and electric wires into the dining room and of his being almost unable to eat because all space before him and around him was taken up by his paraphernalia, that it was here we first took a stand. It was not just that Joey was entirely encumbered by his gadgets, or that we were kept busy helping him carry them about and in their proper arrangement; it was that he could not have eaten if he wanted to. Whenever he seemed ready to take a bite, some little thing was out of place; or he had moved and the insulating paper had come loose and must be rearranged; and if this was righted, something else had no doubt gone amiss.

So we chose to risk not letting him bring more than a small tube or part of a motor to the dining table; no more than a token for the real McCoy. When we told him of our decision he was frantic, as we expected, and claimed he could not eat without them. But despite many shattering explosions we stood our ground. We felt that he ate so little at the table anyway that not much would be changed if he ate nothing there at all.

Our decision was eased by the fact that after a few weeks with us he let us hand feed him, mostly candy, of which he ate large quantities at night, hidden under his blanket. Later he carried a blanket with him and liked to eat at any time the candy and cookies we fed him while he was all covered up by the blanket. If our decision had proved too risky we could always have reversed it. But we felt that human preventions (our interference) were to be preferred; we hoped that by turning his anger on us he might become active in a human relation. There we overestimated his ability to interact with other human beings.

It soon appeared that to have his eating run by actual motors was not so important. True, he made a big show of being unable to eat without them. But once he realized that it did not make us anxious, most important, that we did not force him to eat—that is, did not "run" him—he began to eat without mechanical help. After all, his elaborate preventions around eating at the table had originated in the parochial school where he felt he had to guard against his very life (his body) being run by mortal enemies. If he was now run by machines they were at least partly in his control, since they worked only if he plugged them in. As we imposed no rules on Joey's eating, he could dispense with some of his preventions. By otherwise taking his machines seriously we gave credit to his chief way of asserting minimal autonomy. As if to stress that he had not given up these self-created devices, he simply relied on imaginary machinery for eating and connected himself to imaginary wires, as already described.

There were, however, two special preventions around eating that he did not give up: he could drink only through straws, and he could eat only in a "dining car." If he was contradicted about the dining room being a dining car, he would not eat. Why this need to eat only in a moving object and to drink only through a tube was not clear till much later.

Though we slowly restricted the use of his various apparatuses in other areas of living too, we could not remove them entirely before replacing them with human "connections." For a long time it was still hard to know at any one moment what Joey's tubes and motors meant to him, or whether they were benign or destructive in a particular situation. On a playground near the School, for example, is a very low slide that Joey liked to use. Eventually his weird grin and trembling lips showed that this was another of his dangerous activities, and we declared it out of bounds. As usual, he long and frantically objected until he was convinced our decision was final. Only then did he tell us it was not gravity at all that moved his body down the slide. At the top of the slide he had connected his tube to it with powerful electronics: this, plus electricity, pulled him down. Unfortunately, as he slid off at the end of the ride the circuit was broken and this "exploded" him.

Here, then, was another meaning of his explosions. As long as he was "plugged in" to what gave him life, the symbolic flow of current that stood for being connected, he was at least in contact with something. When this contact broke, when he lost his imaginary source of warmth and energy, then the anger at his actual isolation exploded, destroying him and all others who had once again deserted him.

After many months we dared to separate him from the motor he carried everywhere except to meals. Next, when we felt he had acquired some trust in our good intentions, we told him we would no longer replace broken tubes, and warned him not to "explode" those he had left, if he wanted to keep some. In this way we offered him a chance to hold on to them if he was really not ready to live without them. But his explosions continued and in two months all tubes were gone. He threatened horrible things if we did not replace them but again, when he was sure that all his pestering would not move us, he told us how much their emotional impact had ravaged him.

Slowly he began to admit that machinery and tubes also hurt him. Now there were good and bad tubes. It was a first bringing of human order into his inflexible world of machines. While before this all were necessary for survival and all were also destructive (as he needed his parents for survival, though their emotional impact had been ruinous), he now separated his tubes into ones that were helpful and others that damaged. While before this the world he lived in was "without form, and void; and darkness was upon the face of the deep" he now "divided light from the darkness." But it was not only a separation of darkness from light. Joey was beginning to know good from evil. And whoever does that is committed to live a human existence on earth.

Because if the world has good in it and not only bad, then it is worth exerting oneself to add to the good and to limit the bad. Which side, he now wondered, were we on? For weeks he now talked of how his parents let him expose himself to danger and that we had to do the same. And if we refused, it would not make any difference. Because when his parents came to visit they would get him the tubes they knew he had to have.

As we stood our ground, though his pleas became more frantic, he continued to tell us we were wrong and that only his parents understood his need for tubes, until one day he told us that his parents let him have "tubes with poison inside." From this realization it did not take Joey long to accuse them of being willing to let him get hurt. Always in his voice was a great admiration for them and desperation about himself. He admired them for their power (which the negligence proved); the desperation was for his own helplessness against it.

But our not budging made a difference to Joey, despite a more intense barrage than what led his parents in desperation to furnish the tools for his inhuman existence. It enabled him, a few months later, to ask us to protect him from a temptation he felt too weak to resist by himself. "You should keep the small person (Joey) locked up in the School. Otherwise the small person walks by shops that have tubes," he said with a note of deep helplessness and irritation. He then told us what we already knew: that he threw light bulbs or otherwise made explosions when he was very frightened, both at his helpless isolation, and his anger about it. So his explosions were statements about his state of mind. But they were also meant to arouse feelings in others. If we would not share his positive feelings he would force us to share his explosive fright and anger. Only it did not work. If we responded with positive emotions, we were totally out of tune with what he felt (that no one liked him). And had we responded with negative ones we would have added to his anger and anxiety.

For months he returned to his fear of and desire for tubes, each time bringing out more of his resentment at his parents. When he could thus voice his feelings he became enough of a person to use personal pronouns, which from then on he used freely and correctly. "If my parents were here, I would kill them; it's not the School that's bad; it's my parents' fault. If they were here and I had a fan, I'd put their fingers in it while it's whirling, and I'd cut them to pieces." This was the first indication he gave us of some of what lay behind the interest in fans of his earliest years. It may also suggest what destructive fantasies he may have had as he watched propellers whirl in his infancy.

Typically he could open up about his angry fantasies years before he could recognize their true source. He could tell about the fan as a tool of destruction; he could talk about how bad his parents had been to give him poisonous tubes; in short, of things his parents had done to hurt him.

But how long it can take to discover the longing behind the anger is suggested by the fact that it took several more years for Joey to admit to himself, and then to us, that in his mind the fault of his parents was not the bad things they did to him, but the contrary. That they had not even cared enough to do that.

One day, years later, he said he so often wanted to hurt himself because he was so angry at the world, particularly at his parents. Then he narrowed it down to his mother. He was so angry at her "because she didn't punish me for my angry feelings I had about her. I had to punish myself." It was as if he were complaining that his deepest anguish—of which by now he was fully aware—was that all his feelings, even of violent rage, had been nothing to her. It took still more years for Joey to recognize the desperate longing for her which, with his anger, made for the vicious circle of his life. The cause of such delay is that to admit anger is safer because it shows one's own power; it threatens others first, though they may later threaten us back. Anger states our feelings; it asks for nothing directly. In exposing our longing we reveal how much we want, and how defenseless we are if our plea for love is denied.

Joey did not, of course, abandon the use of tubes simply because we stopped buying them. He just fabricated them out of cellophane, cardboard, masking tape, and pieces of wire. But since he himself produced them, and knew exactly what they were, he controlled them in a way, instead of the other way around. This, we believe, was the most positive gain in our withholding of real equipment. It forced Joey to assert himself in more direct ways—at least to the degree of forging the tools he felt he needed for living. We had created a situation that made him indeed *homo faber*, man the tool maker. It started him on the long trek of transforming, first material things, to fit them to the needs of his life, and later himself too, so that he could not only have the things but also the life that he wanted.

We ourselves were for a long time affected by Joey's utter dependence on motors. When an emergency arose and we had to reach him quickly, we too in a semiconscious process fell back on motors instead of human relations. One day in the park, for example, Joey attacked some other children and had to be stopped. He then turned on his counselor in a fury, kicking her legs, biting and scratching. Her efforts to hold him or carry him, which often stopped the violence, were useless. Since he seemed to want to run from the "explosive" situation, the counselor offered to run with him. But he shouted, "Stay away!" and dashed into the street in front of oncoming cars.

Calling or running after him seemed hopeless, even dangerous, because he might have rushed into a car. Almost automatically, then, the counselor lifted his big motor and held it high for him to see. This worked and Joey came back at once. Thus even those persons who worked with Joey most closely, when they needed to penetrate the wall around him, relied on motors and tubes. It was from these he drew the emotional strength to stop his self-destructive venture.

In order to understand further why Joey had made himself a machine-sustained child, we have to return again to his first experience with human beings. I shall not discuss the airports again. It is true that his parents' letting him have a fan for a toy must have made a deep impression on him. Essentially, however, Joey must have felt that his emotional demands on his mother were a burden to her, of which he should free her by not asking for affection any more. There were many reasons why machines were better than people. Some I have mentioned, others will be discussed later. But like a leitmotif there were two things he said over and over again in the most varied contexts: that machines don't feel and hence can't be hurt; and that they can be shut off at will. Or in Joey's words: "Machines are better than people. Machines can stop. People go farther than they should." Most devastating to Joey were his fear of emotional hurt, and that he could not stop his own longing for affection.

When in answer to his requests for more tubes his counselor told him she liked him and wanted to take care of him, he would panic. Such a statement threatened his entire delusional system. It aroused too many feelings he felt powerless to stop and which would surely lead to endless disappointment. So his desperate response was, "I don't want to stay in this place. I'm afraid of people. You mustn't like me." First, the very place of temptation must be shunned. Temptation leads to disappointment, disappointment to avoidance, and avoidance to fear. And if all this fails to kill the longing, then he must invoke the cosmic law that ordains it.

But Joey had known other experiences that became linked in his mind with things mechanical. On the basis of material that came to light only years later, and from memories not fully recovered until he was fifteen, it became clear that the explosions and machine noises Joey came to us with were also defensive reactions to fighting he thought he witnessed between his parents, as well as to primal scenes he was exposed to as an infant. When he could finally remember, it turned out that these memories too had been hidden by a mechanical contraption.

First he saw closed jalousies blocking his view; he remembered himself all alone. Then slowly the jalousies began to turn open and from behind them came memories of noises and fighting. Only later did he also recall parental intercourse, watched in silence and fear. "I do remember when I was two years old. I was in a room with my parents. I was sleeping with them in the same bed. I woke up in the night. I got scared and thought it was a ghost who did all those horror things." Four days later he recovered more memories: "I was thinking of another experience I had with myself. I woke up and my parents were already up and my father had something around his penis. I wondered what it was. Then I realized that my father was mating with my mother. He put his penis in my mother's vagina; then when he took it out it was sticky and he wiped it off."[4]

When Joey first experienced all this, all he knew was that these were terribly exciting and dangerous events. The noises he heard had not acquired any human connotations, much less specific ones as yet. But later they seemed to have coalesced with the terrible noises heard at the airport. What were here the explosive emotions of his parents, he experienced (or changed into) the explosions of inanimate objects. Perhaps he remained a machine for so long to protect himself from realizing that it was his parents who loved or fought each other so intensely: parents who seemed so deeply involved in each other and so indifferent to him. But what if the terrifying noises he had heard at home in infancy were the explosions of machines? Then he would not have to believe they originated in his parents' fighting or loving each other. Also, if these were mechanical explosions, they had to obey universal laws: hence they were predictable and he could avoid them by preventions.

§

A Machine-Powered Body

When Joey came to us, going to the toilet like every other move in his life was surrounded by elaborate preventions. We had to go with him to the toilet; he had to take off all his clothes; he could not sit but

4. Such stilted or precious language as the use of the term "mating" in this context, is rather typical of autistic children. It comes of their only "having experiences with themselves," to use Joey's language. Often this language is precise enough, but it lacks the shaping that comes of daily experience with how others express themselves. Basically these children talk only to themselves, and in ways that avoid coming to grips with emotion. Precious language protects them from any sense of immediacy about what is being said.

only squat over the seat, and he had to touch the wall with one hand in which he clutched the tubes that powered his elimination. With his other hand he had to hold on to his penis when defecating, and close his anus when urinating. This was our first indication of how he feared that by opening his body too much he would lose all body content, that all his "stuffing" would spill out. The terror he experienced when something left his body showed how fearful he was of losing anything from this closed system.

Here it should be stressed that Joey's past experience around elimination and his present anxieties about it must be viewed in terms of what happened in his life before elimination became a conscious act, long before toilet training began. Whether we apply the classical Freudian models or the revised ones given us by Erikson, the experience of the anal stage is essentially conditioned by what happens in the oral period before it. Or to lift it out of these somewhat arbitrary divisions, the infant develops within a continuous flow of living, experiencing, and the building up of a personality. Each development in turn flows naturally out of the interactions of the child with the world in general, and the mutual interactions of parent and child in particular, until such time as he reaches true maturity, which in present day society is rather late in life.

To use Erikson's terms, it is the basic trust born of initial good experience that later enables the child to trust that toilet training is not an effort by the parent to disembowel him nor to impose his will on the child's most intimate bodily functions. Rather, it enables the child to see it as a further step in lifting a relation of mutuality to a higher social level; to enlarge his autonomy from the sphere of eating, for example, to that of elimination.

Though I find it little mentioned in the literature, toilet training has a precursor long before it is formally attempted. Just as some infant mammals must have their anus licked by their mothers before they can start to eliminate, so the sensations the parent provides around the anus will condition how the child will experience toilet training. Hence the so-called anal stage of development begins at the moment the infant is cleaned after his first bowel movement, and is moved along with each later cleaning up.

Such cleaning can be done with loving concern for the child's tender skin and his feeling of well-being, with pleasure in the child and what one can do for him; with satisfaction that his body functions well. Or it can be done in a businesslike way, as a necessary service provided matter-of-factly. It can be done with disgust, whether conscious or unconscious, open or repressed, but still without hurting the skin; in which case the handling is emotionally harmful but not physically so. Or it can be done (or left undone) so that the handling is both emotionally and physically hurtful to the infant. However it is done will have far reaching consequences for what happens later on when toilet training begins, or when the child becomes aware of defecation. Other events around feeding, such as how the mouth or hands are cleaned, will also affect how things in later life are perceived, as will those around bathing and being dried.

That such early experiences around cleanliness can be destructive to the child should be obvious, if for no other reason than that every year some infants die in consequence of being scalded in the bath, and many more are so severely burned as to carry scars for life. While water that is too hot can kill outright, the daily painful experience around diapering can be equally killing to the infant's emotional life. One can only wonder why so much attention has been paid to the dangers of rigid toilet training, which hits the child relatively late in life, and so little to the fact that this process starts right after birth. Maybe the reason is that for so long Freud and his followers relied on what their adult patients could remember and put into words, while the experiences I speak of cannot later be recalled in clear images and put into words.

If, then, Joey feared he might be swallowed up by the toilet when he lost to it the content of his bowels, this need not have been directly related to elimination. Such fears came from the over-all experience that his mother did not hold him securely riveted to this world by her attachment. More than anything else, it was Joey's shaky connection to others that made him think he might go down the drain altogether. Because electrical wires are a poor way to be held in this world. It was the mother's lack of interest in and pleasure that he, Joey, ate; her not caring whether he enjoyed it; her lack of satisfaction that he, Joey, eliminated—these are what made him think of his body as a long tube where machines put things in at the top, moved them through, and extracted them at the other end (Figures 12 and 13).

When in this section I then discuss "anal" material, it must be borne in mind that this was the anal experience of a boy unlike other children. He was not a child who felt surrounded by human beings who, though potentially dangerous or powerful, were in fact mainly gratifying persons. This was a boy who was convinced that strangely powerful things had complete control over him, even including his intake and elimination.

Thus with elimination it was the same as in all other respects: our main problem was to restore to him the feeling that it was his own body that functioned autonomously so that it would no longer be a process

FIGURE 12. Man drawn as a single, long tube (digestive tract). Food is pushed in at the top (mouth, neck) and extracted at the other end.

FIGURE 13. The same conception of man, showing how wireless electricity is received at the top; this powers the machine which extracts the content of the bowels. It also shows how encased an existence this figure lives, and the vast quantities of excreta he produces.

where "they" extracted something from a hapless machine. As a first step we encouraged Joey to eliminate where, how, and whenever he pleased.

Here our task was reminiscent of Marcia, though hers was a story of lifelong constipation while Joey's bowels moved well because powered by machines. As a matter of fact, Joey's early childhood contained an upsetting experience with diarrhea that he could not contain and which, the parents told us, "went all over the place," sending Joey into panic. Only one wonders why an occurrence that happens in most children's lives should have terrified him so, and why it seemed important enough for each parent to stress it independently—unless it was already part of a badly damaged attitude toward commonplace events in the functioning of the body. To Joey it was just more proof that he was better off without a body that ran by vital processes instead of by machines. Small wonder then that once, at the School, when he had had a hard stool, he concluded that he needed better machines to heat them so that they would soften to the right consistency.

In a vague way he seemed to feel our good intentions when we encouraged him to act in line with his anxieties. Thus a first use of his freedom at the School was to spend hours squatting on the toilet, holding on to the wall for dear life. There he eliminated in extremely small amounts over a very long time, to make sure he was not losing his guts in the process. Later we offered him a metal wastebasket in lieu of the toilet. For months from then on, he spent most of his days either squatting on the toilet or more often squatting, and later sitting on his symbolic toilet, the wastebasket. Often he used it as a real toilet, defecating into it in the dormitory, or after he had dragged it to the bathroom.

Despite this usefulness of the wastebasket, or perhaps because of it, he often kicked it angrily or threw it around as he did his tubes or light bulbs. Then he would shout "Crash!" and "Explode!", angry at his need to depend on such things for security. These were also the first signs he gave us of some link between explosions and elimination. By this time he was no longer squatting precariously but could sit down on the wastebasket—perhaps because he could now kick it and throw it around; in short, because he controlled it. How much he feared annihilation as he eliminated was further suggested by his screaming "Explosion!" at the moment when feces left his body, as if it were both a grandiose and devastating event. Its nearly cosmic effects were inferred from statements like: "I'm plugging in my tube. I'm going to make a bowel movement; I'm going to light up the lights outside."

At this point I might carry our speculations a step further, most of them supported years later by early memories. And here I present only those of our many speculations about Joey, over years of close living, which he himself could later validate to a degree.

I have suggested before that this machine-like existence was in part a reaction to his parents' indifference, to their ambivalent involvement in each other, and to particular experiences such as that of a primal scene. Here I might add what seems to have been one source of connection between elimination and explosions, and/or the lighting up of things. The sight of parental intercourse, with what to him seemed machine-like behavior and machine-like noises, had excited him. And this excitation, he recalled, induced a bowel movement. Thus "machines" were what produced feces, no doubt against his will. But elimination was only the first in a sequence of events.

Joey's defecation led the parents to turn on the light and clean him up, probably with bad feeling at the interruption. Thus his bowel movement produced light. Something happening outside rather than something going on in his body produced his bowel movement ("I'm plugging in my tube—I'm going to make a bowel movement"). Producing feces, on the other hand, produced something on the outside ("I'm going to light up the lights"). Many of his drawings and paintings showed how fire and light, or huge explosions, begin: by feces being lighted up, ignited by a light or a burning cigarette (Figures 14 and 15). Other paintings show how feces are produced by light, by a lighted tube, and so forth.

Other aspects of his behavior, too, suggest his conviction that each event in the outside world depended on his doing something with his body. At one time he developed a blinking tic, a very fast opening and closing of his eyes, which persisted for some time. If he said anything in explanation it was, "The lights are going on and off." That is, in order for light to go on he had to open his eyes; to turn it off he had to close them.

He would also sway back and forth, saying, "Now the earth is moving." Even the rotation of the earth depended on what he did with his body. In a strange way he retained all the omnipotent ideas that psychoanalytic theory ascribes to the satisfied infant, but without any of the feelings of security and self-importance such fantasies should confer. The rotation of the earth depended on his rocking, but it gave him no feeling of power or importance. On the contrary, it meant enslaving obligations.

He had to become terribly important to some person before he could give up his fantasies of power over inanimate objects, and the related conviction that he was helpless in their power. Or to put it differently, the infant must first become important to a human being he can therefore influence, and who therefore becomes important to him.

Lacking such a sense of mutuality with other human beings, many troubles can derive from the kind of sequence of events Joey experienced at an age when he could not clearly distinguish between what came first and what second, between cause and effect, reality and imagination—and when, because of overwhelming emotions, he could no longer clearly separate what went on inside from what went on outside. Only the prior experience that we and other persons mutually influence each other permits a sense of causality to arise.

In this particular situation the outside world was represented for Joey by the noises of the propellers as well as those of his fighting or love-making parents. Since the human noises were too threatening, he translated them into electrical noises. But if such an outside world is then viewed as running one's body, then if something goes wrong on the outside it means that something is also wrong with one's body. The result was that any mishap in a piece of electrical machinery threatened Joey's very existence.

Once, for example, when a night light in his dormitory (small blue bulbs of low wattage) burned out it threw him into a panic. He was convinced that his body was falling apart. He insisted that the School was "against the law" because the bulb had burned out, that its inner connections had given away, that the ceiling was caving in on him, and so forth. It jeopardized his life when machines went awry.

In the same vein, he treated his body and mind as things mechanical, consisting of parts that must be discarded and replaced if they did not function well. On a hot summer day he cried, "I must drain out all my blood because it's too hot." If he lost something, or forgot something, "My brain isn't working right. There's a forgetfulness part in my brain. You have to cut it out because I don't remember," and he hit his head with his fist or banged it hard against the wall. If he spilled something, "I must break my arm; it doesn't work right," and he would pound at the defective arm.

Next best was to be (or be like) a machine. Once, in a fury, he cried, "My knees must be absolutely stiff so I can't bend them." And he took a piece of cardboard and tried to wrap it around him so that the knee joint could no longer bend. When we asked him why, he said, "So my body won't hurt." To become rigid, unfeeling, machine-like, was the only protection he knew (Figure 16).

Or again, he bumped into a pipe on the jungle gym and kicked it so violently that the teacher stopped him and warned that the pipe was much harder than the foot; it would only hurt him. "That proves it," Joey cried. "Machines are better than bodies. They don't break. They're

FIGURE 14. How feces (painted in "shitty" brown) become ignited by the fire of a lighted cigarette.

FIGURE 15. The resulting world-destructive explosion (painted in bright red).

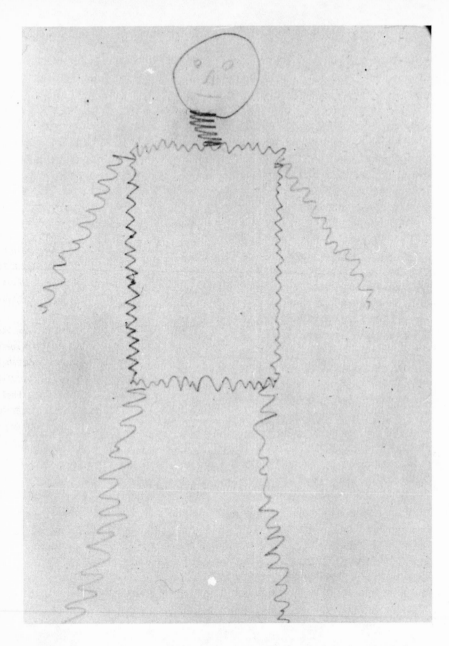

FIGURE 16. A man (Joey) who consists mainly of a head, and whose body has no substance but is formed of electrical wires.

much harder and stronger." To him, the most frightening events came from being human and from having a human body.

Behind Joey's anger at this poorly functioning machine lay also the hope of relief by eliminating parts of himself that were bothersome (such as those that were inhibited in their function by anxiety or repression) or of replacing them by spares that worked better. This was also reassuring because if parts of his body could go bad at any moment, lost parts or defective ones were easily replaced by new spares.

Through many statements he made about what he thought should be done with nonfunctioning parts of his body, we began to understand what had seemed to be contradictory behavior: his holding on for dear life to motors and tubes, then his suddenly destroying them in a fury, only to cry out urgently for new and better tubes. These motors and tubes powered and regulated his life—in short, "lived" him. If he could not live (felt unbearable pain or frustration), it proved that his present set of motors and tubes were worn out. This being so, he could finally take his vengeance on them. So he destroyed them in shattering explosions.

At such moments, the sorcerer's apprentice became the old master himself, as it were. As the master sorcerer he had long ago invented these machines to run his body which he felt could not run by itself. But long ago too, the machines had taken over and were now running him. Overpowered by machines that controlled his body and mind, and exasperated by how they ran him by their own laws and not his own wishes, Joey reasserted himself in a fury. When "exploding" the light bulbs or tubes that powered the Joey-machine he became for an instant a real person. Tossing them away, he threw off his bondage. It was the one supreme instant of his being alive. But as soon as he had shattered the machine all life ebbed away and anxiety set in. The circuit was broken. His self disintegrated, drained of all emotion, all vital energy. Everything was spent in the explosion.

Joey took a big step forward when, after much encouragement, he was able to accept less powerful objects for running his elimination. Eventually he accepted a flashlight, a gadget he could visibly control by flashing on and off. While the flashlight still ran his elimination, he himself ran the flashlight. By then he no longer needed to close his anus when urinating. Instead he clutched his penis in terror when he urinated, often stifling a scream, deathly afraid he might lose the penis with the urine. But even when showing such open anxiety he seemed strangely detached.

This lack of human response had to do with Joey's continuing inability to separate what was human and what was not. Just as his motors and tubes had to move his bowels for him, they had their own to move too. And he was terribly concerned that they should. But since they were vastly more powerful than men—as some machines truly are—he was also terrified at how much his tubes would produce if they did move their bowels. So much, he was afraid, that the smell would suffocate him, that their feces would fill out all space and leave him no room to live. Always he was caught in some hopeless contradiction that did not permit him to move.

Much later he also told us that as anxious as he was about losing body content in the toilet, he was just as anxious to be sure that his bowels were working well. This he tested when he spent hours trying to eliminate. Only he could not do it often enough or well enough to be satisfied that he was "getting rid of all the waste material." Because the contrary fear of losing his insides kept him from letting go freely. Sometimes he tried to puncture his body so that "waste material" would come out there too, instead of only out of his penis and rectum. He would clutch at his ribs trying to pull some out.

When we tried to assure him that his body was fine, when we refused to let him hurt himself, he became very angry. Probably our efforts showed how little we understood the complexity of his problem. He knew how alien he was from his body, how inadequate he felt it to be. Our implied wish that he accept it as it was became another unbearable annoyance from those stupid "big persons." So he hit and scratched us, bit us, and kicked us. And if he was stopped in his violence, he tried to vent it on himself.

§

World of Mire

While we could not help Joey yet to feel better about himself, our readiness to accept his toilet habits and our willingness to go to great lengths to make elimination less frightening helped him at least to put his fantasies down on paper.

Among the first things he drew were dinosaurs. The emphasis was on the inner skeleton—the digestive tract, which he painted brown—and on elimination leaving the body (Figure 17). Drawing these fantasies was a first step in visualizing and objectifying what concerned him at the moment. That in doing so he also let us in on his thoughts, however remotely, seemed less important. Still it suggested how closely related were his trusting us a little more and his ability to begin to deal on his own with what disturbed him. It began a process lasting more than a year in which, in his life and his drawings, stools in general and his own in particular, became the center of interest.

In putting his fantasies on paper, Joey let us see them, though often only for a moment. Since he never told us right off what they meant, they remained vexing riddles for some time. Then he would draw them again, and after many repetitions would occasionally drop a clue to their meaning. Usually he did not tell us outright till after we had guessed it correctly.

Perhaps Joey was acting out on us his own experience of things fleetingly seen, without understanding, but with deepest anxiety. Perhaps he tried to master this experience by imposing on us what was once imposed on him: to glimpse something extremely important or threatening, for a bare moment, and with no notion of its hidden meaning.[5]

For some time Joey continued to draw dinosaurs. Indeed, the fascination of these huge extinct animals for many psychotic children is quite remarkable. Typically they get interested in dinosaurs when they begin to guess what must happen if they are to lay the ghosts of their past: that they must first exhume and put correctly together those skeletons in the closets of their minds; that they must understand what the skeletons meant when they still roamed through their lives. Freud likened the work of psychoanalysis to archeological discoveries. Maybe these children have found a better analogy than the reconstruction of dead buildings and artifacts from buried places. Their need is to unearth something that was once very alive, very huge, and overwhelmingly stalked them.

I have written before [1950] of how extinct animals may stand for a complexity of fears, often those around elimination. Because in addition to being dangerous and huge, they are something that was once alive but is now dead, much as some of these children view their stools.[6] To Joey they also stood for something that is buried and can be dug up again. He may even have seen petroleum ads showing that dinosaurs roamed the earth so long ago that the plants that grew at that time have since turned to oil.

But for Joey the hugeness of the dinosaur (and its elimination) had

---

5. Most drawings he destroyed right away; others he kept for a while before destroying. Only a few of his innumerable drawings and paintings did he let us keep. So the examples we have are only what we could salvage from a wealth of production, and not necessarily his most imaginative or illuminating pictures.

6. From further experience I would like to add here one more aspect of the ambivalent fascination with dinosaurs. Children are often told that dinosaurs grew too big for their own good and hence became extinct. So they also represent the warning not to let go, not to relax controls or to let their wishes "grow too big."

FIGURE 17. A "dinosaur," with emphasis on the inner skeleton (viewed as a digestive tract, painted brown) and on elimination leaving the body.

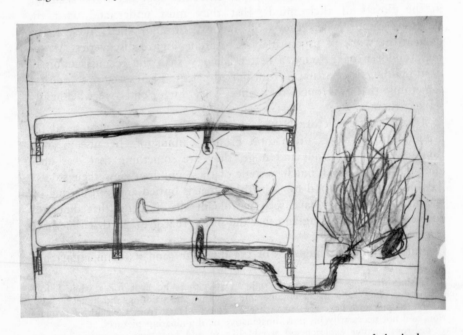

FIGURE 18. The dangers of elimination: the intestines come out of the body like "a cable," leaving the person disemboweled, but providing fuel for the furnace (right).

FIGURE 19. Trail-tracks exploding, showing a man (boy) painted in "shitty" brown, the feces spurting out of his body at various places to ignite and explode the entire world.

still other implications. During this period, the growing freedom he experienced with us around elimination induced him to begin to think of
this function freed of crippling restrictions. And this applied first, to his
machines. Powerful as they were, his machines too, were restricted
severely. Before he could free his own elimination further the machines
had to become freer. For a time he had worried that if they did, they
would inundate the world with their feces. But the greater freedom we
had made possible for him gave him hope: since we had shown him
there can be freedom with safety, we might also keep the elimination of
machines in safe bounds. So he now permitted them, in his fantasy and
drawings, to eliminate at will.

The result was that Joey now saw feces coming out everywhere.
Though there was little change in his actual toilet behavior, he now saw
the world as containing essentially nothing but feces.

This was another step in externalizing his problems. Up to now they
had been so huge that he had denied their existence. Now he could afford
to look at them because he no longer had to face them all alone. For
some time he did not trust us enough to admit it was feces he saw, and
talked instead about oil wells and oil. He saw it spouting up out of the
earth in high geysers. Our jungle gym was a derrick and the drain pipes
were oil lines. Oil was pulled out of the earth, huge quantities of dirty,
black, sticky oil that came spurting out to envelop him and us. So while
he still closed his anus to keep everything in, feces spouted all over.

Because we were deeply interested in, and accepted these fantasies
without forcing ourselves on Joey as participants, or for some other
reason, he began slowly to include us.[7] Later they changed from mere
illusory thought to weird fantasy games. As long as these games extended
all over the place, we had little chance to deal with them constructively.
So we tried to locate ever more of his play in our large sandbox. There
it became real play with sand and mud. He liked to feel the mud, to let
it run through his fingers.

Our joining him in his fantasies about oil wells, his letting us, and our
changing them together into childlike play, convinced him that his fantasies could be acted out in reality, with enjoyment, and most important,

---

7. It is sometimes difficult to become as emotionally involved in these fantasies
as we must, if the child is to open up about them, without being drawn into a kind
of *folie à deux* that would be harmful to therapist and child. What helps here is
our system of having the child's regular counselor also spend time with him in
individual session, because as counselor she has to do so many real things for him
that it serves as a safeguard. So does the fact that the child watches the same counselor
deal on a much more realistic basis with other children. Thus he recognizes that if
the counselor is involved in his fantasies it is for his sake and not for any needs
of her own. This also helps him to know that she enters his fantasies not to placate
him but to help him master them.

with other persons. During that spring and summer he spent most of every day at such play, messing with sand and mud in the sandbox or on the beach, in the presence of his counselors or in their company when he allowed it.

Like other autistic children, Joey became preoccupied with his stools in the early stages of becoming aware that he had an independent existence. For Joey, too, it was the problem of self versus nonself that he explored around fecal matter because at one moment it is part of the self and the next it is not. In his case things were much more complex because stools were something he produced.

In Joey's system only machines produced things. So becoming aware of elimination posed nearly insolvable problems. If he produced feces, was this further proof of his being a machine? If, on the other hand, he was a human being and the stools were his, then how could something that was part of his body be outside of his body? Where were the boundaries of his physical existence? Did this mean that his body had no limits?

I do not know how correct these speculations are. What counts is that Joey could become aware of elimination (as opposed to the mere panic of losing his body in the process) and tried to master its psychological aspects exactly to the degree that he slowly gave up seeing it as run by machinery and could recognize it as a bodily process and product. For a long time he continued to view his body as a machine. But if this Joey-machine eliminated, wasn't it logical to assume that all other machines did, too? Thus the particular form in which Joey wrestled with the problem of self versus nonself around elimination was this: either this is not my elimination or else everything eliminates.

In a new development—and after he had come close enough to one person to call her by name and could let himself wish for infantile care at her hands—oil (and feces in general) changed to what he called "trail-tracks," a neologism for his own feces. With this private word, he hoped to make us believe they were the feces of others, or of animals. Trail-tracks too, began as imaginary figments. After some testing and after he felt sure of our interest and respect for these products of his body, the trail-tracks became real—mud marks he made, pieces of paper he had dirtied and deposited everywhere. Playing the trail-track game was now our best chance for personal contact.

Again we could see how Joey used elements from the world at hand to make them serve inner needs. As he had used the fan his parents offered, to weave around it a mechanical existence, so he used the tracks we provided at Easter, as guides to lift himself out of that existence. Of the many holidays we observe at the School, Easter is among the more important. Its connotation of resurrection and rebirth can be a symbol of hope for our children and we do our best to accent this meaning for them.

On Easter morning when the children wake up they find bunny tracks, pieces of cardboard cut to resemble a bunny's paw and differently colored for each dormitory. These lead from the dormitories to the place where each child will find his Easter presents. Clearly these are tracks that lead to something enjoyable, something also connected with a new and better life. It was around the notion of such tracks that Joey wove his trail-track game.

It indicates, too, how responsive even autistic children are to the intentions behind the fantasy material one offers. The fan was offered to quiet Joey down, to reduce his need for personal interaction. The only purpose of the bunny tracks is to amuse the children and let them know they are not beholden to us for their presents. The presents are not from us but from the Easter Bunny. Hence they will not hurt our feelings if, in spite of our efforts, the presents are not to their liking.[8]

After a year of the trail-track game, it and the oil wells that preceded it turned into what had always lain hidden behind these symbols of Joey's. They became "diarrhea," both his own and that of others, and the world was a mire of feces. As we willingly played out his fantasies with him, he told us that the original oil and then the trail-tracks were really feces, dragged out of him and out of the earth by derricks. No longer was there any pretense. When later he imagined that he himself could drag feces out of the earth, it was the first thing he felt he himself could do.

For a time now, Joey became excessively clean, as if in reaction to feeling surrounded by feces. When he came to us, his attitude toward washing and bathing was indifferent. It was just something that happened to a body from which he was alien. During those first months he often got very dirty, and in washing up or taking a bath, he got clean or let us help him without much ado. But during the period now beginning he insisted on long baths and on being scrubbed with meticulous care. It was in the bathtub, surrounded by the comfortable warm water

8. Here I might mention the behavior of one autistic girl who for years, and particularly at holidays like Christmas and Easter, threw all her presents in the trash can. We accepted it without question or criticism and protected her from the other children's critical comments. Only after years of this did she finally believe that the presents we gave her were to use as she pleased, and not in any so-called "right way." Until she was sure of this she could not accept them because they threatened her barely existing autonomy. Before she came to us she had too often been given things to buy her off, so she found it hard to believe they could also express affection.

as his counselor washed him, that he first spoke of some of the anxieties he felt about human beings.

Unlike his usual erratic talk, it was now he who began to tell her how forgetting (repression) impoverished his life, made him so dissatisfied with his body and mind that in desperation he wanted to get rid of some parts. A few weeks later while again sitting in the tub being gently washed, he talked for the first time about his feelings for another person, his favorite counselor. This he could only do by talking in opposites, as he still did with all emotionally loaded issues: "You have to stop liking me. This has got to stop."

It took another year, and again while being bathed, before Joey could finally tell his counselor how he felt that nobody, not even she, could possibly like him. The command to "stop liking me" then turned out to have been his effort to put in assertive form the desperate cry, "Nobody likes me, nobody *can*." By now he could talk openly about his despair, how his feelings were always hurt, and how no one had ever loved him enough or ever could. But he could only speak so directly about his deepest feelings while surrounded by the yielding, protecting warm water, and while feeling the pleasant tactile sensations of being washed.

As he also talked more freely about the diarrhea that lay everywhere, he told us of the vast obligation this put him under. He was obliged not only to produce these enormous quantities of feces (either from his own body or by pulling them out of other bodies) but to arrange for their disposal. Up to then he had only ruminated in secret about elaborate sewer systems and how they worked; now he no longer needed to hide this. While all solid surfaces were covered with diarrhea, all openings became sewers. Windows or floor gratings were sewers to be carefully watched, kept in good working order. He would test their condition by dropping objects into them or other openings and anxiously watch them disappear. All his elaborate machines were needed for the immense sewage system that moved these enormous masses of feces.

While before this Joey had no body and no power, now his body was everywhere. Every opening became one with his body opening. From being nothing he was now everything. He was still a machine, not a human being in a world; there was still very little of a self. But his nothingness had at least been given up.

With the extending of elimination from real or symbolic toilet (the wastebasket) to his whole world, he began to eliminate freely wherever he happened to be; the whole world became his toilet. But with it the real toilet became less dangerous. He used the wastebasket less often and rarely sat there or on the toilet for hours any more. Perhaps our best sign of his greater security was that he now sat securely on the toilet seat; no longer did he squat. In a further step defecation became the first physiological process he could perform—or in his view, a process that took place in his body—without the help of even a flashlight.

It must not be thought he took pride in producing these all-important feces. To take pride implies that one accomplished a feat of one's own volition. Joey did not feel himself an autonomous person yet, one who could do things on his own. Nor could he take pride in what his body produced; on the contrary, he felt it completely worthless. Feces, their production and disposal, were still all-important by some binding cosmic law.

Was it the law his parents imposed on him when he was toilet-trained? There he got the idea, not given up till much later, that feces had to be produced and disposed of in line with some unexplained law governing the universe. But to repeat: all children are toilet-trained, many as early and rigidly as Joey. Why, then, in his case these delusional exaggerations? The answer, as suggested before, may lie with his parents' emotional disinterest, particularly his mother's.

Many children are forced against their wishes to eliminate when and how the parent dictates. Ordinarily this loss of body autonomy is more than compensated for by a psychological gain in autonomy. It becomes clear to the child that he holds the power to confer pleasure or pain on the parent by doing or not doing as told. This changes what seems an insensitive, absolute law (to defecate where and when told) to an event where one's own doing affects others. Around such an act personal relations are built up, sometimes more satisfying, sometimes less, but always rooted in interactions between people. Since this did not happen to Joey he did not relate to us yet; his despair that anyone could like him ruled that out. We can relate when we can hope to be liked or respected, or both.

Just to be taken care of—and we took good care of Joey—is not enough. It is a necessary but not a sufficient condition. Otherwise, the greater the comforts we can offer, the greater should be the ease in relating. In fact the reverse would seem true, though in fact this is not quite the case. At the extreme opposite where no comforts exist, where utter scarcity reigns, relations are also disturbed.

To think that physical comfort makes for human relations is an error we make because the absence of all comfort interferes with good relations. But we base it on the correct observation that when the parent takes pleasure in going out of his way to provide comfort for his child, the child takes it as proof that he is lovable and deserves care and respect. This feeling enables him to trust—we can trust our well-being to persons who find us so important. Out of such trust in their intentions toward us, and our importance to them, develop first fleeting and then permanent relations.

This is where a society of plenty can make it harder for a child to relate. If comfort for the child can only be gained, by the parent, with a certain amount of trouble, he will very likely feel pleasure when he offers it to his child. It is this, the parent's pleasure, that gives the child a sense of worth and sets going the process of relating. (Of course, there are many pitfalls, such as when the parent feels his effort is too great, and creates guilt in the child as the comfort is offered.) But if comfort is so readily available that the parent feels no particular pleasure in being able to provide it, then the child cannot develop self-esteem around the giving and receiving of comfort.

Of course, this may happen around other situations where the child can see that he gives pleasure to the parent. But matters are then no longer so simple and direct. The child who feels he gives pleasure around events where he does not receive comfort may feel he is mainly at the giving end of pleasure and not far more at the receiving end, where he should be. That he should give pleasure, he might understand. But this is not likely to make him feel he is lovable as a person; on the contrary, he may feel he has to give to be cherished; that while his giving is of value, he himself is not.

Among our difficulties in helping Joey to relate was precisely that when comfort was received there was no pleasure involved. Therefore the basic issues around which personal well-being is formed—touch, early feeding, the encouragement to act, and the experience of good bodily care—these never became vehicles for relations.

Joey's toilet training, we surmise, was rigidly enforced without his obedience giving emotional satisfaction, or his disobedience inflicting pain on the parent. He had to do as told, but beyond that it had no meaning. Joey had to produce feces from somewhere, and had to dispose of them. But none of it gave him pleasure, just as his obedience, we conjecture, gave the mother no pleasure. No other person was emotionally involved in his toilet training. That he became trained was simply an event that saved labor, as our machines save us labor. As a machine is not loved for its performance, but replaced if it does not work well, so Joey had to work well or be discarded. But like a machine he was neither liked for it, nor could he come to like himself.

Again, the whole thing must have started long before toilet training began; not even so much around eating or being cleaned, as how he was received into the world. Since his arrival had given no pleasure, everything was mechanical and gave the infant no pleasure either. He had to obey unfathomable, if not plainly capricious laws. As he put it, "I have to eat leaves so there will be leaves in my bowel movements." Things (food) were put into him and he had to return them unchanged.

Why leaves? As with all his his other symbols, leaves were highly overdetermined for Joey. Explosions lead to fire and the end product of fire is ashes. Watching leaves burn always excited and depressed him beyond his usual state of dejection. At the School he had muttered for two years about ashes and ashcans without saying what he meant, until one day he talked about "ashes of veep. These are German words. Only Germans can understand. Veeping is burning and tearing somebody's eyes out." ("Veep," given my accent, is how my pronunciation of "weep" sounded to Joey. And if I were too dense to know he was talking about weeping and me, he specified that this was something only Germans can understand. Here he gave me too much credit, because it took me years to understand what he was telling me.)

Did Joey really know that he had, so to say, wept his eyes and heart out till they were nothing but ash? That the fire of his emotions had not even sparked enough interest in others to be extinguished, but was just left to burn itself out? It must have been something like this because about a year later when speaking of his anger at his parents he said he felt like ashes and that "my parents put me in an ashcan. They threw me down the sewer."

Mixed with all this was the old misery with eyes that wept human tears. They should be torn out; not only his, but someone else's. This was not simple retaliation, but because he did not know yet what was self and what was nonself. Was it he that wept or somebody else? Was it he who had burnt himself to ashes, or had his parents? If one has no clear feeling of self, one is never sure if an experience is one's own or someone else's. It was the same confusion as to whether he had to produce his own feces or somebody else's.

But in the trail-tracks game he knew it was he who played it. And as we played it with him and in this way joined him in his symbolic elimination, he stopped asking us to accompany him to the toilet and no longer needed to shed all his clothes. Only then did he tell us he had always removed all his clothing there because he was terrified of defiling them.

Here too it seemed that parental admonition became divorced from its purpose and was conceived of or changed into an absolute law. The common "don't soil your pants" became an abstract principle, separating once and for all and absolutely, clothing from any act of elimination. The freedom with which we, as parental substitutes, played with him in the mud, handled his trail-tracks, did not mind if it touched our clothes—more important, that nothing terrible befell us, who so openly flouted this law—gave Joey the courage to reduce it from an absolute dictum to the sensible practice of trying to avoid soiling one's clothing.

In another great effort at self-assertion he began to urinate standing up. But it took him all of three years at the School to acquire the courage, and later to take pride in, directing the stream of his urine into the toilet bowl from a distance.

Such "phallic" pleasure and achievement took a long time to gain. Even when it was finally an act of will and no longer the result of electrical forces, many of his urethral problems were still to be solved. What he achieved remained for several more years the mere freeing of an isolated body process that was not yet an integral part of his person. Defecation, for example, remained a severe problem for years after he gained relative freedom in urination.

§

The Body Autistic

Perhaps at this point another brief discussion of what may make for a mechanical man should be interpolated. I have spoken before of an important point in Erikson's model: that while in each stage of infant development, one zone and one mode is dominant, the functioning of any one body zone requires the participation of all other modes, at least in an auxiliary manner [Erikson, 1950]. Which raises the question of why most children are able to achieve an integration of modalities automatically, as it were, or one might better say in an autonomous way, and why the autistic child does not. Perhaps the steps needed for Joey's improvement may refine some of the answers to this question given earlier in this book.

Perhaps it is the inner cohesiveness of the parents' emotional investment in these zonal functionings that binds them together into the unity that alone makes for a full human personality. That the parents react with positive feeling to some aspects of the functioning of these zones and modes and negatively to others, still ties them into a unit via emotion.

Since the parents' feelings about Joey did not "hang together," what they reacted to did not hold together either. None of their reactions to his doings flowed from a unitary interest in him, unitary because deeply bedded in their emotional investment. Disinterest, on the other hand, though a uniform attitude, does not make for a unifying experience. Only selective emotional interest does this, because it selects out some aspects and binds them together positively, rejects others and binds them together negatively; the two together becoming a unity. That is, the positive accentuation of one type of behavior has no meaning without the negative accentuation of another behavior. The very qualities, positive and negative, exist only by comparison with each other; else one would have to ask, "positive, compared to what?"

The more logically opposite the behavior that is positively accented from what is negatively accented, the more the personality "hangs together" and the more the child can make it his own. What is thus positively invested by the parents may then become positively invested by the child (or negatively so, in counterreaction). But either way it is unified with all other behavior by feelings.

To use Erikson's model again, neither the incorporative mode, the retentive, the eliminative, or the intrusive were tied together for Joey by any unitary response from his parents. Since they were only interfered with in a mechanical way to meet the parents' wishes, they remained mechanical functions.

In the same way the various organ zones or functions—oral, anal, phallic, and genital—did not acquire any unitary meaning. They were not parts of one body, subordinate to and integrated with its total functioning. Instead each became a function, existing separate from the others. The alienation of all autistic children from their bodies—their astonishment at recovering each part, the relative ease of doing this, compared with how terribly hard they find it to unify those parts with the rest of the body, its functions, and the emotions to fit them—attests to the soundness of such speculation.

How early this process of alienation sets in may be seen from the fact that all autistic children we have worked with had to learn to eat. When they came to us some were anorexic, others devoured food like animals, tearing it with teeth and hands. Some poured large amounts of salt or mustard on all food before they would touch it. Very few chewed. They would bite off chunks of food or put it in their mouths to be swallowed in large pieces. Thus while they all fed, some extremely daintily and meticulously, none of them ate freely or with enjoyment. Eating, the most basic life function, was not experienced as such. All of them took a long time to gain cognizance of it, to enjoy it, to know it was they who were eating.

What was true for eating was true for all other basic functions. In a back-and-forth process, with many ups and downs, each functioning had then to be cleared of its fearful or hated connotations. The isolation of functions in which each one was subject to separate "laws" or "preventions" had to be made personal and subject to the individual's will. Then each one has to be linked to the others; each in turn had to be moved from isolation to a concerted human functioning.

Two functions at least were already tied together for Joey when he came to us—eating and elimination. But they were linked in a way that did not help us. They were not two functions bound together by serving the needs of a human being; on the contrary, they served only themselves and each other. Eating existed simply for elimination, as a machine is fed gasoline to make it run, though the car is only a vehicle for our use. Joey's eating had no purpose except to power elimination. It was all one big mechanical totality, powered by the same mechanical process.

As to its importance, eating could not compare with elimination. Only years later did we learn why this was so. By coming out of a body, Joey hoped to be reborn, to get a new life for himself. Preferably it would be out of the body of someone who would want to rebear him. But if there were no one who loved him that much, his own body would do. Eating to him seemed to offer no such chance. Hence eating as such had little merit to him, had no independent meaning. In all respects it was subordinate to elimination, which at least held out chances for a fecal birth.

All his preventions safeguarding intake were connected to, and dependent on, his anxiety about output—and both were based on the conviction that his metabolic processes were run by mechanics. However complex his symptomatic behavior around eating, even this had no independence. The need to "insulate" his body with paper (so that the electricity that powered his digestion would not be lost nor his clothing get dirty) and to press close against the table, were reduced duplications of the need to undress entirely when eliminating and to hold on to the walls at the same time. The inability to suck liquids except through a network of straws was to make sure it was only part of the mechanical system that continued down his esophagus to the combustion chamber.

In Joey it seemed that a reversal took place in what we consider the normal sequence of physiological and psychosocial development. Though he mastered some functions like toilet training and speech, he achieved them separately and kept them isolated from each other. Eating had not led to a wish to incorporate, identify, relate to other persons, not to speak of enjoying their company or the satisfaction that normally comes with being fed. Toilet training had not gained for him a pleasant feeling of body mastery along with the power to please his parents. Speech had not led to communication of thought or feeling. On the contrary, each of these achievements seemed to have steered him away from mastery and integration.

Eating served only elimination. Toilet training, instead of putting some of his bodily processes under his control, had enslaved him. Speech, instead of leading to human relations, interfered with his and our ability to relate to each other, with his neologisms and talking in opposites. With each of these stepping stones toward humanity, it seemed as if he and we had to wrestle separately. In Joey's language, we had first to free them of their negative charges before they could be carriers of growth. Thus whatever he had learned did not put him at the end of his infantile development, but further behind than he was at its very beginning. Had we understood this sooner, his first few years with us would have been less baffling for us.

Autistic behavior is, after all, an adaptation of the organism to an environment that was experienced as unsuitable. However much we adjust the new environment of the School to the particular needs of the child, it is still one to which his old autistic ways are maladapted. The difference between his home environment and the one we create is that the first one seemed to permit him no adaptation except autism, while ours offers other possibilities. And we try to make the offer as attractive, even seductive, as we can.

When we succeed, then the old adaptation turns out to be useless and has to break down. The result is that for a time the child becomes even less adapted, less protected, less able to manage, than he was in his autism.[9]

Maybe what happens to all of us when our adaptation to one environment is suddenly not viable any more may illustrate the autistic child's predicament. The foetus is adapted to the environment of the womb, but upon birth, this environment is suddenly withdrawn. The newborn must quickly adapt to an entirely different environment in which, for example, he must breathe for himself. The organization of the neonate, as he enters life, has to break down because it is no longer adapted to the new environment outside the womb. Weight loss is only one indication of this process. More telling is the loss of prenatal motor abilities that seems to take place about eighteen hours after birth, such as in the hand-mouth coordination and in various kinds of motor activities. These are given up because in their old form they are no longer adaptive to the postnatal environment with the new stimulations it offers and the new demands it makes.

What takes place here is not only a breakdown but also a readaptation. And so it is for the autistic child. As he surrenders his autistic

9. This is why one has to proceed with such care in the treatment of these children. There is always the danger that as they loosen up, and give up their autistic armor, their despair too will be freed because all the preventions that contained it are weakened. They may then commit suicide, usually in ways that are looked upon as "accidents" but that always indicate their newly won freedom. Such children may then suddenly fall out of a window, drown in a swimming pool, jump into one that is empty of water, and so forth. These, at any rate, were the means used by three different autistic children in ambulatory treatment that I know of. We at the Orthogenic School have been fortunate so far in protecting autistic children from such dangers. But for a short time each child we were able to wrest away from his autistic isolation went through such a suicidal phase. In Joey's case running out into the street was one of several incidents that were typical of him during this period.

adaptation, namely his defense against feeling and relating, he becomes excessively vulnerable. Old ways of coping break down fast and building new ways is tremendously difficult.

§

Chinks in the Wall

So far Joey's story has dealt only with one aspect of his efforts at readaptation: how he had to gain mastery of his bodily functions at a very late age, and could only then develop the bare rudiments of autonomy and a minimal feeling of self. I have said also that the autistic child, like the infant, needs concerned caretakers to do this, though only the child himself can take the necessary steps. My account of Joey would therefore be incomplete without something of what, at his late age, had to take the place of the loving care that must accompany each step of the infant towards autonomy if he is to achieve it.

Events discussed in this section began late in Joey's first year at the School, some time before he invented the trail-track game. With emotional acceptance and devoted care he became master of his feces to some small degree and was then ready to begin to master feelings too. So he dared to experiment with relating.

It began around a suicidal attempt of the past in which he had deliberately put his arm through a window. Up to now, in his many desperate moods, Joey always ended up by turning his anger against his body. At such times he would threaten to break his bones or his head. But later he would scream, "Give me a knife so I can rip my hand to the elbow again" (alluding to the suicide attempt). After which he would frantically ask for more tubes to run him better.

Eventually however he felt saved from his suicidal impulses not by tubes but to some small degree by his favorite counselor. Unlike the definitive way he spoke about machines and explosions, this real past event he could only talk about in a tentative way. First he tried to escape into talk of explosions. But then he asked to be taken to his bed to wet it, to make it explode. (At this time his bed was still a machine that ran him at night. If he were to wet it, the wires would be shorted and explode him.) Until now, it was never Joey who caused tubes to explode. But the recognition that he could do things (produce stools) brought the dim awareness that it was also he who generated feelings (explosions). He said *he* would wet his bed and thus produce an explosion. In his symbolic language he seemed to be saying that because of the good will and affection poured out by his counselor his defensive armor was giving way, that feelings were welling up in him that he recognized as his own. And these he tried to explore around an emotional experience involving his sister in which emotions had proved as deadly as he imagined his explosions to be. He had once dared to feel, had dared to crave the affection that other children normally get and that he saw his sister getting. He had dared to hate her because she enjoyed what he so desperately longed for.

Sitting on his counselor's lap as she cuddled and fed him, he began: "You have to learn how to leave me alone. I have to hurt myself." As he repeated again and again, "I have to hurt myself," he fixed his gaze on the old scar on his arm. We assured him we would always do our best to take good care of him and not let such accidents occur, that we were sorry it had happened. So he went on:

"There were seventeen stitches. You know I have no feeling in this hand here.[10] The small person's things were all over and I was rampaging, kind of wild and hard, and I went through the glass; that small person's things were scattered all over. The small person, gosh darn it; my parents have had her for a long time."

At this point he broke into a shrill laugh and said nothing for a long while. When he continued, he tried to deny the emotional import of what he had said and tried to withdraw. But the counselor remarked that if his sister's things hadn't been strewn around he wouldn't have hurt himself, so it was really her fault. "Yes," he said, "the small person's things were all over the place. And then there was a tremendous television tube and one of the small persons had a sledge hammer. It was a big tube, and it was so round. It was the biggest thing I ever saw. We were visiting another small person's house."

It was a turning point in Joey's life when he could tell how his suicide attempt happened in part because he hated his sister; how it was not only anxiety but also hatred that led to explosions. As far as we could piece it together later, he had first tried to vent his hatred against an object—the TV tube that he smashed to bits with what to him seemed a sledge hammer. A small hammer would have sufficed to play havoc with the tube. When he was punished for his vandalism, safe outlets for his hatred seemed closed and in desperation he tried to destroy his own self.

He had tried to punish an electrical device for having flooded him with overwhelming feelings. Had his "explosion" found acceptance, as it later did at the School, he would perhaps have felt drained, and things might have rested there for the moment. But when he was punished for wrecking the TV set it proved again that his parents

10. Some fingers of his hand were actually still numb. It took almost another year for all feeling to return.

counted machines more important than his feelings. He was expected to keep his feelings in check for the sake of an electrical device, and once again this flooded him with feeling. Since parental punishment kept him from taking it out on a machine, there was nothing left to take it out on but himself. As he had shattered the TV by breaking the glass tube, so he tried to destroy himself by breaking glass with his arm. Perhaps he saw himself bleeding to death, as in fantasy he made his tubes bleed to death when they failed him.

Both the destruction of the TV set and his suicide attempt were rather late expressions of feelings that had their origins at the very beginning of his life. But they reinforced the conviction that for his own safety he had better be a machine, without feelings that explode.

By this time too, Joey had a vague understanding of another reason why he felt machines to be better than humans. His parents had either lacked control of their feelings, or else the feelings they had were of no comfort to Joey. If one is starved for affection and never gets it, it is better not to hope; better to believe that feelings do not exist, should not exist, or are so bad that one is better off without them. This, as likely as not, had been Joey's inner experience with feelings. The trouble was that Joey did have feelings, and they did get out of hand. Feelings are just not as easily shut off as machines. So whenever they overwhelmed him, what more natural than to wish for better machinery, to become more of a machine that could better control feelings? He lived in terror that his own feelings might destroy him. Hence it took great courage to admit to having any, and it was a sign of new strength that he dared to face them.

However much another person may reach out to a child, and however much comfort this brings, the child will not recognize this other as a person (as opposed to a mere source of comfort) until the child has in some way reached out to this person on his own. This crucial step Joey took when he let at least one favorite person know his feelings. After which he began slowly, and ever so minutely, to respond with feelings to others who thus began to seem like human beings. From having acquired a feeling of selfhood to becoming a person, he moved to recognizing others as persons and then to interacting with them.

A few days after the events just described, he spied his counselor unexpectedly, and in surprise called out, "Oh, there's Fae." It was the first time he had called her by name. Even more exciting, this boy who wanted only to be left alone, who for so long had warded off all efforts to reach him, now reached out to her. He felt secure enough in having something of a self that he was no longer afraid to share an experience with somebody else, that it would mean the loss of his self. So he invited her to join him. Two important firsts.

At the moment he was standing in one of his preferred positions, isolated at the top of our jungle gym where he surveyed his "oil fields." "I am way up high and can see lots of things," he said. "I can see the whole oil world. Come up and visit with me." Delighted, she climbed up, and he explained, "You see the machines and drills over there? They're working very hard and they're pumping up lots of good oil." But that was as far as it went. Then his machine noises resumed and he lost all awareness of her presence.

But two days later when his counselor was again trying to play a game with him and introduced a stuffed kangaroo, he accepted her invitation and the infantile care it implied. He said, "You are the kangaroo. I want to be a little kangaroo and ride in the kangaroo's pouch."

His counselor told him that while she had no pouch, she would like to carry him in her arms and after some hesitation he accepted. To her offer to take him in, he responded by taking her ever more into his confidence. That was the night he began to substitute trail-tracks for oil. Again he said he was going to wet his bed, and this time he believed her when she told him that was perfectly all right. Using the opportunity, she also explained something about the elimination he was so afraid of. "Yes, I know it all," he told her. "That is a cable that comes out of my behind. It is also my intestines" (Figure 18). It was the first time he told anyone of his belief that intestines were lost when he eliminated. It was a dangerous admission and to protect himself he demanded tubes and returned to shouting about explosions.

His counselor said, "You're afraid everything will explode because we won't take care of you, and you'll get hurt." At which he gave her his first human little grin and said, "Yes, I do. I think everything will explode." And then he added, "Vagina. Somebody's vagina will explode. Explode us all."

Surely nothing good can have come from an exploding vagina, and his life was certainly no good.

§

Regression as Progress

Like Joey, most children are fascinated by the marsupial mother who carries her infant in a pouch. To normal children this can help them to understand life before birth, to visualize how they grow in the mother's womb. Nearly all psychotic children we have worked with also engage in elaborate fantasies about kangaroos, but for another reason. What they feel they missed out on was not so much life inside the womb, as the warmth, the total protection and indulgence after birth that they think the marsupial baby enjoys in the mother's pouch.

There is another reason why they prefer the lot of the marsupial baby to the uterine existence. The marsupial baby can enter and leave the pouch more or less at will, at least after reaching a certain age. This is even more attractive because it combines a measure of independence with the always available security of the pouch. The psychotic child wants the chance to venture out at his leisure, but is too afraid to, unless he knows that the protective walls of his defenses will not be closed to him because of it. It took small ingenuity to see that it was this kind of freedom to venture out, with his preventions intact, that Joey wanted.

While some autistic children wish only to have another babyhood and infancy of this kind, most want to be reborn altogether. This second desire can often mean trouble since some of these children, to make sure they will have a new life, try to shed their present one first. They try to die in order to be reborn, and this may mean another period of suicidal danger. During such a time they need to be watched and protected most carefully. Things did not go that far with Joey this time. But he did feel that to enjoy a good life he would have to start all over again on a human basis.

Do these children somehow know that basic trust, on which alone we build satisfying relations to others, is best acquired during the infant's utter dependency on his mother, through the good mothering he receives? It is hard to believe they can know it, but something inside them must exert a powerful push in this direction, since they all want it so much and go to such lengths to recreate the situation.

But was this the right time for Joey and us to rebuild his life on the deepest—because normally the earliest—level of experience? In encouraging a child to relive emotionally the very beginning of life, timing is of paramount importance. If not timed correctly things may go wrong and irreversibly so.

Only two dangers may be mentioned. The first is that the child may find the experience so comforting that he wishes never to leave it again. The more so because physiological developments no longer provide the push and support for the steps in personality growth. The chronology of physical and neural maturation is by that age out of gear with the structuring of basic personality and personal relations. Thus the task may seem beyond him and the child settles for being dependently cared for, the rest of his life. In the autistic child this may merely lead him to exchange a total and inhuman isolation for a more comfortable but nonetheless unhuman existence.

The other danger is that he is seduced into experimenting with emotional experience when he is not trusting enough to give up his defensive armor. Then the longing for infantile emotional experiences may still induce him to be like a baby but with much of his armor intact. This armoring will prevent him from experiencing true mutuality. And without it, nothing he gets from us will produce the deep trust in some adult that he should have experienced in infancy. It might even prevent him from truly enjoying the care itself. Although yearned for and hence partly accepted, it will fail to humanize; worse, may even debilitate him further. Because there are ministrations at all age levels which, if they occur within a relation of deepest mutuality, are the most humanizing ones, while outside of such a context they can degrade and humiliate. Instead of leading to a sense of worth, and so to the development of a self, they have the opposite effect.

If a child has once had a bad time of trying to effect a new beginning, he is not likely to venture it again. By inducing total dependency too soon we can lose forever the chance to induce it again at the right time. Therefore it must be a "regression" that does not merely bring id satisfaction but leads to ego development. In short, it has to be a regression in the service of a still nascent ego, which is really no regression at all. It is a recapturing of early experience through a partial re-experience that will support a very different development.

When I speak here of regression I am using a term that is no longer restricted to the technical meaning Freud gave it, but has entered the common language. This has neither improved its precision nor an understanding of its meaning. It is one of those terms that everyone, without too much thinking, is sure he understands, and that even the dictionaries are not much help in defining. The confusion arises because one seems to be able to return to a point in space, but not in time. But we may even question if there can be a return to the same place. As far back as Heraclitus men knew that one cannot step twice in the same river. For a return to the same place is not a return to the same thing, precisely because time has elapsed. (I understand from some physicists that it is now possible to think of time as flowing in both directions, but I doubt that anyone has this in mind when they speak of regression.)

If we then find regression defined even in a psychiatric dictionary, as "the act of returning to some earlier level of adaptation," [Hinsie and Schatzky, 1953] we can only wonder at so superficial a view of human nature that it assumes there can be such a retracing of steps in time. To cite a common application of this term in the psychiatric literature: an infant wets because he has no bladder control. The older child who wets again after attaining control, perhaps because a sibling was born, is then said to regress. But it is not that the older child wets because he has again become an infant or "regressed" to wetting. He has progressed to a deliberate wetting as a means of conveying a need to his parent, which is certainly a step forward in adaptation. Or he has done it to express specific feelings, or to gain relief from new pressures, all of which are movements forward in time and adaptation to new needs.

As commonly used now, the term regression seems to suggest a state of mind in which we are unable or unwilling to see the adaptive purpose of a behavior. Behind this lies a narrowly conceived idea of progress that interferes with our recognizing the immense variations in how people deal with new problems. It is a concept that, even at its most technical, harbors the connotation that certain behaviors are or should be, restricted to a specific age level. So long as it is our common feeling that "going backward" is undesirable, and "going forward" desirable, no matter what the cost to the individual, the concept of "regression" will not be free of value overtones that should have no place in our efforts to view human behavior with empathy and objectivity.

If all this is so, why not dispense entirely with the term regression? Why is it used at all in psychoanalytic literature? The reason is that the term seems to have a cautionary value. For all of us there is a continuous struggle to maintain our socialized behavior against the asocial tendencies within us. It seems easier to avoid the problem of when, and to what degree, we should give them their due. So if giving in to them is always and forever "regression," then in our "forward" oriented culture this is a heavy brake on the giving way of social controls. But in taking this stance we avoid the real problem of when, and for what gains, we ought to strip away social adjustment for the sake of our personal development.

Why then do *I* not refrain from using the term regression? Because it has its use when it is clearly understood that what we are talking about is how a behavior looks to the observer who knows nothing of what it means to the person who enacts it. Thus the dictionary definition would be entirely acceptable if it were to stress this important qualification. It would then have to read about as follows: "Regression is what simulates a return to some earlier level of adaptation."

As suggested before, there are as many reasons for what seems like regressive behavior as there are persons and situations. Still, at least two of them should be differentiated. To use a gross analogy: A ship in dire distress may jettison all, including valuable cargo, and set itself adrift on the seas. This is far preferable—and represents a much higher achievement—than to let men, ship, and cargo go down altogether. It can be likened to "regression" in which an aged person stops investing his energy in socialized behavior in order to husband his depleted resources for sheer survival. It is the kind of regression that is too often the only one available to patients in our mental hospitals.

But there is also an entirely different type of regression: that of the adolescent who regresses out of deep inner need, or the regression we try to help our children engage in when the timing is right. The analogy here would be to a ship with a leak in its hull that throws overboard a cargo of little value—or one they can easily replace or retrieve later on. Here the purpose may be to raise the hull so that much needed repairs can be made once the leak is more accessible, or to lighten the ship to where she can make her harbor in safety. In this case energy is required not just for survival, but to achieve a significant goal.

Precisely because socially acceptable behavior has been contrary to the autistic child's deeper needs, his "regressive" shedding of it becomes a most important step in acquiring a true personality. Thus when Laurie and Marcia and Joey began to soil again it was tremendous progress. Before this they went to the toilet mechanically, as told, without daring to question if it tallied with their needs, if it made sense to them; and if so, why; and if not, why not.

If such development is viewed as "regression," I can only wonder what progress is. Too often children's progress is viewed not in terms of a move toward autonomy, but of the convenience of a society that cares less about autonomy than conformity, and of parents who prefer not to have to clean their children's underclothes, no matter what.

It is a reflection of the progress we are slowly making that for adolescents this is beginning to be recognized. Erikson [1959] stresses the need of many adolescents for a psychosocial moratorium, and that their seeking it against society's pressure for "progress" does not mean they regress but that they are searching for autonomy. It would be nice to have this insight extended to where it would do the most good: to the child in his first years of life.

Just because it is the most important progress the autistic child can make, the time, place, and conditions for a symbolic re-experience of earliest infancy, if not of life in the womb, must be his own spontaneous choice. It is the essential safeguard against his permanent fixation at this way of experiencing the world (because it proves too desirable) or against a premature effort at mastery (the child is so well defended that the experience is meaningless).

Here is only one of the many tragic contradictions in the treatment of autistic children. To rebuild their lives without danger, they must choose such a course on their own. To do what they must to gain autonomy, they have to exercise a quality they barely possess.

Thus we cannot tempt or induce the child to take such a course. All we can do is create the most favorable conditions for so extreme an emotional venture. These conditions, more than anything else, are the child's conviction that if he should start life again from the beginning, should "rebear" himself, so to speak, the world will not disappoint his trust; that he will not be hurt though he has made himself utterly vulnerable; that we will answer all his needs in a way that will not peg him to a level of helpless dependency but will help him to develop his own self. In short, he must have the conviction that his rebirth is self-chosen and self-regulated; that his development as a person from there on will proceed autonomously, with us as helpers, not controllers.

And this Joey was not ready to believe. He was still far too controlled by his anxieties and the machine existence they drove him to live. Even if we had had it in us then to give Joey the infantile care he longed for, and without reservation, he could not have felt it that way. More likely it would have been one more case of being overpowered by adults. Though not hostile this time, or for the convenience of adults, overpowering it would have been, and hence not likely to further real trust.

As for ourselves, we were sure we were not ready for this. None of us on the staff felt capable of carrying through by day and by night the emotional closeness required. To accept another person as one's baby, to give him the warmth, the total care an infant needs and enjoys after birth, takes a particular emotional relatedness that Joey's counselors did not feel they could continue for the needed length of time. He was still too strange, too mechanical. Even for our counselors it is not easy to take electric tubes to their hearts, as it were. Though more than ready to give babying care under difficult conditions and to mean it, they were not ready to do this with Joey because they cannot mean it if the child does not respond a little humanly.

If the counselors had decided at this time to induce Joey to go all the way back, if need be to a womb-like existence, the decision would have come out of theory and not from the conviction that "this is what he needs, and this is what I am eager to give him. Whatever he may think at first and however he may try to resist, soon we both will enjoy it very much, he the getting and I the giving." We do not believe that total dependent care does any good unless it is given with this conviction, and we have seen some very bad results when a child gives up his defenses without it.

For this and other reasons we had to wait until Joey was ready himself. But if he was to gather the courage, he had first to believe that good human relations were waiting for him to enjoy. He had to work out and humanize his machine life, to humanize his preventions. Most important of all, he had to get free enough of his anal concerns and misconceptions so that his birth would be a human one, not anal. At this time the vagina was still exploding. It was still too dangerous to be a safe place from which a baby could emerge into the world. So much he had told us himself.

Joey too gave indications that he was not ready for such closeness, though he wanted it. A short while later, at the end of his first year with us, he told us he was living on Mars, sometimes Jupiter, but always on another planet than we. Feeling drawn to his counselors, he had to defend himself from the emotions welling up in him by putting planetary space between them. If he got closer, he told us, the warmth would burn him up.[11] But though he warded off his budding attachment, he began to see us a bit more as persons. Now he called not only his favorite counselor by name, but also his second counselor and his teacher, the three persons working with him most closely.

Since we did not overpower him, either by asking that he conform or by expecting more closeness than he could afford, he no longer had to see us always as machines controlled by him or his gadgets. Occasionally it was safe to view us as persons who acted on our own and had an independent existence. At such moments we were human and hence he called us by human names.

Still, Joey was not yet functioning as a person who had integrated the various steps in development. On the contrary, the dominance of a mechanized elimination over all other psychosexual stages and modalities (to return to Erikson's conceptual structures) was due partly to his failure to master stages and modalities that came before it and after. Though he was most preoccupied now by problems of elimination, he had far from mastered them, nor could he do it alone. Because the mastery of each stage requires the appropriate social experience around it. It would not work, trying to help him with the earlier stages, so long as he remained beholden to a *depersonalized and mechanized* taking in (through his motors and wires) and giving out (his anality).

Why, when the essential damage to Joey's development took place around the earliest part of his life, did he get so preoccupied with elimination (as did Marcia and Laurie) in response to our therapeutic efforts? Before he came to us most of Joey's preventions had to do with taking in, with acquiring vital energy. It was only later that anality began to assert itself so openly, first with his eliminating in wastebaskets, then in diarrhea that engulfed the whole world. True, he arrived with countless anal preventions too; but they were minor at the time, compared with the overriding problem of ensuring his flow of electrical input.

11. I do not further discuss Joey's using space to ward off dangerous closeness since this particular psychotic mechanism has been discussed much more fully than I can here, by Ekstein [1954] and Ekstein and Wright [1952, 1954].

I believe the emergence of anality as a dominant issue had to do with two factors already discussed: First that the autistic child needs a minimal amount of autonomy to start life anew, and second that elimination is a much more assertive act than intake.

To be born does not require a decision, though to grow up successfully requires that the infant become active very early in the process. Why then, if activity and autonomy fail to develop or have withered away, can the older child not regain them around intake? And this, though I have stressed the importance of the nursing infant's activity in rooting for the nipple and in sucking? I believe the answer here, as it was there, is that however active the infant may be, neither eating (nor being stroked during the bath) can be as clearly self-assertive as elimination, because they depend on what another person gives.

It is true that many of our children, autistic or not, try to assert themselves around intake by grabbing food away from us, though we offer it freely. The idiosyncratic way in which some autistic children eat only a very limited and often strange diet and reject all else we may offer, plus their strange ways of eating, while due mainly to anxiety, are also token strivings for autonomy around intake. But somehow the thin bit of autonomy they win here has never, in our experience, gained them autonomy writ large as it does around elimination. Hence even for the child who will only eat what he grabs from another person, grabbing never conveys so strongly the feeling that "it's me who did this, and nobody else" as he gets when his own body pushes out feces.

From the beginning we had offered Joey both dependent care and chances for self-assertion. But he seemed unable to assert himself within a dependent context. Where he did use it to advantage was by eliminating as he pleased. Though we encouraged him to soil, he knew quite well this was not the way of the world, just as Marcia did. Though he took us up on our offer, there was little doubt in his mind that it was *he* who took us up. Defecating in our wastebaskets, or urinating on our floors, was not something we requested. It was something we readily accepted, which is quite a different matter. By soiling, he knew far better than a Marcia did that he was defying the customs of the world. Moreover his defiance was much more decisive than it could ever be by eating, however deviant his eating behavior.

This has been true of other autistic children; that though some responded quicker than others to infantile care, or to the much more effective tender, loving care, they all experienced some assertion around elimination long before they experienced it around intake, kinaesthesia, or any other physical or emotional satisfactions we could offer them. My speculation seems borne out by the fact that Joey could dispense with motors to run his elimination long before he felt there were things he could do to assure himself of the food he took in.

This is why the tender loving care Joey was offered, and which he wanted when he asked to be carried in the pouch, could not yet come to fruition. He still lacked the autonomy.

Some readers might now ask: how come I do not discuss phallic phenomena here; the phallic modality more than any other being that of aggressive self-assertion? The answer is simple: we have never worked with an autistic child who had progressed to this stage of psychosocial development before our work with him began.

In Joey's case it was not so much that he lacked the experience of self-assertion, but that it had not yet become a shared experience. We had tried for this, and he too had tried, by inviting us to join him in his oil wells and trail-tracks. But we were somehow too human, too much what we were. We were simply not depersonalized enough to be fit companions in his solitary mechanized world.

We had offered him our company, but we were still planets away. Nor could we join him as machines. Much as we appreciated their importance to him, we could not transmit vital strength to him through wires. We felt empathy, but that was as far as we could go. He himself could not join our human company and so we stayed, one on a side. The longing for company had been rekindled by the good care he had known now for an extended time. He was ready for company. But he could only join another person who was somehow more like himself. It had to be a person who was largely beholden to that zone and mode in which Joey now functioned; who, in some real or symbolic form, was an electric tube like himself.

If companionship could be found without having to relate in a human way, how much simpler for Joey to find a companion in his anality. So now that he was somewhat anxious for companionship he found it in another boy.

§
Kenrad the Terrible

There was just such a youngster at the School then, one who had merely been another "small person" but who suddenly became terribly important. It was the first time Joey showed any interest in another child, and typically it began around bowel functions.[12] A few days

12. One might ask: why did Joey need such a child companion when Marcia did not? Why could Marcia's counselors do it all for her, while Joey needed other

earlier Joey had made a painting of how he made trail-tracks (defecated) and how the trail-tracks exploded (Figure 19). At long last his explosions were linked to their human origin, defecation. This magic in his bowel movements he now extended to the other boy: "Something happened today. I saw one of the small persons in the bathroom. I knew that small person's name. I was peeking underneath the door. While he was having a bowel movement there was a big flash and an explosion."

Ken, the boy thus observed, was some three years older than Joey. He was immediately fused with Joey's most powerful tube, a Kenrad, the one name applying henceforth to both. It was the first time Joey had called anyone by name except his three favorite persons, and the first time he called another child by name, though a fabricated one.

While Joey had always hated "small persons," Kenrad the boy-tube he venerated. Ken himself had once been schizophrenic, and in that phase he too had focused on world destructive fantasies and preventions against them. He did it not through electronics but complicated number systems. Not as sick as Joey, Ken's magic took the much more sublimated form of mathematics. By now he was still much concerned with anal phenomena and their derivatives, but more by way of a compulsive personality and not delusionally. Their common anal focus, though expressed very differently, may explain Joey's choice of Ken and why Ken, with embarrassed reluctance, accepted Joey's advances.

Joey's relation to Kenrad was his first entirely self-chosen interest in another human being. Ken, for his part, seemed indifferent, if not annoyed at Joey's advances, and sometimes he really was. But at other times he enjoyed the idolatry. Probably too, he liked Joey's blatant acting out of an anality that by now was only latent in him.

A few weeks later Joey announced with elation that he knew Kenrad's surname; it was "Conflict." This conflict was soon acted out in bitter battle between Joey-and-his-tubes versus Kenrad Conflict. In the end Kenrad beat up the tubes till they were "a bloody sight" and the battle so decided, Ken, the boy, was Joey's god for nearly six months.

children as adjunct therapists, so to speak? First, there are differences between human beings, and Joey and Marcia were certainly different. So were their main caretakers. But we also believe that the different course taken by the history of these two children at the Orthogenic School has something to do with what we learned from working with Joey and other autistic children. Joey came when we had only recently begun to concentrate on trying to understand autistic children, and to develop our own methods for working with them. Marcia came about six years later, during which time we had learned much from him and others.

In point of time, Joey's tentative efforts to relate did not neatly begin with adults and then turn to children, but proceeded side by side. While they began with his getting closer to Fae, it was soon Kenrad, the boy, who became more important. Then, toward the end of the Kenrad period his other counselor and his teacher became more and more important to him too. Events described in the present section, for example, began while the trail-track game was still in active progress.

On approaching Ken he was reverent, sometimes crossing his hands before him in adoration. Violence was no longer committed by Joey; all destructive power was vested in Kenrad. But it was difficult at any one time to know if the Kenrad, whom Joey threatened would kill us, was the tube or the boy.

Soon all other powers and preventions such as trail-tracks and then diarrhea were first linked to, and then relegated entirely to this powerful, destructive alter ego. For a long period though wholly submissive to the imaginary Kenrad, Joey had small interest in what Ken, the real boy, was doing or feeling. This stood out in situations where Ken was most annoyed and embarrassed by Joey's behavior. When Joey approached Ken face to face there was veneration; this Ken pretended to ignore though it secretly pleased him. But whenever Joey approached from behind, or when Ken's back was turned, then Joey had to move Ken's bowels for him. Approaching him no less reverently, Joey pumped or drilled feces out so that "Kenrad won't get constipated."

Joey would stand as close as he could, or Ken permitted, to Ken's buttocks, making drilling or extracting motions with his hands, and then move slowly backward, as if extracting feces. Here again the pantomime was so good that the observer could almost believe it was happening. It was still beyond Joey's comprehension that anyone could possibly move his bowels "on his own steam." Only machinery could do that. He was contemptuous whenever we showed we were too stupid to know this, and delighted in his own secret knowledge.

Next, everything that happened in Joey's world, everything true or imagined, good or bad, that took place around the School, but especially bad, was all Kenrad's doing. If another child scratched himself or got a small cut, if a ball hit someone, or landed on the roof, Kenrad did it. When Joey's foot slipped, he complained, "How slippery it is. Kenrad was having diarrhea and it is very slippery." It was Kenrad's diarrhea that covered all the sidewalks and streets of Chicago, which was why Joey could not walk securely. But what Kenrad supposedly did was as nothing, compared to what Kenrad might do if he wished: Joey threatened that he would mutilate or kill us, destroy the School or perhaps the whole world. It was Kenrad now, not Joey, who would set the School on fire because we did something Joey did not like, a fire that would spread from the School and destroy the whole world. At other times he only threatened what would happen if we didn't watch out.

As Kenrad's power magnified, Joey became more "no good." Having transferred his ideas of grandeur about himself onto Kenrad, he could admit more and more to his own utter wretchedness. Protected by Kenrad's powers for revenge, he became more openly desperate about his inadequacies, and each time it hit him he ended up wanting to destroy himself. When he choked on a piece of popcorn he raged, "Take my lungs out; cut it off; you have got to do it; I am no good. Take my windpipe out; get rid of me." Kenrad was all-wonderful; Joey was all feces. "I am all waste material," he said. "My brain is all waste material. You have to knock it out."

Despite all of which, the two boys failed to relate to each other. Though Joey wanted companionship, first of all in his efforts at viewing the world through his anal preoccupations, but maybe even in efforts to broaden his view of the world, it did not work. The older child merely suffered Joey because it fed his badly depleted narcissism; he was not available to Joey in a flexible give and take relation. No solution could come from their comradeship because it was not the socializing experience Joey needed. He remained as isolated as ever.

Autonomy just cannot be gained outside of human relations. The process can begin around the experience of being in charge of one's defecation, but it cannot mature outside of a satisfying relation, and over time. Even if Joey should have been ready for mutuality, Ken was certainly not willing to consider such a relation with Joey.

And yet the comradeship was not without gain. Joey had further externalized his inner concerns and by projecting them onto a person made them more human. It is true that with his destructive powers projected onto Kenrad, Joey was more vulnerable than ever. But this too was a step toward humanity; instead of denying his vulnerability behind a machine existence and covering up, behind a screen of anal omnipotence, his desire to live in a satisfying dependence, he now faced it head on.

The courage to let himself feel helpless came from the security Joey had gained at the School. He now knew we would not trade on his weakness, punish his destructive wishes, let anyone he attacked take revenge, or let him hurt himself or others. Without all this he might have been afraid to shed his fictional powers. Moreover, he had vested his destructive fantasies in someone else and was less afraid he would enact them himself and be destroyed in the process.

§

Human Papoose

So when Kenrad had been doing Joey's dirty work for about six months and nothing disastrous happened, Joey began to show more infantile behavior. It began with squirting water through the nipple of a

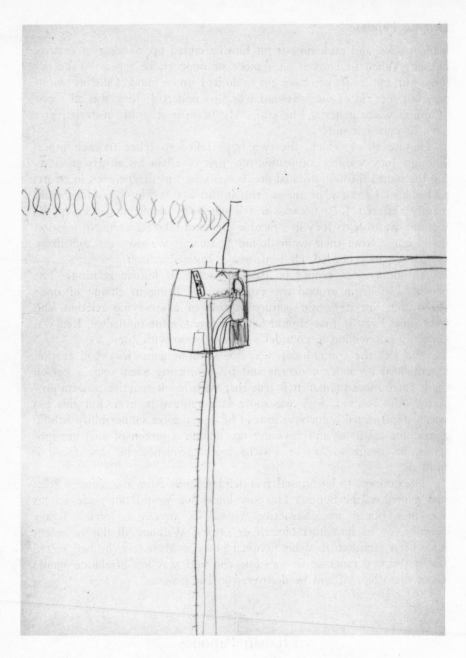

FIGURE 20. Joey as an electrical papoose, terribly small and lonely and wholly encased. He is suspended in empty space, run by power received through wireless connections from an unknown power on the outside.

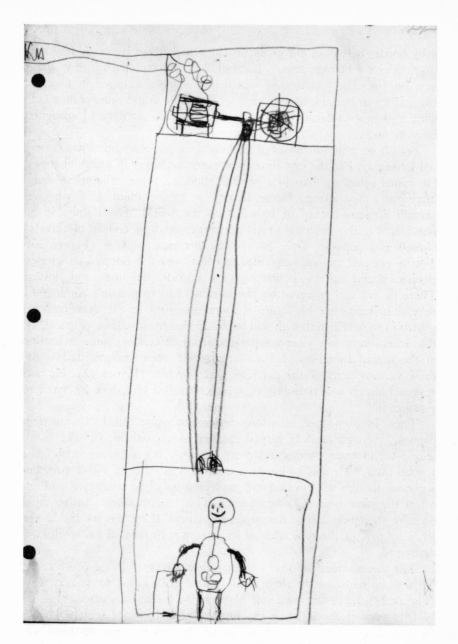

FIGURE 21. The same electrical papoose, but now grown in importance, and directly connected with the machine that "lived" Joey. The machine is now visible, and the papoose fastened much more securely to its supports.

baby bottle; he would not go so far as to suck from it yet. A few days later, he put a blanket around his shoulders and cuddled up in it. From now on for many months he was nearly always wrapped in blankets, covered up as he said, like a "papoose." Still he could only permit cuddling and other infantile care so long as he did not have to recognize them as such.

For about a month he lived entirely as a papoose; but then came a red-letter day. For the first time Joey expressed anger in a childlike way. He joined other children in a pretend shooting game, holding an imaginary gun and shooting, "Boom, boom," at another child. At last he was playing at guns instead of blowing up the world. The change in his fantasies was also reflected in his drawings; he drew endless pictures of himself as a papoose. Only he was an electrical papoose (Figure 20). Totally encased, he was suspended in empty space connected to wireless electricity and run by powers on the outside, unknown and unseen. There he sat, and powered by the current, had to produce elimination. Several months later his figure is more dominant in the drawings, has grown in importance though still haplessly run by machines (Figure 21). But urination is now clearly separated from defecation; some separation of the special functions of body organs had been recognized. He also drew various parts of the machine that ran him (Figure 22). He was approaching an understanding of what controlled him since he dared to visualize it.

Then Joey engaged in a long-drawn-out game called "Connecticut papoose," though he only played it when alone with his favorite counselor. As he once condescended to explain, "It's a person with glass around them." He was no longer a collection of wires in a glass tube but a person, though still encased and protected by glass, connected and cut off at the same time (Connect-I-cut). This fantasy threw further light on why shattering a tube destroyed the world. If he was the inside, the working part of the tube, then if its glass was broken all his world was destroyed.

The Connecticut papoose was therefore a way of living protectedly. Though he said that the shelter was brittle glass and drew it that way, (Figure 23), he in fact used soft blankets for his actual shelter.

In a parallel development the figure in his drawings acquired hands that do things and he himself began to try tentative masturbation. On the day he finally explained what a papoose was he began to masturbate in earnest. But here too he could only approach bodily freedom by first mechanizing himself. He moved his penis as if it were the handle of a machine and called it "cranking up the penis."

As time passed, we learned more about the Connecticut papoose. "It's

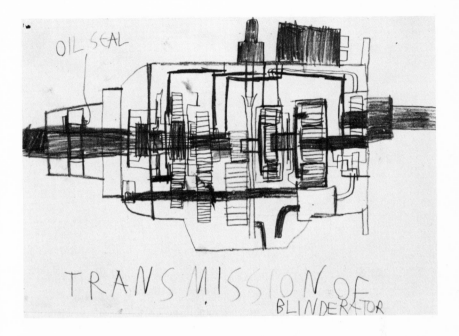

FIGURE 22. The machine that ran Joey by remote control, showing (as marked by Joey) both the "oilseal" that protected him somewhat from total disembowelment, and the "Transmission of Blinderator" which makes blind (prevents seeing and understanding).

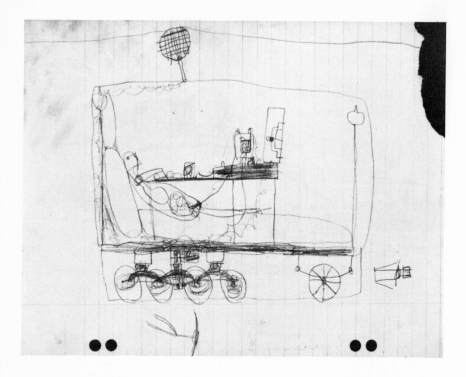

FIGURE 23. The Connecticut papoose; a way of living in relative safety. Here for the first time the papoose is not merely an entity run by a machine; it also runs the machine, since its arms and legs handle the controls.

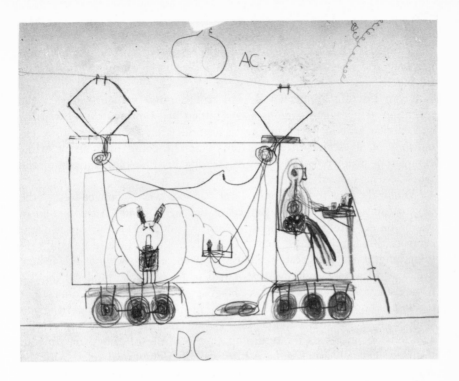

FIGURE 24. The papoose is definitely in the driver's seat in a hennigan wagon, with the machine relegated to a secondary position.

FIGURE 25. Nests in a tree, where infants can safely be hatched; the original is a colorful picture in varied hues.

a person in a glass tube with food." Elaborate structures called "hennigan wagons" were added, though the riddle of this term was not solved till much later.

From his talk about wheels and trucks now, we guessed that the invention of hennigan wagons also signified his wanting to be cared for and carried around in a baby carriage. Still later, the papoose took excursions on a "scenic cruiser" from which it could look about while completely protected. Was Joey recreating his first observations of the world, as he viewed it from the carriage?

While the key to the Connecticut papoose was "Connect-I-cut," the key to the hennigan wagon seemed to be "hen-I-can." In this hennigan wagon he definitely sat in the driver's seat (Figure 24). But the hen is a creature that hatches eggs. Joey was finally ready to believe he could do something about his greatest emotional need: to be reborn into a new life. This idea was so daring that it had to be carefully hidden behind a neologism, revealed only in secret language. It was as if the Connecticut papoose stood for the negative aspect of his wish, with he hennigan wagon as its positive counterpart. To survive, he had to cut off his emotional connections by returning to the inside of tubes, or papoose blankets. Through the hen he could rebuild an emotional relation to the world. He did not say yet what it was he could do. But since hens lay eggs out of which new life emerges, the "hen-I-gan" represents the hope of regaining the very life from which he had cut himself off. He was merely feeling more strongly that the only way to do that was to start all over again by being reborn.

In Joey's case the human womb had proved disappointing, since the life he began there was not a viable one. From the time he recognized that life at the School might be worth living, he had been searching for a better way to be born. Since machines were better than men, what more natural than to try to be reborn by them? This seemed to be the deeper meaning of his papoose period when he was enclosed, as in a womb, but by mechanical devices; nourished and kept going not by a mother, but by electricity.

Later, his relations to his counselors who were living beings may have started him wondering if it would not be better to be born of something living—as it turned out, a hen. Perhaps the hen seemed the best choice because what it gives birth to is all enclosed in a breakable shell, like his tubes. Life without a shell was still unthinkable to Joey.

But maybe oher children managed to live without a shell. If so, how did they do it? Perhaps to learn how they managed, Joey now became fascinated by Mitchell, a boy who was then the most adequate youngster at the School.

§
Mitchell the Good

The wish to be reborn is not the result of feeling the misery one lives in; otherwise the wish would be easy to induce. On the contrary, autistic withdrawal is a defense *against* feeling one's desperation; if one permitted oneself to feel its depth, one would prefer to die. The wish for a new life is predicated on the hope that one can have a better one, and the despair that such a better life cannot be grafted onto the present one.

That adults can have a better life is not very reassuring; this the autistic child knew all along. Even that other children can live more successfully he is dimly aware of. It is why he hates them, and out of envy will have nothing to do with them. But that other children who were once as withdrawn in misery as he is, now have a better life—this may seem reassuring. If such children can have wrested from their misery a satisfying life, there is reason for hope. This is why a once disturbed boy who was now doing well became so reassuring an object of identification.

While Kenrad remained important, he was not all-important any more; in a slow evolution Mitchell, who was also a few years older than Joey, received ever more attention. This boy, who was much healthier than Ken, was by then fully rehabilitated and soon to leave the School. For some time he had been very nice to Joey, even somewhat paternal. Joey recognized him as a real person and began to call him by his real name; nor did Mitchell share his name or identity with a tube. Nevertheless it seemed that in each personal relation Joey had to begin with defecation. This time it was not an actual observation but a dream, which he told to us as soon as he awoke. Joey had dreamed, "I was in the boy's bathroom with Mitchell. He was sitting on the toilet having a bowel movement and I was kneeling in front of him."

As Mitchell became more important, all of Kenrad's protective powers were transferred to him. Though Mitchell too was all-powerful, he dispensed only good things; all the powers of destruction remained Kenrad's. Just as Joey had stripped himself of his megalomanic powers and projected them onto Kenrad, he now divided these powers into good and bad, Mitchell and Kenrad.

Eventually he began to create for Mitchell and himself an imaginary family, the "Carr" family. Why a "Carr" family? One element was that in a car there were hopeful possibilities. One was not only passively driven around, but could actively drive. To get well Joey would have to use dependent satisfactions (being driven about) as a stepping stone to autonomy (drive by himself). Far more important was how he used this imaginary relation. Because now he made an autonomous effort to neutralize a bad experience of the past, a car accident that took place while his father was driving. This event had come to stand for what he viewed as the danger and destructiveness of his parents.

While drawing pictures of Mitchell and the Carr family, he worked through what to him had seemed deliberate abuse by his parents, if not a homicidal attempt, ending in his being pushed to seek solace in tubes. His (correct) description of the automobile accident was: "My parents were in the car once and the car went smash. Everything went all over. There was gas all over everything. And one time when my arm hurt badly (pointing to his scar) my parents told me to think of tubes—little tubes, big tubes, all kinds of tubes." Thus he connected the car smashup that might have killed him with his own suicidal attempts and with being shunted onto tubes. The Carr family stood for a good family where such things do not happen.

Having acquired a good imaginary family, he could recall more about his real family. One day he suddenly remembered something from his infancy "about light," adding a new aspect to his interest in light and electronics. Perhaps he was re-experiencing his first sensations of light and dark. Were these the most important stimulations he experienced as a baby, since he was left so much to himself? As he remembered it, "When I was a baby in a double bed, there were venetian blinds and I could see a light." As noted before, it took years for these blinds to open, revealing his parents in intercourse. This was merely the first time the fateful and screening blinds were remembered. After a long and thoughtful silence he added, "Wanda (the school nurse) and Mitchell are husband and wife, and I could be born from them."

So now he had told us in words that he wanted to be reborn, to begin his life over as the child of persons who lived at the School. He speculated how this might happen, asked again to be told stories about kangaroos and how they carry their young in their pouches. But that kind of a rebirth was not something he thought possible for himself. For that he was still too isolated, too beholden to things mechanical. Instead he had a dream about trees in which there were big nests. That his rebirth would have to occur from an egg in a nest we did not know then. Hence we overlooked the significant sequence of thoughts about birth at the School being followed by a dream about nests in trees. (This tree with nests he painted, the first picture he ever did in pleasantly bright colors; Figure 25.)

His excursions into fantasy about babies were usually short-lived, and from these he would turn to ruminating and drawing pictures of mechanical papooses. But as with his questions about kangaroos, he occasionally branched out to talk of animals in the uterus of the mother, and eventually this led to tentative talk about real babies in utero. He asked to be shown pictures and asked us to draw them. We were careful always to show the baby in utero as part of the mother, not as a uterus in limbo. But when Joey drew them, it was still a fetus disconnected from the mother (Figure 26).

Though his figures remained disconnected, he had grown impatient with isolation since he was no longer so terrified by human relations. With Mitchell, they began to be tempting, though still too dangerous to try. Except for Mitchell he still called no other children by their real names. Especially taboo were the names of his parents, or the words "father" and "mother." For that reason he could not even play the game "Mother May I?" But as he moved more and more toward relating, not all persons seemed as threatening as his parents any more. The task now was to free himself of their overpowering influence, and this he set to work on by being critical of them. Nor was it easy, because it threatened his system.

Being critical of his parents implied that he did not control them absolutely. To believe he controlled them meant to feel secure; it was why he created a machine world. So for his own security, he had to counteract each thing he was critical about in his parents by insisting it was all his own doing, not theirs. Despite the back-and-forth swings, it was a step in self-assertion. At least it was he, and neither machines nor his parents, who was now the prime mover, if only in creating his own misery.

As he outspokenly asked to be punished for his critical thoughts they came ever more to the surface. Slowly he began to recognize that his anger had to do with his own past and his parents, not with us or other children, and still less with motors and tubes. The day even came when he was angered by another child and was able to stop himself, saying he wasn't going to take it out on the boy "because really I like him." He had recognized another child as a person in his own right.

Since others began to be persons rather than objects run by his machines, he might get energy from them instead of his tubes. To be liked, and because of it like back, starts the infant on the human venture. Joey had been liked now for a long time by those who took care of him. But they were too much like parents for him to like them. Just to be liked is a passive thing; it gives comfort, maybe strength, but not autonomy. This can be gained only from actively liking another person oneself. Since he could not yet like adults it was crucial for Joey that he could like another child. Mitchell was the first person from whom he thus gained strength (still viewed as electrical energy) through touching some object that gave Mitchell

FIGURE 26. A fetus in
"limbo," disconnected,
but distinctly human,
not a papoose any more.

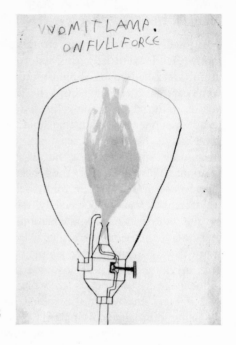

FIGURE 28. "Vomit lamp
on, full force."

FIGURE 27. A house built around its sewage system with elaborate
flywheels (left) regulated by Valvus. The chain (center) controls the
"abdominable" valve.

energy—his drinking glass, dinner plate, or some other object related to food.

As he got ready to try to connect with a person in a relation of some mutuality, he replaced electrical circuits with human closeness. Among the infant's early attempts to contribute to mutuality is to put things in the other person's mouth, to feed his mother as she feeds him and to eat in turn from her plate, out of her hand. Thus he replaces with objects around eating (pieces of food) the earlier prototype of all mutuality: that of breast feeding and being fed from the breast. So Joey "fed" from Mitchell's plate, recreating for himself the infant's closeness to another person in a feeding situation. While we had long been feeding him by hand, the activeness was ours.

Later he even dared to go up to Mitchell and touch him directly, climb on him or pet him. With greater physical closeness there was less talk about Mitchell's diarrhea. Getting energy from Mitchell, Joey began to find energy and security in food instead of electronics. In lieu of the tubes we did not replace, he had been carrying flashlights. Now he also carried candy.

Branching out from Mitchell, he began to talk to a few other children. He asked them to do things with or for him. Any slight rejection—any simple "no" or "wait a minute"—was an unbearable frustration that led to wild screaming and acting out with machines. But certain children he stopped referring to as "that person," and began to use "he." It preceded by some time his occasional use of the child's name. His own feelings, however, continued to be mechanical and dead. If Mitchell rejected some of Joey's interest in his elimination, Joey's reaction was, "He broke my feelings."

While Kenrad continued to do all the evil, Joey put more and more distance between himself and this bad alter ego. He now began to imitate the good Mitchell. He wanted to look like, to dress like, to be as big as Mitchell was. If he wanted or liked something, his way of letting us know was to say, "Mitchell will like this." It was enough interest in a person to further reduce his concern with diarrhea and machines.

Glad as we were that Joey reached out to a person, we had misgivings about this relation to Mitchell. Partly we felt we could help more if Joey had selected one of his counselors to reach out to, and partly we knew that Mitchell would soon be leaving the School. It was as if human relations could never work out happily for Joey.

Though he knew of Mitchell's impending departure and we had tried to prepare Joey, the trauma was severe when it came. That day he took to bed saying, "I have pneumonia; Mitchell left," and he returned to being run by machines. For some time he had been going to the toilet without mechanical help; now he frantically needed it again "to push out the bowel movement." If he was abandoned by Mitchell, he would abandon this world; and he went back to living on Jupiter or Mars. Icy worlds of dead space had to stand between himself and his feelings. It was still the only defense he knew against a deep disappointment in human beings. But by now he had a dim realization of what machines can do and what they cannot: a body split off from feelings is not much more than a machine, and smooth functioning is all one can expect of it.

§

A Boy Just Like Me

Though his mourning was great, Joey recovered from Mitchell's leaving in a few months. During the following year Mitchell's occasional visits were big events but not unduly so, and after two years Joey paid them little heed. His way of mastering the loss was to extend his fantasies about the Carr family and to concentrate on an imaginary companion called "Valvus."

Valvus was a boy "just like me." Valvus was neither all good nor all bad, neither totally helpless nor all powerful. Like a valve, he could turn himself on and off as much as needed or proper; in short he could regulate himself. From then on, for two years, both Valvus and the Carr family played a prominent part in Joey's life and ours.

Through Valvus he achieved autonomy, that is personal control of his own elimination. A mechanical device (valve) no longer ran his body, but was used to permit functioning in line with his own needs and desires. Valves too, belong to a system of energy. The selection of a valve suggests to us, as did the earlier electrical system, that Joey was somehow aware that more was needed than just self-regulation (the plugging in and out, or the switching on and off of electricity). Also needed was a back-and-forth flow, that would join him to some other person, and some day to humanity. His belief that such a union was only possible with someone "just like me" shows how beholden he still was to his autism. But that this alter ego was somebody outside himself is also an index of the desire to now escape that autistic isolation.

If one were to translate Joey's symbolic language into psychoanalytic concepts, one might say of his imaginary alter egos that Kenrad was all id and Mitchell part auxiliary ego, but mainly superego. Valvus, who had open access to either of the two institutions and could regulate their admixture, functioned much like an ego. True, it was still an externalized and mechanized ego, but ego nevertheless. This ego regulated what flowed from various parts of the system; it permitted them to influence each other so that Valvus was neither all good nor all bad. But this was still Valvus, not Joey. And it was still a self-contained system, not a flexible interacting with environment and people. In Valvus, Joey found for himself an externalized structure for an inner personality. But it was not yet a true personality, because that cannot develop through imaginary contact with others.

Therefore his fantasies about the Carr family remained of the old mechanical nature though in a slow process they acquired more normal features. Not always did the members of this family live in a car driven by remote control; no longer were their feces always mechanically extracted. Occasionally they lived like other people in a house. Only these were strange houses. Their most prominent feature was an elaborate sewage system with a "flywheel valve for sewage" that Valvus regulated (Figure 27).

While Joey wanted more and more to start life over, he could not comfortably anticipate another infancy in which he was totally helpless. Self-regulating Valvus was the safety device he had needed. He could now dare to recapture those corrective emotional experiences that would free him from the past for a new future.

As with other developments, this too began with a flare-up of his old preoccupations with tubes and lights, this time "incandescent lights." These lights were still powered by his body's elimination, as electricity had once provided the energy for his body. But the source of this energy was still a rather involuntary activity of his body, since the lights were powered by his vomit (Figure 28).

Whatever the source of their power, these lights were terribly important, because "burglars need to see babies. Babies need light; otherwise they get blind." Thus they were both necessary and dangerous: because of these lights "babies get blind." Here too he was caught in a vicious circle of opposites with no exit: bright lights blind us, but so do their absence.

Perhaps babies who in the middle of the night see things they are not supposed to see are like burglars, stealing their parents' treasure—adult secrets. But while babies need light, they get blind with or without it. Is that because what they see is so absorbing or so frightening that they can think of nothing else and become blind to the world? And yet if they don't see (don't understand), they are also blind. Bad people, like burglars who steal, can see the baby in the night. What did these burglars steal? Did they rob Joey of his humanity by not permitting him to feel? If there had been light in the bedroom his parents might not have had sexual relations and Joey would not have needed to blind himself.

These questions may serve as greatly simplified examples of Joey's ruminations, circular, incredibly complex, their origin remaining unconscious. They engaged him to the exclusion of nearly everything else, although he allowed nothing to come to consciousness (come to light) except the cryptic kind of statements I have quoted. His reasons for keeping them rigidly in the unconscious are implied by the little he did say. For babies to live in this world they need light; that is, light would have to be shed if they were to understand what goes on in the darkness of their unconscious. But if there were light, what they found would be so terrible as to make them go blind. Either they would be blinded by the powers that be, for shedding light on issues that should be kept hidden in darkness, or they would have to blind themselves since no one can live with such knowledge.

Alas, Oedipus! For those who seek and find the hidden truth the punishment is blindness. Better not to search. But this again means to be blind to the truth. So to be blind is inescapable.

I doubt that Joey was familiar with the myth of King Oedipus and may never have heard it at all. Yet he spoke of the need of babies to have light—as Oedipus would never have slain his father if he had been enlightened to know Laius for his father. Hence the story of King Oedipus tells us more: that tragedy awaits parents and child if the parents desert their child by denying him a place in their intimate life.

All autistic children feel deserted in this sense. Only by being totally "out of touch" with all others do they protect themselves from Oedipus' fate. Since they do not know who their parents are—because, emotionally speaking, it is only intimate relations that make the biological parent a true parent—every person they meet might be the one. In which case they had best not come close to anyone at all.

Here then was another circle in which Joey was caught: the wish to see, to understand, to shed light; and the converse anxiety of being punished with blindness. Was this another reason for his choice of electricity to express his central problem? In our day electricity is *the* source of light, short of the sun. If babies need light and the parents do not provide it, what could be more important for survival than to secure it for oneself?

Something else is true of electrical power. Electric motors are driven by alternating current, the source of energy continually changing its valence from positive to negative. There is never any rest, any solution. Neutralized energy is never available—to use the term psychoanalysis borrows for describing the ego energy we use in dealing with the external world. All such energy Joey used up in the longing to see, to understand, and the fear and avoidance of understanding.

With his interest in incandescent lights came also a fascination with headlights. During this period Joey could hardly see where he was going for his concentration on the headlights of cars. Often it was hard to get him away from a parked car whose lights he would fondle and pet. From other children we knew that headlights (like overhead lights) stood for breasts, and years later Joey told us they meant that to him. It was still another connection between lights and the elements giving life.

Now the power of tubes declined further and their character changed. So much had he made them his very nature that when he himself became softer, began to feel, they went through a parallel development. He came to think of them not as something that produces energy but gets it. Like infants, they began to depend for their functioning on the mothering care of machines. When he now talked about tubes and about infants, how vulnerable they are and how they need to be cared for, it was often hard to know if he was talking about tubes or real infants.

We felt that tubes were no longer a source of deepest anxiety to him or a block to his knowing human beings. So there seemed little reason to withhold them any more. Since he had never stopped asking for them fervently, we let him have some. Once he had a real tube again he reverted instantly to old behavior. Just holding one in his hand seemed to incapacitate him and he lost the new body control he had acquired. Walking upstairs, which he was now doing safely every day, he stubbed his toe. This he blamed on the tube and swore again he would break his leg off and replace it by a spare. But it was all very short-lived. His excessive pleasure at getting the tubes was more pretended than real. He had asked for them too often to let us know too soon that they were no longer important to him.

But neither was he quite through with them yet. Just as he had divided his powers between Kenrad and Mitchell, so he now divided tubes into bad "abominator" tubes (which burned out and smelled like diarrhea, also bad now) and life-giving tubes (which provided light and warmth to hatch eggs). Good tubes later became "persimmon" tubes. By naming them for a uterus-shaped fruit he came closer to letting us know what tubes had symbolized all along: his desire for the closeness to a mother he had known only in utero; his hope of getting from a tube what he could not get from human beings; his desire to again live in a womb, and his fear of it.

Finally he got tired of all tubes. "They feel just awful," he said. And turning off the imaginary machine that fed tubes he said, "The tubes were burning too long. I don't need them any more." With which he settled in his counselor's lap and talked of his coming birthday and the presents he would get. Wholly content for the moment, he concluded by saying, "We sure did lots today." Life, freed of tubes, was no longer empty. Very occasionally it even held out pleasant expectations.

But such moments were rare and fleeting. He remained extremely sensitive to any negative feelings or ambivalence on the part of staff members. Once, for example, his counselor wavered about something and Joey instantly attacked her, hitting and screaming. Then he became terrified and quieted down, but all feeling had left him. "I need to freeze," he said. "My arms and legs have to turn to ice," and he tried to break them off.

These were the occasions when he demonstrated how it was not parental rejection or ambivalence that made him turn himself into a dead machine, but his own reactions to them. As long as we suffer we do not dehumanize ourselves. Only as we inhibit our actions and stop ourselves from feeling, do we cease being human. Others can destroy us, but we alone can turn ourselves to ice or become a machine. The autistic child then, is the child who keeps his feelings from being felt, from coming to consciousness, and thus prevents himself from acting in line with his feelings.

Still, Joey's desire to freeze implied the recognition that at times now there was warm blood in his veins, that he was becoming more alive. There were periods now when despite what he said and did he no longer needed most to be protected from a horrible world. Instead he needed to be shown over and over again that there was much in the world to enjoy, and that all of it might eventually be his.

While he did not want it known that he was beginning to play and enjoy it, he did learn to do a few new enjoyable things. Even when he chewed gum or ate candy, he was anxious to keep us from knowing he enjoyed it. If he felt observed he would surreptitiously let the gum or the candy drop from his mouth.

Since he was now aware of his feelings and could no longer see his body as a machine, freezing up did not work as easily or well. It was his body now that had to protect him from feelings. As soon as he began to feel his body, he became deeply dissatisfied because it seemed to give him nothing but trouble or pain. He was convinced, for example, that no one else had ever had earaches.

When in good contact, he could recognize that he had earaches only when there were certain feelings he did not want to hear about or recognize. But it proved again that machines were better. So he insisted he could only hear through machines because them he could turn off as needed. We assured him we would help, told him that all people suffer from bad feelings and still manage to survive, but this scared him. Still he did want to talk, and since feelings were so dangerous, he had to take precautions.

First he spoke about his feelings only over the (imaginary) radio where there was no connection between him and the other person. Then he agreed to use toy telephones connected by wires. Meeting up with feelings was so risky that he also had to sit in a certain place and go through a long ritual to make sure that not only he, but his counselor, was situated safely. But with feelings and persons safely separated he could vividly describe how things moved from bad to worse in his world, how a mere device meant at first to protect him from too much feeling ended up by destroying him as a person.

Hearing, we may assume here, stood for all contact with others: "First you get wax in your ears. That protects you and closes up the ears so that you cannot hear things you do not want to hear. You get more and more wax to make sure you do not hear it; this makes you deaf. Deafness spreads so much that everybody gets deaf and nobody can hear. It spreads to blindness. Then people are deaf and blind and have blind battles. Horrible things happen with your feelings. Feeling kills you."

Remarkable insight into how his own defensive armoring ended in total paralysis. Even more remarkable to understand that by making himself blind and deaf to the world, it then seemed inhabited by people as insensitive as he had become. When people have lost all emotional rapport with each other and then meet, horrible battles ensue because they are blind and deaf to each other. The result is emotional death.

We agreed with Joey that often we do not want to recognize our feelings, are afraid of them: that maybe what made him so angry was that he felt everyone was deaf to his feelings and needs. "That is how it was at home," he said, "like with my parents."

This recognition of how he lost his feelings if not also his humanity he achieved a short time before the second anniversary of his coming to the School. It turned out to be a very important date because to celebrate it Joey let others use his name for the first time. Later that day he went further by sending a message to the other children on his new telegraph set, and signed it. The taboo on his name had been lifted.

It was after this that he returned to insisting he could only do things in moving vehicles, that our dining room was a dining car; that he could only eat in a moving vehicle. His bed was again equipped with elaborate, skillfully copied automobile motors, carburetors, generators, and wheels. But this time it was not so much to be run by machines—that delusional system was in decline—as because he could only sleep in a moving car. We guessed he was trying to reproduce uterine conditions, where the baby "eats" and sleeps while the mother carries him around.

He liked to put a towel between his legs as if it were a diaper, and to urinate and defecate into that. This he called "playing baby." Soon he was taking a bottle of pop into bed with him, sucking through a straw. It was self-feeding, not a passive being fed as before. He kept the bottle on his chest, hidden under the blanket so that he looked like a baby who sucked liquids from his own body.

Activities once shunned were now attractive if they could be made into symbols of infantile care. For example, he suddenly wanted to play cribbage. His interest in the game had to do mainly with the two hidden words in its name, "crib" and "bag." A container called "cribbage" became very important and was carefully locked with a key. In this "cribbage" went all kinds of "papoose objects." When we commented that all of them were things babies like to play with, he grinned and nodded.

He became more interested in childish toys, particularly stuffed animals. He played with dolls and hand puppets—took them to bed with him, cuddled them, and rocked them in a cradle. He dared to enter active games with other children for longer times at a stretch.

Independence led to new difficulties. Up to now Joey had always stayed close to his counselors unless extraordinarily upset. Now he often strayed, and a few times the two were separated as he suddenly began to wander off in stores or on the street. Having lost sight of a counselor, he grew frightened and angry and would afterwards threaten, "I am not staying in this world." If we were to lose him he would lose himself again.

With his new relative independence Joey could finally let go of the last of his "preventions" at the dinner table. As he dispensed with these rituals, what they had protected him from became clear. He knocked things over, broke dishes, threw and spilled food—very mischievously, and much as a baby in a high chair might do.

§

The Miraculous Egg

Active ventures into the outside world were accompanied by an ever-increasing interest in the world of the egg. Much more important than tubes now were books on chickens. Looking through books about the birth of babies, and knowing they described human birth, he said his only interest was to learn more about chickens and eggs. Bertha, the only female in the Carr family, turned out to be a person who lays eggs: "You know, very few people do."

He could not have indicated more clearly that he was leaving his autistic isolation than by saying "only very few people do." He himself, as it turned out, was this Bertha, since he was the person who laid eggs. Since it was himself he referred to when he said he had important things in common with a few people, he was saying that a common bond now existed between him and at last these very select few.

At this point he did not quite dare to let us know he was talking of himself, so he called the person who laid eggs Bertha. Why Bertha? We knew of no one by that name in his past or present life who had any significance to him. But Joey had always played on the words hidden within words—encapsulating messages within words as he himself was encapsulated in a tube. Hence one cannot neglect that the name Bertha contains the word "berth" (perhaps the safe berth eternally sought) or that berth and birth are identical in sound. And if one breaks Bertha up and puts the last letter first, the solution to the riddle of this name emerges as "a berth."

Holidays and other types of anniversaries were always significant dates for Joey, around which new developments took place. Just as machines ran his life so the calendar ran the major steps of his inner growth. At his second Christmas (when he had been with us about twenty-one months) he suddenly added an "egg wagon" to his car-park. The explanation was that it had to be warm for the egg to hatch. And there it rested until Easter, soon after his second anniversary. Then he began to talk about hens, to imitate chickens, and said that I was a chicken who laid an egg. Sitting close to his favorite counselor he picked up her skirt and said, "I want to build a nest by you. Let's build a nest in there."

Joey's second Easter was the first big holiday he really enjoyed at the School and may have strengthened his hopes for a better life. He was very pleased with his Easter eggs. On his own initiative he made a large incubator, copying one he had seen at the Museum of Science and Industry. His big concern was keeping the temperature correct, regulating it so that the eggs were not too warm or too cold. This was also when his tubes changed and the purpose of good tubes became mainly the nurturing of incubator eggs. To this end he now used all his "incandescent" lights for giving light and warmth instead of for destruction.

He was also making cryptic remarks about henpox and chickenpox. He could not tell us what they meant but one day he wrote one of them down (Figure 29). He said it was "the most important word in the world," and laid it out as follows:

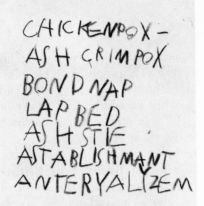

FIGURE 29. CHICKENPOX cryptogram as Joey drew it.

FIGURE 30. The chickenpox, dated two years before Joey came to the School.

FIGURE 31. The chickenpox, dated some time after Joey's coming to the School.

FIGURE 32. The chicken-hen, showing the womb exploding.

FIGURE 33. The hen electric, pregnant with the electrical fetus. (Compare its front compartment with that of the Connecticut papoose and the hennigan wagon.)

CHICKENPOX
ASH CRIMPOX
BONDNAP
LAP BED
ASHTIE
ASTABLISHMANT
ANTERYALYZEM

We did not know what to make of this at the time, but the following interpretation agrees with his own later thinking about it, and with the way he broke down the words into separate lines: CHICKEN–POX / ASH–CRIM–POX / BOND–NAP / LAP–BED / ASH–TIE / ASTABLISHMANT / ANT–ERYALYZ–EM. Thus the chicken box is the place he retired to in order to start a new life. He had become ash, because of the crime (either the one he committed, or the one committed against him). In this box he formed a bond to the person who let him nap on her lap as if it were a bed. Ashes refer again to his burnt-out feelings. The rest is more difficult to decipher. He was now tied to (was living in) an establishment and there, as regarded his feelings, he hoped to "realize them."

As things became better for Joey, his talking and writing in riddles became more and more playful. When he felt good he called his favorite counselor "hen" or "pox." At rare times, when extremely pleased with her, he used the single name "henpox."

All these more or less spontaneous events were paralleled by a growing ability to relate. In order to do this he seemed to have to begin the way the infant does: he wanted to be fed like a baby. Where he had rejected all baby foods before, he now ate them with pleasure. And again his tubes served him, instead of the other way around. They all became "osterizer" tubes that mash up and prepare baby food. From this he went at last to accepting the nursing bottle. He wanted it "just like the baby drinks," with the milk warmed, and given to him in bed where he lay comfortably. He welcomed having his counselor hold him and rock him while he sucked from the bottle in passive enjoyment.

About the same time he began to play with toys in an infantile way. He pushed little cars around on the floor as if he perceived them as independent from himself and as if he were interested in their functioning apart from himself.

Life was definitely better for Joey, and one day he told us, "Now the lights are pretty much the way they should be. It isn't real hot and it isn't real cold, so I don't mind too much. I don't bother about the lights so much anymore." Even planning to destroy other people seemed less important. "I used to think when I'm sixteen, I'll get up on a tree and fall down like an angry bear on all the bad people and kill them. But the bears here are pretty nice so I won't have to do that now. His first remark shows an identification with his teddy bear, which for two years he had thrown at others when angry. The second comment about the bears who were pretty nice referred to the children and counselors he lived with since the boys in his dormitory group called themselves the "Bears."

After Joey had been with us about two years and four months, he made a series of drawings over a six-week period, showing the development of the chickenpox, year by year. This culminated in the chicken-hen and a hen electric, pregnant with the electrical fetus. (Figures 30–33) During the weeks he was making these drawings he behaved more and more like an excited hen, flapping his arms like wings, stuttering and cackling, fluttering about as if he were trying to take off and fly. When he had finished the drawings, he also told us what they meant.

On this day his cackling, his flapping of wings, and his stuttering reached a paroxysm. Suddenly he became very still and crawled under a table over which he had draped blankets so that he was entirely hidden beneath them. There, by his own statement, he gave birth to an egg out of which he pecked his way newborn, into the world. "I laid myself as an egg, hatched myself, and gave birth to me."

Chickenpox had not been the disease. It was the box inside the hen where eggs grow; the womb out of which he had hoped to give birth to himself. He told us how he and Valvus, his alter ego, "pecked our way out of the shell when we were born. We weren't joined together, but we were very close." Later he added, referring to his original birth, "I was hatched from an egg and a criminal broke it with a hammer and cracked it open."

As if to specify exactly what happened, he gave himself a riddle. He wrote several sentences, some of them nonsense words, and gave himself the task of checking the ones that were false. This he did, and the remaining sentences read: "The bomb exploded. A cannibal exploded." Between these two he had checked as false: "A hen died." He then corrected this sentence to read: "A hen is living."

Obviously he had feared all along that in the process of exploding the bomb and the cannibal, the life-bearing hen that carried Joey might die. That was one of the reasons he had waited so long, testing us out. When at last he felt sure that the egg would not be destroyed if he exploded the bomb and the cannibal, he broke through and came into this world. He was no longer a mechanical contrivance but a human child.[13]

---

13. For the story of another child of the Orthogenic School who gave birth to herself, see the story of Mary [1955].

All this poses many problems, not all of which we feel we can solve. One of them is the question of why Joey chose to be reborn from a chicken's egg. The protective shell I have mentioned often. A main reason for favoring the bird (nests in trees) and chicken for his new origin is that birth by egg comes closer than human birth to a fecal theory of procreation. Since everything of importance in his delusional world consisted of feces and derived from them, it would not be surprising if he thought people too were created from fecal matter. Indeed, this may have been the origin of his belief in the fecal nature of the world, and not the other way around. If birth (his birth) represents the birth of the world and began in a cloaca, why not assume that the world thus born consists of feces?

His fear of the vagina has been mentioned before. Out of the cloaca of a chicken both feces and eggs are sent into the world. The vagina that explodes can be dispensed with if birth is from the cloaca (only one changed letter makes a bomb out of a womb). Also, if he felt he had to give birth to himself, such a birth could only take place out of a body opening he possessed. If this opening was the rectum, then all was well.

Another element may have favored an egg birth. If the mother is the crucially dangerous person, then to be nursed by her is like being poisoned (his parents gave him tubes "with poison inside"), while the infant's rage changes the wish to nurse into the wish to devour (the cannibal). Thus a birth entailing nursing might have seemed too dangerous to Joey. But if he were born out of an egg, he could fend for himself the minute he crawled out of his shell. There would be no need to nurse from the breast.

What about the cannibal that had to explode before Joey could stop being a mechanical boy? Joey told us: "I'm a cannibal." What are cannibals? "People who eat each other." Because it is only a mother's wish to carry her baby, her desire to feed him from her body, that makes his taking from her not a robbing. The unwanted baby is indeed like an intruder and his feeding from her makes him a cannibal. As a baby in utero he had been a cannibal eating his mother. This he still wanted and feared. But if he was a cannibal, so was everyone else. To become a person, to stop being a machine, meant to be eaten by others. His solution of getting sustenance from wires was not only the wish to be fed through an umbilical cord, but a way to avoid the closeness to human beings that could tempt him to eat them or be eaten.

When Joey gave birth to himself and crawled out of the egg, all these problems were solved. But a newborn who is already close to twelve has lost an awful lot of time and has a vast amount of living to make up.

§
"No More Pox; No More Ash"

Many conversations followed these events, talks about coming out of the chickenpox, the dangers involved if he did it permanently, the difficulties he would have to master if he gave up living inside a shell. Joey pondered and pondered. But by Christmas of that year he quietly set himself the task "no more pox, no more ash." And so it was.

As if to underscore his feelings he developed what for a time seemed an obsession, his playing a record of the *New World Symphony* over and over again. Joey was quite open about the reason for his interest; he wanted to enter a new world.

When Memorial Day came round Joey, like the other children, took part in a little parade. Recalling his "Radiant TV" float of the previous year, he decided to do something entirely different. He made a float for his favorite teddy bear and had him carry a big sign that read: "'Feelings are more important than anything under the sun."

During the next months Joey cried at his unhappiness. Up to now he had cried very rarely, and only in violent rage. Now he cried because: "How can I be like other children if they do not like me? I want to be like them, I want them to like me."

It took him nearly a year from learning to cry to being able to laugh. But having learned it, his reaction to mishaps changed radically. Before this Joey had only one reaction—some part of his body should be destroyed or at least punished. Now when something went wrong he expressed astonishment and pride because "I did not hurt myself." He (his body) had become something of value, to be cherished and protected from harm.

To recount the further vagaries of Joey's attempt to make up for twelve lost years, to be an adolescent when he had never been a feeling infant or child, would take as long again as the foregoing account. The next years of our work together were a true "research into times past;" so many steps in development were lost out on, at the time when they come natural to the growing child. Nor did he succeed in regaining them all; and even those he did regain were not all as rich as if he had known them at the appropriate time. Sometimes Joey set to work with a will; at other times he regretted that he ever came out of his shell because life was so difficult for him. But he never once wanted to resume his mechanical life.

Since the intention here was not to follow the child after he has given up the autistic position, but to discuss the nature and treatment of infantile autism and what we can learn from it about human development, my task is substantially done. Only one of Joey's efforts to recapture the past may round out his story. It pertains to the kind of experiences that normally come so early, that happen so all by themselves that they are hardly remarked upon, though they took Joey years to achieve: in my example here, the courage to defy another person through a temper tantrum and to find, after it was over, that their closeness stood intact as before.

Joey had long allowed his counselors and even Lou, his teacher, to hold him and carry him, had sat in their laps and let them cuddle him. But it turned out that for Joey this was something entirely different from asserting his own aggressive feelings in closeness to their bodies. Sitting on their laps had enabled him to get hold of them as persons with bodies that had something physical to offer his body, but only when he was passive. Therefore it now became important to find out if he was also accepted in physical closeness when he was aggressively self assertive.

It began with a series of elaborate procedures wherein Joey put blankets over himself and Lou—his preferred adult after Fae left the School. This, for Joey, was something entirely different from our covering him or both of us with blankets, or Joey alone wrapping himself in a blanket. It was Joey himself trying to become part of a twosome, as opposed to our doing the trying. It was his reaching out to a Thou, rather than us doing the reaching that he only tolerated at first and later even enjoyed. By now he recognized he had feelings and knew he wanted to be liked; but he was still afraid of them because he dreaded disappointment. Hence the temper tantrum, a back-and-forth between longing and anger, because anxiety stopped him short of his goal. Nevertheless, he was now going beyond just having feelings for another person, to taking action on his own to express them, and in their whole range from passive dependence to aggressive assertion. He had progressed from just wanting to be liked to truly liking another person.

This venture entailed any number of safety devices. Once the blankets were over Lou and himself he imposed numerous restrictions. Only much later did he tell us why: Joey was convinced that unless Lou was securely tied down he would get very angry if Joey were to touch him, and would leave. The purpose of the elaborate maneuvers was to so tie Lou down that he could not possibly escape. After innumerable experiments at binding the loved person fast, Joey finally approached. But as he came closer to touching Lou he became terribly excited. This time the excitement no longer led to explosions, but to what he called a "rumpus" which had all the hullabaloo of a tantrum. He now made rumpuses early and often, as he used to make explosions when he first came. Having emotions exploded him then. Now they excited him beyond his capacity to contain them. So having touched Lou he rushed to the farthest corner of the room shouting wildly, only to approach and reapproach, touching and retouching again. Reaching out for touch on his own was that unbearably exciting.

Then came many months of far greater daring when his behavior had less the character of a tantrum and more of a conscious seeking of body closeness. He would put an arm around Lou's shoulder, or sit in his lap for a moment—after which he would rush away. But now the adult was no longer supposed to stay put as when Joey had tied him down. Now he had to rush after Joey and catch him, so that Joey could know that his touch had been welcome. Here, late in Joey's development, appeared the "chase me" game that stood at the beginning of Marcia's development. In so different a sequence do autistic children go about regaining late in life the early experience of closeness and of feeling themselves desirable to parental figures.

There is a reason why the chasing appeared so early in Marcia's rehabilitation, and so late in Joey's. Though Marcia was chased by us, for a long time she was just a passive object in the chase. She did not begin by touching us; she did not initiate the physical contact. That Joey could and did is why the account of his life can stop here.

Because to be born again, to be able to feel, even to wish to be liked, is not enough for a full human existence. What is still lacking is the ability to be active: to deliberately reach out to others for warmth and affection, to dare on one's own to close the gap between self and other; to reach out and change one's physical apartness into closeness between body and body; to be a lover and not merely to enjoy being loved. All this Joey achieved in his rumpuses.

When he had reached this point with us he wanted to try for greater closeness with his parents. On his own he let us know that now, after nine years, it was time for him to leave us, and so he did. Joey returned home and resumed life with his family. From there he completed his education in a technical high school, making good use of his persisting but now more normal interest in technical matters.

§

A Visit: Three Years Later

When Joey finished high school he asked his parents, as a graduation present, to have a visit with us. He traveled to Chicago by himself and during his stay with us visited old friends on his own. Fae was now married and a mother, and he visited with her in her home. Lou was still with us and they had a happy reunion, as Joey did with other staff members he had come to care for and who were still at the School. Unfortunately he could not visit with Barbara, who had moved to California.

It was obvious that during the intervening years Joey had made continuous progress in learning to live in society, though it did not always come easy. He had already worked out plans for his future, namely to continue with his study of electronics while holding part-time employment. It was on this visit that I asked for permission to publish his story and to transcribe the interview that follows. This he gave me graciously and without hesitation, as he did once before when I published a short account of his development. As is natural on such occasions, we reminisced and I found our conversation so interesting that I decided to include portions of it here. I told him I was awfully glad he had come to visit us, and that we were all very proud he had done so well. "Tell me," I asked, "how does it feel to see the old place?"

JOEY. Oh, I can remember some very wonderful times and also some very hard times. Like for example that time when I was scared of why I was here and had to run away from it.

B. B. And how has life been treating you since you left us?

JOEY. Oh, it's felt very different and there was lots of anxiety at times, about going into a new life and doing things more for myself. For example, I can remember when I used to feel I needed somebody to help me make friends, and now I do it all myself.

B. B. Good. And do you now have a better understanding why you came into such trouble as a child?

JOEY. Yes, I do. I think a great deal of it had to do with the fact that I was afraid to tell any person how I felt.

B. B. And that's why you kept it all to yourself? Wouldn't talk with anybody?

JOEY. That's right.

B. B. Why were you so afraid? What did you think might happen if you had told people how you really felt?

JOEY. As I remember it, I had a feeling, a long time ago, that I would find out that somebody wouldn't like me. Or something like that.

B. B. If you told them what you thought?

JOEY. Yes, I think I also, deep down inside, felt that I might not be liked. I think actually the feeling stemmed from loneliness, of not telling anyone how I felt for such a long time.

B. B. This terrible loneliness of yours.

JOEY. Yes, it was very much a terrible loneliness. And it showed very much whenever my parents would have company. I would worry about it and feel I had to be in on it. I felt I just had to, even if I stayed up way long into the night, when I was only a very young child.

B. B. And why did you make all these explosions? Do you remember the explosions?

JOEY. Yes, I certainly do.

B. B. Why did you make them?

JOEY. Well, it stemmed primarily from a feeling of anger that I had . . . that built up as a result of having to keep these feelings so much to myself. It was just like a feeling of being sorry for myself— that I was cheating myself out of the comfort I could have by talking to people about how I really felt.

B. B. But you just couldn't get yourself to talk about it.

JOEY. Yes, that's right. It was very hard.

B. B. Who was the first one to get you to talk about your feelings?

JOEY. Fae was.

B. B. Fae was. Do you want to see her?

JOEY. Yes, yes. I'm hoping to see Fae while I'm still here.

B. B. Well, we have to arrange that today.

JOEY. Yeah.

B. B. Tell me, how did it feel to come back after all these three years?

JOEY. Oh, in certain ways it felt the same and in others it felt very different, primarily because I know I'm no longer a boy in high school. I'm ready to go on for further education, get a job for myself, and earn my own money. And I'd be buying my own clothes and other things that I need. Another very important factor is—and this happened after I left here . . . but I was really becoming able to tell people much more freely how I felt . . . like when I first *start* having the feeling, instead of waiting until long after. Because then I might find myself expressing it either by making a terrific explosion or trying to do something to hurt myself or getting all upset when something went wrong.

B. B. And how else did it feel—being back?

JOEY. It felt good and it stirred up lots of anxieties about being away from it for so long.

B. B. Yeah? What were the anxieties?

JOEY. Well, mostly that there was a chance . . . the anxieties were about a chance to talk to what I feel are my best friends.

B. B. Who?

JOEY. Like Lou and Fae and others.

B. B. And how did you feel after talking with Lou?

JOEY. I felt a much greater feeling of satisfaction.

B. B.   Good. Now, is there anything else you want to tell me? Do you think there's anything we should do differently at the Orthogenic School? So we can learn for the future.

Joey.   There's a very interesting thing I was thinking of. I can remember the time when Fae and Barbara would feed me at the dinner table. Well, I remember having a much greater feeling of comfort whenever this happened.

B. B.   When they fed you?

Joey.   Yes.

B. B.   By hand?

Joey.   Yeah.

B. B.   That was an important experience to you?

Joey.   Yes, it was.

B. B.   Very good. When was this? Right at the beginning?

Joey.   It was just a little after that. I think it started just before the anniversary of my first year here. And they also did it with baby food, starting the same time.

B. B.   Where did they give you baby food, in session or at the dinner table?

Joey.   They gave me the baby food in session and in the dormitory, on my bed.

B. B.   At night or during the day?

Joey.   At night particularly.

B. B.   And that made you feel very comfortable?

Joey.   Yes, at that time . . . yeah.

B. B.   Well, I'm glad. This is very useful and will go into my story. Is there anything else you think I should put in the story?

Joey.   Well, another thing is that this very same comfort I can get for myself by talking to my friends about how I feel about any certain situations that come up.

B. B.   That is, the same comfort you experienced then by being fed with baby food, you now get from talking with your friends about how you feel. Is that it?

Joey.   Yes, yes.

B. B.   I just want to understand it correctly because that's very important.

Joey.   Yeah.

B. B.   Tell me, do you know how your interest in electricity developed which you still have, after all?

Joey.   Well, as I remember I was interested in electricity or anything that was mechanical, I think, when I was as young as two years old. At least this is what my mother tells me and I can remember being interested in mechanical and electrical things almost as far back as I can remember.

B. B.   Yeah, but you don't know what made you so interested? What kept you so interested in that?

JOEY.   No, I don't.

B. B.   Remember how you made these machines on your bed?

JOEY.   Yes.

B. B.   How did you call them? Remember, you had a name for them?

JOEY.   No, I made a car.

B. B.   That's right. But you made it out of your bed, remember?

JOEY.   Yes, that's one of the main things I made out of the bed.

B. B.   Yes, and why did you do that? Do you know? Why did you like this idea?

JOEY.   Well, I knew of course that a car is something that moves and it takes people places. After all, that's the whole reason it was invented; so people could go places faster. And also it was something in which a person was enclosed.

B. B.   You liked this idea of being enclosed; it was important to you?

JOEY.   Yes.

B. B.   Why? What were you afraid would happen if you weren't enclosed?

JOEY.   Well, I think the main reason behind my wanting to be enclosed was I think when I started coming closer to people, I very often . . . I'd have fantasies about a car or anything that moved on wheels that was enclosed and I'd have a fantasy that I was in it myself. Well, I'd always picture that somebody else was in it with me.

B. B.   So it wasn't just to protect yourself against others?

JOEY.   No . . .

B. B.   It was also to have somebody with you all the time? Who wouldn't leave you?

JOEY.   Yes. You know, it was just a few months after I first came here that I started to have such a fantasy. I know I never had a fantasy like that before, except on very rare occasions.

B. B.   But before you came you didn't touch people enough, is that right? Didn't act like you wanted them to stay?

JOEY.   Yes.

B. B.   And after you came you wanted people to stay with you?

JOEY.   Yes.

B. B.   Who was it that you wanted to stay with you in your car?

JOEY.   Well, one person was Barbara, and it was right after I'd been here a year and a half that I had put up a device on my bed to make it look like a car. I told her to get on the bed while I pretended to drive the car.

B. B.   And where did you pretend to drive it?

JOEY.   As I remember, it was just within the city of Chicago. But on other occasions I pretended to drive home, you know, to where my family was. And mostly, I think, it was a way of thinking of the time when I would be living with my family and would trust people enough to want them.

B. B.   Now, I wanted to ask you, remember you always walked around with tubes?

JOEY.   Yeah.

B. B.   Transformers and so on.

JOEY.   Yeah.

B. B.   Why did you always like to have these tubes in your hands?

JOEY.   Well, it was just the feeling that I didn't really have ideas of my own, you know, like a human being, that I could feel comfortable with.

B. B.   And? How did they make you feel comfortable?

JOEY.   Well, they made me comfortable in that . . . well, as a means of protection against the fear, I would pretend that I was a machine. Especially when I was eating.

B. B.   Why? Why did you need to be a machine especially when you were eating?

JOEY.   Well, I think because food was something I really wanted, you know, not just because it serves some purpose. I felt like it was a necessity more than a real one . . . like the tubes, I felt, were kind of . . . and this reminded me of my having a fear of having wishes and desires like other people, you know. I was afraid to have a real feeling that there's something I really want.

B. B.   The food you really wanted?

JOEY.   Yes.

B. B.   So why did you then have to pretend you were a machine?

JOEY.   Yeah, well, just for the same reason. I had these fears about having a real feeling of wanting something from other people.

B. B.   Why? Why were you so afraid of wanting something from other people? Why was that so dangerous?

JOEY.   Well, I think one reason was because I had hidden my feelings for so long until it got to a point where I would be scared of wanting something from another person.

B. B.   Do you have any idea why you started to hide your feelings so much? What caused it?

JOEY.   My ideas are that I might have had some very unhappy experiences that I don't remember.

B. B.   You don't remember them?

JOEY.   Yeah. Although my mother does tell me that just after I was an infant I had these severe stomach pains every time I would eat something and then I would be very hungry and I'd want to eat something again. And I'd have severe stomach pains again and it would keep going on and on like that.

B. B. You think that might be the cause?

Joey. Yes, it might. It just might, because when I think of it I look upon it as being a very unhappy experience for me, even though I don't remember it.

B. B. Remember when you wrote these secret messages and cryptograms, you know?

Joey. No, what do you mean by cryptograms?

B. B. Well, you used certain letters of the alphabet and made long words out of them. Remember that?

Joey. No, I don't.

B. B. Well, do you remember the rumpus you made with Lou, when you tied him down and all that?

Joey. Yes.

B. B. What was that all about? Do you now know, or can you tell me about it?

Joey. Yes, it was a feeling, I think . . . it was a desire of mine to show him that I wasn't afraid of people. But I still wasn't sure about just going ahead and telling him how I felt.

B. B. How did you feel?

Joey. I felt very strongly that I wanted to have his love and companionship but I still felt afraid to do that quite yet and so I tried to rumpus, to see if I could show him at first in an indirect way.

B. B. That you wanted his affection and companionship?

Joey. Yes. And then I was getting much less afraid to want it and have it.

B. B. Now, why were you afraid of showing that you wanted companionship? What were you afraid would happen if you showed it openly?

Joey. Well, at first I was afraid I would find out that I couldn't have it, or that it would be very hard for me to get.

B. B. And that would have been too upsetting and painful?

Joey. Yes, that's why I was afraid of it at that time.

B. B. Well, what other experiences can you remember that brought you out of your withdrawnness and your interest in machines only? What brought you to be interested in people?

Joey. Well, another thing was that to play with other children my age seemed to help a lot, too.

B. B. Yeah? And why did you play with things that rotated like propellers? Can you remember? Why did you have rotating things? Why were they so important to you?

Joey. I think one of the reasons was the fact that I felt my own life was going in a vicious circle and this was the way to express it.

B. B. Oh, and what vicious circle? What was the vicious circle in which your life went around?

JOEY. Well, one example, you know, is with my fears of wanting something from another person and where that would lead to. I would keep feeling afraid of that. And because I felt afraid of it in the past, I would be scared of it again.

B. B. So the vicious circle was what exactly? Can you tell me?

JOEY. It was a matter of, you know, of being afraid to do something and then just saying to myself, "Oh, this is too much" or something like that.

B. B. So you wanted it, and you said to yourself, "This is too much"?

JOEY. Yeah.

B. B. And that seemed to you like these rotating blades of the propeller?

JOEY. Yeah.

B. B. Tell me, do you remember anything from the nursery school you went to?

JOEY. Yes, I remember that I used to pay attention almost only to machines. And I would take almost any item and pretend it was a machine. Such things as blocks, tin cans, anything of almost any shape or description.

B. B. Now, why did it give you some security to think of them as machines?

JOEY. I think . . . well, one reason I used these things was because I was so much thinking about them that the shapes, the very shape of them, had certain ways of suggesting something mechanical.

B. B. Yeah, but why? Why were you so interested in machines? What made them so attractive to you, the machines?

JOEY. Well, one thing was the fact that they did have these rotating blades.

B. B. Can you think of any other reason why they were so attractive?

JOEY. I can also remember that they seemed to be a way of showing that I was intelligent and know something. Because I was very much afraid to show it in any other way.

B. B. Why were you afraid to show it in any other way? What were you afraid would happen?

JOEY. I think I was afraid that maybe I would have to do things on my own and not be liked for what I did. In other words, as if the people wouldn't want to take care of me.

B. B. If you showed some independence?

JOEY. Yeah.

B. B. What were you afraid they might do?

JOEY. That they'd walk away and leave me. At least this is a feeling I remember having when I went to nursery school. That if I showed my intelligence in any other way than machines, I would feel too independent.

B. B.   And they would leave you?

JOEY.   Yes. I think this is another reason that I would take something of almost any shape and make it suggest some form or another of a machine. That's why there was such a variety such as a tin can or a block or even a stone.

B. B.   And when did you begin to realize that people cared for you and wanted you to have a real life of your own? What made you realize that, and when did it happen?

JOEY.   I think this happened very shortly after I first came here. I remember my counselors encouraging me to have fun with other children.

B. B.   And when did you start to like it that people touched you? You know, at first you were afraid of that. When did you start to begin to touch and to like it? Do you remember?

JOEY.   Yes, it was . . . I can remember first signs of it, just shortly after I came here. I remember with Mitchell I used to have a desire to touch him and this was a first sign. Now, this didn't come on suddenly at all. It came very gradually over the nine years.

B. B.   Why do you think you selected Mitchell? Do you have any idea?

JOEY.   Well, let's see now. I think it was first Ken. And that was still connected with machines. Kenrad happened to be the trade name of a company that made radio tubes. With Mitchell I feel it was because he was heavy, he was fat.

B. B.   And why did that interest you?

JOEY.   Well, at that time it seemed to remind me very much of when my mother was pregnant. In fact, this was the main reason. Because I wanted to express the feelings I had at a time that I had much resentment about not being with people or not having people. That was when my mother was pregnant and ready to give birth to my sister.

B. B.   And why were you so interested in defecation and stools and so forth? Do you know?

JOEY.   Well, I think mostly it reminded me of letting something go.

B. B.   That was your feelings about it?

JOEY.   It reminded me of the fact that there was something very much missing from my life.

B. B.   Namely?

JOEY. The human company I wanted from other people.

B. B.   And that's why you did or didn't want to let go?

JOEY.   That's why I didn't want to let go.

B. B. You didn't want to. So the interest in stools was that you didn't want to let go of them.

JOEY. And it was a way of expressing that I was afraid I was letting go of something. Every time I would use the bathroom I had this very strong feeling of letting something go.

B. B. And were you afraid because you had so little, or what?

JOEY. Because I had so little.

B. B. So you couldn't afford to let go?

JOEY. Yes.

B. B. So actually this touching of Mitchell was anger. Because he was so fat and like your mother? Or how was it?

JOEY. Yes, there was . . . there were many anger feelings mixed with it as I very well remember. See, every time I went up to Mitchell, there was the fact that, you know, he did remind me of my mother's pregnancy.

B. B. And what did you want to do to him when you touched him?

JOEY. I was really wanting to express the fact that at that time, and also at the time that I was touching him, I wished my mother was pregnant with me again.

B. B. So you wanted to start life all over again, is that it?

JOEY. Yes, it was a way of starting life anew.

B. B. By then you were ready for that?

JOEY. Yes.

B. B. Did you have such fantasies of being born again?

JOEY. Yes, I did.

B. B. By whom did you want to be reborn? Do you know? Who in your fantasy would re-bear you?

JOEY. Well, I fantasied that my mother would re-bear me.

B. B. And what are your feelings for your mother now?

JOEY. I would say that I still love my mother very much.

B. B. And your father?

JOEY. Yes, I love him, too.

B. B. So, if you loved them so much, why did you disappoint each other so much when you were a child?

JOEY. Well, I . . . what it was is, feeling two ways at the same time.

B. B. Namely?

JOEY. I felt so angry that I had to have some way to let go of it.

B. B. And why were you so angry?

JOEY. Because I kept so many of my feelings to myself.

B. B. Yeah, but that's a vicious circle, you know. You were so angry and you kept it to yourself. But what made you so afraid that you had to keep them to yourself?

JOEY. I . . .

B. B. Do you have any ideas?

JOEY. I thing that this, too, after I was just a baby, I think I just . . . It's what I said before. My mother tells me I was only about two or so when I got interested in machines and . . .

B. B. Well, thank you very much, Joey. Is there anything else you want to tell me? No? Well, this will do very beautifully for my understanding better what went on with you. I thank you very much, Joey.

JOEY. You're welcome.

B. B. And I hope you will visit us again sometime.

By the time of this interview there was little Joey could tell us that came as news to us. Only what we had come to understand before his departure was put in his story. What we had not known before the visit was that Mitchell was also important because he reminded Joey of pregnancy. Nor did we know before that he hoped to be reborn by his own mother.

In some respects his memories as he spoke of them on this visit did not go far enough; in others the full interpretation was not available to him. As to his wish to be reborn by his mother, I am still doubtful. Knowing Joey, his desire was to make a good impression on this visit, to show us how reasonable he had become. He may therefore have shied away from admitting that he wanted to re-bear himself, may have felt this was too crazy an idea. So for semiconscious or wholly unconscious reasons he may have replaced it by the much more acceptable idea of being reborn by a woman, particularly by one's mother.

But far beyond what he told us of the past, and of his present ability to manage, we were deeply impressed by the two things he selected to bring with him to show us. One of them was his high school diploma.

The second thing was an electrical machine he had constructed himself, and which he demonstrated to each of us who was willing to listen. It was a very heavy thing, and he was weighed down with it just as tubes and motors had weighed him down in the past. But with this machine there was triumph and satisfaction in the way he carried it. It was a rectifier and its function was to change alternating current into direct current. And he showed us again and again how this device he had constructed himself changed the eternal back-and-forth of the alternating current into a direct continuous flow.

Joey had truly freed himself of the vicious circle in which he rotated forever between longing and fear. All by himself he had altered the course of events till he was now meeting life in a straight-forward direct encounter.

Part Three

WOLF CHILDREN

Persistence of a Myth*

WITH UNCANNY INSIGHT Shakespeare tells us why the myth of feral children finds belief. It is *The Winter's Tale*, and Leontes, the king, wants his infant child to be burned to death, but dares not commit the murder himself. So he orders Antigonus to do it. But Antigonus is horrified and pleads for the infant's life until the King agrees that it need not be killed but should merely be set out to die. Then Antigonus can only pray that some animal will find the infant and suckle it, though

> . . . a present death
> Had been more merciful. Come on, poor babe:
> Some powerful spirit instruct the kites and ravens
> To be thy nurses! Wolves and bears, they say,
> Casting their savageness aside have done
> Like offices of pity.

Thus Shakespeare understood that behind a belief in feral children stands the fact that some parent wishes his child to be dead, but too afraid to kill it he exposes the child to a fate just as deadly.

Myth, according to Benedict [1933], expresses "a people's wishful thinking and remodels the universe to its dominant desire." This chapter does not deal with the fearful delusions autistic children create. It deals with the myths adults have invented to explain why such children exist.

* A shorter version of this chapter was published as "Feral Children and Autistic Children," *American Journal of Sociology*, LXIV: 1959, 455–67.

§
The Uses of Myth

Long before Darwin gave us rational evidence to show that man and beast are closely related, ancient tales of how lost or deserted children were succored by animals made a bridge between the two. These tales also gave some assurance that children who become lost to us are not invariably destined to perish. Thus the feral myth reflects the larger desire to believe in a benign nature that in some fashion looks after all of its children.

What concerns us here even more is that the myth also serves to explain children who seem most unlike other children. In a strange contradiction the same myth that brings the species closer together also divides a single species: it further separates normal man from his most severely disturbed young. On the one hand the myth says (in Darwinian fashion) that man and animal can be as closely related as a mother and the child she brings up. On the other hand (contradicting Freud), it says that certain aspects of our nature are so bestial they cannot possibly be innate to man, but must have resulted from animal rearing. Where does myth end and error begin?

Myth turns into dangerous error when it stops the search for knowledge by lulling us into thinking a problem is solved when in fact it is not even recognized. The problem I refer to, of course, is that of infantile autism. There are many ways in which it goes unrecognized, one of the oldest being to consider these children feeble-minded or brain-damaged. But even this belief is very young compared to the ancient one that they were mothered by animals.

Among the purposes of this book is to do away with a few widely held notions about autistic children which we believe to be in error. Because in science especially, the correction of error can often do more to solve a thorny problem than some new discovery or theory. Often, too, erroneous ideas can keep the valid knowledge we already have from being put into use. The knowledge I refer to is what we already know about autistic children. In preceding chapters I have presented the bases for our conviction that these children are not feeble-minded, but suffer from a disturbance we believe to be functional and which we know to be reversible in many cases, if treated early and radically enough. In the following chapters I shall discuss the contrary view that infantile autism is organic in origin and irreversible, to show that evidence supporting it is not yet convincing to us. Here in this chapter I hope to show how the task of helping autistic children was circumvented in other times and other cultures by belief in a myth: that these are feral, or animal-reared, children.

Having lived with autistic children for many years, both the very wild and extremely withdrawn ones, I had long felt that most so-called feral children were more probably children suffering from the severest form of infantile autism, while some were possibly feeble-minded, as Pinel thought to be true of the Wild Boy of Aveyron [Itard, 1932].

Except for the report on this boy, most earlier accounts of feral, or feral-like children were so vague that no real diagnosis could be made. Yet the more detailed the accounts of the children's behavior, the more likely did they seem to have been autistic. Fortunately, in the case of Amala and Kamala, the two famous wolf girls of Midnapore, a fairly accurate description of the behavior of Kamala, the elder girl, and of the steps in her partial recovery, became available in 1940 [Singh and Zingg, 1940; Gesell, 1940]. Her story closely parallels our experience with some of the most autistic children we have treated, children who were reared from birth on by human beings and had never lived with wolves.

The similarities were so definite that it was hard to reach any conclusion but that the two wolf girls, too, had been suffering from severe infantile autism. From what we know of autistic children, it seemed most unlikely that they could or would adjust on their own to any environment or be able, of their own volition, to live with any other creatures, including wolves. Certainly their desire for sameness and their avoidance of close contact make either event most unlikely. Knowing next to nothing about the habit of wolves, I cannot even speculate about whether wolves can live with autistic children. The experience is certainly very trying even for the most humane of beings, to which the Reverend Singh and our staff at the School would bear witness. But none of this seemed to preclude the possibility that Amala and Kamala had been found in the company of wolves.

According to Singh's account, he discovered the two children living with three grown wolves and two wolf cubs in the hollow of a "white-ant mound as high as a two-storied building." He claims that he had the grown wolves flushed out of their home and the mound broken open. Within, he says, were "the two cubs and the other two hideous beings there in one corner, all four clutching together." To the question, "How often do wolves den in deserted ant-mounds?" Singh replied that "this was the only white-ant mound known to be lived in by wolves" [Singh and Zingg, 1940].

Though I was dubious of Singh's account of how and where the girls were found, I was probably more ready than most to believe his report of how they behaved and developed in his orphanage. All of us at the School were only too familiar with exactly such behavior.

Then in the fall of 1957, Professor William F. Ogburn sent me a manuscript he had just written about a new outcropping of reports on a feral child. Since he was familiar with the work of the Orthogenic School he wondered if this child might not be like some of the children we work with, and he invited my comments. While in India, Ogburn had read in a newspaper of the finding of a wolf boy named Parasram, near Agra. He visited and observed the six-year-old child and spoke with the couple who claimed Parasram as the son who was stolen from them in infancy by wolves. Later he interviewed the man who actually found the lost child roaming wild, far from any place where wolves were known to live or prowl.[1]

When Ogburn's story showed to my satisfaction that a boy widely believed to be a wolf child was not a wolf child, and when his description of the boy's behavior suggested he was another autistic child, my former doubts about wolf children were enforced. Now an alternative explanation became all to possible: Singh's account of his close association with the girls could be, and I believe was, entirely correct; his interpretation of their behavior, in terms of its assumed feral origin, I am convinced was not. In his interpretations, I believe he was carried away by his imagination, as he was about the one single event that makes or breaks his interpretations, namely, the way the children were found. I was now ready to argue the children's past and the interpretations based on it by Singh, Gesell, and others.

I cannot begin to enumerate the various animals which, according to legend, have nurtured human infants. But that children were cared for by wolves has been claimed more often than for any other animal. Evans and Evans in their *Dictionary of Contemporary American Usage* [1957], and elaborating on Benedict's definition, state that "In sociology and anthropology, a myth is a collective belief that is built up in response to the wishes of the group instead of a rational analysis of the situation to which it pertains." They also inform us that the term "feral in its literal sense of 'animal' has been applied by some anthropologists to those children who are alleged to have been reared by wolves, bears, baboons, and the like, and if the supply of children or credulity holds out, it may become established as a technical term."

But if feral children are indeed a myth, why did man wish for such

---

1. Professor Ogburn's investigation was later published in short form as "The Wolf Boy of Agra" [Ogburn, 1959], together with my companion piece on "Feral Children and Autistic Children," *loc. cit.*

a myth, and what made it plausible enough to persist up to now from the most ancient of times?

The answer may be that in earliest times, feral children served to warn man of the dangers of being bestial to his children, and also satisfied that other purpose of myths: to respond to the wishes of the group. In this case the strange and perturbing behavior of some children could be explained on the basis of wish instead of by rational analysis.

In more recent times, feral children have been used to support the theory that man is nothing more than the product of circumstances. Embodied in certain theories of behaviorism and social anthropology is the wish, not so much to view society as man's creation, but to see man as wholly created by society. If infants raised by wolves were to become, to all intents, wolves, then we would have to accept that man is nothing but the product of his surroundings and associations. It would mean that there are no inborn functions; no potentials that can either be developed or not by the circumstances of life, but never altered entirely. This psychological view of man as the creature of society—conditioned only by what he has learned, by what was imprinted on him, by what conditioned his responses—then met with the bias of some anthropologists that man is infinitely malleable by the conditions of his life.

Psychoanalysis, on the other hand, has shown how much the human being can and does resist the forces of society, and that no known society has ever done more than to modify innate characteristics. At most, as this book tries to show, if the modifying forces are very strong and are present at critical periods in infancy, they can stunt and modify these innate characteristics most radically.

Thus rational analysis does not support the contention that man is shaped entirely by what happens during his life in society. But because some theories carried the wish to hold on to such a belief, there was need of facts to support it. Now while theory cannot generate facts, it can so reinterpret them in its image that the facts thus interpreted will come to validate the theory. This purpose I believe the myth of feral children has been called on to serve more than once.

There is still another reason for discussing feral children in this book. If environmental influence could change a human child into a wolf cub, or nearly so, then little could be learned from the study of autistic children about human development in general. We could infer nothing about normal children from the autistic predicament nor its causes, beyond the small group of autistic children in our population. But I contend in this book that if the environment is too atypical early in life, and if the endowment is particularly vulnerable to its influence, human development will be arrested in general, and even those aspects of personality that develop somewhat will be too severely deflected to be of much use.

It is not that the extreme environment, as I call it, would cause the infant to develop whichever way the environment pushes him, any more than living with wolves—if such a thing were possible—would make him develop more along the lines of a wolf. It is that infants, if totally deserted by humans before they have developed enough to shift for themselves, will die. And if their physical care is enough for survival, but they are deserted emotionally, or are pushed beyond their capacity to cope, they will become autistic. That is, their development, in essential respects, will just not take place, and in other respects will deviate severely.

Recently an ingenious analysis of all serious longitudinal studies available on human development was published by Bloom [1964]. It demonstrates in what ways, and how much, environment can influence certain human characteristics, particularly intelligence. It shows that the effects of an unfavorable environment act mainly to arrest these characteristics. Some it may also deflect; but it cannot produce any traits that are not present in all human beings.

Or to put this in terms preferred by Rapaport [1958]: we are born with a set of given apparatuses for relating to reality. If these apparatuses do not receive adequate nutriment, or receive nutriment befitting the environment of a wolf cub, personality will fail to develop. Because the human infant's constitution, his ego apparatuses, cannot utilize wolf-cub nutriment for the purpose of human development.

For several years now we have been working with a child who during her first years of life was raised *with* dogs, though not *by* dogs. Both parents had more feelings for their canines than for their child. Dogs were not only safe from the mother's hostility but were even treated with affection. The mother's rejection went so deep that the very thought of living with her daughter "made her so sick that she couldn't sleep or eat." She did not "want any girl child around" because "I'm afraid of myself," that is of what she might do to her child. Interestingly enough, her biggest complaint about her own childhood was that her mother treated her "like a trained dog."

The mother's rejection of her baby began as soon as she knew she was pregnant because "there was just no place in our lives for a baby. I hated it." From before the baby was two, she was boarded around with whoever would take her in. But by then it was too late, nor did the parents allow any favorable placement to last. When at home with her parents, the child was beaten severely with a strap and locked in a dark closet for long periods of time. One boarding mother reported that when the child was three she already identified with a dog, because dogs received better care than she did. As usual, the parents soon removed her from this home because, as the boarding mother stated, "they thought we gave her too much love."

It was at or before the age of two that the girl began to act like a dog. She crawled under furniture like the dog and chewed up both furniture and rugs. Along with the dog she chewed on bones and lapped the dog's water. At age four she was placed by the court, which by then had taken custody on grounds of neglect. In her specialized foster home she again identified with the family dog and ate its dog biscuit. When efforts were made to interfere she "fought like a little tiger." She had, of course, neither bladder nor bowel control, kicked, bit, and scratched at anyone within reach. Most important, in the present context, she "picked up and carried things with her mouth only like a puppy, picking up tinker toys with her mouth from the floor without using her hands at all."

In short, she used her constitutional apparatuses as much like a dog as her human endowment permitted, but only that much and no more. She never did anything canine that another human being could not do who put his mind to it.

After she came to live with us and was exposed to the best care we could provide, all dog-like behavior disappeared very soon. In its place came a violent anxiety whenever she spied a dog, even afar. But by then she was six. It had been easy enough to have her give up the dog-like behavior which, given her human inheritance, cannot have been easy to develop. But the devious uses to which she had long set her ego apparatuses made it very difficult to convert them to average human use. In important respects this has so far proved impossible for her to do. A human being can go just so far in trying to live a dog's life because it seems so much safer and superior than a human environment which, as in this case, had no use for the girl.

Returning to feral children, I should mention certain similarities between Singh's story of how he found the two wolf girls and the wild fantasies we spun about some of our most violent autistic children when we first met each one of them. Our speculation was born of efforts to find emotionally acceptable answers to the near unexplainable and wholly unacceptable behavior of the children we were setting out to treat. Upset by their strangeness, we let ourselves be seduced into speculating about what fantastic experiences might have caused such unheard of behavior; and this was long before we met the "dog girl" just described. I must even admit that some of what we imagined these children must have suffered at the hands of their parents was, in its way, just as fanciful as

Singh's account now appears after Ogburn and Bose's investigation [1959].

Later, we came to recognize that most of our own speculation sprang from two different psychological needs. First, it served to safeguard our narcissism. We were unwilling to admit that these animal-like creatures could have had a past similar to ours. We also needed to believe that only the most incredible circumstances could reduce a human child to such subhuman behavior. It was a remnant of the same narcissism that rebelled at the theory of evolution.

Secondly, these speculations served our need to understand and explain. The more unusual, the less acceptable a phenomenon, the more our anxiety and narcissism requires us to find an explanation. Maybe, too, the more revolting the behavior, the less thought we wish to give it. We tend rather to explain it by an emotional reaction, or in so simple a form that it calls for little more thought. This may have been why Singh was tempted to explain the girls' animal-like behavior as a consequence of animal rearing.[2]

In our case, these flights of imagination were short-lived. In each instance, as soon as we had established a child's history, it turned out to be one of extreme emotional deprivation, often one of unusually severe traumatization, but most critical of all (as Shakespeare knew) of a parent's wish that the child should not live. Bad as this was, it was nothing like what our unbridled fantasies made out. It was no more than what Shakespeare alluded to with his "they say" and sprang from our emotional unreadiness to take a rational view of the children's so irrational behavior.

But even after we knew what the past of these children had been, again and again, the knowledge became lost to us when one of them had severely bitten, scratched or otherwise badly harmed a staff member, had jumped on him with wild cries, torn off his own and our clothing, or defecated on us. Then it would flood in on us how they also urinated and defecated without so much as knowing it as they walked or ran about; how they could not bear clothes on their bodies but would run about naked; how they did not talk but could only scream and howl; how they ate only raw food. And such "animal-like" behavior would provoke a temporary renewal of fantasies about their past.

When Ogburn's report rekindled my interest in the whole subject, a rereading of Singh's account made it altogether likely that out of sim-

2. For a few years during World War II the inhuman behavior of the Nazis was explained in like simple fashion. Emotions held sway over reason because our emotional reactions were so strong. Since the Germans behaved so inhumanly, they were viewed as subhuman; theories that all Nazis or the leading ones, were insane found ready acceptance and were defended by psychiatrists.

ilar needs he wove an equally fantastic myth and came to take it for the truth.

After Ogburn finished investigating the Parasram myth he conducted a further investigation to verify Singh's account of how he discovered the two wolf girls. This he did not find to be true. Since then, publications have begun to appear in which feral children are dealt with as fable, but the myth dies only slowly. Even Ogburn concluded carefully that if Amala and Kamala were not wolf children, it did not prove that others might not have been. The belief that children can live with wild animals is not easily given up.

For example, three years after the appearance of Ogburn's report, Professor George Humphrey in his introduction to a new edition of Itard's *The Wild Boy of Aveyron* [Itard, 1962] wrote that "*Wolf Children and Feral Man* by J. A. L. Singh and Robert M. Zingg . . . is indispensable for psychologists, sociologists, and others who wish to study the effects of different environments on very young children." And "in contrast to the wolf child, Itard's boy had probably not even the advantage of hearing such patterns as the howling of the wolves in the cave."

A year later, and despite Ogburn's great standing as a sociologist, Professor Quinn [1963] discusses feral children in a textbook of sociology and comments, "One of the better authenticated stories of this type concerns Kamala, a Hindu girl about eight years of age, found living with wolves." Thus despite Ogburn's careful demonstration that this girl had never lived with wolves, Quinn seems to need such a belief to explain her "animal-like" behavior. Nor should we too easily dismiss that Gesell [1940] who was then the most renowned American student of child development, backed Singh's account with his authority.

Even more reason to ask, how is it that these myths found so much credence? And since the myth will remain until the riddle of feral children is solved we must also ask, who were they—if they were not feral children? Only by studying them can this question be answered.

§
In Lieu of Evidence

Starting with the stories of how these children were found, we find important similarities. For Parasram, it was claimed that two experts vouchsafed the truth about his finding—one a psychologist, the other a physician. Both had supposedly examined the child after he was discovered; neither had been interviewed at the time, nor could they later be found. The physician had "moved to Lucknow where it would be difficult to find him;" the psychologist replied that "he had not made a report, but planned to do so later" [Ogburn, 1959].

In the finding of Amala and Kamala, two "reliable" witnesses supposedly corroborated the story. A judge's affidavit precedes Singh's account [Singh and Zingg, 1940] because the feeling was that it, more than anything else, proved the veracity of the story. In addition to the affidavit, the judge had the following to say about two of the named witnesses to the girls' feral origins other than Singh and his native helpers: "the two Anglo-Indian friends of Singh who accompanied him at the time of the rescue are not at Khargpur; Mr. Richards is dead and Mr. Rose is not to be found."

The Judge's affidavit reads as follows:

The Reverend J. A. Singh has placed before me all the documents and evidence relating to the so-called "Wolf-children" of Midnapore, which I have studied carefully.

I know Mr. Singh personally and I am convinced that every word that he has written regarding the children is true, to his knowledge. I have also spoken to several people who saw the elder of the two girls on several occasions in Mr. Singh's Orphanage and they have confirmed Mr. Singh's accounts of the manner (for example) in which the children walked and behaved.

There is not the least doubt in my mind that Mr. Singh's truthfulness is absolutely to be relied on.

In this affidavit it is almost explicitly stated that because several people who saw the elder of the two girls on several occasions have confirmed Mr. Singh's account of the manner in which the children behaved and because the account of the children's behavior turned out to be trustworthy beyond expectations, we are therefore to believe that "every word he has written regarding the children is true;" hardly a sequitur. And this, although it is stated that the witnesses saw only "the elder of the two girls" and thus could not confirm "the manner in which [both] the children walked and behaved."

Since I am convinced that both children were autistic, and Singh's description of their behavior correct, this point is made only because the judge's use of the plural here is another example of how far even witnesses learned in the law and in rules of evidence can be carried away to believe anything claimed about these children, because unheard of as it was, it was found to be just as described.

The mechanism at work here may have been that the rational mind, which at first disbelieved in the story of Kamala's behavior, turned out to be an unreliable instrument. Therefore its critical voice was silenced altogether as far as these stories were concerned, and henceforth everything was believed as told.

This is not surprising to us. Many times when we have described the behavior of some of our extremely autistic children even to persons quite familiar with very disturbed children they have reacted with polite or not so polite disbelief, unwilling to grant that any children could be quite so strange. They were convinced that we were grossly exaggerating and dramatizing our experiences, and afterwards told us freely about their initial disbelief. But later, on meeting these children, their doubts changed to utter belief; so much so, that they would have been willing to believe almost anything we might have told them about the children or their past. Precisely because they could not believe what did not jibe with their experience before seeing the children, and now having found correct the accounts they had doubted, they were ready to believe whatever else we might have chosen to say.

This I believe happened to Singh. All testimony favoring his story is based only on the truthfulness of his description of the girls. Character witnesses are accepted in lieu of evidence. The crucial affidavit of Judge Waight is based entirely on such circumstantial evidence: Singh had been found truthful in some matters; hence he was in all matters trustworthy. Only witnesses could have corroborated the story of the finding of Amala and Kamala. Such witnesses were named, but they could not be found when the effort was made.

Thanks to Ogburn's investigation we know that Parasram was not found in the company of wolves, though such had been widely believed. Thanks to his investigation of how Amala and Kamala were found [Ogburn and Bose, 1959] Singh's account on this score is now known for a fiction. But just as it was true that Parasram was found wild, there seems no reason to doubt that Amala and Kamala were found living wild in the forest, as was the Wild Boy of Aveyron. The various accounts of the wild children of Europe—children found roaming in various places on the continent—sound true enough, too, though hardly any of them were thought to have been raised by wild animals.

How these wild children were used to support the tenets of behaviorism may also enter the history of psychology some day under "the myth of behaviorism." For example, in the story of the two Hessian wolf boys we will see how the wish can be father to the thought. Singh and Zingg [1940] in many of their accounts of European feral children, rely on Rauber's *Homo Sapiens Ferus, oder die Zustaende der Verwilderten* [1888]. But Rauber, in his critical analysis of the story of the Hessian wolf boys demonstrates convincingly that we are here confronted not with two different boys, but only with two different accounts of the same boy.

The first of these accounts, written by the official historiographer of the Counts of Hesse, is very short and to the point. It has nothing to say about the boy's ever having lived with wolves.

The second, which claims that the child was raised by wolves, was written in Latin by an unknown monk. According to the monk's story, the wolves not only "always brought the boy the better part of their catch, but made him a bed of leaves to protect him against the cold." Furthermore, the wolves (who seem to have heard of conditioning) "forced him to walk and run on all fours."

This and more led Rauber to the conclusion that the monk's account was in the nature of a fairy tale and deserved no credence. He continues: "The monk used the occasion to condemn man with his heart of stone by comparing him with the kindness of the wolves. Possibly, the wolves are an addition due to rumor and exaggeration, never absent when unusual events occur. In this case the real event was no more than the finding of a wild boy by hunters in the forest who brought him to the castle [of the Counts of Hesse]. In the same forest also some wolves may have been roaming." [Rauber, 1888, my translation.]

Confronted by such doubts, well-founded in Rauber's study of the original German reports, Zingg [Singh and Zingg, 1940] has the following to say: "Rauber's doubts . . . would likely be set at rest by the evidence of the wolf children of Midnapore."

Here we see circular reasoning at its height: an apocryphal story, told as such by Rauber, who states clearly that it did not deserve belief, and could hence support nothing, is used to support the veracity of the feral origin of the wolf girls. The alleged truth about the girls, thus supported, is then used to dispel Rauber's doubt that the Hessian boy was raised by wolves.

This, incidentally, should have made us skeptical about the two Indian girls, since their behavior, in significant aspects, was described as being similar to that of the many wild children found in Europe. Which raises the interesting but still unanswered question of how Amala and Kamala survived, all alone in the wilderness, and how they got lost in the first place.

As to the first question, I tend to believe, from our experience with autistic children, that these wild children could not have survived for very long by themselves, even allowing for the clemency of the Indian weather. Neither their haggard look nor the absence of clothing nor the "hideous ball of matted hair," prove they had been lost for very long. Some of our autistic children keep their wild looks for months. They can and do tear off all their clothing in minutes. Even after years with us the well-groomed hair of one of our autistic girls could, within hours, turn into a "hideous ball of matted hair," glued into an ugly mass by the saliva, remnants of food, dirt, and whatnot rubbed into it. In her case this process was further speeded up when the hair was glued together with chewing gum, an item hardly available in the forest.

With quite a few children, we have often had to resort to cutting off their ball of hair, and to keeping the hair trimmed short to avoid the formation of hair balls. Some of them are most resistant to this, and we had one autistic girl whose face we did not manage to see in its entirety for months because she kept it well out of sight behind a curtain of hair.

We are a bit more sure of our grounds in regard to the second question: how do such children get lost? In the case of the Indian children, Ogburn thought they might be lost children, feeble-minded, or the children of prostitutes. His hunches are as good as any. My own guess would be that they were simply children who were emotionally (and probably also physically) abandoned.

In the report on the two children of Midnapore we are told by Bishop H. Pakenham-Walsh that "The very primitive people who inhabit the parts where these children were found, who are not Bengalis, do fairly frequently expose baby children" [Singh and Zingg, 1940]. If these people are ready to expose normal babies, is it so farfetched to believe that they may also expose older children who act like babies (as autistic children do) or children who seem extremely abnormal to them? Also, how old are "baby children"? At what age do these people normally stop exposing children? All these questions remain unanswered in the account of Amala and Kamala. And while Pakenham-Walsh, who knew the area, spoke only of baby children, R. R. Gates in his introductory remarks to the report on the wolf girls mentions that in the jungle areas of India "female children are still occasionally exposed." [Singh and Zingg, 1940.]

From our own experience I would like to enlarge on this by adding that the girls in question were probably children who were utterly unacceptable to their parents for one reason or another. This characterizes the background of all autistic children. It is independent of how, or how soon, the parents manage to disengage themselves from such offspring. But the manner in which the parents do this depends on economic and cultural conditions. The morals in regard to one's offspring are different for the culture of poverty than for the middle classes.

Nowadays, in the better-educated middle classes, the parent's disengagement from his autistic child is emotional. But these parents continue to care for the child physically, and in many cases secure psychiatric treatment. This is so common to the group that Kanner came to look upon autism as a disturbance restricted to children of the better educated middle classes, as I shall discuss in the next chapter. In the less educated middle-class family, and in the better-off lower classes, the disengagement is also largely emotional. Physical disengagement is only possible if the parent can believe his child to be brain-damaged or feeble-minded, which permits him to place the child in a state institution.

Among poverty-stricken populations, the disengagement requires less complicated maneuvers: the child is simply set out, or allowed to wander off. In this connection it should not be overlooked that the wild boy of Aveyron was found in 1799, at a time when the French country-side was in revolutionary turmoil; still earlier, wild children were found in regions of Europe wherever and whenever poverty was rampant. In India, where abject poverty is still widespread and child neglect still common, we may thus expect to find wild children—that is, children who in our setting would be viewed as feeble-minded by the less for-tunate groups in the population, or autistic by the others. With the increase in standards of living, in feelings of obligation toward children, and in psychiatric knowledge, we are going to be confronted with ever more autistic children who will be "recognized" as such. In poverty-stricken countries some of these children may continue to be set out to fend for themselves in the wilderness, or more likely will not to be searched for very quickly or persistently when they run away.

Our experience with the parents of autistic children, many of them well-educated, good middle-class people, leaves little doubt that in their deepest emotions, they wished themselves free of these children and, as the child grows older, for very good reasons. Such wishes they could not afford to become conscious of, or to act on, because of the stringency of their conscience, the behavior expected of parents in America, and the near impossibility of a child's getting physically or permanently lost in our cities. But there is hardly one such parent, living in twentieth-century America and conscientiously on the watch, whose wild autistic child has not managed to get lost several times after the age of about three or four, though it happens to some of the quiet, with-drawn ones too. We learn from these parents how their children dis-appear, how they must search for them for hours, only finding them eventually because the police or some stranger has happened on the child and made his whereabouts known. Quite a number of these parents have to maintain the most unremitting vigil over their autistic children who will otherwise, incredibly, have vanished in a flash.

It seems perfectly reasonable, therefore, to assume that in the case of Parasram, some Indian parents "lost" such a child. Whether deliber-ately, or for reasons they were not aware of, they probably left him behind or failed to catch up with him when he ran away.

Even without the complex emotions these children arouse in their parents, and with all our precautions, we have again and again met with difficult times when these children have disappeared because our watch-fulness lapsed for a moment—and I mean literally a moment. Within less than a minute they would be gone, and it would take us hours to find them. Many times we have had to send out several search parties, on foot and in cars, only to find them in a neighborhood where one would not believe that a child could get lost. Fortunately, we have never lost an autistic child for more than a short time. Their strange behavior makes them easy to spot as being entirely different from all other children. Strangers who pay no attention to ordinary children will watch this one because of his unusual behavior, and can tell us where he has gone. Or they will call the police who then pick him up and return him to us. But however easy it is to spot them, getting them in tow has sometimes been as difficult as the capture of other wild children described in the literature, where it took several adults to subdue them.

One example may do for many. Anna, one of our wild autistic girls, had again run away and her absence was known to us exactly one minute after she vanished. Within minutes (since we are used to such emergencies) three search parties on foot and one in a car were out looking for this ten-year-old girl, to no avail. She was finally found only because she had torn off much of her clothing and had violently attacked people on the street who then called on a policeman for help. When the officer found himself unable to subdue this frail ten-year-old (since he did not wish to club her) and after she had kicked, scratched, and bitten him, he sent in a call for help. With the aid of another policeman he managed to get her to the station.

Since we had notified the police (another precaution we have learned to take as soon as such a child is missing), they called to inform us that the girl had been brought in and asked us to come for her immediately. When members of our staff arrived there a few minutes later, the little girl had managed to throw the station in an uproar; the two policemen who caught her had by then been fought to a state of exhaustion, their uniforms torn. She had been found on the platform of a suburban railroad station, exactly five and a half city blocks away. At this time she had hardly any speech. Retracing her steps, we learned that she had torn off some of her clothing within two blocks of the School; we never could figure out how she managed to pass through the constantly attended turnstile that leads to the passenger platform. On other occasions she was found as far away as thirty blocks from the School.

When this is possible in the city of Chicago, where the utter strangeness of such a child makes him instantly conspicuous, it would seem an easy thing for such children to get separated from their parents under more primitive conditions of life. If one can draw any conclusions from our experiences with some of the parents of autistic children, it is reasonable to assume that their efforts to find their lost children have been more than lax. So much for how feral children may get lost.

But why is it believed that there are feral children in general, or wolf children in particular?

Three factors certainly promoted this belief. Firstly, many such children are not dumb but do not talk; and speech, as much as anything, separates humans from animals. Animals cannot talk; hence these children must have something in common with animals. Secondly, all children even feeble-minded ones, need human care, reach out to other people; but these children shun human company. Thirdly, some of these children are ferocious in their attacks, using claws and teeth, like animals. Beyond that, I can offer only speculation.[3]

I have already suggested the role that human narcissism may have played in making credible the stories of feral children. On this I would like to enlarge here, and also to draw on our experience with severely autistic children. In centuries past, when we still believed that the insane were possessed by devils or ghosts, their "wildness" was less of a shock to our self-image as human beings. Even now, we seem to need to ascribe to extrahuman forces those unwelcome aspects of our nature, or those potentials of human nature from which we have grown alien in the process of civilization, but which break through in certain psychotic processes.

The wildness in the girls of Midnapore was ascribed to their having been raised by wolves. How tempting this path is we had to learn by experience when we tried, in this or other ways, to separate the children's wildness from what was human about them; to ascribe the first to external circumstances, and to see in the latter the true human nature of the child. It taught us that living closely with such children can seduce those who work with them into developing just such beliefs, and spontaneously, if only very briefly.

One typical example, which again must stand for many, comes from a staff member's report on her reaction to one of our wild girls—not just after the first encounter, but after having worked with the child daily for several months. When the girl had once again severely attacked the worker, "I felt the most intense anger at the demon in her which, in spite of her, caused her to hurt me." Needless to say, this worker did not believe in demons or possessed people. But in order to go on living with an autistic child, she needed something that would enable her to suffer the child's scratching, biting and tearing off of her

---

3. Unfortunately, I do not know the religious beliefs current in the region where the two girls of Midnapore were found. But if the people there believed in the transmigration of souls and were confronted with the behavior of the girls, isn't it possible that they thought of them as having been wolves in a previous incarnation, or of now representing an incarnation that was part wolf, part human? Such beliefs were unacceptable to the adult Reverend Singh, but perhaps they were part of his ingrained thinking before he became a student of Bishop's College in Calcutta. If we have once believed that a human soul, in a previous incarnation, may have inhabited the body of a wolf, maybe it is easier to believe that in a previous life the two girls dwelt among wolves.

clothes without either rejecting her or becoming punitive; something that would also allow her to grasp the meaning of the child's behavior. Therefore in her emotional experience of the situation, though not in her rational evaluation, she had to split the child's behavior, as it were, into the part caused by demons, and that other part, the child's human self that was untouched by demons.

The origin of the subhuman, animal-like behavior of these children, in our enlightened age, is no longer sought in the world of spirits, but in their nature-given endowment, or their environment. In this day of reason, we look first for organic damage and then think, of course, of the early environment of the children as explaining their behavior. Normally, we trace autistic behavior back to the extreme emotional isolation they experienced, to the inhuman ways they were handled, or to other specific or nonspecific traumatizations they once suffered. But on first encounter with their wildness, and thereafter with their total withdrawal, their "contrariness," their violence, we too are thrown back for moments to feel they are possessed, that they are "animals."

To quote another typical reaction to a mild sample of Anna's behavior: "As I watched her continual application of saliva to all parts of her body, her biting and chewing of her toes, I thought to myself she is an animal, destructively washing herself." So if observing these children seems naturally to lead to the thought, "They are (like) animals," then the easiest solution to the problem posed by their behavior is to believe it results from an animal upbringing; they must have been reduced to such animal behavior by having lived with animals.

This was precisely the reasoning used by the parents of the six-year-old "dog girl" referred to above.

Or to cite Anna again, she reminded even those who knew her most intimately and liked her very much, of an animal. Her bodily movements, for example, were described as follows:

She has an extremely flexible body, but she does not walk or run like a human being. She runs in a hopping motion. It sometimes turns into a loose-jointed lope like an animal's running; and when she falls into that, running as hard as I may, I have a very hard time keeping up with her; usually I am unable to overtake her.

About the walking of the two girls of Midnapore, Singh has the following to say:

Gradually as they got stronger, they commenced going on all fours, and afterwards began to run on all fours. When their health improved, they would run very fast, just like squirrels, and it was really a business to overtake them.

Other of our autistic children have spontaneously been likened to other animals by staff members. One boy who (like Anna) could neither walk nor run like a human child, but could only leap wildly, or hop or jump, was often referred to as a gazelle. Another child reminded us all of a bear because of his lumbering gait, his growl and the sudden wildness with which, on his rare emergence from a state of total withdrawal, he hugged his "caretaker."

A further example of Anna's behavior lends itself even more easily to the belief that this girl had once been fed by wolves, or some other wild animals:

This afternoon, she was sitting, watching other children, some of whom were chewing gum. One fourteen-year-old girl sat next to her. Suddenly she reached over, put her arms around her neck, put her face close to the girl's face, and tried to open the girl's mouth, first with her fingers and then with her teeth, to take with her teeth the gum from out of the other girl's mouth.

It wouldn't take much imagination to believe that here re-enacted was the feeding of a child from the muzzle of a mother animal. It would indeed make a good story.

But beyond this kind of generalized behavior, such as animal-like locomotion, there are other and more specific reasons to suggest comparing these children with animals. Their biting and clawing of us I have mentioned repeatedly. It is so marked, that during one year a single staff member needed medical care more than a dozen times for human bite, not to mention the numerous times when she and others were bitten but not badly enough to require a doctor's care. As part of this behavior the children regularly bare their teeth when they are angry or annoyed.

Different, and again reminiscent of animals, is their prowling at night, in marked contrast to their quiet withdrawal into a corner during the day. One of these girls could only be reached and brought to accept human closeness when her favorite counselor roamed through the building with her for many hours each night, feeding her as they went, since it was the only occasion on which she would take food from us.

Another piece of marked animal-like behavior is the great preference shown by some of these children for raw food, particularly raw vegetables; some of them will go to almost any length to get raw onions or raw lettuce, and so forth, and will rage uncontrollably if such foods are not provided at once. Others lick salt for hours, but only from their own hands. Again others build themselves dens in dark corners or a closet, and sleep nowhere else, preferring to stay there all day and all night. Some build caves out of blankets, mattresses, or other suitable objects they can collect. They permit no one to touch either them or their abode, and at least two of them would eat only if they could first carry their food into these self-created caves or dens, where they would then eat without any utensils.

But it is not only the unwillingness of these children to mix with human beings, or their ferocity, that suggests a close affinity to animals. Some of them on seeing an animal will respond as to a beloved, lost friend. One of our girls (not the "dog girl") always became extremely excited when she saw a dog. She showed a strong desire to run toward it, and cried or howled like an animal; particularly like a wolf. She fell on all fours, jumped like a dog with her head down, and made biting gestures. She also broke into wolf-like howling at mealtimes, often for hours during the night, and at other times, too, when excited

Had we believed in the feral origin of this girl—whose total history was quite familiar to us—we would probably have been convinced that seeing a wolf-like creature like a dog kindled memories of her happy times among wolves, and that she was here reverting to what they had taught her. The same could be said of those children who would eat or sleep only in their self-created dens or caves.

And yet, despite such similarities between the behavior of some of our autistic children and that of the feral children described in the literature, it remained possible that all this was sheer coincidence; that the similarities were only superficial and that closer inspection would reveal important differences between the two.

Moreover, there are other children believed to have been reared by animals, such as Parasram, who showed none of this animal-like wildness; and even our wild children do not show this behavior all the time. It predominates in our minds because of its inhuman qualities, and not because it is present very much of the time. Our experience with the most violent of these children has been that their tearing off of clothes, their making of animal noises, biting us, and the like, all subside during the first or second year of our working with them, to return intermittently for another year or two in times of great stress. While such behavior is the most dramatic expression of infantile autism, it is not characteristic for the disturbance; it is incidental, not essential; it is neither persistent nor all-pervasive when compared with the children's disturbance of contact and with their seemingly total unrelatedness to the environment. These are characteristic for all autistic children, most of whom show no animal-like behavior except for their shunning of human company. And this trait is by no means characteristic of all animals.

How to decide, then, whether Amala and Kamala were autistic children? We can be sure of our grounds only if a comparison reveals that what was viewed as the most characteristic behavior of the two girls is like the behavior most characteristic of autistic children, and like what the literature reports to be typical of infantile autism.

§

The Wolf Girls of Midnapore

Singh, in describing the children's behavior, states as most typical of the two wolf girls first what he calls their aloofness, and second their shyness or fright. These he describes as follows:

From the very beginning their aloofness was noticeable. They would crouch together in a corner of the room, and sit there for hours on end facing the corner, as if meditating on some great problem. They were quite indifferent to all that was going on in the room. Their attention could not be drawn to anything. They sat there musing the whole time. If we tried at times to draw their attention to anything by touching them or pointing to something, they simply bestowed a forced look as if looking at nothing, and would quickly turn their eyes again to the corner.

We never kept them alone, but always purposely kept a few orphanage children in the room for two reasons; first, to guard them, so that they might not run away; second, to associate them with the other children. The children would be playing, chattering and moving about in the room, but those things did not interest them at all. They remained quite uninterested and indifferent.

They were shy from the beginning. This shyness I counted for fright. The presence of others in the room prevented them from doing anything, even moving their head from one direction to the other, or moving about a little, changing sides, or turning about. Even a look towards them was objectionable. They wanted to be all by themselves, and they shunned human society altogether. If we approached them, they made faces and sometimes showed their teeth as if unwilling to permit our touch or company. This was noticed at all times, even at night.

Compare this with what one of our staff child psychoanalysts wrote of one of our ten-year-old autistic girls when I asked him to put down what he considered most characteristic of her: "Her most pervasive behavior trait is her overwhelming panic reaction to the slightest interference from the outside, often occurring without visible external motivation."

Singh continues,

For nearly three months . . . there was a complete disassociation and dislike, not only for us, but for their abode among us, for movement and play—in short for everything human.

This is behavior typical for all autistic children; but how do the authors explain it? According to them the children withdrew from all contact with the surrounding world because:

> After their rescue and subsequent capture they were looking for the cubs and the wolves. It was noticeable that they wanted their company and association, but finding that they could not get them here, they refused to mix with the children or with anybody. [And:] They could not find their mates in the jungle; they could not prowl about with the wolves; they missed their cosy den, and could not get to feed on meat or milk. Consequently, the thought of their old environment preyed heavily on their mind, and their thought was to regain their former habitation and company. This fact made them meditative and morose.

If outstanding scholars (Professors R. R. Gates, A. Gesell, F. N. Maxfield, K. Davis, R. M. Zingg, and many others) had not put their seal of approval on such accounts, it would seem like belaboring the obvious to point out that one must be careful not to ascribe thoughts or wishes to the minds of mute autistic children unless they are based on the most assiduous observations and are supported by all aspects of the child's behavior in various stages of his development. But even then they remain conjecture so long as these children do not, some time later in their development, verify them unequivocally. The latter is impossible in this case because nowhere in the account of Kamala's later development (Amala died much too soon) are we told of any stated recollection of her life among wolves.

I do not know how it could have been "noticeable that they wanted the company of wolves," though I am quite ready to believe that "the thought of their old environment preyed heavily on their mind" or at least that of their past terrifying experiences. Those once mute autistic children whom we have helped to reach the point where they could tell us about the past have only had dim notions of the vague and terrifying fantasies that occupied their minds in a state of total withdrawal. They recall only having been in vague states of terror. Things are quite different for talking autistic children like Joey in whose case the images are much more definite and complex.

Here too the circular reasoning of Singh and Zingg should be pointed out. The assumption that the two girls were reared by wolves is used to ascribe content to their thought and to explain their behavior. Then the behavior, so interpreted, is used to support the assumption that the girls were reared by wolves. Because why else, for example, would they "meditatively and morosely" think back on their happy feral existence?

Before comparing Singh's account with the literature, and with our own experience, I would like to quote the only eyewitness account of

Kamala's behavior beside Singh's that appears in his book, because it is more concise and less adumbrated by speculations about the girls' feral origins. We owe an excellent description of Kamala's behavior some six years after she was found, when she was estimated to be about fourteen years old, to Bishop Pakenham-Walsh. He was also, as far as one can tell, the most highly educated person who ever saw the girl. He reports:

When I saw Kamala, she could speak, quite clearly and distinctly, about thirty words; when told to say what a certain object was, she would name it, but she never used her words in a spontaneous way. She would never, for instance, ask for anything she wanted by naming it, but would quietly wait till Mrs. Singh asked her, one by one, whether it was so and so she wanted, and when the right thing was named she would nod. She had a very sweet smile when spoken to, but immediately afterwards her face resumed an appearance of unintelligence; and if she were left alone, she would retire to the darkest corner, crouch down, and remain with her face to the wall absolutely listless and with a perfectly blank expression on her face. She had an affection for Mrs. Singh, and was most amenable to her directions during the time I saw her. She was not interested in anything, nor afraid of anything, and cared nothing for the other children, nor for their games. She walked upright, but could not run.

I saw her again two years later [when her age would have been about sixteen], and except that she had learned a good many more words, I did not notice any mental change.

How does this compare with what is described in the literature as typifying the behavior of children who suffer from infantile autism? In his classical accounts of this disease, Kanner [1943, 1944, 1948, 1949] states that its most characteristic features are a "profound withdrawal from contact with people, an obsessive desire for the preservation of sameness" that nobody but the child herself may disrupt on rare occasions, and this with "the retention of an intelligent and pensive physiognomy." Equally characteristic is either "mutism or the kind of language that does not seem intended to serve the purpose of interpersonal communication." The children seem unable to relate to people, sometimes even to objects. They are referred to as self-sufficient, behaving as if people were not there, and giving the impression of silent wisdom.

Kanner's first case, Donald, at the age of five displayed "an abstraction of mind that made him perfectly oblivious to everything about him. He appears to be always thinking and thinking, and to get his attention almost requires one to break down a mental barrier between his inner consciousness and the outside world" [Kanner, 1943]. This sounds like Kamala's crouching in a corner for hours as if meditating on some great problem, indifferent to all that was going on, so much so that her attention could not be drawn to anything. Or like what Anna's mother said of her: that when she was not screaming or being violent, she was doing nothing, "thinking, thinking, sitting by herself and thinking her own life."

About Kanner's Case Nine we are told that

The most impressive thing is his detachment and his inaccessibility. He walks as if he is in a shadow, lives in a world of his own where he cannot be reached. No sense of relationship to persons. He went through a period of quoting another person; never offers anything himself. His entire conversation is a replica of whatever has been said to him" [Kanner, 1943].

The similarity to the wolf girls' aloofness and shyness is striking, and this boy's never talking spontaneously is like the description of Kamala's language behavior which we owe to Pakenham-Walsh.

As for the children's being reminiscent of animals, Kanner has noted of Case Eight that "he is called a lone wolf," while of the boy cited in Case Nine he writes: "When he is with other people, he doesn't look up at them. We had a group of people visiting. When Charles came in, it was just like a foal who'd been let out of an enclosure" [Kanner, 1943].

That one of these children was described by someone as a lone wolf proves nothing, since the metaphor is common. But can we as readily dismiss the second animal comparison? I think not, if we draw on our own experience with some forty or fifty staff members over a period of years. Hardly ever do they liken the behavior of our nonautistic children to animal behavior—difficult and destructive as some of these schizophrenic and delinquent children are—while typically and spontaneously falling back on animal comparisons when describing autistic behavior.

This was and is true to some degree even for the very quietly withdrawn autistic children. They are often described by analogy with the turtle withdrawn into its shell, or the permanently clammed-up oyster. Much more frequent however, is the use of animal comparisons for describing the wildly acting out ones.

If an intelligent and interested layman such as Pakenham-Walsh had observed most of our autistic children during their first year with us (and a few of them even during their second or third years) for about the length of time he spent with Kamala, his description might have tallied exactly with the one he gave of this wolf girl.

Interestingly enough two of our mute autistic children began to say their first words after about a year with us, which closely resembles what was reported of Kamala, namely that she said her first words after thirteen months, when she began to "prattle like a baby." From our experience, as well as from Pakenham-Walsh's description, I doubt that she prattled like a baby, which is the result of a voluntary reaching out, and an enjoyment first of vocalization and later on of verbalization.

These mute autistic children, even after they have acquired the ability to say a few words—or perhaps I should say, have overcome their reluctance enough to at least say a few words—prefer not to. They prefer to let us do the talking for them, as was noted of Kamala after six years. The soft, hesitating, often echolalia-like saying of preferably short, single words, as it characterizes the speech of these children, is very different from what develops out of the usual happy prattling of babies. It is also in stark contrast to their wild, ear-piercing "inarticulate" screams. This makes their barely audible, unclear (or overclear), strained enunciation of single words seem, by contrast, to be even more minimally invested with the positive wish to talk than might otherwise seem true.

§
Feral or Autistic?

It is hoped that my excerpts from the literature suffice to show that the types of behavior most characteristic of the wolf girls as described by Singh, are the same as those listed as characteristic for autistic children by Kanner. Those excerpts and the comparison with our own group of autistic children may seem brief. But they comprise the essentials of infantile autism and these have been spelled out throughout the book.

What, then, of some of the specifics of Kamala's behavior? (Amala was so much younger, and died so early, that very little of Singh's account deals specifically with her.) Perhaps the specifics are so different from the behavior of autistic children, as observed by us and by others, as to justify the belief that the etiology of Kamala's behavior may be feral after all.

To find out if this is so, I have tried to make a content analysis of the wolf children's behavior on the basis of the descriptions given by Singh, disregarding his interpretations and those types of behavior that even he does not link to a feral past. I have done this either by comparing the behavior of the wolf girls with what we observe in autistic children, or by assessing the intrinsic character of such behavior.

Among these descriptions only one stands out as very strange, and it is the one repeatedly referred to as explainable only by the children's feral experience. It is also the only one for which we have no parallel among our autistic children. This is the inability of Amala and Kamala to walk erect when first found. While several of our autistic children have preferred to crawl on all fours for some time, none of them was unable to walk erect when first we met them. This is a crucial issue, because if walking erect were only a learned behavior, and not the result of an inborn "apparatus"—one that begins functioning at the appropriate age, given the appropriate stimulation—then all our thinking on inborn ego apparatuses would be in need of revision.

Singh tells us that the children were captured on October 17, 1920, and immediately placed in "a barricade made of long poles, not permitting the inmates to come out. . . . The area of the barricade was eight feet by eight feet. There were two small earthen pots for rice and water placed on the side of the barricade, so that the keepers could pour in their food and drink from outside." This, we are told, the keepers failed to do because they immediately deserted the children.

Singh left them there for five days, to return on October 23. In this extremely narrow confine "they had been left to themselves without any food or drink." On his return, Singh reports,

I found the situation very grave . . . the poor children lying in their own mess, panting for breath through hunger, thirst and fright. I really mourned for them, and actually wept for my negligence. The feeding was a problem. They would not receive anything into their mouth. I tried by syphon action. I tore up my handkerchief and rolled it up to a wick. I dipped it in the tea cup; and when it was well soaked, I put one end into their mouth and the other end remained in the cup. To my great surprise, I found them sucking the wick like a baby.

As soon as seemed feasible, and when the girls had recovered a bit, that is on October 28, a journey of seventy-five miles was undertaken, the children being transported "in a bullock cart, in which there is a good bit of jolting." Midnapore was reached on November 4, and nobody learned of this journey but Mrs. Singh. This suggests that for most, if not all of that time, the children remained in the cart; another seven or eight days spent in narrow confinement. When they arrived at Midnapore "they were so weak and emaciated that they could not move about, so no one could suspect anything with regard to their extraordinary history."

If this had happened to some of our autistic children, we would have been ready to assume that their being utterly deprived of food, drink, and a chance to move about for at least five days and nights—and possibly up to the time they reached Midnapore, that is for nineteen days—was traumatic enough to explain total collapse including the inability to walk, or to eat in any way except by sucking. Even if the restraint on movement was lifted on Singh's return, it was repeated again on the trip to Midnapore. This was another traumatization, since the children could not fathom why they were thus being restrained and moved about.

Most of the descriptions we have of their way of walking refer to the time after their arrival at Midnapore. In an entry dated November 24, 1920, we are told about the "extensive corns on the knee and on the palm of the hand near the wrist which had developed from walking on all fours." Of these sores they recovered by December 5, but only "on the nineteenth of December, 1920, we found them able to move about a little, crawling on feet and hands."

Thus no moving about was actually observed after they were placed in the barricade, and probably none took place from that time until sixty-two days later. Only by then had the children emerged enough out of what I infer was a state of total collapse to again move about. Little wonder that after such an experience they crawled like infants.

That the corns were due to habitual walking on all fours I consider pure conjecture, no less than that their walking on all fours was due to having lived among wolves. It seems equally reasonable to assume that these corns prove the children had not been living with wolves. If they had indeed been running on all fours since infancy they would more likely have shown the horny, tough skin people develop who walk barefoot all their lives. Corns on hands and knees suggest to me that the girls' moving about on them was rather recent. But this kind of temporary return to crawling after severe traumatization we have frequently observed in some of our autistic children. Also witness Laurie's collapse after a much less severe traumatization than that of the Indian girls when they were deserted or "lost."

When the girls were then placed in the barricade and left without food or drink for days, this added trauma further reduced them to a stage where they would no longer bite or chew, but only suck. Thus the return to crawling and the corns could just as easily be explained by the very recent traumatization of getting lost and by their experiences after capture, as by anything that happened before then.

R. R. Gates, in a footnote to the description of the children's crawling, mentions that A. Hrdlicka in his book *Children Who Run on All Fours* [1931] collected 387 such cases, mostly of white children born of civilized parents. This suggests that crawling in children is neither unheard of, nor necessarily due to feral rearing. Here I might mention two of the many facts (or stories, if one does not wish to believe these accounts) that Ogburn unearthed. A schoolmaster who claimed to have served in Singh's orphanage for twelve years stated that while Kamala was very different from other children and would answer only by means of single words, there was nothing wild or ferocious about her, and that Singh would beat her to make her walk on all fours [Ogburn and Bose, 1959].

I have devoted so much space to the children's walking on all fours because this, with the possible exception of the glare of their eyes, is the only characteristic of Amala and Kamala which we cannot match from our experiences with autistic children at the Orthogenic School. Nor shall I discuss the glare of their eyes, because it seemed controversial even to the authors, and even they do not correlate it with the children's feral past.

A characteristic definitely attributed to that past is their eyes being wide open at night, like those of a cat or dog. We are also told they could see better by night than by day, though no objective tests support the assertion. This unusual acuity of vision is reported as of December 20, the day after they first began to move about again, when they were barely emerging from their deepest immobility and debility. How Singh could be sure they could see better at night than by day, at a time when they could hardly move or do anything else, I do not know.

Kamala's later ability to find her way about in the darkness is reported as unusual, and likewise due to her feral experiences. But this finding one's way in the darkness is nothing unusual for many of our autistic children who, in general, rely very little on their sight for getting about. Recall, for example, the period in Laurie's life when she kept her eyes shut tight for days. This in no way impaired her ability to find her way about, even when we tentatively put some obstacles in her usual pathways, hoping to induce her to open her eyes. This she did not do, but sensed exactly the place where the obstruction was put and circumnavigated it.

Another capacity linked to the girls' feral past is their ability to smell meat or anything else from a great distance, like animals. Hardly anyone who has worked with psychotic children and reported on them in any detail, has failed to remark on the strange hypersensitivity of these children to sensations of smell and touch, which are in stark contrast to long periods of unresponsiveness to those of sight. That is, they react much more with the senses of closeness than of distance. Hearing often takes a middle position; sometimes it is blocked out, while at other times or in other cases, the sensitivity is increased. In general, the senses of closeness (touch and smell) and distance (hearing and seeing) are invested in psychotic children inversely to what is usual in normal persons. Elsewhere I have reported on the extremely acute sensitivity to smell of schizophrenic children, who could smell what we could not [1955].

Amala and Kamala were also reported to have eaten and drunk "like dogs from the plate, lowering their mouths down to the plate." To which statement a footnote is attached saying, "Their methods of eating were conditioned reflexes learned from the wolves." But so did the girl described earlier who identified with dogs (as opposed to being conditioned by them) and so did Andy, a boy whose history is given later in this chapter. Andy had never, to our knowledge, eaten any other way before he came to us and still ate only that way after more than a year at the School. Other autistic children eat only by shoveling food into their mouths with a paw-like motion, while again others feed only from their own skins.

We are told that "the perception of cold or heat was unknown to them." To which, in a footnote, is added that this was "another conditioned reflex from their experience with wolves." Some of our autistic children have sometimes tried to run out into the street stark naked even in Chicago winter weather where the temperature is quite different from that of Midnapore. Though we always caught them quickly, they seemed totally insensitive to the experience and never had so much as a cold to show for it. In another context [1950] I have reported how and why some schizophrenic children behave as if they were totally insensitive to heat and cold, as did Amala and Kamala, whose response to temperature is therefore not unique and proves nothing about a feral past.

Insensitivity to pain is similarly different in psychotic children than in normal children as discussed at various points in this book and in the literature on childhood psychosis [Mahler, 1952]. It has to do with the nature of the disturbance, not with a feral past.

Other behavior which is cited as evidence of the children's feral past is their preference for raw foods, their unwillingness to wear clothes, their preference for running about naked, their avoidance of light and their preference for roaming at night, all of which I have discussed earlier and shown to be equally true for some of our autistic children. This leaves only one inhuman characteristic in my catalogue: the girls' inability to laugh. But this, too, is quite characteristic for most, if not all, autistic children. As clearly as I can recall, none of our autistic children has ever laughed until such time as we believed they had definitely moved from infantile autism to a less severe pathology and with it to a more benign degree of emotional disturbance.

Actually this catalogue of animal-like behavior is thin. Comparing it with what animal psychologists such as Lorenz [1952, 1963] can tell us about the wide variety of animal behavior, not to mention the incredible variety of human behavior, even our most autistic children show only a few characteristics that lend themselves to comparison with animals. They are the few characteristics, or types of behavior, that are so shocking to us that they assume an importance entirely out of line with their frequency or significance in the child's total life.

If we were to catalogue the behavior of even wildly acting-out autistic children, two things would stand out: first, that most of the time they do nothing and avoid any stimulation (the aloofness of the wolf children) and second, that even when they briefly leave off doing nothing, they do so very few things compared with normal children their age. Because they occasionally engage in animal-like behavior, which hits us so hard, we tend to be so overimpressed that we lost sight of the rest.

Here I would like to return for a moment to the Wild Boy of Aveyron because now his characteristics can be compared with those of other children I have mentioned. Unlike Pinel, who thought the boy feeble-minded, I tend to agree with Itard's original opinion: that this boy was not feeble-minded but, likely as not, was reacting to the conditions of his life with what we now would call infantile autism.[4]

That he rocked incessantly, as do many autistic children, is not conclusive, since feeble-minded children do that too.

Quite different is the story of his selective lack of sensitivity. Itard remarks repeatedly of Victor (as he named the boy) that "It was not only to cold but also to intense heat that the organ of the skin and touch showed no sensitivity" [Itard, 1962]. His hearing, too, was highly selective and idiosyncratic. "The sound of a cracking walnut or other favorite eatable never failed to make him turn around . . . nevertheless, this same organ showed itself insensible to the loudest noise and the explosion of firearms. One day I fired two pistol shots near him, the first appeared to rouse him a little, the second did not make him even turn his head." Like Marcia, even the most autonomic reactions were lacking. "I have often succeeded in filling the exterior cavities of his nose with snuff without making him sneeze" . . . although "the organ of smell was very highly developed in other respects."

Unlike feeble-minded children and very much like autistic ones Victor was, when emotionally involved, very intelligent in getting the better of those who wanted to put something over on him. Itard gives many examples, of which I shall quote only one.

Wanting to stimulate both anger and joy, Itard tried to evoke the anger by giving the boy a light electric shock with a Leyden jar. The next day, though he could see that Victor was apprehensive, Itard again placed the Leyden jar between them.

4. Others too [Silberstein and Irwin, 1962], on studying Itard's account have come to the conclusion that the Wild boy's behavior, as described, was "probably quite like the picture of Amala published in *Wolf Child and Human Child* by Arnold Gesell."

Seeing the uneasiness which the approach of the instrument caused him, I thought he would move it further away by taking hold of the handle. He took a more prudent course which was to put his hands in the opening of his waistcoat, and to draw back some inches so that his leg would no longer touch the covering of the bottle. I drew near him a second time and again replaced it between us. Another movement on his part, another adjustment on mine. This little maneuvre continued until . . . it was no longer possible for him to make any movement. It was then that, seizing the moment when I advanced my arm in order to guide his, he very adroitly lowered my wrist upon the knob of the bottle. I received the discharge.

Repeatedly, Itard remarks on how the senses of closeness were markedly more invested than those of distance, as is so often reported of autistic children. Even when specific efforts were made to develop them "sight and hearing did not participate in the improvement."

I have mentioned before the peculiar animal-like running of some wild autistic children, including the so-called wolf girls. Victor, too, would only run; so much so that "It was impossible when I took him with me to go on foot. It would have been necessary for me to run with him or else to use most tiring violence in order to make him walk."

The other similarities are many between what Itard reports of Victor and our experience with autistic children, such as deliberate withdrawal from the world of people, long periods of doing nothing, and so on. Among them is the fact that while he eventually achieved a wide range of appropriate emotions and was able to relate positively to his caretakers, it was not possible, to any comparable degree, to restore intellectual and other ego functions to the boy.

If I refer here in passing to Kaspar Hauser it is because no discussion such as this would be complete without it. His story posed concisely, for the first time, the problem of what happens to the person who is raised in emotional isolation, with a minimum of stimulation. Kaspar Hauser was by no means a wild autistic person, and if autistic at all, of the quiet type [Feuerbach 1832, Wagler 1928]. But since he was about sixteen years old when he was found, and thus hardly a child any more, I shall not discuss him further, particularly since an entire literature has grown up around him which is readily available.

§

The Known Past

Returning to the wolf girls, and having examined what were considered proofs of their feral past, we approach our last problem: namely, what the actual past of these children may have been. If feral experiences do not explain their behavior, what past experiences do? I know nothing about the past of the two wolf girls. But perhaps the past of our autistic children may suggest what the actual, as opposed to the alleged past of the two girls was like.

Before presenting this material, I must stress that while these histories, strange as they were, offer a part explanation of the children's disturbances, they may or may not be the full explanation. While there are no grounds as yet to say for certain what causes infantile autism, we are pretty sure by now about the very important role of certain discernible factors in the children's past.

In comparing the two wolf girls with the autistic children known to us through the literature and through our clinical experience, it should be stressed again that only a small minority of known autistic children are "wild." For example, only a few of Kanner's cases showed some of the traits that characterized Kamala and possibly also Amala. Most of his cases were much more like Parasram. We have worked with both types of autistic children, those more similar to Parasram, and those more like Kamala. Both groups have all the essential features in common, with the one exception of the animal-like wildness of the latter.

We wish we knew more about what causes this difference in behavior. For a time we thought it might originate in the difference in home backgrounds. All of Kanner's cases are children of highly intelligent parents, and this is true for some of our group of autistic children, including some of the very wild ones. On the other hand, some of our quieter ones who are very like those described by Kanner come from lower-middle-class backgrounds, the parents having had little, or at best moderate, education. Some of our wildest autistic children had unusual experiences in infancy, as will be seen from the life histories of Anna and Eve. Anna's parents would hardly be described as highly intellectual, and in Eve's case, only the father could be viewed as such.

Since we are here concerned with feral children, and since animal-like behavior traits are used to support notions about their feral past, I shall here sketch only the life histories of this type of child.

Again, since the preceding discussion involved three wolf children —two of them girls, Amala and Kamala, and one boy, Parasram—I shall restrict myself to presenting only three examples of the life histories of our autistic children, two "wild" girls and one "wild" boy. (Though Andy, our autistic boy, was "wild" and Parasram was not, the latter's animal-like traits and alleged feral past make him a wolf child no less than Amala and Kamala.)

§
Anna

Some of Anna's behavior has already been described. She entered the Orthogenic School at the age of about ten, but for years, before then, her wild, uncontrollable behavior made life unbearable for her family. Her brother, considerably younger than she, had been in constant danger for his life and had to be guarded at all times. Neighbors had had to call for police protection because Anna's violence endangered their children.

Before she came to us, several efforts at placing her in treatment institutions had failed. For example, in one well-known institution for disturbed children she lasted barely half a day, for in those few hours she managed to throw the institution into so much turmoil, and created so much damage, that she could not be kept. Even in a psychiatric hospital she could remain only a month because it too, was not equipped to handle such a wild child. There she had to be placed in a maximum-security room, that is, a room without any furniture, where she spent her days naked because she tore off any clothes that were put on her. Most of the time she crouched in a corner in total withdrawal; from this she emerged for short periods of wild screaming, running, jumping, and pounding on walls and door. Since her behavior made it impossible to keep her in the children's ward, the hospital was forced to place her in the adult maximum-security quarters; it was felt that such an arrangement was too unsuitable to be continued.

Anna's life began in a dugout under a farmer's house in Poland, where her Jewish parents were in hiding to escape extermination by the Germans. Her parents were ill-mated. The mother found the father utterly unattractive and had rejected his courtship for years. Both parents felt they were of opposite temperaments and background. By the time World War II broke out the father had given up hope of winning the mother, but the invasion of Poland suddenly changed things.

Foreseeing what would happen once Germany had occupied Poland, the father collected a large amount of wool and made arrangements with a gentile peasant friend to staple it in a dugout under his farmhouse, together with a loom. When the Germans began to exterminate all Jews, Anna's father took permanent refuge in his small earthen cellar. But first he tried once more to persuade the woman he loved to join him. This proposal she again firmly rejected. She had no use for him, she said, and would sooner be killed by the Germans than be his wife.

Soon things worsened and most of her family was killed. The father, who could no longer leave his hiding place, sent word to her again through his peasant friend, asking her to join him. By this time she was homeless and alone. So very much against her will she took refuge with the father, since he alone could offer her safety in his hole under the ground. There, his friend was willing to let both of them hide out. Her condition for accepting was that they would have no sexual relations.

The father managed to support himself and her, and in part also the peasant who hid them during the whole of the German occupation, by weaving in his underground hole. The peasant sold the sweaters that were woven, and by spending what he got for them (clothing being at a premium) he and the couple in hiding were able to live. But the dugout was so small there was not enough space for the parents to so much as stretch out at night unless the loom was taken down. Only then could they bed themselves down for the night, using the wool for both cover and bed. So every night the loom was taken apart, and every morning it was reassembled. Several times the Germans searched the farmhouse but never stumbled on the two in their cellar; it was secured by a trapdoor covered with stamped earth, like the rest of the floor in the farmhouse. At least once (or according to other stories they told us, several times) the Germans shot into the farmhouse.

With the passing of time, life under these conditions became ever more difficult, the two being forced on each other without respite. Nevertheless, Anna's mother refused her body to her husband for more than a year. She rejected him because physically he repelled her and both culturally and socially she felt him beneath her. According to the father's account he respected her wishes and did not force himself upon her, though embittered by her continued refusal.

About what then happened, the parents' stories differ. According to the father, they had to tremble for their lives every day, but he at least had his work to keep him going, while his wife was beginning to lose the will to live. In desperation he decided that if she had a child, it would restore her interest in living and might even make her accept him. So he convinced her to have a child, and she agreed to have sex relations for this purpose alone. These were the circumstances in which his wife became pregnant.

According to the mother, the father had never ceased his sexual pursuit. After a year of this, he was no longer willing or able to stand the presence of a woman whom he wanted so much and who rejected him, so he threatened to drive her out of their refuge. Either she slept with him as his wife, or she had to leave—which was tantamount to a death warrant. Under such duress she gave in.

As one can imagine, both before and after Anna was born, there were many fights—the mother screaming how she hated him, couldn't be his wife, had no use for him, and he fighting back in bitterness. To make matters worse, the peasant feared for his life if they should be heard, and threatened to kick them both out unless they remained absolutely still and kept their peace. So life proceeded, the two hating each other and yet thrown together by the unrelenting danger they shared. Only on rare nights did they dare to venture outside their hole for exercise or air.

When Anna, the child of this relation, was born, she did occupy the mother and give her some interest in life, but it made living still more difficult in their narrow confinement. When Anna tried to cry, as infants do, one of the parents had to hold a hand over her mouth since any noise, particularly a baby's crying, would have given them all away. The peasant, who had reason to fear for his life if it were learned he was harboring Jews, became more and more fearful and angry when the infant made any noise or otherwise complicated matters. So the parents and the farmer, each afraid of the Germans, did their best to see that Anna was totally still at all times, and as little bother as possible in all other respects.

As long as the mother could nurse Anna, the infant had at least enough food. But her milk gave out before Anna was a year and a half old. Then all the parents could feed her were raw vegetables or such like, since they could not cook in their dugout. Only in 1945, when the Russian occupation replaced that of the Germans, did things improve a bit. But by that time Anne was unmanageable. She would run about nightly, jump up and down and scream, sometimes for hours, sometimes all night. She never fell asleep before two or three in the morning. When she was not screaming or being violent, she was doing nothing, "thinking, thinking, sitting by herself and thinking her own life."

Things were finally a bit better when the parents managed to reach Germany and entered a DP camp. But once in Germany and relative freedom, the mother took a lover. When her husband learned of it he was beside himself, and new and violent fighting broke out. The mother wanted to leave her husband once and for all, taking Anna with her, but her lover did not want the child. So Anna stood in the way. Then the mother was ready to give up her child and start a new life, but was not ready to let the father have Anna. So she suggested that her own mother should care for Anna. This the father refused to agree to; he wished to emigrate to the United States where he had relatives, and to take Anna along.

During the years in Germany, the parents frequently considered divorce, but at the last moment the father could never accept it. He was too afraid that the mother would get custody of the child, and felt she had no more use for Anna than for him. This period was characterized by violent outbursts in front of Anna. As the father said of his wife: "I so often gave my life for her and she only betrayed me."

Long before Anna came to this country, and before her brother was born, she was examined by an American physician in one of the German DP camps and immediately recognized as an autistic child who needed to be placed in a treatment institution. Since we are here concerned with what the background of so-called feral children may have been, and since Anna was recognized as both wild and autistic when she was five or six years of age, nothing more needs to be said here of her later life.

§

Eve

The second wild girl, Eve, was a war baby too, the child of displaced persons. But her misfortunes had little to do with this fact, and much more with the death of an older brother and the impact of that event on her parents, particularly the mother. The parents were gentiles living in Germany as displaced persons from one of the Baltic states. But they were fairly well off, since the father's professional skills were needed by the Germans. The marriage went well until their only, dearly loved son died suddenly at age four.

The boy's death sent the mother into a depressive state, but it also made her try to become pregnant at once to replace him. In this she succeeded within a month of his death. Only it did not lift her depression, which continued with little interruption for most of the pregnancy.

The child, Eve, was born prematurely in the eighth month of pregnancy. By then, Germany had lost the war and the parents were in a displaced persons' camp in Germany. Eve was very small and was placed in an incubator, where she did well. But the mother went into a post partum depression, perhaps because she had had a girl instead of the wished-for boy. In addition, she needed surgery. So she stayed in the hospital for four months. There Eve, too, remained for the first four months of her life, though apart from her mother.

Mother and daughter then left the hospital, where Eve had done well, and began living together. But within two or three weeks Eve was brought back to the hospital in a state of total collapse. The symptoms were severe vomiting and diarrhea, anorexia. and such severe loss of weight that the child was found to be in an extreme state of marasmus. To be kept alive at all, she had to be put on a prolonged regime of intravenous feedings and blood transfusions. Month after month she lay in the hospital unmoving and unreacting. Only very slowly did she recover enough to return to her parents. By that time she was eighteen months old.

After her second return home from the hospital Eve was restless and rocked incessantly. She could not sleep, did not talk and never sucked. She ate fairly well, although only a few types of food, preferably raw vegetables and salt. She learned to walk at the age of two, and by four she began to say a few monosyllables though only when prompted; never spontaneously. She never spoke any sentences, never said "mama" or "daddy."

At the age of four, when she came to the United States, she was diagnosed as autistic and on a physician's advice was placed outside of the home. Several foster-home placements were attempted but did not work out. Then an attempt was made to have her live with her parents again and receive psychiatric care. This did not work, either.

Eve's failure to develop seems definitely related to the mother's depression, though we cannot be sure how far it impressed itself on the child in the short period of two or three weeks when she was brought home the first time, or when she returned again at eighteen months of age. But that the healthy baby of four months who left the hospital was in deep marasmus three weeks later is certainly impressive.

After Eve's return to the hospital at five months of age, her severe vomiting and refusal to take food suggests how painful or physically uncomfortable it was for her to eat. Later, when prevented from biting, pinching or scratching others, or when attempts were made to stop her incessant and violent rocking, she immediately turned to self-destructive efforts which were as marked as her wild behavior. For example, from the age of four on, when her outbursts against the world stopped—and possibly even earlier—she turned her aggression against herself. She bit and pinched herself just as much as she did others, so much so that her body was covered with bruises. She tore her hair out by the handful until large areas of her head were almost bald.

Eve's history certainly raises the question of how far her mistrust and total rejection of life was the result of painful early experiences and what was the influence of parental depression and rejection when experienced so very early in life. Nor can we disregard the mother's depression during her pregnancy and the possibility of its prenatal influence on Eve's endowment.

From our experience we can say with conviction that it is pure chance that our two wildest girls were foreign born and first saw the world in time of war. It is not the strange and unusual externals that make for autistic withdrawal and animal-like behavior. Thousands of children were born in DP camps and developed normally, while most of our autistic children were raised in what, before investigation, seemed like good middle-class homes. These children seem, in general, to be potentially very bright and very sensitive. Perhaps it is why they react so strongly to parental attitudes which they somehow comprehend and feel as a threat to their very existence. Or so it would seem.

§
Andy

The native born son of native born parents, Andy is an example of a wild autistic boy of highly intelligent and ambitious parents—exactly the type of parents Kanner believes to be typical of all autistic children.

When we first met the parents, nearly nine years had elapsed since Andy's birth. By then, what they recalled of their attitudes toward him as an infant was highly colored by their guilt feelings about having neglected him so badly during infancy. If the intensity of those feelings was any index of reality, his case must have been one of extreme neglect and isolation. Still some facts stand out, irrespective of how the parents viewed them years later. Also, the earliest investigation of Andy's past took place when he was not yet three years old. Since then several more psychiatric studies preceded his coming to the Orthogenic School and our interview with the parents. From each of them emerged the same picture of Andy's early life.

Both parents underwent psychotherapy, starting a few years after Andy's birth. They gave us permission to confer with their therapists, and according to the latter, both parents gave us a truthful account of their early attitudes, and handling of their son. Their accounts also tallied with their personalities and with their past and present attitudes, as those emerged during treatment.

Andy was born within ten months of the parents' marriage. At that time both parents were overburdened and were physically as well as emotionally exhausted. The father was a graduate student and was also holding two jobs (one a night job), to support himself and his family. Understandably, he was always on edge. The task of caring for a baby frightened both of them. As was typical of the father all his life, when in fright he attacked. The mother's reaction to having a baby was one of fear and panic, which increased the father's anger at the baby. What he called his anger and fighting back at the baby is described by the mother as his violent rages, of which she lived in continuous fear. Then, she said, after living in "fright and trembling" for some time, she suddenly rebelled and began a "counteroffensive," at which point her husband was viewed simply as an enemy to be conquered.

While the mother stated that she was "thrilled at the idea of having a child," the father reports that her total attitude toward having a baby changed immediately after Andy's birth. She became depressed and developed great fear, if not panic, in regard to nursing him. She became afraid of everything about Andy, particularly about whether he would get enough to eat. At the same time she worried about her sore nipples and was confused about how often she should feed him.

Andy was obviously not a happy baby. He rocked a great deal, scratched his face severely, and cried a lot. He was collicky, and by the end of his first month in life both parents were fed up with him. At that moment they accepted a pediatrician's advice to leave him strictly alone, particularly when he cried. The mother, who had previously felt that the infant's demands on her were monstrous in their excess, was glad to follow this advice rigidly. She behaved distantly toward Andy, leaving him strictly alone, although he had prolonged spells of crying every day. After a few weeks of this regime he stopped crying, but was still left alone most of the time.

The degree to which his presence was (and could be) ignored may be illustrated by the following incident, as reported by the mother: "We again had a violent quarrel one day. We screamed and physically fought each other for half an hour, or longer. Before the fight started, I had just put Andy on the potty, and it all took place within his hearing. He just sat there on the potty without moving or any reaction." This particular incident took place when Andy was about six months old.

When he was not yet a year and a half old, the mother went to the hospital to prevent an impending miscarriage and Andy was placed in the pediatric ward for the period of her hospitalization. During this time he resumed persistent thumb-sucking and rocking, and stopped saying the few words he had already learned. Some weeks later the mother aborted and had to be hospitalized for a time; yet despite the bad effects they knew it had on Andy, he was again put in the pediatric ward for the sake of convenience. By then both parents had lost interest in him. The father withdrew entirely into his work; the mother became engrossed in a new pregnancy. Andy spent most of his time alone, either in the yard or at a nearby beach. He had no one to play with and did not move about. He spent all of his waking day simply clinging to one or another toy, such as a ball.

The parents first became aware of how serious were his difficulties when he was two and a half. At this time the birth of a brother intensified his symptoms of twirling, twiddling, rocking, thumb-sucking and lack of speech. When they tried sending him to a nursery school, his total withdrawal became even more apparent. Treatment was attempted, but failed.

The parents wished to believe that Andy's difficulties were organic, but complete physical examinations at three outstanding medical centers revealed no evidence of any organic cause for his disturbance. The conclusion reached each time was that his difficulties were emotional in origin. The findings agreed on Andy's severe intellectual retardation and the severity of his emotional disturbance. These were evidenced by his total withdrawal and self-preoccupation, his seeming inability to relate emotionally, or to make any meaningful contacts at all despite attempts at physical contact by others. He was and remained withdrawn into his own autistic world. There was no tangible evidence of fantasy content to his solitary infantile play or to his primitive hand-and-mouth activity. The low affect responses and reactions, the emptiness of his emotional and intellectual life indicated the presence of a primary psychotic disorder, in which at no time was there any but the earliest and most primitive ego development.

The diagnostic impression was once psychosis of childhood, twice of infantile autism. Treatment away from home was recommended, and when Andy was not yet four he was placed in an institution where he remained, with little change in behavior, until he was admitted to the Orthogenic School.

By then he was a child who had never again made articulate sounds, though he understood simple commands. He tore his food with his hands, licked food from his plate like a dog, and attacked others in all ways including clawing and biting. In short, he behaved like a "feral" child.

To summarize then: a comparison of so-called feral children, with known and well-studied autistic children, the wild as well as the quiet ones, suggests that their behavior is due largely, or perhaps entirely, to how they reacted to an extreme emotional isolation combined with experiences which they interpreted as threatening their very existence. It seems in large part their reaction to some persons' (usually the parents') inability to parent one of their children, and not of some animals' humanity to the child.

This discussion of the many myths that have been woven around autistic children would be incomplete without mention of those other tales—those that tell of how man tried, out of curiosity perhaps, to create autistic children.

In Herodotus [1958] we read that the Egyptian king Psammetichus

took two new-born children of humble parents and gave them to a shepherd to be brought up among his flocks. He gave orders that no one should speak a word in their hearing and that they should sleep by themselves in a lonely hut; at the proper times they should be fed with milk by the she-goats and given whatever else was needful.

The purpose of this experiment was to find out what language the children would develop on their own, since this would have to be the oldest of all. We are not told how (or if) these children developed, who were raised under conditions so inhuman.

Perhaps the German Emperor Frederick II meant to repeat this experiment. Or perhaps Salimbene of Parma [1944] wanted to teach us by cautionary tale, and took this story of Herodotus' for his text. But he tells in his *Chronicle* that the emperor Frederick wanted to find out

what kind of speech and what manner of speech children would have when they grew up if they spoke to no one before hand. So he bade foster mothers and nurses to suckle the children, to bathe and wash them, but in no way to prattle with them, or speak to them, for he wanted to learn whether they would speak the Hebrew language, which was the oldest, or Greek, or Latin, or Arabic, or perhaps the language of their parents, of whom they had been born. But he labored in vain because the children all died. For they could not live without the petting and joyful faces and loving words of their foster mothers.

Thus as early as the thirteenth century man knew that no infant deprived of emotional closeness can live, or not at least as a human being. Fairy tales about the human empathy and compassion of the beast just do not stand up under scrutiny. Even Little Red Riding Hood knew better.

On the other hand, if wolves do not rescue lost children, man is now ready to do so. But this rescue will not be undertaken if we continue to believe that the autistic child's disturbance is irreversible. So a final discussion follows, to examine the myth about the hopelessness of their future, just as this one explored the myth of their feral past.

Part Four

A DISCUSSION OF THE LITERATURE
ON INFANTILE AUTISM

Etiology and
Treatment

No EFFORT WILL BE MADE HERE to review the entire literature on infantile autism in a historical or systematic way. To present and do critical justice to the major publications on this subject would fill a tome many times larger than this one.

My purpose in this book was to set forth the experience of a group of people who have worked intensively for many years with autistic children, to tell what we learned from it about the nature of the disturbance, about treating such children, and about early personality development. This I felt I could do better if I also discussed some of the thinking of others on infantile autism.

Since I did not intend this as a handbook on the disease, the task I set myself in these last two chapters was limited: to discuss selected pieces of the literature, as they may clarify those views I derived from the foregoing clinical experience.

§
On the Origins of Autism

Autistic children have been known and described in past centuries, and in this one too, before Kanner gave a name to their disease. As early as 1809 Haslam described the case of an autistic boy who was admitted in 1799 to Bethlehem asylum [Vaillant, 1962]. And in 1921 a four year old autistic child was studied [Darr and Worden, 1951] at the same Johns Hopkins hospital from which, some twenty years later, came Kanner's first description of infantile autism. To Kanner also we owe the first systematic investigation of the disease ever published [1943]. While one may question his conclusions as to the origin and treatability of autism, questions he has somewhat changed his mind about in the intervening years, his description of the syndrome itself remains classic.

Part of it I have already discussed in the chapter on feral children. In reviewing it here I shall not try to cull from his original paper what he considered most typical of the disease, but will quote instead a more concise statement from his later writings [Kanner, 1951-52]:

The characteristic features consist of profound withdrawal from contact with people, an obsessive desire for the preservation of sameness, a skillful relation to objects, the retention of an intelligent and pensive physiognomy, and either mutism or the kind of language that does not seem intended to serve the purpose of interpersonal communication.

This behavior differs from ordinary obsessive ritualism in one significant respect: the autistic child forces the people in his world to be even more obsessive than he is himself. While he may make occasional concessions, he does not grant this privilege to others. He is a stern and unrelenting judge and critic. When one watches such a child for any length of time, it becomes evident that, unless he is completely alone, most of his activities go into the job of serious, solemn, sacerdotal enforcement of the maintainence of sameness, of absolute identity.

In Kanner's original paper [1943] he presented eleven case reports that established infantile autism as a diagnostic entity, and concluded:

We must, then, assume that these children have come into the world with innate inability to form the usual, biologically provided affective contact with people, just as other children come into the world with innate physical or intellectual handicaps. If this assumption is correct, a further study of our children may help to furnish concrete criteria regarding the still diffuse notions about the constitutional components of emotional reactivity. For here we seem to have pure-culture examples of *inborn autistic disturbance of affective contact*.

So while Kanner felt sure at this time that autism was an inborn disability, even in this very first paper he stressed its potentials for learning more about crucial aspects of the development of the psyche, namely our "emotional reactivity," or the capacity to relate to other persons.

In the same paper he also differentiates this disturbance from the group of schizophrenias. Such a distinction was particularly necessary since Bleuler [1911] felt that autism was not a separate disease, but one of the secondary symptoms of the schizophrenias.

Inasmuch as Kanner used the concept *autism* as Bleuler defined it in 1911, perhaps that definition should be given. Although Bleuler recognized that "In the outspoken forms of schizophrenia, the 'emotional deterioration' stands in the forefront of the clinical picture" [Bleuler, 1950], his definition of autism stresses not so much the disturbance in affective contact as in relation to reality.

The most severe schizophrenics, who have no more contact with the outside world, live in a world of their own. They have encased themselves with their desires and wishes (which they consider fulfilled) or occupy themselves with the trials and tribulations of their persecutory ideas; they have cut themselves off as much as possible from any contact with the external world. The detachment from reality, together with the relative and absolute predominance of the inner life, we term autism.

Kanner, however, recognized from the very beginning that while the schizophrenic withdraws from the world, the autistic child failed to enter it in the first place:

While the schizophrenic tries to solve his problem by stepping out of a world of which he has been a part and with which he has been in touch, our children gradually *compromise* by extending cautious feelers into a world in which they have been total strangers from the beginning [Kanner, 1943].

Unfortunately, because Kanner concluded that this disturbance is inborn, he failed to ask the question which, especially since Freud, we consider essential for understanding a psychological behavior; namely, Why does a person behave in this way instead of some other? Such a question cannot be avoided unless we assume that behavior is engaged in without the person's having any choice in the matter, as in the movements of a spastic. But if one fails to ask this question, one fails to understand the person's motivation, and is easily tempted to ascribe to some inherent defect what does not make obvious sense in terms of conventional behavior.

Thus when Kanner [1943] initially wrote about Donald, his first case, he said, "Many of his replies were metaphorical or otherwise peculiar. When asked to subtract four from ten, he answered: 'I'll draw a hexagon.'"

Fifteen years later, when writing again of this case, Kanner stressed what is crucial here, namely that the boy "obviously knew the answer" [Kanner and Lesser, 1958], which put his saying "I'll draw a hexagon" in an entirely different light.

Even as early as 1946 Kanner wrote: "The autistic child has his own private, original, individualized references, the semantics of which are transferable to the extent to which any listener can, through his own efforts, trace the source of the analogy." Here the language of autistic children is viewed not as a symptom of organic defect, but as a meaningful expression of the child's idiosyncratic experience of the world.

Nevertheless Kanner did not comment on the fact that Donald's answer also constitutes an ingenious solution to the problem confronting the boy: how to show that he understood the question, could readily have answered it, and that his intelligence even exceeded what the question required. By his response he showed that he not only knew the answer, but could even give it in Greek. He further asserted his independence by replying on his own terms instead of those of the questioner. So he offered to draw a six-sided form instead of answering "six."

The original description of Donald's case ends with a quotation from a letter by his mother: "Another of his recent hobbies is with old issues of *Time* magazine. He found a copy of the first issue of March 3, 1923, and has attempted to make a list of the dates of publication of each issue since that time. So far he has gotten to April, 1934. He has figured the number of issues in a volume and similar nonsense" [Kanner, 1943].

This "hobby" was declared nonsense at the time, because it was not seen in the context of Donald's preoccupation with the passing of time though that interest was duly reported as follows: "He was inexhaustible in bringing up variations: 'How many days in a week, years in a century, hours in a day, hours in a half day, weeks in a century, centuries in half a millenium,' etc. etc." [Kanner, 1943]. Such obsessive ruminations about the passage of time, as well as desperate efforts to somehow capture the past and bring to it some orderly sequence, are typical of some autistic children. They feel their life is empty, if not also that they have never had a past, and want desperately to fill the emptiness with something (the collection of old magazines). They fear that time is eluding them, and that there won't be time enough left for them to live. Hence their ruminations about what might have happened in their empty past, and how much time they have left.

It is regrettable that in his second publication on autism Kanner [1944] dropped the name that identified it as a "disturbance of affective contact," a fact that cannot be too strongly emphasized—since when it has been known as "early infantile autism."

While Kanner never deviated from his conviction that these children do not relate to people, details of his descriptions reveal that they do indeed relate not only to objects, but also to people, except not in ordinary ways. Or I should begin by saying that Kanner, from his very first report, and in all his later writings on autism, stresses the peculiar nature of the parents of these children.

In his authoritative textbook on child psychiatry, for example, Kanner [1948] writes:

> There is one other very interesting common denominator in the background of these children. Among the parents, grandparents, and collaterals there are many physicians, scientists, writers, journalists, and students of art. It is not easy to evaluate the fact that all of our patients have come of highly intelligent parents. This much is certain, that there is a great deal of obsessiveness in the family background.

So while some inheritance factor is implied, Kanner himself does not see the behavior of the children as a response to parental behavior, which would contradict his thesis that they do not relate to people. But his careful qualification leaves the possibility open that they do indeed relate, but can do so only in their own way.

Later, when writing with Eisenberg, his frequent collaborator, he went further in implying a relation between these children and their parents. In the same symposium [1955] in which I suggested that childhood schizophrenia might be a reaction to extreme situations, they [Eisenberg and Kanner, 1956] spoke of how "emotional refrigeration has been the common lot of autistic children." More explicitly, they said:

> It is difficult to escape the conclusion that this emotional configuration in the home plays a dynamic role in the genesis of autism. But it seems to us equally clear that this factor, while important in the development of the syndrome, is not sufficient in itself to result in its appearance. There appears to be some way in which the children are different from the beginning of their extra-uterine existence. Indeed, it has been postulated that the aberrant behavior of the children is chiefly responsible for the personality difficulties of their parents who are pictured as reacting to the undoubtedly trying situation of having an unresponsive child. While we would agree that this is an important consideration, it cannot explain the social and psychological characteristics of the parents which have a history long anteceding the child.

It is difficult to see how the "emotional configuration in the home" can play "a dynamic role in the genesis of autism" if the child does not respond to it because he does not relate to people. The only way these two statements can be reconciled is to assume that the parents' behavior does not permit or induce the child to come out of his shell. That is, the only way one can accept Kanner's thesis that the home affects the disturbance and still hold his view that the child cannot relate would be to assume that the parents fail to evoke any response in the child and that he therefore remains in his original autistic state.

When Eisenberg [1957] writes alone then a somewhat different view emerges of the etiology of autism.

They rear them, if according to any plan, by a caricature of Watsonian behaviorism, a doctrine they find congenial. Such interest as they have in the children is in their capacity as performing automata. Hence, the frequent occurrence among autistic children of prodigious feats of recitation by rote memory. Conformity is demanded; what is sought is the "perfect" child—i.e., one who obeys, who performs, and who makes no demands.

Eisenberg seems convinced that these children conform in ways that are also rebellious, since they do not obey blindly but through a form of behavior that punishes the parents for their insensitive demands. Both the obedience and revolt show that the parents are very important. Because unless we relate, or wish to do so, others are just not important enough to make us respond to their demands with such consistent behavior.

Eisenberg [1956] goes even further. He says it can

be argued that their cognitive potentialities were, from the first, limited [but that] it would seem inevitable that a child whose contact with the human environment is so severely restricted must undergo irreversible intellectual deterioration when opportunities for growth are barred by the exclusion of normal experience, a concept that is supported by animal studies.

Though Kanner failed to recognize the wish for relatedness behind the children's extreme isolation, some of his later writings show that he no longer viewed autism as wholly inborn, but also as a result of intention. For the first time, then, the children's unrelenting demand for sameness is viewed not as an inability to do otherwise, but as the result of some decision:

The patients find security in sameness, a security that is very tenuous because changes do occur constantly and the children are therefore threatened perpetually and try tensely to ward off this threat to their security [Kanner, 1951a].

But while Kanner is impressed by the great skill autistic children show in respects such as memory, he continues to stress an innate impairment of affective contact. Unlike Eisenberg, he is not willing to assume the possibility that inadequate and overwhelming emotional experiences in early childhood may create severe changes in relating to or comprehending the world, and that if these are not corrected early enough, they may become irreversible. He is therefore hesitant to link autism to the environmental experience and continues to view it, in the main, as inborn. It is another question whether such extreme and early withdrawal from the world, such a far-reaching unresponsiveness to emotional stimuli will only impoverish the mental functions in a temporary way or become permanent.

Nor is Kanner alone in concluding that infantile autism is due to an inborn impairment, though others view it less as an impairment of affective contact than of the capacity for abstract thinking.

Benda, for example, sees the source of autism not in an inability to form affective relations but in an inability to abstract, a suggestion first made by Goldstein et al., to which I shall shortly return. Benda [1960] writes:

In distinguishing childhood autism from other forms of mental deficiency, we must say that the autistic child is not mentally retarded in the ordinary sense of the word but rather is a child with an inadequate form of mentation which manifests itself in the inability to handle symbolic forms and assume an abstract attitude. In these children we have, therefore, a specific disorder of abstraction which is an important part of human intelligence but not identical with other forms of intellectual defects or of focal brain damage. . . .

At the same time, we realize that the autistic child although seemingly withdrawn is not lacking in emotions, affection or even the intensity of personal contact. The child reacts emotionally to his surroundings: and if he seems confused, he is confused because he cannot orient himself in this world and in his contemporary age group. He cannot handle abstract material, speech and communication on the level required by his age. . . . Their drawings reveal circumstantial evidence that the lack of abstract attitudes is not a particular pathology of a circumscribed brain area but a developmental disorder of integration which involves the whole contact of the child with his environment.

Bender [1959] does not see autism as an inborn impairment of the central nervous system, but as a defensive reaction to one.

I have long argued that autism is a defense mechanism frequently occurring in young schizophrenic, or brain damaged, or severely traumatized, or emotionally deprived children, who thereby withdraw to protect themselves from the disorganization and anxiety arising from the basic pathology . . . in their genes, brains, perceptual organs or social relationships.

Goldstein [1959] too views autism as a secondary defense against an organic deficiency. The impairment, he feels, is the autistic child's inability to engage in abstract thinking. Autistic behavior is likened to the reactions of brain injured patients and "represent expressions of protective mechanisms, occurring passively as a means of safeguarding the patient's 'existence' in situations of unbearable distress and anxiety." Autism is then how the so impaired child avoids a catastrophic reaction.[1]

As mentioned at the start of this book, I began to work with a mute autistic child in 1932, more than ten years before Kanner published his first account of the disturbance or gave it a name. So I was unaware at the time that I was dealing with a child suffering from infantile autism. While such ignorance was not bliss, it certainly protected me from giving up too soon in despair.

When, in the 1940's, I became acquainted with Kanner's account, it fascinated me because he described in detail so many features of the child whose recovery I had struggled for. But by that time I could not accept his conviction that for her and others like her it was "an innate inability to form affective contact" [Kanner, 1943], or that theirs is a "disability to relate themselves in the ordinary way to people and situations from the beginning of life" [Kanner, 1944]. The way this child reacted in later years to any temporary absence of those who took care of her, the joy she showed on their return, and her appropriate response to other emotionally significant events ruled out such an assumption.

I find it equally hard to accept as proven that autistic children are different "from the beginning of their extra-uterine existence." Despite the most careful scanning of the literature, and study of the many cases that have come to our attention at the Orthogenic School, we found no tangible evidence that autism was recognized at birth or right afterward. While some parents do make such claims, none that we examined stood up under scrutiny. On closer examination it always appeared that what was later recalled as being present at birth, was behavior not actually observed for the first time until weeks or months later.

Bosch [1962] came to a conclusion we arrived at on the basis of different observations: that the observable onset of infantile autism must have something to do with events that take place during the second year of life, as opposed to those who wish to see evidence of autism immediately after birth. This is so important that I would like to quote:

While it may be thought that possibly a more careful comparison of these children during the first year of life might show deviations from the norm in regard to expression and behavior—van Krevelen refers to the strange staring gaze during early infancy of one of his cases—we nevertheless have to give serious thought to the question of why, in a large number of autistic children, these differences in behavior became apparent exactly at the beginning of the second year of life, though we have to make allowance here for a number of

1. Thus both Goldstein and Bender view infantile autism (in my opinion, correctly) as a defense against unbearable anxiety. Only I believe—unlike these authors —that the source of this anxiety is not an organic impairment, but the child's evaluation of the conditions of his life as being utterly destructive.

cases where in the parents' recollection these first clear differences in behavior were observed only in the second, or at the latest in the third year of life."[2]

This dating of when infantile autism becomes apparent is further supported by the observations of Schlain and Yannet [1960] who note of fifty autistic children that "most of the parents dated the onset of the abnormal behavior during the second year of life."

My own belief, as presented throughout this book, is that autism has essentially to do with everything that happens from birth on; nor can we rule out the possibility that some prenatal deviation in development may be a contributing factor. But since I also believe that autism is basically a disturbance of the ability to reach out to the world, it will tend to become most apparent during the second year of life when more complicated contact with the world would normally take place.

Typical of how uncertain even parents are about when (or how soon) they notice strange behavior in the autistic child is Kamp's report [1964] on a pair of identical twins. It is a specially good example, because Julie, one of the twins, became autistic while her sister, Coby, developed no disturbance. Hence at all times the parents had an identical image for comparison, which should have made it easy to spot some deviation in one of the twins. But

the mother reported that Julie showed the most favorable development during the first few months, but remained behind Coby during the later half of the first year of life. The father believes that Julie made a somewhat less vital impression from the onset. He denies any abrupt alteration in Julie's development.

By way of explaining the discrepancies between his own opinion and his wife's, the father thought it "possible that the mother confused the two highly similar looking children at some time during the latter half of the first year of life." But both parents agreed that "when she was about ten months old, Julie began to respond less well to approaches. She withdrew into herself, showing nothing of the functional development apparent in Coby."

Identical twins also constitute a crucial test of the innateness of infantile autism. Rimland [1964] discusses fourteen cases of twins with autism that came to his attention, eleven of them monozygotic and all twenty-eight of the children suffering from autism. This, he feels, provides "one of the strongest lines of evidence against psychogenic etiology of autism."

Yet even where both twins are autistic, it does not invalidate a hy-

2. In the absence of an English translation, all quotations from Bosch in this and the following chapter are my own English renderings.

pothesis of environmental origin since both may have been subject to an identical or very similar home influence. And if there were even one instance of identical twins in which one was autistic and the other not, it would throw serious doubts on any theory of inborn origin, while it would not weaken the environmental hypothesis since parents may react differently to each twin.

Fortunately, two such instances have come to light. The twins on whom Kamp [1964] reported have by now been studied intensively for five years by the department of child psychiatry of the University of Utrecht. According to a private communication [Kamp, 1965] "The twin sister has shown no signs of maladjustment, is doing well at school and is getting along alright." Vaillant too [1963] has reported on a set of identical twins who were discordant for autism.

As Kanner notes, some authors speak of the autistic child's innate inability to respond to mothering and ascribe to this the strange behavior of their parents. For example, there is reference to an alleged lack of anticipatory response to being picked up.

What is meant by "anticipatory approach behavior" Call [1964] describes as follows:

In the course of making observations of newborn infants, we . . . observed a hungry two-day old breast-fed at the eighth feeding open his mouth, bring his free arm against the force of gravity from his sides to the region of his mouth and the mother's approaching breast when he was handed to the mother and placed in a nursing position close to the mother's body but prior to any contact with the mother's breast, clothing, or other stimuli on the infant's face.

Recently, when studies of animal imprinting showed the importance of earliest experiences on later socialization, these findings have been called upon to explain infantile autism. Since some animals do not show anticipatory gestures but rather following behavior, the two behaviors were assumed to be equivalent and the absence of an anticipatory response in babies was viewed as a possible cause of what made them be (or become) autistic. For example, the question was raised "whether infantile autism might represent failure of visual attachments to the mother to develop during an early critical period, due either to defects in the intrinsic neural organization or to aberrations in infant-maternal interactions" [Garrard and Richmond, 1963].

Here the authors do not commit themselves either to an inborn defect in the child or to unresponsiveness in the mother as the definite cause of autism but consider both possibilities. Yet the question is: What exactly does the maternal behavior have to consist of in order to keep visual attachment from developing in the infant?

Actually I know of no uninvolved observers who have seen lack of anticipatory behavior or an absence of visual following during an autistic child's first days of life. And thereafter it may already be a response to what mothering the baby has experienced.

Some of the observations we do have of newborns (see pages 16–19) may explain why this is so. Certainly, with observations like those of Call, Fantz, Wolff, et al., we may question even more than we once did, any claims about behavior being present or absent at birth because of observations not made till weeks later. For example, anticipatory behavior has been observed in babies as early as at the fourth feeding [Call, 1964].

In nine out of eleven breast-fed babies Call observed, this occurred not later than the eleventh feeding; while in four out of six bottle-fed infants it was observed, too, as early as the fourth, and not later than the fourteenth feeding.

The two instances in which no anticipatory approach behavior was observed in the breast-fed infants were both primaparous mothers with nipple problems ("flat" nipples and "inverted" nipples on one side). . . . In both cases . . . the infants were fed while lying flat on the mother's lap with minimal body contact.

If things go wrong because such anticipatory behavior is not met by an appropriate response in the mother, the relation of the infant to his environment may become deviant from the very beginning of life. Thus an infant's later fighting against or autistically withdrawing from the world may be caused by what happens so early in life that unless the first few feedings have been carefully observed, it may seem to be the consequence of inborn behavior.

This is not to say that herein for certain lies the *Anlage* for infantile autism. But neither is there reason to exclude the possibility until we have explored it more fully. These babies failed to show anticipatory responses to being picked up, as some have claimed to be typical of newborns who will later become autistic. But, after all, the anticipatory response has the purpose of securing survival. What then, if the infant's experience of being put to the breast is that far from securing survival, it may mean suffocation? I refer to Gunther's example (pages 17–18) in which the mother's own breast obstructed the baby's nasal passage, cutting off his air supply. Isn't the baby's then fighting the breast the best adaptation to the experience he is capable of?

The same example shows that if the baby doesn't get what he wants he will fight or become apathetic, so that both ways are possible. And even those who fight, if their struggle isn't recognized as legitimate, may turn apathetic.

While these observations date from the first days of life, Call reports on an infant for whom things went well in the hospital but worsened in the home.

A third infant showed anticipatory behavior of the usual kind during the lying-in period, but began consistently turning away from the mother at five and a half weeks. The mother held this infant fairly close in the first few days of bottle feeding while in the hospital; but when she got home, she consistently held the infant in her left arm away from her body with inconsistent head support. seldom looking at its face. The father, who fed about one-third of the time, held the infant close to his body well supported in his right arm, and consistently looked in the infant's face. The mother also engaged in a teasing game which consisted of brushing the nipple across the infant's mouth, having him reach for it with his mouth, only then to take it out of reach. From five and a half weeks to eight months of age, the baby continued turning away from the mother when she fed him and turned towards the father when he fed him. Further study of this case and follow-up of other apparent pathology that has developed will be subject to another report [Call, 1964].

One wonders if this infant was not protected from an even more severe pathology by the father's positive support. This the fathers of autistic children seem unable to provide, though it would counteract the mother's lack of responsiveness to her infant's needs. Because it seems that behavior once thought to be instinctual, or inborn, may turn out to need environmental releasers if it is not to go radically astray.

If this is so, then what Kanner viewed as an inborn disturbance of affective contact may very well be what happens when the inborn ability to relate does not meet the appropriate releasers at the appropriate time.

This seems also the view of Bowlby [1952] since he compares maternal care to the chemical organizers during embryonic development.

In dealing with the embryology of the human mind one is struck by a similarity with the embryological development of the human body, during the course of which undifferentiated tissues respond to the influences of chemical organizers. If growth is to proceed smoothly, the tissues must be exposed to the influences of the appropriate organizer at certain critical periods. In the same way, if mental development is to proceed smoothly, it would appear to be necessary for the undifferentiated psyche to be exposed during certain critical periods to the influence of the psychic organizer—the mother.

Unfortunately we have far too few observations, made right after birth, or any follow-ups on how such children developed later on, to say anything about autism for certain, on their basis.

In discussing feral children, I indicated that we have been aware since at least the thirteenth century that infants brought up under atypical conditions can be damaged severely. From the beginning of this century, reports have told consistently about the incredible mortality rate of infants raised in hospitals or institutions of low standard, or under extremely "sterile" conditions. Among the first to report on how radically this can interfere with the infant's intellectual development were Durfee and Wolf [1933]. They found that while life in a bad institution did not seem to interfere with the infant's intelligence at three months, those who remained longer than eight months could no longer be tested for lack of an appropriate responsiveness.

Spitz [1945, 1946, 1951] was the first to study this problem psychoanalytically. It was his conclusion that emotional deprivation and an absence of appropriate stimulation leads to anaclitic depression and severe emotional and intellectual retardation. In extreme cases the results are marasmus and death.

Goshen [1963], extending these studies to the private home, stresses the impact of the mother who fails to stimulate the child or to evoke meaningful signals during critical periods of life, particularly between the ages of six and eighteen months. As a result the child may fail to grasp the significance of language and eventually reach a state of mental retardation.

Goshen was here concerned with mothers who were ordinarily capable and conscientious with their children but because of a temporary state of depression were

unresponsive to them, and consistently disinclined to assume any initiative in meeting the children's needs. [While] they tended . . . to be nearly the sole person to take care of them . . . the nature of their participation was silent, mechanical, resentful, gloomy, and lacking in any spontaneity. Most significantly, there was a minimum of interest expressed in eliciting any emotional response from the children and a maximum interest expressed in keeping the child quiet and inactive. These attitudes or activities were colored by a powerful effort to control in a restrictive, negative way.

These mothers whose depressive and self-involved attitudes, according to Goshen, are highly correlated to their children's mental retardation show characteristics that are strikingly similar to those of the mothers of many of our autistic children. And these children, when they came to us, all tested mentally retarded. Still, the children Goshen describes were not autistic. Perhaps for one reason or another the mother's unconscious motives were not experienced by the child as a threat to his very existence. In any case, we have here reactions to an absence of stimuli, a situation that has been reproduced artificially in recent sensory-deprivation experiments.

Other studies take us into the prenatal environment. Sontag [1941] reports that fetal movements increased significantly while the mothers were undergoing emotional stress. When the mother's upset lasted several weeks, fetal activity continued at an exaggerated level throughout the entire period. More recent studies have stressed the impact in general of the mother's emotional attitudes on childbirth and the newborn [Ferreira, 1960; Davids, Devault and Talmadge, 1961]. While these authors make no claims about long-range effects, Sontag felt that prolonged emotional stress during pregnancy might have an enduring impact on the child.

Bergman and Escalona's study [1949] of the reactions of very sensitive infants are also relevant here. They suggest that some infants have what the authors call "too thin a protective barrier" and that because of it they may develop ways of protecting themselves. Too much protection, however, may result in "delayed and possibly all-too-delayed ego formation." And while the authors speak here mainly of a barrier to sensory stimuli, I shall assume this refers equally to emotional stimuli, since at this early age it makes little sense to differentiate between the two.

In a more recent publication, Spitz [1964], who initially stressed the damaging effects of an absence of stimulation, expresses equal concern for the opposite conditions. He writes:

Recently I was struck by the obvious: in the etiology of all psychotoxic disturbances the *wrong* kind of emotional supplies is conspicuous. Some of the psychotoxic disturbances (three-months colic, infantile rocking, etc.) show in addition a specific etiological factor, in essence the diametrical opposite of emotional deprivation, namely, a surfeit, an overdose of affective stimulation. After years of trying to formulate this problem of "too much," I now suggest to call this factor *emotional overload*. An example of this, for instance, is encountered in undisciplined parental behavior, one that is unlike genuine object relations, because it is the outcome of the parent's own unresolved emotional problems, such as repressed hostility, guilt feelings, narcissistic needs, etc.

In those children destined to become autistic their oversensitivity to the mother's emotions may be such that they try, in defense, to blot out what is too destructive an experience for them. Little is known about the relation between the development of the child's feelings and his cognition. But to blot out emotional experience probably impedes the development of cognition, and it may be that the two reinforce each other till autism results.

This is a view akin to Eisenberg's thinking [1956], since he wrote:

One wonders if there may not be, parallel to intellectual inadequacy, a syndrome of affective inadequacy. Just as intellectual inadequacy may be the outcome of structural limitations or of cultural deprivation, so may affective inadequacy reflect organic dysfunction, affective deprivation, or a combination thereof.

Assuming a possibly heightened sensitivity in autistic children to all or a wide variety of stimuli (perhaps because of their potentially superior intelligence) wouldn't it follow that because of their low threshold to stimuli they avoid some of them as too painful until such time as they learn they are pleasurable?

The foregoing indicates why I believe that stories about autistic children being unresponsive from birth on do not, in and by themselves, suggest an innate disturbance. Because it may be a very early reaction to their mothers that was triggered during the first days and weeks of life.

What is difficult to know is what triggered the reaction. The more intimate the relation, the more difficult it is to know what belongs to which partner. If we assume that the investment in the mother is both intense and disappointing, then it may cause the child to turn his back on the world. That part is easy. What is much more difficult to say, at this shadowy age of the mind, is what made things go so sour for the child.

Social workers who place newborn infants in foster homes are well acquainted with the fact that some infants do not eat, or remain totally unresponsive to their foster mothers. But when, for that reason, they are moved to another foster home many will perk up at once. It shows how early an infant can respond with radical rejection or withdrawal to feelings in the mothering person, and that the cause of it lay in the interaction with a particular mother and not in the infant alone.

Despite the foregoing, it would be very hard to know if what goes on between the infant and his surrounding world is due to his heightened sensitivity, to overstimulation, or to an absence of stimulation.

Balancing the two opposite possibilities of what causes the damage, it seems obvious that the child who has known pathogenic deprivation or pathogenic overstimulation, and reacted to either in a sensitive way, will in some way be scarred for life. But depending on the circumstances and the endowment of the child, these scars may be barely noticeable or severely handicapping. Certainly we know of children whose deprivation or other pathogenic histories were every whit as bad as those of children who became autistic, but where the former group only developed severe neuroses.

It seems that the newborn (and probably also the fetal) organism is equipped only for dealing with what, in the normal course of development, are average environmental conditions. As Hartmann [1958] puts it:

The question is whether, and to what extent, a certain course of development can count on average expectable stimulations (environmental releasers) and whether, and to what extent, and in what direction, it will be deflected by environmental influences of a different sort. . . . No instinctual drive in man guarantees adaptation in and of itself, yet on the average the whole ensemble of instinctual drives, ego functions, ego apparatus, and the principle of regulation, as they meet the average expectable environmental conditions, do have survival value. . . . The proposition that the external world "compels" the organism to adapt can be maintained only if one already takes man's survival tendencies and potentialities for granted.

But what if survival tendencies were severely stunted, either from birth on, or shortly thereafter?

[While] strictly speaking, the normal newborn human and his average expectable environment are adapted to each other from the very first moment, that no infant can survive under certain atypical (on the average not expectable) conditions does not contradict this proposition. [Hartmann, 1958.]

Autistic children simply did not meet up with what for them was an average expectable environment, either because of their native endowment, or because of deficiencies in their environment—including too much or too little stimulation—an environment that in some fashion was too unresponsive to them.

Referring specifically to autism, Escalona [1963] feels that

The controversy as to whether infantile autism is "due to" inadequate mothering or "due to" inborn deficit loses its significance. It is a result of a lack in experiences which may come about through extreme variations in either intrinsic or extrinsic determinants, or both. But autistic psychosis in childhood is not directly caused by a maternal deficit or by a deficit in the child. It is caused by the absence of those vital experiences in early childhood which we regard as the necessary condition for ego synthesis.

Which is perfectly true as far as it goes. But it remains difficult for me to accept such correct and well-reasoned explanations of our problem. Because what we need to know is exactly how it comes about, in the lives of some children, that these vitally needed experiences do not occur. The controversy of what came first, the chicken or the egg (the child's or the mother's inability to respond to each other) seems fruitless. But neither is it answered by saying that the whole thing is the result of an interaction, which it certainly is.

What we need to know are the minutiae of the steps in these interactions: what particular response to what particular event will, for example, result in autism instead of neurosis; what are the specific intrinsic determinants in the infant that will predispose to autism instead of another type of childhood schizophrenia—or to no disease at all? Since all personality development, normal or abnormal, results from the interactions of a particular inheritance with a particular environment, to state that the interaction causes autism is a truism—unless, of course one subscribes to a simple hypothesis that autism is due only or mainly to an organic impairment *sui generis*. It does not answer the question: What is the particular inheritance, and the specific environmental factor which, in their interaction, create autism?

In any case there is reason to question the inborn nature of autism until such time as it is actually observed in newborn infants before mothering can have made a difference; or until such time as organicity is established not on the basis of speculation but of objective neurological findings or other incontrovertible evidence. The more so since we now know of at least two cases of identical twins discordant for infantile autism.

A neurological theory of autism has indeed been proposed by Rimland in a recently published monograph. Since it is also, to my knowledge, the only book-length report in English on infantile autism and the most recent one at this writing—a German monograph will be discussed later—I shall be referring to it again in this chapter.

Rimland holds that the source of the autistic disturbance is to be found in the reticular formation of the brain stem. But a careful study of the evidence presented in his book failed to convince me that autism has anything to do with an inborn dysfunction of this or any other part of the brain. And even if a specific neurological dysfunction should some day be found to correlate highly with the syndrome of infantile autism, it would still be compatible with the psychogenic hypothesis.

First, the possibility exists that if certain neural systems are not appropriately stimulated within a specific period of life, they may suffer permanent impairment. Hence the absence of certain emotional experiences at a very early age may account for the later dysfunction of some part of the central nervous system.

Second, and more important, we were able, through psychotherapeutic treatment, to reverse the course of the disturbance. As illustrated in this book by Joey's history, we have helped him and others to free themselves of all those symptoms that are viewed as typical of the disease, suggesting that infantile autism is not caused by an inborn dysfunction of the central nervous system.

What, then, of the reticular formation and its arousal function? To begin with, Hebb [1955] explains that sensory events have at least two functions: to provide cues for guiding behavior, and to arouse. But our observations suggest that the autistic child, through his own efforts, achieves a state of nonattentiveness to stimuli which has all the appearances of a state of dysfunction of the system serving arousal, possibly that of the reticular formation. This he does, for example, by his monotonous, continuous self-stimulation which arises, in part, from his motor behavior. In a sense, any stimulus from the outside is then lost, either by being blotted out, or in the concentration on inner sensations alone.

I will return to the functional aspects of such behavior in a moment. But first a consideration of normal neurophysiology may be helpful. Of the sensory impulses—those conducted by the long afferent pathways subserving touch, light, and those serving inner sensations— few ever gain conscious recognition. Many sensory impulses bring about activity at spinal and brain-stem levels. Others pass to the thalamus and cerebral cortex directly. Still others influence the activity of the cerebral cortex by way of collaterals to the brain-stem reticular centers.

Recent studies emphasize the significant role of this brain-stem reticular formation in regulating the background activity of the central nervous system. But the autistic child, with his self-imposed structures of unvarying, repetitive stimuli, and of shutting out external stimuli, prevents the reception of extrinsic sensory input. If he maintains a state of wakefulness, it is not an alert attentiveness to the outside, though possibly he is attentive to his own inner sensations.

But we do not have to look to neurological theory to support the idea that infantile autism is linked to some failure in the system serving arousal. That the failure does not reside in the central nervous system is amply demonstrated by children like Marcia, and there were quite a few others who showed similar symptomatology. By closing their ears and even their nostrils with their hands, by covering their eyes with their hair, they try to ensure that nothing from the outside will arouse them. Such children also cover themselves with blankets, retire to dark corners, turn their backs to the world, and so forth. Even their loud screaming has the purpose of drowning out what they might otherwise hear.

If their arousal function were impaired, as Rimland assumes, then their shutting out of stimuli would be incomprehensible. It is exactly because they can be aroused, but do not wish to be, that they try to block out stimuli through motor behavior like twiddling, or to drown them out through music which they hear as "white" noise without content. Or else they quite simply cover up their sense receptors.

These children derive no pleasure from the blocking out of stimuli, nor from their sensorimotor behavior. Their emotions, as revealed in their expressions at the time, show us clearly that these children desperately narrow their orbit of experience because they feel they must. Their defensive maneuvers afford them, at best, only a timeless existence —which is also the paradox of treatment. Through their shutting out of sensation they are neither confronted by a frustrating reality, nor are they gratified in their timeless existence. Both must be introduced to motivate them to change. But change represents a threat to their very existence and they appropriately defend themselves against it.

Whatever the case, I do not see it as my task to weigh hypotheses of an organic etiology of infantile autism. If the condition should become curable through pharmacology or any other nonpsychological treatment of the central nervous system, we shall cease our efforts to cure it on a psychological basis, but not before.

Even now, with the many research papers devoted to it, and with book-length reports such as Rimland's, Bosch's, and the present volume, far too little is known about infantile autism to settle this question of organicity versus a psychogenic origin. As heuristic hypotheses both have value in the sense that by following both, no possibility is overlooked. While I do not accept the hypothesis that autism is due to an original organic defect, I do not feel I can rule out its later appearance. On the contrary, I tend to believe that far from being organic in origin, infantile autism, when persisting too long, can have irreversible effects. This applies not to the affects—since we could restore full affective functioning to nearly all the autistic children we worked with for long enough—but to the intellectual or ego functions.

Thus my essential disagreement with Rimland, for example, is not with his approach, but with his insistence that the psychogenic approach should be discarded; and this though he does not claim certainty for his ideas. I think it most important to investigate the hypothesis of an organic etiology. I can only wonder why he decries what he calls "the all too common practice of blatantly assuming that psychogenic etiology *can* exist or *does* exist" and that to do so "is not only unwarranted but actively pernicious."

Actually, I believe that in earliest development, soma and psyche are so little differentiated that to a more enlightened time the entire controversy between organic and psychogenic hypotheses at that age may appear moot. The infant's brain needs stimulation through sensory-emotional experiences to fully develop its cognitive functions and the ability to relate, even if the infant was born with a normal potential for mental and emotional functioning.

There are some points on which I can agree with Rimland: one is that it serves no good purpose to make the parents of autistic children feel guilty as having caused the disturbance. Firstly, we cannot be sure that their attitudes and the handling of their infant was, in and of itself, sufficient cause. While we believe it to be a precipitating factor, this makes it only a necessary but not a sufficient condition. We cannot even be sure whether, or to what degree, they handled the child as they did because of his unusual responses to them. But even if it turned out one day that the parents' contribution is indeed crucial, they did as they did because they could not help themselves to do otherwise. They suffer more than enough in having such a child. To make them guilty will only add to the misery of all and help no one.

Nevertheless, it is one thing not to wish to make parents feel guilty because it makes them miserable and gains nothing for the child. It is another thing not to wish to find out what experiences may have caused or contributed to infantile autism, because to do so is "pernicious;" that is, may turn out to be painful to parents.

There is another point of agreement: Rimland expresses a view which, as much as anything, motivated me to work so sustainedly with these children and also to write this book. He quotes Sarason and Gladwin [1958] who feel that "The importance of these cases [of early infantile autism] to the development of the science of psychology would seem to be vastly beyond what their relatively rare occurrence in the general population would suggest."

There is one further aspect of the investigation of infantile autism which the present volume represents, and which I found largely absent in the literature. While a great deal is written about the nature of the autistic child's parents, we know far too little about what can be learned about the disturbance through the child's own uncovering efforts. Though Mahler, Rodrigué, and some others do concentrate on uncovering treatment Rimland inveighs against it, while others seem to feel it is not worth the trouble.

Our understanding of hysteria, neurosis and even much about psychosis would be at the pre-Freudian level had Freud not concentrated on having the patient himself find out what lay behind his symptomatic behavior. I believe that the royal road to the understanding of mental disease is the patient's own uncovering of the hidden meaning of his overt behavior, and what caused it. To demonstrate that even autistic children can do this was in fact another main purpose of this volume. In their case, too, knowledge makes them free.

It is therefore distressing that Escalona [1965] though she uses infantile autism as the example to support her ingenious model explaining individual differences, does so without regard to what the autistic child can tell us about why he developed so differently.

While she tells us that "child psychiatrists have been gravely puzzled by the etiology of a severe form of pathology, referred to as infantile autism," she is convinced, on the basis of her model, that "all autistic children have lacked in their concrete experience that which we have summarized as mothering."

Although her model has a great deal to be said in its favor, infantile autism is again explained by means of an investigation that disregards the autistic child's own discoveries about what caused him to take recourse to autism. It is as if Freud had assumed he could discover the nature of the unconscious, of dreams, of hysteria and neurosis, by constructing an ingenuous model of the workings of the human psyche. In fact he made his discoveries, including an entirely new model of the human mind, by working strictly the other way round. His models grew out of what he learned from his own dreams and from examining the workings of the mind, both his own mind and those of his hysteric and neurotic patients. And what he learned there, I believe, will stand the test of time. The models he then constructed on the basis of his therapeutic investigations will change and be improved exactly to the degree that we push forward in our own therapeutic investigations. And while Freud had doubts about how effective was psychoanalysis as treatment, he never doubted that the psychoanalytic investigation of the disturbance with the patient would vastly increase our knowledge.

If Freud was correct, then whether we learn to understand infantile autism depends on whether or not we treat autistic children in ways that parallel Freud's, a method that permitted him to treat and explore the nature and cause of the disturbance in a simultaneous process. Such a method permitted him not only to help many of his patients, but to learn much that was so far unknown about the mental workings of all men.

§

On Treatability

Wherever infantile autism is viewed as an inborn impairment, of whatever variety, the resultant attitudes toward treatment will be defeatist. Among those, on the other hand, who trace the causes of autism at least in part to the environmental influence, outlooks will be more optimistic because of the not always valid but convincing belief that what environment has caused, environment may also be able to correct.

Nor is the pessimism limited to those who embrace the organic hypothesis. Study of the literature suggests it is also dominant among many who accept a psychogenic hypothesis, even in part. In my opinion the pessimism is unwarranted and may be ascribed to the fact that all too few efforts at treatment were intensive enough, and even more important, were sustained for the requisite number of years. Thus when Kanner [1954a] and Kanner and Lesser [1958], state that infantile autism has not been influenced by any form of therapy, I can only explain it by the fact that the therapy was not appropriate in terms of methods used, or of intensiveness or duration of treatment.

That this may indeed be the case seems born out by data which Professor Eisenberg [1965] was kind enough to furnish at my request. Since his follow-up study of autistic children [Eisenberg, 1956] is the outstanding one of its kind in the literature (see page 413), it was important to know how much treatment these children had received. The most intensive treatment received by any of the sixty-three children reported on was in three cases of outpatient treatment where the children were seen in once- or twice-weekly sessions, for not exceeding two years. It is significant that while a "fair" or "good" outcome is reported for only seventeen out of the entire group of sixty-three (about 28.5 per cent), the story is very different for the three who received the most intensive treatment. Although the treatment they received was by no means as concentrated as it should have been for children suffering so severe a disturbance, the outcome was rated fair or good for two of them (or about 66 per cent).

The largest group (twenty) of the sixty-three reported on were placed in private institutions where care was essentially only custodial. Fair or good outcome was reported for five of these twenty. The next largest group (sixteen), was placed in training schools or state hospitals. None of these sixteen showed fair or good outcome.

Given the small number of children in this group of sixty-three to receive appropriate psychiatric treatment, and that only of relatively low intensity and limited duration, one may assume that opinions about the treatability of autistic children would change radically, if larger numbers of them were to receive intensive treatment of appropriate duration. But since the data described here were all that Kanner and Eisenberg could base their conclusions on, both their pessimism and their wavering views on treatability become understandable.

Kanner himself, for example, convinced of both the inborn nature of the disturbance and the parents' contribution, has been somewhat vacillating in his opinions about therapy. Never optimistic about its chances, he has not entirely denied them either, witness his comments of 1956: "Insofar as our data permit evaluation, psychotherapy seems in general to be of little avail, with few apparent exceptions" [Eisenberg and Kanner, 1956]. But a few years earlier he seemed to feel more strongly that the evidence on treatment results was by no means yet in.

In discussing Darr and Worden's report on an autistic girl, twenty-eight years after she was initially studied, Kanner [1951b] wrote:

The first reaction to the story of the patient Jane is likely to be a reminder that Jane has never been treated adequately. Would appropriate therapy have altered the development of her psychosis? . . . . The paper by Drs. Darr and

Worden tells us what has become of one autistic child who has reached adult-hood. The two decades before us ought to tell much about the destiny of those now observed and variously treated.

Those two decades are by no means over, and perhaps the present volume will in some part answer Dr. Kanner's questions.

Rimland shares none of Kanner's doubts, but states apodictically that "no form of psychiatric treatment has been known to alter the course of autism." How right or wrong he is the reader will have to decide after reading the case histories in this volume, or if he goes to the trouble of reading some of the sources Rimland refers to himself. For example, he quotes Eveloff [1960] five times in support of his own theories, but fails to mention that Eveloff's is a report on the excellent progress of a three-and-a-half-year-old autistic girl after only several months of outpatient treatment. (Though the therapist favored placement in a treatment institution, he was opposed in this suggestion by the parents.) Nor does Rimland mention that Eveloff concludes his article by saying: "There is no question that she has improved greatly, and there is considerable evidence to support the contention that this improvement is the result of psychiatric treatment."

Rimland asserts further that "recovery in those cases where it has occurred, has apparently been spontaneous" and that chances for such recovery are slight. Whether, for example, Marcia's recovery, or Joey's, were spontaneous or the result of intensive treatment the reader will have his own chance to decide.

It is true, however, and our experience confirms it, that trying to rehabilitate autistic children while they continue to live at home, or by treating mother and child simultaneously, is a questionable procedure. It has been our experience that this works only when the disturbance is relatively mild and the child still very young.

Though never explicitly stated, childhood schizophrenia has been viewed as not much more than a negligible appendage of maternal pathology—occasionally so much so that reconstructions and study of the assumed cause of the disturbance (the mother) seem to have taken the place of the study of the disease itself. And this is even more so in regard to the severest form of childhood psychoses, infantile autism. Direct connections have been established between maternal attitudes —about which relatively much was known, and which were easy to study—and the behavior of the schizophrenic child, about which little was known and which was difficult to understand.

Partly this may have happened because one can get fairly adequate information from a relatively well-functioning parent who at least talks, compared with what can be gleaned from an autistic child. But given such an attitude, some students of this disturbance have concentrated mainly on the mother, not only for understanding but also for helping the schizophrenic child. Thus the child, who suffers most of all from not having acquired an autonomous existence as a person, is again not regarded as an autonomous being even in treatment efforts designed to help him become a human being in his own right. And as if to crown the irony, some treatment methods rely on efforts to understand and help the schizophrenic child through the very person who (it is assumed) kept him from developing normally in the first place—his mother.

It is unfortunate that Mahler [1952], who was among the first to discuss infantile autism from the psychoanalytic viewpoint, was kept from recognizing infantile autism as an autonomous response on the part of the child by her belief that the young child is "only half an individual" [Mahler, 1965]. Thus she views his way of experiencing life as an outlook conditioned by the mother instead of his autonomous way of reacting to his total life experience, including the mother.

Convinced of the paramount importance of the child's symbiotic relation to the mother, Mahler sees it as a major tool of treatment "to reconstruct the mother-child symbiosis of the original unit" [1965]. And guided by this conviction, she tries to treat mother and child simultaneously, as do many others who follow her lead. Just because it is so extraordinarily important for the infant's initial well-being and later healthy development to have a good mother, it is erroneously assumed that any mother-child relationship is so valuable that it must be salvaged, even when it is damaging to the child.

Thus while Mahler is skeptical about the cure of childhood schizophrenia, she speaks [1952] of

the insuperable plateau of arrested progress, which usually . . . frustrates . . . the hopes of the parents. Impatient reactions and pressures are then exercised and progress forced. [Yet] if the autistic child is forced too rapidly into social contact, and particularly if the newly formed symbiotic relationship causes frustration, he is often thrown into a catatonic state and then in [a] fulminant psychotic process.

But why should the psychotic child be treated under conditions that expose him to impatient pressure from parents? Why should he be forced too rapidly into social contact, and why should the newly formed relationship cause frustration? It may, for example, cause frustration if restricted to only a few office hours. But then this would be an important communication from the child about treatment.

All this would soon be apparent if we would just listen carefully to what the schizophrenic child tells us, at least those who talk. They will let us know readily enough what kind of treatment they need—which is another example of how it is only through the study and treatment of the child, not his mother, that we can understand and help him.

In order to present findings beyond my own on this most important problem of how the schizophrenic child should be treated I shall quote Anna Freud [1954b]. Speaking of a schizophrenic adolescent girl, she reports:

After several months of struggles in the treatment, during which relations to the analyst went up and down, wavered, threatened to dissolve, to peter out, to extend to other figures in the environment in turn, the girl said to the therapist: "You analyze me all wrong. I know what you should do; you should be with me the whole day, because I am a completely different person when I am here with you, when I am in school, and when I am home with my foster family. How can you know me if you do not see me in all these places? There is not one of me, there are three."

Here, then, we are given the essence of what must form the treatment of the schizophrenic child. But Anna Freud continues:

It struck me that here, disguised as a piece of technical advice, we were offered some insight into the basic deficiencies of her ego structure. There had been, in her past, no opportunity to introject any one object sufficiently to built up inner harmony and synthesis under the guidance of a higher agency, acting as a unifying superego. Her personality shifted, following the promiscuity of her relationships. She was well able to adapt herself to the varying environments in which her life was spent, but in none of these relationships could she build up a real feeling of self, or correlate the self experienced in one setting with those of another setting. What she asked the therapist to do was, as it were, to offer herself in the flesh as the image of a steady, ever-present object, suitable for internalization, so that the patient's personality could be regrouped and unified around this image. Then, and only then, the girl felt, would there be a stable and truly individual center to her personality which she could transfer and offer for analysis. . . . We are faced with the technical question whether such preparatory assistance, if undertaken in all earnestness, would be compatible with later analytic work.

Here treatment requirements, clearly stated by the patient, are recognized as valid by the analyst. But then, instead of arranging for treatment along these lines, the issue is dropped in favor of discussing the problem of whether, if such treatment were begun, any later analytic work would be possible. On the basis of many years of experience with exactly the type of therapy this girl requested, my answer is: given the treatment she asked for, she may not need later analysis; not given this treatment, likely as not there will be no occasion for later analysis.

Schizophrenic children do indeed need a therapist who "offers herself in the flesh as . . . a steady, ever-present object . . . so that the patient's personality could be . . . unified around this image." From experience I can add that, after a few years with such a person, most schizophrenic children will relate and acquire a relatively stable and truly individual center for their personality. They will be able to live fairly successfully with this personality, and will feel no need to transfer it, or to offer it for analysis.

Much the same, incidentally, was suggested by Kanner [1948] when he advised that autistic children should be placed outside the home with some warm, understanding persons.

Here I wish also to comment on current efforts to deal with infantile autism through operant conditioning—that is, by creating conditioned responses through punishment and reward. Temporarily this breaks down the child's defenses against experiencing the frustrations of reality and arouses him to some action. But the actions are not of his devising. They are those the experimenter wants; that is, they are conditioned response actions. Which means that autistic children are reduced to the level of Pavlovian dogs.

According to a recent description of operant conditioning [Lovaas, Berberich, Perloff, Schaeffer, 1966]:

Training was conducted six days a week, seven hours a day, with a fifteen-minute rest period accompanying each hour of training. During the training sessions the child and the adult sat facing each other, their heads about thirty cm apart. The adult physically prevented the child from leaving the training situation by holding the child's legs between his own legs. Rewards, in the form of single spoonsful of the child's meal, were delivered immediately after correct responses. Punishment (spanking, shouting by the adult) was delivered for inattentive, self-destructve, and tantrumous behavior which interfered with the training, and most of these behaviors were thereby supressed within one week.

It is not claimed that such "training" of mute autistic children leads to speech, but only to "verbal imitation," that is to echolalia, which is no less a symptom of psychosis than is mutism. Hence all the training does is to add one more symptom to the old ones.

Our procedure centers on the acquisition of only one aspect of speech, the acquisition of vocal responses. The development of speech also requires the acquisition of a context for the occurrence of such responses ("meaning").

But this is true only if the symptom of echolalia (which is typical of psychosis) is viewed as a response; otherwise it cannot be said that such training leads to vocal responses. Thus the authors must recognize that their "training" the child does not lead to purposeful talk. Speech in the sense of communication simply cannot be forced out of children. It can only be acquired as the outcome of personal relations. Forcing them into echolalia by bribing, shouting, or spanking will only lead to a greater dehumanization.

Efforts like these reflect the correct observation that in infantile autism the child avoids being confronted with reality. Without asking the question of why he does so—that is, without interest in why the disturbance—operant conditioning is meant to achieve some results, whatever the permanent injury it may cause. These unfortunate children are treated as objects. They are viewed from beyond any frame of reference that would embrace the totality of the human experience. Observing correctly that autistic children do not allow a painful reality to enter their world, the decision is made to force an even more painful one upon them.

To shock mental patients is, after all, one of the oldest of answers, and finds supporters in every age. This is so, firstly (and often recognized as such) because it produces results. While stripping the patients of whatever humanity they still have, it makes them, whether out of fear or an intensity of pain, much more pliable. Here it matters little whether this is done, as in past ages, by dunking or whipping or chaining them, or in a more technological age, through medical procedures like lobotomy or electrical shock.

Secondly, but not often recognized, it satisfies a desire to punish these recalcitrant objects: because to view them as persons would preclude any use of such procedures. To create conditioned responses in the patient deprives him just as effectively of the human freedom to make choices, as does the destruction of part of his brain. Perhaps we may say of the operant conditioning procedures what has been said of lobotomy: that "lobotomy changes a functional disorder that is potentially recoverable into an organic one for which there is no treatment" [Freeman, 1959]. It was exactly because this is so that lobotomy was forbidden as early as 1951 by the Ministry of Health, U.S.S.R. (Order Prohibiting Lobotomy, 1951). And this, in a country far behind the Western world in its recognition of the unconscious processes, and their treatment based on discoveries by Freud.

Any stripping away of defenses, without concern for why the person needs to defend himself, or from what, will produce reactions. But it will never lead to cure; that is, to a human existence involving choices. In the case of infantile autism this requires that the child's positive experiences convince him it is now safe to slowly give up his autistic defenses. He gives them up because new gratifying experiences are readily available and not because a machine dispenses candy. He does it not because levers are conveniently located, but because satisfying human relations are within easy reach. This, as the preceding histories have shown, takes a greater expense of spirit than delivering electrical shocks, or the offer of candy in return for the pulling of levers.

In a way, the conditioned response shaking-up of autistic children reminds one of Harlow's [1958] initial conviction that a terrycloth mother is not only as good but even better as a source of security, than a live one. Only it turned out that monkey infants reared by terrycloth objects did not grow up to be viable monkeys. Conditioned-response regimes may turn autistic children into more pliable robots, and the behavior of an Anna was devastating at times. But better to let even such a child decide what reactions she needs to feel able to live at any particular moment than to train her to live a conditioned-response existence because those around her find it more convenient.

Returning to the question of the treatability of autism, what counts from a human point of view is which theory of causation offers the better chance of relieving the distress of children who suffer from it today. To my knowledge none of those who propose a neurological or organic theory of causation have claimed significant improvement in children treated by methods based on their theories. But from the work of the Orthogenic School alone we can report that the majority of those clearly autistic children we could work with for several years were returned to society, as will be shown in detailed figures below.

If we at the Orthogenic School had worked with our autistic children intermittently, or for only a few months or at most a year or two, our outlook on treatment might have been very different. It is only when, after years of frustrated attempts, these children begin slowly to respond to treatment efforts based on psychoanalytically oriented hypotheses on the nature of the disturbance, that the psychogenic explanation becomes more and more convincing.

This tentative hypothesis gains in conviction as the psyche of the child slowly unfolds and he recaptures those fundamental steps in personality formation that other children took in early infancy. When at last the once totally frozen affects begin to emerge, and a much richer human personality to evolve, then convictions about the psychogenic nature of the disturbance become stronger still.

Only after such progress did it also turn out that events that had unfolded much earlier had been greatly significant, events that sometimes dated from the children's first months or even weeks at the School. Such was the case, for example, with Marcia's pouring water on our floors for months, for what seemed like no particular reason.

The same example, incidentally, may explain why some types of treatment efforts go wrong. There are reports on the study or treatment of autistic children which indicate how some of their symptomatic behavior was interfered with because for one reason or another it was not acceptable to the staff—or to the parents, where the child lived at home. If this happens, not much progress will take place and the pessimistic prognosis will again be confirmed. Had we stopped Marcia from flooding our floors, she would probably have withdrawn and stopped her water play. It would then have been viewed as another mystifying expression of infantile autism without deeper meaning, and lent support to the theory that something was organically wrong with this child. Thus our attitudes, while these children are being studied, can greatly influence their development and hence our opinions on treatability.

§

Follow-up Data

The best known follow-up of autistic children is the one already referred to, by Eisenberg [1956]. As a close collaborator of Kanner's he had access to the earliest studies of autistic children and could hence base his assessment on the longest follow-up period. He reports:

The follow-up evaluation was classified into three catagories: "poor," "fair," or "good" outcome. By "poor," we mean a patient who has not emerged from autism to any extent and whose present functioning is markedly maladaptive, characterized by apparent feeblemindedness and/or grossly disturbed behavior, whether maintained at home or in an institution. By "fair" we mean a patient who is able to attend regular classes in public or private school at a level commensurate with age and who has some meaningful contacts with other people, but who exhibits schizoid peculiarities of personality, sufficient to single him out as a deviant and to cause interference with function. By "good" we mean a patient who is functioning well at an academic, social, and community level and who is accepted by his peers, though he might remain a somewhat odd person.
Of the total group of sixty-three, three can be said to have achieved a good adjustment, fourteen a fair one, and forty-six a poor one. Thus, a little less than a third are functioning at a fair to good social level.

In order to evaluate our results in a comparable way I shall use here exactly the same categories as Eisenberg, though our results, unlike those he reported, are based on the most intensive and sustained therapy we were able to provide. Altogether we have worked with forty-six autistic children, all of whom showed marked improvement. But for purposes of comparison the following remarks will be restricted to only forty of these forty-six because one of them (Laurie) was withdrawn after a year; one, unbeknown to us when we accepted her, had been subjected to a long series of electroshock treatments a year before she came to us, which precluded effectiveness in our treatment methods; and four others, at this writing, have not been with us long enough to make valid assessments.

Applying Eisenberg's categories, there were eight in our forty for whom the end results of therapy were "poor" because, despite improvement, they failed to make the limited social adjustment needed for maintaining themselves in society. For fifteen the outcome was "fair" and for seventeen "good." Thus while Eisenberg reports only 5 per cent good outcome, our experience shows that intensive treatment can raise this figure to 42 per cent. While he reports only 22 per cent fair improvement, we can report 37 per cent. Most important, while he found 73 per cent poor outcome, we had only 20 per cent poor results. Certainly failure in a fifth of the cases is disappointing. But certainly also, the difference between Eisenberg's findings and ours justifies us in offering autistic children the chance to succeed—though we admit a still limited chance—through intensive institutional treatment.

On the other hand, I must reluctantly agree that as yet the prognosis is closely related to the child's willingness to speak. Eisenberg [1956] and Eisenberg and Kanner [1956] have reported much better recovery in speaking autistic children:

It soon became apparent that those children who were so isolated from human contact that they failed to develop, or, once having developed, lost the ability to communicate by speech did much more poorly than the others. If we choose as the line of separation the age of five, the total series can be divided into thirty-two speaking and thirty-one nonspeaking children. (The category nonspeaking includes mute children, those who exhibit only echolalia, and those who may possess in addition a few words, usually employed in a private sense. Its meaning in this context is unable to communicate verbally with others.)

The outcome of the first group of thirty-two [speaking children] can be classified as good in three, fair in thirteen, and poor in sixteen instances. Contrariwise, the outcome of the thirty-one nonspeaking children were fair in one and poor in thirty cases. Thus sixteen of thirty-two with useful speech at five years of age have been able to achieve a fair to good social adjustment, whereas only one of thirty-one nonspeaking children can be so classified [Eisenberg, 1956].

While our results are again much more favorable, the fact remains that of our eight failures, six were once nonspeaking (in Eisenberg's terms) while of the thirty-two who showed fair and good outcome only eight were nonspeaking. Thus while Eisenberg reports that only one out of thirty-one nonspeaking children showed meaningful improvement, our figures are eight out of fourteen, or the difference between 3 and 57 per cent. This difference is even more marked when comparing good outcome among the speaking group. There Eisenberg's data showed

50 per cent fair and good outcome, while our data for this outcome show twenty-four out of twenty-six speaking autistic children, or 92 per cent.

Despite our experience that the prognosis for autistic children who talk is much better than for those who do not, there is reason to assume that as we improve our treatment methods and gain a better understanding of the disease, our results may improve even for mute autistic children.

The seventeen children whose improvement we classified as "good" can for all practical purposes be considered "cured." Most of them still have some "quirks" in their personality, but none that would prevent them from functioning well on their own in society.

Nine of the seventeen are gainfully employed. Since eight are still in high school or college, this means that all who are not still completing their education are presently self supporting.

As for the academic level they had reached at the time of this writing: Five of the seventeen had finished college and three of these five had, in addition, earned higher degrees. Four others are still in college; one dropped out of college in his third year to seek employment; three graduated from public high school; one is a senior in a prep school; the other three are still high school students. Two of the seventeen are married and one has a child.

The fifteen classified as "fair" results are no longer autistic, though eight of them should now be classified as borderline or schizoid, since they have only made a fair social adjustment. The remaining seven do much better and suffer only from more or less severe personality disorders, which limitation has not kept them from making an adequate social adjustment.

Generalizing on both our failures and successes, we are impressed that for all forty-six children the so difficult establishment of affective relations—first to significant persons and then to the world—was achieved far more readily than what we might call ego-functions. In cases classified as "poor," ego-functioning remained at a low level, while most progress came in the emotional sphere.

Marcia's case may illustrate here, since she gained the whole range of affect in relation to people and the world. But while her ego-functions —including reasoning, reading comprehension, and mastery of the non-affective aspects of reality—showed marked development, they never reached normal levels. Or to put it in psychoanalytic terms, while Marcia and others like her achieved full recovery in the libidinal sphere, the same is not true for the ego sphere. Their egos seemed to remain pegged on a much lower platform than is normal for their age.

These findings, incidentally, suggest again that in infantile autism we are not dealing with an inborn disturbance of affective contact, but rather with an inborn time schedule that cannot be delayed for too long. That is, if the child does not soon enough achieve affective contact with the world it may be too late for him—even if he does so later on—to build up all the ego functions that seem to require the relatedness in order to develop. This is true for the children we classified as "poor" results, and for some of those classified as "fair," though the latter achieved much higher levels of ego functioning.

Some of the fifteen whom we classified as "fair," while completely able to feel in a two-way relation, show a capacity for empathy that is less than normal. This applies to the eight whom we classified as "fair" but who are presently borderline or schizoid, and two (or possibly three) of the seven classified as "fair," who do better. That is, while they have normal or better awareness of the nature of their feelings for others, and an average or better awareness of how other people feel about them, they are not responsive where the feelings of others do not pertain to themselves.

For example, Marcia understood completely how her counselors and teachers felt about her, most of all Karen. But she was largely insensitive to Karen's feelings for her husband. This was not simply jealousy, because it was just as true in other situations. And the same is by and large typical of children in the "poor" and "fair" groups as compared to those in the "good" group. They may understand very well their own feelings, and those of others toward them. But they cannot project themselves into the feelings of others about issues that do not directly concern themselves, and on the basis of this projection understand how others feel. For that they remain too self-involved, though the ones classified as "fair" manage despite it to get along in society on their own.

§
Parental Background

Our data do not confirm some reports in the literature about the social backgrounds of autistic children (as summarized by Rimland) without necessarily contradicting them. The same is true for reports on the sex ratio of autistic children and their place in the sibship.

Rimland postulates that "Children stricken with early infantile autism as a primary disorder were genetically vulnerable to autism as a consequence of an inborn capacity for high intelligence." This statement is based on Kanner's original observations on the intelligence of the parents of autistic children. Since other pertinent literature is mentioned by Rimland I need not repeat it here.

There is reason for discussing evidence in the literature where it suggests that high intelligence is universal among the parents of autistic children. Because if autism is due to some specific defect in the newborn, and if it is inherited, then there must be something specific in the parents which the autistic child inherits. The only specific quality in the parents that has been mentioned in the literature and that could affect their offspring is their high intelligence, since emotional coldness and self-involvement are not viewed as hereditary traits. (I should note too, that nowhere in the literature are there reliable measures of the intelligence of parents. Only occupation is reported, and occasionally academic achievement; hence these are all I can speak of here.)

Of the three cases detailed in this book, two at most, of the six parents, can be considered as falling in the high intelligence group: the fathers of Laurie and Marcia. Marcia's mother displayed driving ambition, but no signs of superior intelligence. Joey's parents were of good intelligence, but not in any sense superior. Nor were there any persons of outstanding intelligence among the children's grandparents.

Turning from them to the entire group of forty-six (which includes the three histories) four of the children were illegitimate, given up by their mothers for adoption right after birth. Three of the four were adopted; the fourth was not, but was raised from birth on in a variety of foster homes. True, in one adoptive family both parents were of better-than-average, perhaps of superior intelligence, and in a second family this was true of the father. This may speak for the psychogenic hypothesis, since pathology is based on the personality of those who nurtured the infant, and not on heredity. But it gives little support to the supposition of an inborn impairment of the brain related to superior intelligence in the parents. Because from what is known of these four children's natural parents (as learned from the placing agencies) there appeared to be no superior intelligence in the mothers, and none was claimed for the putative fathers.

Three other of our forty-six children were given up for adoption right after their first years of life. Up to that time they were raised by their lower-class parents, none of whom was of superior intelligence.

The parents of the thirty-nine remaining cases distribute themselves as follows: In eleven cases, one or both parents may be considered of better-than-average, and possibly of superior intelligence. Only one parent, a father, showed intelligence and achievement that we would generally acknowledge to be superior, since he is a scientist of international reputation. None of the others have shown achievements that would lift them out of the ordinary. There are two physicians among them, two lawyers, and one college teacher; thus the intellectual professions are well represented in this group. For the twenty-eight remaining children the story is different, all their parents being of average intelligence. They have only twenty-seven sets of parents because among them are two sisters (not twins). To these twenty-seven should be added those four children given up for adoption at birth and the three who were given up later, since their parents were not of superior intelligence either.

This leaves a parental ratio of thirty-four average to eleven sets of better than average or superior intelligence, only one of whom has shown outstanding achievement—hardly an impressive validation of the alleged superior intelligence of parents of autistic children. Among our group of thirty-four sets of parents of average or below-average intelligence are day laborers (two of them more often than not unemployed), farmhands, a post-office clerk, but also one high school teacher, two accountants, etc. The largest single category is of people in business who are either self-employed or salaried (seven parents), followed by white-collar workers (four).

Rimland also presents an evaluation of parental data based on a personal communication to him. He quotes Van Krevelen as listing parental occupation in his ten European cases to include the following: elementary school teacher, clerk, florist, salesman, horticulturist, and police sergeant. By European standards these five are definitely not of high or superior intelligence on the basis of occupation alone (and no test results or other information are given). Nothing is known of these five in regard to other characteristics that Kanner posits for the parents of autistic children, such as that they are cold, reserved, and efficient.

About the other half of Van Krevelen's sample we cannot be certain, since their occupations are listed as constructional engineer, industrial lawyer, civil servant, and government official. (Although Rimland speaks of ten cases, he lists occupations for only nine.) Since ranking for the civil servant and the government official are not given, it is impossible to know if one or both belong in the high intelligence group. But even if both are considered of high or superior intelligence it certainly does not hold for the first five, based on occupation alone. Hence from the information Rimland provides, the distribution of this group may be viewed as five quite average parents to four who might possibly be of high intelligence. Despite which Rimland concludes that "Van Krevelen's data clearly support Kanner's."

This they do not. Nor does another group of European autistic children who have been studied intensively. Bosch presents five detailed case histories in none of which does he mention superior intelligence in the parents, though he is quite familiar with the importance of this factor in Kanner's views of infantile autism. Though he says about the father of Karl B. that he was intelligent, this in common German usage does not denote superior intelligence, but only what Americans would call good intelligence. It would tally with the father's occupation as bookkeeper.

Since Bosch mentions for all his parents those traits that Kanner also stresses when present—such as that some of them were cold, distant persons, others withdrawn, or wrapped up in their work—one would expect him to refer to superior intelligence, if present. One parent, the father of Dieter E., possessed considerable drive, since he put himself through night school and late in life managed to graduate from technical college and become a civil engineer. Another father (of Hans R.) was employed by the mails in what Bosch terms a mediocre position, certainly not a sign of superior intelligence, nor of high drive. Nothing that is said of the parents of Fritz K. suggests high intelligence. Only the parents of Richard L. might fall into Kanner's category of superior intelligence, since Bosch says of the mother that she was intelligent (see again my remarks on its connotation in German) and that the father was a chemist. Neither description in itself would suggest superior intelligence. But since it is the only case in which Bosch speaks of a very cultured parental milieu, with its interest in chamber music, painting and literature, it may be reasonable to view these parents as matching those features which Kanner (and Rimland) describe as typical for parents of autistic children.

Thus like Van Krevelen's, both Bosch's group and the one at the Orthogenic School fail to support the assertions of Kanner, Rimland and others as regards the parents' superior intelligence. Nor does the case of the twins discordant for autism reported by Kamp [1964] since her father is described as "a skilled laborer." In addition, Professor Kamp [1965] writes in a private communication that "the parents of autistic children who were of definite superior intelligence do not account for more than 25% of the total sample from our outpatient department [Department of Child Psychiatry, University of Utrecht] and my private practice."

Moving from these children who are described in some detail to mere summarizations I might quote from one report of a group of fifty autistic children studied at the Southbury Training School. "Our impression was that the educational and socioeconomic background of the parents were similar to those of parents of other categories of severely retarded children in the institution" [Schlain and Yannet, 1960].

Bruch [1959] too, reports that the autistic twins she studied did not conform to Kanner's findings in regard to parental intelligence.

"The parents did not comply with the description of the superior intellectual ability and academic achievement in a high proportion of parents."

What can account for the strange difference between these data and those of Kanner and others? One explanation may be found in recent sociological research which tries to identify those groups of the population who seek out and have access to psychiatric service. The evidence is overwhelming that it is the educated, middle and upper classes who do, and the uneducated and lower classes who do not. We have known of autistic children who were declared feeble-minded early in life and thereafter disappeared into state schools for the defective. This seems to have happened much more often when Kanner was compiling his data than might happen today. Just because of Kanner's pioneering studies and other publications, physicians and particularly child psychiatrists have grown much more sophisticated about recognizing infantile autism. So by now, whether or not a child is recognized as being autistic, or is treated as feeble-minded or brain-damaged, depends largely on whether he was examined by a competent child psychiatrist.

Perhaps the autistic child I worked with in Vienna may illustrate what was more usual at that time. The child's mother, who came of an upper-class American family was told by many specialists she consulted here that the child was feeble-minded and the advice was to commit her to an institution. Unwilling to accept such a verdict, she went to Europe to consult specialists there, most of whom confirmed the diagnosis of feeble-mindedness. Since further efforts were still within her means she refused to give up, decided to consult Freud, and went on to Vienna. There it was eventually recognized that this was definitely not a feeble-minded child. Such persistence was still necessary then; but how many people could have been so persistent?

Kanner says that children are brought to his clinic for diagnosis from every state in the union and from all parts of the world. This fact may explain things best of all. If children are brought to him from the four corners of the earth, doesn't it suggest that a preponderance of them are the children of highly educated or successful parents? How else could they have learned of Dr. Kanner and made the trek to Baltimore?

Bender [1959] arrived at similar conclusions: "It is not clear what he (Kanner) means by saying that there is evidence that autistic children have greater intellectual potentialities, unless he is referring to the family background of his colleagues, professors and intellectual sophisticates who have selected his service."

Although Bender is convinced that autism is the result of an inborn impairment, she thinks it wrong to trace it to an inheritance of superior parental intellect.

Experience with unselective services of large city and state public facilities shows that as many autistic children come from a background of defective or mediocre intellectual attainment, with all kinds of social, family and personality constellations, as come from families of cold and over-controlled intellectuals described by Kanner.

Her experience is based on New York City where even the children of underprivileged families are more apt to reach the attention of physicians or be brought to hospitals than in less sophisticated centers.

Though Bender, like Rimland, is an outspoken proponent of the organic etiology of autism, Rimland does not quote her views on the parents of autistic children. Perhaps the reason is that if autism is due to an inherited defect in the central nervous system, then it must relate to the only genetic trait that is emphasized in the literature. Hence he disregards evidence suggesting that high intelligence is by no means preponderant among the parents of autistic children.

But there may be another reason why, in earlier days, many more autistic children of intelligent and conscientious parents came to the attention of early workers in the field. In a different context I have mentioned the autistic child's seeming lack of sensitivity to ordinary pain. The normal child, when afflicted by diseases that evoke obvious pain reactions will alert even an inattentive parent to the fact that something is very wrong with his child. Autistic children tend to show no such reaction, and can fail to alert their parents, even when seriously ill.

It is my belief that many autistic children who are not carefully and conscientiously watched over by intelligent parents die in early infancy because various afflictions go undetected—the more so if they come from homes where good medical services are not a matter of course. With the extension of medical care we see ever more autistic children from underprivileged families. This liability of autistic children to die of undetected illness may also explain the reports that those who are studied are particularly healthy specimens. It may be that they alone survive.

According to published reports, the sex ratio among autistic children is about three to four boys to every girl [Kanner, 1954; Keeler, 1957; Anthony, 1958], with first born males said to predominate [Rimland, 1964]. But the report of the Southbury Training School states that "Thirty-one males and nineteen females were studied. This sex distribution is in contrast to the experience of Eisenberg and Kanner who found eighty males and twenty females in their one hundred cases" [Schlain and Yannet, 1960]. (The hundred cases here referred to are the same group which were reported on by Eisenberg in "The Autistic Child in Adolescence," but only sixty-three of them could be contacted for follow-up purposes.) In our own sample, the sex ratio is certainly not four to one, since it consists of thirty boys and sixteen girls, or slightly less than two to one.

Neither does our sample show the claimed degree of a dominance of male first-borns. If we exclude the four children given up for adoption at birth (since we could not verify their being first-born or later born children) the remaining forty-two autistic children consist of twenty-three first-born, fourteen of them males, and nineteen later-born children. Thus while our sample definitely shows a dominance of boys over girls and of first-born over later born children, it shows it much less markedly than the reports in the literature. The twin girls reported by Kamp, incidentally, were not first born either; an older daughter preceded them.

Since both Kanner [1954] and Rimland stress the large percentage of Jewish children among reported cases of infantile autism I might mention that the same is true for our sample, since twenty-one of the forty-six children had one or two Jewish parents. But this may have much to do with which parents are able to send their children to the Orthogenic School (since there are never enough scholarships for tuition), and which are also the parents who consult psychiatrists who then refer the children to us.

It is telling, for example, to trace the origins of schizophrenic children with whom we have worked over the years, or those who came to us because of a severely delinquent symptomatology. Among them too, the number of Jewish children about as far exceeds the percentage of Jews in the general population as does the number of Jewish autistic children. And no one has yet claimed a greater propensity of Jewish children toward delinquency. At Southbury Training School [Schlain and Yannet] no particular racial group was conspicuously present. Also nothing that Bosch says, or does not say, suggests that any of the children in his group were of Jewish origin.

Until such time as a large random sample of the population will have been studied as to the incidence of infantile autism, it is my opinion that we ought to disregard claims as to the ethnic origin of such children, and as to their parents' superior intelligence and professional achievements. This is because the sample that comes to the attention of child psychiatrists is much too skewed by factors I have mentioned (which parents keep autistic children alive, which of them are not satisfied with the still common diagnosis of feeble-mindedness and/or brain damage, which ones seek psychiatric evaluation for their children, and so on).

My guess is that in a study of all three-year-old children in one of our metropolitan areas there would be startling results. They would probably reveal that the disturbance is more frequent than is generally assumed, and more evenly distributed among all groups of the population. But this too, in the absence of facts, is no more than a guess.

On the Nature of Autism

D ISCREPANCIES are great among the opinions of what causes
infantile autism, and of whether or what the parents contribute. So
it is reassuring to find much greater agreement on the kind of behavior
that characterizes autism.

§

Kanner, Rimland, and Others

Nearly all reports mention that where the children talk at all they
do not use the pronoun "I." Kanner [1946, 1951–52] called this phenomenon "pronominal reversal"—where the child uses the pronoun "you,"
but correct grammar would require the "I." He also spoke of "delayed
echolalia" and "affirmation by repetition" as when, for example, the
autistic child is asked "Do you want milk?" and replies "You want
milk" (meaning "I want milk" or "Yes, I want milk").

In my opinion the concept of pronominal reversal is misleading. Because the issue is not that autistic children reverse pronouns, but that
they avoid using them, and that they avoid them the more, the more
directly the pronoun refers to themselves.

Cunningham and Dickson [1961] studied the language of one autistic boy whose development had been normal to about two years of age. He began to speak at about one year and continued to acquire and retain new words up to the age of two, when his mother entered a nursing home to have her second child. From this time on he began to lose many of the words he had learned, and by three years had stopped speaking. He was admitted to a children's residential unit at age five, at which time he was still not speaking at all. As a result of treatment there he became slowly less withdrawn. His first word was recorded after three months in the unit; after seven months he could say a number of single words. From then on he gathered words fairly rapidly and began to put them together in short phrases or sentences. When he was seven, and had been at the unit twenty-one months, his language was studied.

His speech was then at about the two-year-old level. It was therefore compared with the language of normal children who were thirty months old, with particular attention to the frequency of certain parts of speech in the total vocabulary. There was little difference in how often the normal controls and the autistic boy used most parts of speech: verbs, articles and so forth. The story was different, for nouns and especially pronouns. He used considerably more nouns, since the ratio of nouns was about 28 per cent for the control group to 36 per cent for the boy. But the differentials were most marked in regard to pronouns, where the count was 19 per cent for normals, 5 per cent for the boy. For personal pronouns alone, the difference was 4 per cent for normals, less than 1 per cent for the boy.

While the study shows that this particular autistic child avoided the personal pronoun "I" to the same degree that he avoided personal pronouns altogether (using them only about a fourth as often as normal children with speech as developed as his), I believe this to be the exception and not the rule. Our own findings confirm those of Kanner and others who report that while these children avoid using personal pronouns, they do not use "I" at all, or not until much later in their development.

Arieti [1955] comments that: "It will be easier for George to think 'You, George, eat'; than to think 'I, George, eat,' because when he says 'you, George, eat' he verbalizes an attitude of his mother's which he has not accepted and therefore has not transformed into 'I, George, eat.'" This will be so if the adults in his life are anxiety producing or extremely rejecting, because then he "has difficulty in incorporating attributes, feelings, points of view about himself which come from others."

It has also been commonly observed that these children avoid the word "yes" as much as they avoid the word "I." This behavior Rimland explains by saying that "the children appear to have done all they could with language—repeat it rather than understand it." Unlike Kanner, he is convinced that such language behavior is due not to a disturbance in the child's affective relations to the world, but to organic brain damage. This he further deduces from "the fact that the children willingly memorized . . . lists of presidents, foreign lullabies, and nursery rhymes 'with great facility.' "

It is astonishing that Rimland and other writers who discuss the same phenomena have not also observed that while autistic children readily repeat such statements as "You want milk," to indicate that they want it, they will never repeat a statement such as "I want milk" if they want it. If we were dealing here with no more than echolalia, it should be as simple for them to repeat "I want milk" as to repeat "you want milk." We have tried this with all our autistic children, and always the result is the same. They will readily repeat "you want" such and such but never, before they have also begun to say "I" in other contexts do they repeat a statement containing "I."

When, for example, Karen asked Marcia "Do you want to go out?" and Marcia wished to reply in the affirmative she repeated "want go out" or later in more complete form "You want go out." But if Karen said "I want to go out," Marcia, like all autistic children understood immediately what was involved and if she repeated anything at all, it was not a simple echo of the statement. Instead she would say "Karen go out" or later, more correctly, "Karen want go out." Her substitution of "I" in the statement she heard, with the name of the person behind the pronoun, shows how completely she understood the thought. She simply would not use the pronoun "I."

If she did not want to go out, she would say, "don't want to go out" and later "no." This, the much earlier appearance of "no" in the speech of these children, compared with "yes," Rimland disregards, too. But the word "yes" should be no harder to learn than the word "no" if the difficulty in learning it were organically caused. In my opinion, however, the readier use of "no" compared to "yes," is an indication of extreme and deliberate negativism. Kanner [1944] comes close to recognizing that the affirmation is what is not available to these children, while they are quite ready to practice negation.

"Yes" is a concept that it takes the children many years to acquire. They are incapable of using it as a general symbol of assent. One child learned to say "yes" when his father told him that he would put him on his shoulders if he said "yes." This word then came to "mean" only the desire to be put on his father's shoulders. It took many months before he could detach the word "yes" from this specific situation, and it took much longer before he was able to use it as a general term of affirmation.

As to the avoidance of "I," and depending on the case, I believe it is either a denial of selfhood, or denotes an absence of awareness of selfhood—while the substitution of "you" shows some awareness of the selfhood of others. This seems also the opinion of Rodrigué [1955] who writes: "Pronominal inversal," in which the child speaks "of himself always as 'you'. . . is obviously related to the underlying confusion between 'me' and 'not-me.' " That selfhood, at a certain stage of autism is ascribed to the other person, can be seen from how Marcia revised Karen's statement, "I want to go out" to "Karen want go out."

The once-mute autistic child, even after he has otherwise acquired full speech still avoids the use of "I" (and also "my") for a time. This may be seen from the following sentence of Martha's in which the words she substituted for "I" and "my" are printed in italics. "When *she* saw Lucy help Nonnie cook, *Martha* put up a great big fat fuss when *you* were new. *You* hid *your* face."

There came a time when the same girl had moved sufficiently away from the autistic position to freely use both "I" and "my" with the person she trusted most and even with others when she felt fairly free of anxiety. But when anxious, and with others, she still returned to the old way of distancing herself from her own experience and the self. Then like the small infant she again referred to herself by her name.

One day, for example, she had just freely used the "I" when saying "I hate men," secure in the knowledge that any expression of feelings from her was very welcome to us. But only a few minutes later and in telling the same person about an event of the previous day (when she had fingered some toys in a store and been reproved by the clerk) she put it in the following words: "*She* touched the toys in Wolf's toy store. *Martha* did it and Wolf did not like it." Even so slight a rejection by a salesperson destroyed the shaky feeling of selfhood that still rested on total acceptance by others.

It is not alone the autistic child's reluctance to talk, and his avoidance of personal pronouns, that reveal his anxiety about being himself. Communication is not just a matter of words, but of what they are used for and what may come of the words. To name things, these children are much readier to do because this does not commit them or reveal their thoughts. What they are most anxious about is committing themselves. Therefore they are least of all willing to communicate their feelings. So even if they say something, they say it in a most peculiar voice. Most of the time it is like the voice of a deaf person; it has the same toneless and unaccommodating-to-the-ear quality of one who cannot hear his own voice. And indeed they do not wish to know what they say, nor to have the other person hear it. This gives the voice a most bizarre quality. If it shows any feeling at all, it is that of anger at having been seduced into speaking and then the tonelessness changes to an angry screeching-screaming.

Some comments made by Despert [1946] in discussing Kanner's views on autistic language are to the point.

In all young schizophrenic children speech presents peculiarities which, however varied, have one common characteristic—the voice lacks the emotional tone which stamps the individual as himself and unlike others; it is often described as unnatural, peculiar; it lacks expressiveness and often does not seem to belong to the personality.

Pichon, in his studies of language development, has pointed out that the first and foremost requirement for language to arise and develop is what he calls "*la fonction appetitive*"—the appetition for language . . . meaning literally "the direction of desire towards an object or purpose" . . . Appetition for language is manifested in infants long before language is constituted and sentence formation in its most rudimentary form appears. In fact, it can be said that it precedes the first phonetic forms and represents the first stage of speech as a means of communication. This appetition for language is conspicuously lacking in the autistic and schizophrenic child, even though coincidentally the child may have acquired an extremely large vocabulary. . . .

Despert too finds it "highly significant" that

the "I not I" distinction is not established in the autistic child. . . . Since the appearance of the first-person pronoun in language development shortly follows that stage of individuation which corresponds to the child's consciousness as one, whole, and apart from others, the importance of this sign cannot be overemphasized.

To this I would again point out that while the "I not I" distinction is not clearly established, in the talking autistic child the differentiation between the "you" and the "I" is often sufficiently recognized to accept the "you" while rejecting the "I." Despite wide variation from case to case, these children in some fashion seem more ready to recognize the selfhood of others. As a matter of fact they tend to ascribe to them powers far beyond reason, while protecting what stands for their own selfhood by playing 'possum about it. It is only a strangely depleted selfhood he possesses, one that can assert itself only in negation. (Their negation of change by insisting on sameness is just one aspect of this stance, along with their relative ease in saying "no" compared to the long-delayed "yes.")

Maybe what we are here presented with is a most obstinate determination, but also the autistic child's single affirmation: not to commit himself to anything, or to any particular existence that would inhere in statements implying an "I am" or "I want." It is a total refusal to get involved with the world.[1] And since any use of the "I" carries the

1. Or, to quote Rodrigué once more [1955], "by being the other person's echo, he was reflecting the world outside without assimilating it."

minimal implication that "I am in this world," the use of "I" must be avoided. The survival value of such a position is that if "I" do not really exist, then neither can "I" really be destroyed. This self-protective meaning of the avoidance of "I," it seems to me, is more important than all other protections it offers. It wards off the disappointment always expected, by never admitting to having any wants.

On a different level, I might add that the autistic child, by not permitting any change, by not permitting himself to be an "I," by not permitting himself to say "yes" to anything, is complying with what he considers a parental wish that he should not exist. This is why the "you"—those others who are permitted to exist—and the "no" which is essentially a denial of existence, are so much more readily available to him.

Also relevant is how easily autistic children learn to repeat what seem like meaningless lists of states, capitals, presidents, songs, and so forth, even in foreign languages. Far from indicating that the child can only memorize but does not understand the more complex functions of language, it suggests to me that these children understand them very well indeed. Firstly, the repetition avoids any obvious personal commitment. And, secondly, it divulges nothing or only a minimum about the inner thoughts they feel they must hide.

Using the words "yes" and "I" means commitment to a world they wish to have no truck with; it means commitment to one's selfhood. In a way, their not using "I" because they feel lacking in selfhood also bespeaks their deep inner honesty. This was revealed by one of our autistic girls; after she acquired a complete use of language including the "I," she consistently refused to capitalize "I" in her writing. For that, she explained, she still had too little of a personality.

That autistic children use language to hide what they really think, is also Loomis' opinion [1960]. From his work with autistic children he cites the example of a boy who, while he "might not be giving persons the satisfaction of discovering his positive intellectual gifts, he probably was quite bright. . . . However, it seemed that language was not used as a bridge between persons but rather as a way of hiding from other people."

Kanner [1946], too, on some occasions, has mentioned the protective function of specifics in autistic language when he speaks of "the use of simple verbal negation as magic protection against unpleasant occurrences."

Those children who give up speaking and remain mute seem to feel that merely hiding their thoughts behind what seems like nonsensical language is not enough guarantee of safety. Jackson [1950] reports on nine cases of nonspeaking children she has treated, all of whom could be considered autistic because of their withdrawal from human contact and their repetitive and compulsive preoccupation with objects. Mutism in these children is explained as their ultimate retreat in the face of danger.

The three primitive forms of reaction to danger are (a) flight, (b) fight and (c) assuming complete immobility or feigning death; mutism and the ignoring of other human beings can be likened to (c). Silence and the absence of relationships with others are, after all, a kind of death, non-existence as a social being [Jackson. 1950].

As for those autistic children who speak, it is less that they hide their thoughts than that they pose us riddles to solve, and in this way test our desire to understand them, a desire that would also attest to our willingness that they should exist. Viewed this way, it appears that whatever the child selects for endless repetition has deep meaning. This was amply demonstrated by Marcia, as when this nonspeaking daughter of an English-born mother sang day after day, from 'My Fair Lady," "Why don't the English teach their children how to speak?"

The autistic child's feats of memory have an additional purpose. They demonstrate to those who wish to hear it that the child is not feeble-minded. These children know that the world often views them as such but are too afraid to speak freely. Wishing to counteract the world's low opinion of them, they engage in difficult mental tasks such as committing long lists to memory after hearing them only once or a few times. For the same reason Joey converted every object he saw into some form of machinery, as he told us on his return visit, because it "seemed to be a way of showing I was intelligent and knew something."

Thus I believe that the repetition of clusters of words is nonsensical only to us and shows that the children understand the meaning of language very well. But they strictly avoid it except for the posing of one single question in riddle form: "Do you believe I am worthwhile and have something worthwhile to say?" In doing so they use language in its highest symbolic function by performing verbal feats that symbolize their intelligence and pose the most important question of all.

In connection with what I consider the deliberate use—or misuse—of language for defensive purposes, it might be interesting to refer to Rimland's discussion of drug treatment in infantile autism. The only autistic child he reports as having observed himself was a four-year-old boy treated with 150 mg/day of deanol. When, after two years, the dosage was increased to 300 mg/day, the result was that "at the age of seven the picture was one of severe retardation rather than psychosis, and the words 'I' and 'Yes' were slowly appearing."

Thus infantile autism was changed by medication to feeble-mindedness, though autism is a disturbance believed by many (including Rimland) to occur in children of potentially high intelligence. The total but active rejection of selfhood and of all social contact with the world, was destroyed by the drug treatment. Gone too was the extreme negativism, in this case signified first by deliberate mutism and later by the absence of the words "I" and "yes." With this elimination of the higher mental functions, though they had so far served only extremes of defensiveness, the child became feeble-minded.

I believe it is only because Rimland did not study autistic children carefully with the intention of deciphering the messages of their autism that he maintains they can do no more with their language than repeat what they hear others say. He does not even discuss the fact that Kanner [1946], far from viewing the *language* of autistic children as a sign of inborn impairment, recognized it as meaningful to anyone who acquaints himself with the child's experience of reality.

But language is not the only function the autistic child uses deliberately for defensive purposes. The same can be observed in their selective response to sensory stimuli, of which I shall confine myself here to the visual.

In another context, I have said that Goldfarb [1956] stresses the diminished use of the distance receptors, sight and hearing, by schizophrenic children who show no evidence of significant defect in visual or auditory acuity or threshold. He suggests therefore that "the schizophrenic child can hear and see, but he does not talk or listen." We too have observed the persistently dilated pupil and the averted gaze when we approach an autistic child at the beginning of treatment. But we believe these phenomena lend themselves to an interpretation quite different from a simple diminished use of distance receptors.

The normal but highly selective use of distance receptors can be appreciated in the common observations that these children, even in their apparently most heedless outbursts of activity, seldom hurt themselves by bumping into objects or tripping over unseen obstacles, even when the familiar placement of objects in the room is temporarily changed.

Just as the autistic child uses language not in order to communicate but to defend himself, so he uses his senses not for comprehending the world but to defend himself from terrifying experiences. Typical is the example of Frank, who when going for a walk would get very upset and begin to cry for no apparent reason, or so it seemed to us for a long time. On most other occasions he was able to be out of doors without evidence of such disturbance, but also without much interest or emotional reaction. Gradually, several staff members observed independently that the sight of a baby buggy in the far distance, anywhere within a three-block radius, was always associated in time with the onset of Frank's deep anxiety.

It then appeared that far from not being able to scan the distant environment he was alert exclusively to that particular visual experience. So threatening was it to him that for safety's sake no other visual sensations were allowed to come to consciousness. Any or all of them might detract from his single-minded search for the baby buggies he wished to avoid at all cost. We, on the other hand, who were interested in a variety of visual experiences, could not have recognized a baby buggy at such a distance unless we had been searching too, with a concentration that would have "blinded" us to many other things we would normally have seen.

Goldfarb [1956], restricting himself to observations made under controlled conditions could not introduce—because they were not known to him—those significant objects or events to which the autistic child selectively reacts when he spies them in the distance. We too could not have learned of such reactions had we not extended our observations to include things like walks on the street. The discrepancies between Goldfarb's conclusions and ours might be likened to those between what the animal psychologist observes in the experimental laboratory or the zoo and what Lorenz, Tinbergen, Schaller, and others have observed by studying animals in their natural habitat. But perhaps another aspect of Frank's reaction to baby buggies may illustrate.

It has been correctly observed that autistic children do not cry; or they cry only for no apparent reason, i.e., because of inner stimulation. This is true, when one thinks of controlled situations or of only those other situations where normal children are apt to cry; that is, if one does not assiduously search for the cause. But Frank's "crying for no apparent reason" did not occur without the stimulus of the baby buggy. Later on, in fact, when this stimulus-response was quite familiar to us and we would see Frank begin to cry, we would look about for a baby buggy somewhere. And though it was never absent, it was usually too distant for us to have recognized it without the wailing of the child having brought it to our attention.

Another child, who consistently failed to recognize or respond to objects that were "in front of her eyes," would see a car approaching many blocks away, long before it came to our "normal" attention. She would then wait immovably for it to pass before proceeding across the street. Her consistent behavior on this score seems clear evidence of her use of distance receptors to see and look at objects in the distance. In her case, the automobile was viewed as the vehicle carrying a person, but more specifically as the mother who carries the baby, the mother she wished to kill. She was so convinced that she would be destroyed in re-taliation for her wish that she could see nothing else. Only her eternal concentration on watching for oncoming cars seemed to offer her mini-mal safety.

In fact, our impression is that autistic children look only at what is meaningful to them. Thus even the far distant object, if "important," may be very clear to them. But in thus directing their focus, all that (to us) would be clear and at hand is then obscured for the child. And we found the same to be true for auditory stimuli. The reason for such behavior is again, in our opinion, the child's wish to blot out all stimuli that are to him "unimportant." When, however, the autistic child regards his own hand in front of his face—spontaneously and with equally intense moti-vation, as in twiddling, for example—then his concentration prevents other visual stimuli from coming to awareness.

These comparisons, incidentally, between Goldfarb's observations and our findings, point again to the advantages of long term, continuous ob-servation of autistic children in their "natural habitat," including obser-vations made during their progress in treatment.

§
Bosch

Not only an ocean, but a different world view seems to separate the recent American monograph on infantile autism and its counterpart in Europe. While Rimland [1964], a psychologist, seems uninterested in the psyche of autistic children, since he did not study them as persons but inquired only into the neurological structure of their brains, Bosch [1962], a neurologist and psychiatrist, approaches infantile autism from a framework of phenomenology, and studied them carefully as people. His monograph is derived from direct experience with autistic children as director of the Child Psychiatry Department of the University of Frankfurt.

In the center of Bosch's interest stands the peculiar language these children use. Given such an interest, it was natural that he concentrate on the speaking autistic children he came to know in his hospital ward. Though Bosch is familiar with psychoanalytic thinking, he is very little influenced by it. What he tried to understand was the autistic children's thinking process, but not the children's unconscious. His frame of refer-ence derives primarily from Husserl [1913], and from a psychology of language based on Karl Buehler [1934] and Snell [1952].

To begin with, Bosch observes that "exactly those aspects of the intelligence . . . develop in the autistic child which only in a most limited way call for the prior constitution of a common world." This he relates to the question raised by Husserl: To which degree can a solipsistic subject proceed to constitute a world if he has no notion of the existence of the other? Because without that, he cannot recognize himself as an observing and thinking subject. More than that, it prevents him from seeing an object "differently" at times—namely, as another person might see it.

Without this, no common objectivity is possible between persons. Only those experiences that one can objectify through the laws of mathematical logic—such as the principles of mathematics or the lawfulness of a number chain—need no confirmation by others. These logical mathematical constitutions carry their own objectification within themselves and are independent of place, time, and human community. "If, from this viewpoint, we observe the achievements and interests of autistic children, we find they are those that require little objectification through a common world experience."

From these philosophical speculations Bosch moves to a psychological analysis of language. He starts with the division of language by Buehler [1929] into its functions of expression or appeal, of sign or signal, and finally of symbol, three functions that seem to run parallel to the development of language itself.

Language as *expression* or nonspecific *appeal*, begins with the infant's babble or cry, at which time it is still not directed to a listener. It tells mainly about the inner state of mind, or the emotions, of the speaker. But language, even in its most developed form, never loses this aspect, as may be seen from the expression put into it, and the manner and melody of speaking. At first the infant's vocalizing is just an expression of his comfort or discomfort. Even later, the way the child whispers or shouts tells us something about his feelings and hence tallies with the expressive function too, while both his cry and his shout retain the quality of appeal.

Through language as *sign* or *signal* we try to communicate something. Buehler uses the red stop-light to illustrate this function. The red light tells of a danger, but not what the danger consists of. This, only language as symbol can do. At first, the infant's communication, his cry for example, is directed to a vague world at large in hopes of evoking some desired reaction; only later is it directed to a person. When the infant cries, dimly knows that he cries to be fed, and his cry is so distinctive that his mother comes to know it for an expression of hunger, then his cry has become different enough from the other sounds he makes so that the sign or signal function is now added to that of expression or appeal.

Language as *symbol* refers to something outside of the self, the meaning of which is shared by the speaker and any listener present. By forming his sounds to say "milk," the child uses language in its symbolic function. He no longer communicates his wants, needs, and feelings through private signals, valid only to those who have learned to understand their meaning. He has now made them readily understandable to anyone who shares the same culture with him. With this, language is fully developed in all its three functions: those of expression, signal and symbol.

To this descriptive analysis of language Bosch adds from Snell, who traces the same three aspects of language to what he calls the original phenomena of meaning. Language as *expression* then relates to "having" or "owning." Language as *signal* relates to "influencing" and "doing"; and as *symbol*, to "being."

"Having" in this context must be understood in terms of Jaspers' philosophical speculation on what it means to the self to make things one's own. Since property is acquired for future use, the acquisition of property is closely linked to expecting things of the future, and thus to having a sense of continuity, of history.

Here Bosch quotes Jaspers [1948] as follows:

To be a self requires that one have the power to dispose of objects that are not self. This dispositional power is symbolized (and also made real) by property, when delimited against the dispositional power of others. It is the pathos residing in property that it makes possible the existential reality of the self: What makes this (my being a self) possible, is the intercourse with objects that are in my power, and my acting on these things; hence the coming into being of my personal world. [This is a free translation of what it defied my abilities to translate verbatim.]

And lastly, Bosch refers to the views of Cassirer [1953]: that in saying "I" one gives expression to the fact that the speaker has achieved an experience of himself.

On the basis of the foregoing, Bosch now approaches the language of autistic children. Comparing it with that of normal children, he finds most important the absence, or only very late appearance, of the child's saying "I." But he finds the same to be true for exactly those language forms normally connected with the meaning of "having" or "owning," and of "influencing" and "doing." Not only is the saying of "I" delayed, but also essential verbal forms such as those connecting "I" with future, as well as the imperative forms. Also lacking are any statements of intention, an anticipation of procedures, or the purposes of doing. He then shows the relative inability of the autistic child to handle any of these concepts.

Discussing the ideas of Kanner and others about pronominal reversal,

Bosch arrives at the same conclusion that was forced on us by our experiences with autistic children, namely that what looks like pronominal reversal is actually due to the autistic child's constructing a language in which the pronoun "I" does not exist. Far from showing an inability to handle language, it is an effort at circumventing the "I" which as word and concept is absent from the autistic child's world.[2]

We deliberately do not speak of a "pronominal reversal" in Kanner's sense since the use of the pronoun "you" instead of the pronoun "I" does not seem to us at all characteristic, but rather accidental. At least as often instead of the "I" the proper name, or the designation "the boy" or "the child" appears. The essential is, as we shall demonstrate, just the belated appearance of the "I" which is paralleled by a belated naming of the other person as "you."

Bosch observes, in my opinion correctly, that

the absence of saying "I" stands in a close meaningful connection with the inadequate attention these children pay to the other, and with the absence of a clear separation between the speaking, answering, encouraging or demanding person on the one hand, and the other person who hears, answers, and responds to the demand, on the other. That is, one has the impression that there takes place a continuous change in position, or that the speaking person has no definite position, which prevents any clear comprehension of a conversation with its intrinsic bipolarity.

In considering why autistic children show such peculiar use of language, Bosch lays stress on its origin.

Language develops in the encounter with others. Language presupposes that certain developments took place in the preverbal phase that precedes language development. Part of this preverbal phase is a development from touching via grasping to experimental manipulation; from holding and showing the object, to pointing to it with hand or finger. Moreover, in this context one should mention the differentiation between comprehending an expression and the ability to express oneself . . . also the preverbal crying and demanding should be counted into the preconditions of language.

Thus Bosch, like all others who have worked closely with autistic children, is convinced that theirs is a solipsistic language, and that what characterizes autism in general, and autistic language in particular, is that the child does not see himself as a person engaged in an encounter.

Although Bosch concentrates on what is general for autism and its

---

2. In this connection I would like to review a fact too often overlooked in the English-speaking world: that Freud selected the personal pronoun "I" to designate what, in English translation, became the technical concept of the ego. It is impressive how the inability of the autistic child to handle the concept "I" corresponds exactly to the lack of development of the ego, which in the original German of psychoanalytic psychology is also the "I."

language, to the neglect of the particular, he has, in my opinion, so far offered the best discussion of them. I shall therefore review other of his observations and conclusions. Not being of a psychoanalytic bent, he does not pay much attention to what is idiosyncratic in the language of each child, where I consider that to be indispensable. Because only a study of the specifics will yield an understanding of why a particular child remained arrested in autistic isolation from others, was prevented from recognizing the other (and thus himself) as a person.

From his own material Bosch could well have been able to speculate on what the children themselves tell us of why they are autistic. For example: In order to corroborate Kanner's point, and show that the "irrelevant language of the patients can become relevant to the listener to the degree to which it is possible for him to find the key to their private and self-sufficient metaphorical constructions," Bosch quotes the following example from Kanner's [1943] account of the case of Paul:

At the sight of a saucepan he would invariably exclaim, "Peten-eater." The mother remembered that this particular association had begun when he was two years old and she happened to drop a saucepan while reciting to him the nursery rhyme about "Peter, Peter, pumpkin eater" [Bosch, 1962].

Bosch recognizes that Paul's behavior was relevant and that the endless repetition of "Peten eater" originated in a particularly meaningful event. But because he considers only what is general for autism he stops there. He does not go on to ask why this event had such long-lasting consequences for this particular child, nor why the original "Peter, Peter, pumpkin eater" was contracted to "Peten eater." Because contrary to the original verse in which Peter is eating a pumpkin, there is now an ambiguous statement about eating. The child does not specify what is eaten, and it is even possible that someone other than Peter is the "Peten eater."

Nor does Bosch mention that Peter was changed to Peten in the typical way that autistic children tend to hide and reveal at the same time. In changing the name, Paul indicates that he was not quite referring to the Peter of the nursery rhyme, and may even have referred to himself, since Peter starts with the same letter as Paul, and since the names Peter and Paul are so often cited together that he may have thought them a unit.

If Bosch paid little attention to the idiosyncracies of autistic language, he puts great emphasis on comparing language development in the normal and autistic child. Quoting Cassirer and C. and W. Stern [1914], he notes that in the normal child's language the "I" appears first in a context of owning something. Only later is it used in connection with a physical action, and still later in connection with wielding an influence.

Thus according to the Sterns' investigations, the possessive pronoun "mine" by far precedes the personal pronoun "I" (as it did in Marcia's development of language and that of all other autistic children we knew). Bosch adds that

The first appearance of the normally developed "I" can be recognized as clearly as that of separating one's own action from other people's actions. We can conclude in retrospect that during the period in which the subject-free imperative or demanding sentences predominated, the person, too, from whom something was demanded was experienced as relatively undefined and unindividuated. Just as the cry of the infant is at first not directed to anyone in particular, but is a general appeal . . . so we must declare the language of the autistic child as yet undirected.

Discussing how an autistic child will say, to empty space as it were, "He wants to eat,"[3] Bosch remarks that it is not only the absence of "I" and its replacement by "he," but the general manner in which the sentence is constructed that makes it seem as if the child does not make a direct request; certainly not one directed to another person. What seems lacking is a desire to bring something to the other person's attention, a demand that something should take place. Also missing is any direct reference to the desired object (in this instance, bread), or any personalized expression of the demand or desire. What takes place here, according to Bosch, is a reduced expression of the very personal demand "I want" to a mere impersonal statement that something is wanted. The impersonal level of the appeal brings it close to the preverbal cry of the infant.

Convincing as is such an analysis, it does not explain the strange phenomenon of why our autistic children never used the assertive form ("he wants") that seems typical of their German counterparts. Our children began with a mere repetition of enough of the question "Do you want to go out?" to produce the assertive "want go out" if the reply was affirmative.

Next came the ability to object to the offer through a "don't want to go out" long before they said "no." This "no" anticipated an eventual appearance of "I don't want to go out," the "I" appearing much sooner in the negative than the affirmation. But never, when we asked "Do

---

3. Here again the English translation fails to indicate what the child does when he says the same thing in German. The German *"er will essen"* (he wants to eat) requires only a change in the pronoun to become *"ich will essen"* (I want to eat). No change in the verb form is required. Also, our infinitive "to eat" is different from the German *essen* because in German both the infinitive and the imperative are identical in form. Hence the small child's imperative demand, *"Essen!"* remains unchanged when used as a request (*"Er will essen"*), whereas in English the imperative "Eat!" requires that the child add "to" in the change from command to request.

you want to go out?" did we get a reply like "He wants to go out" as Bosch reports to be typical of German autistic children.

I believe the explanation may have to do with an aspect of German usage that has no parallel in English. In German the child is addressed as "thou" by adults, a form that he himself will never use with any but the most intimate adults—certainly not with persons in authority such as a physician. Hence to repeat verbatim the question, *"Willst du essen?"* (Wilt thou eat?) would be both a social affront to the questioner, and an admission of great intimacy with him, because the child would be addressing the adult familiarly as "thou." This the German child circumvents by using "he," probably more to avoid owning to an intimacy he feels toward no one. In this way he uses neither the tabooed "I" nor the intimate or impolite "thou," while retaining the impersonal nature of the reply.

From his analysis of the language of autistic children, Bosch disputes Kanner's view that these children treat other persons only as objects and concludes that "in autistic children, early or pre-forms of personal relations exist, out of which in favorable developments, limited and sparse, but nevertheless true personal relations can develop, even up to friendship and love relations." His prognosis is much more favorable than what we find in the American literature.

Because of his phenomenological approach and his avoidance of interpretations, Bosch does not view it as deliberate negativism and desperate defense that the autistic child talks and behaves in reverse of what we would normally expect. He reports, for example, that one of his children insisted that a red object was green or the other way around, in behavior so consistent that his teachers believed him color-blind. Also when something square was shown to him, he insisted it was round.

These we can match with identical examples, such as Joey's insistence that circles are straight lines, and other deliberate "reversals," as when our autistic children turn the seasons around, bundling up in the summer and wanting to wear flimsy shorts in the dead of winter.[4]

Similarly, Bosch does not try to understand the meaning of nonverbal behavior as he observes it in autistic children. But to us, who approach the problem from a psychoanalytic point of view, his observations are of great importance, particularly since they come from a different cultural area, and one less machine-oriented than ours. It is therefore of interest that his autistic children show the same preoccupation with mechanical things and particularly with rotating objects. For example,

4. One wonders how to attribute to some neural defect such deliberate reversals that are certainly not due to repetition, delayed reaction, or failure of arousal, as Rimland claims them to be, or to an inability to abstract as do Goldstein and others.

Hans R. is reported to have had a large box full of wheels. "In each room he entered he immediately spied circular objects that permitted rotation and practically threw himself onto them. . . . When, with other children from the ward, he visited the airport. . . . He remained fixated to the rotating propellers of the planes. In his drawings, too, he always preferred to represent wheels or circular lines." Dieter E., too, was fascinated with wheels, grinding machines, and similar rotating devices, and like Joey, was preoccupied with electricity and electrical machines, including lights and light bulbs.

Reporting further on nonverbal behavior, Bosch notes that

In regard to the verbal development toward the concept "I" we have shown that autistic children to a large extent lack the ability to actively reach toward the future. In dealing with objects they fail to experiment. It seemed remarkable to us that autistic children are usually very clean, do not dirty themselves, and deal with their toys in a very circumspect way. But this means that they really don't become engaged with objects. They do not destroy, they do not modify, they do not investigate; instead they leave the objects exactly as they found them, or they repeat over and over again the same, once-learned simple activities.

If, he adds, we want to understand the strange ways in which the autistic child deals with objects we must consider that

the objects that surround man are not there for him alone, but for his fellow men too. For the most part, the child experiences their nature and purpose through communication, instruction, and through an understanding of how others use the object.

Many objects are constructed for common use with other persons. In order to clarify such bipersonal constitution Langeveld [1956] uses the example of the see-saw, whose function would not be grasped by a person who knows only himself. It is therefore enlightening to observe an autistic child on the see-saw. Eberhard H., age five, sat on it like a dead doll, and clung to it, but could not participate actively in the movement of the see-saw. He could neither push himself up, nor appropriately react to the activity of the other child through changing his position on the see-saw. Autistic children are also at a loss to know what to do with a ball; possibly it might be rolled, or turned while it is held in the hand; but it will not be caught or thrown back to another person.

It was striking to me to read this account about playing with the seesaw and ball, since we had observed exactly the same behavior in several autistic children. Since they were also receiving treatment, they did not remain arrested at this level and could eventually understand objects that involved the interaction of people. But this "learning" took years.

I have described, for example, how Marcia had to hold a ball many months before she could roll it, and how it took many more months till she would try to catch a ball that was thrown to her. It took still more months before she learned to push it back, and only much later could she play ball with a favorite person. Laurie learned the bipersonal use of objects around accepting that a toy bus was rolled toward her, then rolling it herself, and finally rolling it back and forth with her teacher. Because she left us after only a year, her ability to comprehend the bipersonal meaning of objects stopped there.

Returning to Marcia's story, it took her a long time to understand that the seesaw is an object that needs the coordinated actions of two people. Only in her third year did she even dare to manipulate it alone, like Bosch's Eberhard H. Not until she was interacting more freely with others did she also seesaw with others. And this happened at the same time that she began to play ball more freely. Thus her progress was not related to the complexity of the object, but conditioned only by her developing ability to interact with others and hence to take part in interactional play.

An interesting verbal confirmation was provided for us by Martha, the eight-year-old autistic girl mentioned before, after a year and a half at the School. By this time she was well able to read simple stories, especially from a book she was very fond of except for one of its stories. When she first came to the verse, "A seesaw is fun because you have to have a friend," she read with ease, "A seesaw is fun because—" and then began to hesitate. Very haltingly she continued "you—have—to," and there she stopped and refused to go on. Thereafter, and in repeated readings of the book, she would never start that sentence at all.

Summarizing his findings, Bosch stresses once more that

in following the development of the particular language forms created by autistic children we found throughout a deficiency or arrest of those language forms that refer to "having" and "doing." We tried to demonstrate that in this arrest in development we are not dealing with symptoms that can be explained in isolation as specific disturbances of cerebral function. Instead these are phenomena that must be understood to represent a total structure, determined by the specific form of existence that charactrizes autistic children. We viewed as a specific feature of this autistic form of existence the belated appearance and rudimentary nature of the separation of private world and common world. We tried in this presentation not to describe the autistic child as a deficient being, but to comprehend positively his form of existence and its particular nature. . . . But what makes autistic children special is that besides this deficiency . . . other observations reveal astonishingly good performances, intensively followed interests, and original ideas.

[Autistic children] find no access to the variegated forms of interpersonal relations . . . or to historical thinking, to freedom and responsibility for their own and others' existence . . . but with the help of their rationality they construct a rigid, schematically constructed world that is conditioned through measurement and number, and lacks the meaning and fulfillments through an appropriately developed common world experience. Because of this their world becomes depersonalized, static, and meaningless both as an inner, personal world and with respect to common purposes. Within this world of a rigid rationalism, they think and act in an automaton-like perseverating fashion, but in safety.

Thus Bosch, who understood much about autistic children, came close to understanding that they develop their rigid approach to all problems of living, and subject themselves to a mechanical existence, to gain safety. But since he asked himself only what they are, and never why, he did not find in their desperate need for safety the key to any fuller understanding.

Bosch has gone far in understanding the world of the autistic child, as far as one can go by means of a phenomenological investigation of his language. As I have tried to show, this is very far indeed. But he has given us no understanding of how it feels to be an autistic child. And only if we can feel with him—in addition to understanding him—will we gain access to his being.

It was not that others failed to understand him that drove the autistic child into isolation. Or more correctly, this is not what kept him from leaving his initial isolation. It was because he did not encounter the "other" as a person feeling with him that he could not pay attention to the other as an other. But without the experience of a "Thou" he could not become an "I."

Bosch has not given us an understanding of why infantile autism develops or what its causes may be. Most important of all, he has not given us any suggestions of how we might help the autistic child to move out of his isolation to encounter the other, how to give him a life in the present, so that he can have a past (instead of bondage to the mirage of a past) and a future; in short, how to help him be with persons, so that he can start to be himself.

So much for the literature dealing specifically with infantile autism. But no discussion of autism can fail to consider, at least, the most important of our theories on infant development. Because the autistic child, in my opinion, has the same growth potential as the normal child; it has just not been realized.

As of now, the most important body of theories on child development is the psychoanalytic system of thought. This I need not discuss here, since the whole of this volume is an application of those thoughts to the problem of infantile autism by one group of workers—those of the Orthogenic School. But there is another comprehensive body of systematic thought on infantile development which is independent of psychoanalysis: the observations and theories we owe to Piaget and his co-workers.

§
Piaget

To discuss fully the many parallels between our findings on infantile autism, and those of Piaget on the intellectual development of children would again make voluminous reading. Since my purpose here is not to corroborate Piaget's findings, perhaps a few brief examples may suffice to show the nature and extent of these parallels.

For readers not familiar with his system, I might briefly review, first, the two concepts of accommodation and assimilation that are central to it. These two processes are inseparable and explain in part how the organism adapts to its environment; both are necessary for survival and for any intellectual growth. For example,

the organism must transform the substances it takes in in order to incorporate their food values into its system. An initial transformation occurs when the substance is ingested by chewing. Thus, hard and sharply contoured objects become pulpy and formless. Still more drastic changes occur as the substance is slowly digested, and eventually it will lose its original identity entirely by becoming part of the structure of the organism. . . . In the process of assimilating foodstuffs to itself, the organism is also doing something else. It is adjusting itself to them. The mouth must open or the substance cannot enter the system at all. The object must be chewed if its structure demands chewing. . . . Just as objects must be adjusted to the peculiar structure of the organism in any adaptational process, so also must the organism adjust itself to the idiosyncratic demands of the object. The first aspect of adaptation has been called *assimilation*. The second aspect, the adjustment to the object, Piaget labels *accommodation* [Flavell, 1963].[5]

These two processes apply no less to the taking in of food than of information. Because "if intellectual adaptation is always and essentially an assimiliatory act, it is no less an accommodatory one. In even the most elemental cognition there has to be some coming to grips with the special properties of the thing apprehended." In other words, "assimilation can never be pure because by incorporating new elements into its earlier schemata the intelligence constantly modifies the latter in order to adjust them to new elements" [Piaget, 1952]. Thus Piaget, on the twin process of adaptation.

In the introduction to his study of how the child learns to understand and manipulate reality, Piaget [1954] writes:

5. Here and in the following discussion I lean heavily on Flavell's [1963] discussion of Piaget's system. Against this, I checked my own understanding of Piaget to avoid distortions due to a possible wish to find support in his writings for my notions.

At the beginnings of assimilatory activity, any object whatever presented by the external environment to the subject's activity is simply something to suck, to look at, or to grasp; such assimilation is at this stage centered solely on the assimilating subject. Later, however, the same object is transformed into something to displace, to set in motion, and to utilize for increasingly complex ends.

Compare this, for example, with Marcia to whom at first any object was only something to twiddle, as the closest thing to sucking (because sucking was too traumatic and hence inhibited, while looking and grasping were equally dangerous). And how it was out of her twiddle motions that she developed the ability to string beads, to bounce a ball and to explore objects, as the twiddled object was "transformed into something to displace, to set into motion, to utilize for increasingly complex ends." And how only through freeing these twiddle movements could she reestablish looking and grasping, and finally sucking.

Or, speaking of the infant's inner experience of himself Piaget writes:

It is precisely when the subject is most self-centered that he knows himself the least, and it is to the extent that he discovers himself that he places himself in the universe and constructs it by virtue of that fact. In other words, egocentrism signifies the absence of both self-perception and objectivity, whereas acquiring possession of the object as such is on a par with the acquisition of self-perception.

An exact description of how the autistic child achieves "possession of the object" (Marcia's taking possession of Karen) simultaneously "with the acquisition of self-perception."

Finally, such "self-perception" can be achieved only by the subject's having become active in his own behalf, at a time when his still "radical egocentrism . . . leads the subject to attribute all external events to personal activity." Only then will he make "the transition from a state in which objects are centered about a self which believes it directs them, although completely unaware of itself as a subject, to a state in which the self is placed at least practically, in a stable world conceived as independent of personal activity."

From this statement it appears that to gain self-perception there must have been a prior stage in which all events were attributed to personal activity. But the autistic child does not attribute events to his personal activity because he feels too overpowered by the environment to believe he can change it. Safety resides only in sameness which is the opposite of change, while the essential purpose of activity is to bring about change.[6] Since the autistic child avoids personal activity and change, he

6. To restore objects to their old place is an activity in one sense, and so is insistence on sameness, or the obeying of a cosmic law (Joey). But while objectively these are activities, psychologically they are experienced as the opposite, because the goal of the action is the avoidance of change.

cannot move beyond a state in which the universe centers about a something that is "completely unaware of itself as a subject."

These then are typical examples of the parallels between our observations of pubertal or prepubertal children suffering from infantile autism, and Piaget's observations of children during the sensorimotor stage of development (that is during their first eighteen months to two years of life).[7] Though brief, they will have to indicate how far-reaching are the parallels between the two sets of findings; otherwise they would not support our contention that the study of infantile autism yields significant insights into earliest personality development.

But beyond that they demonstrate how and why this study also amplifies Piaget. His research is devoted to the investigation of the child's intellectual development, and neglects the concomitant emotions that set it going. Our study, on the other hand, centers on the problem of what may have arrested personality at an egocentric level (as Piaget would call it) and what emotional experiences set that development going again. For it is the emotional experience, we surmise, that in the normal infant supports the intellectual development Piaget investigated so admirably.

One parallel, however, is of special importance and needs analysis in more detail. Almost everyone who has written about autistic children has emphasized their insistence on the maintenance of sameness in their environment. So it seems strange that no one to my knowledge has so far remarked on the fact that in Piaget's system the establishment of what he calls the concept of the permanence of the object is crucially important, and then related this to the autistic child's insistence on sameness.

According to Piaget [1954] the concept of the permanence of the object is so central an issue because it is "only by achieving belief in the object's permanence that the child succeeds in organizing space, time and causality." Since Piaget (and most philosophers before and since Kant) accept that these are the categories of reason, and since their attainment depends on the concept of the permanence of objects, then all higher mental functioning depends on acquiring that concept.

I would like to quote Kanner [1951] once more on the fact that there is something in autistic children "that forces them to postulate imperiously a static, unchanged environment," and that

7. Those who are interested in a study of the parallels between Piaget's view of the early development of intellectual functions and of the early development of emotions and personality as viewed by psychoanalysis (a view basic to the present volume) will wish to read P. H. Wolff [1960].

the [autistic] child's memory is phenomenal in this respect. After the lapse of several days, a multitude of blocks could be re-arranged, most astonishingly— in precisely the same unorganized pattern, with the same color of each block facing in the same direction as before. The absence of a block or the presence of a super-numerary block was noticed immediately, and there was an imperative demand on the restoration of the missing piece.

Perhaps this tremendous need to have objects always arranged in an identical way can be better understood with the help of Piaget's thoughts. If the autistic child lacks a concept of the permanence of objects, though he has long passed the age when such mastery comes normally, and if all higher mastery depends on that step, then might not his insistence on sameness stand for a desperate effort to establish in the external world what he cannot establish in his mind?

In this vein, let us consider what Piaget has to say about the establishment of the permanence of the object. According to him the concept of the object begins with a mere perceptual image during the first days of life, and gains in complexity through the first six stages of sensorimotor development. The sixth and last of these stages begins at around eighteen months and extends almost to age three.

To the autistic child, objects exist for him only when he sees them or they are readily available in their customary place; they cease to exist for him when they move beyond his familiar orbit. Recall, for example, Marcia's telling Karen "Miss Lukes all gone" when her teacher was absent for a day. But compare it with the following observation by Piaget [1954]:

At nine months and twenty-one days Jacqueline is seated and I place on her lap a rubber eraser which she has just held in her hand. Just as she is about to grasp it again I put my hand between her eyes and the eraser; she immediately gives up, as though the object no longer existed.
The experiment is repeated ten times. Every time that Jacqueline is touching the object with her fingers at the moment when I cut off her view of it she continues her search to the point of complete success. On the other hand, if no tactile contact has been established before the child ceases to see the eraser, Jacqueline withdraws her hand. It is simply because the image of my hand abolishes that of the object beneath it, unless her fingers have already grazed the object.

This observation, which typifies the fourth stage of sensorimotor development, suggests that to some degree it is the stage the autistic child functions on as far as the permanence of objects is concerned. The need of these children to hold onto the object (as Joey had to hold on to machines in his moments of stress) shows that the concept of the permanence of the object gets lost when things become difficult for them. At such times they have to physically get hold of the object.

Conversely, the child can retain the concept of the object in his mind (as Joey was satisfied with imaginary carburetors and wires) when he is feeling less threatened.

This seems a clear indication that the degree of his emotional vulnerability is what prevents the autistic child from according permanence to an object in his mind. Because unlike the infant in the fourth sensorimotor stage (who can *never* do so) the autistic child can retain a concept of the object if the threat to his existence is not too immediately felt. He only loses it when the threat is more immanent and he has to physically hold on to the object (again: as Joey had to do when evacuating, for fear of being disemboweled in the process). Only during the last stage of sensorimotor development does the normal child become "capable of constructing object when the displacements are not so visible" [Piaget, 1954]; or only then does the object continue to exist for him, even though it is not at the same place as before.

A crucial experiment of Piaget's may be quoted here.

I place the coin in my hand, then my hand under the cushion. I bring it forth closed and immediately hide it under the coverlet. Finally I withdraw it and hold it out, closed, to Jacqueline [who at this time was nineteen months and twenty days old]. Jacqueline then pushes my hand aside without opening it (she guesses that there is nothing in it, which is new) she looks under the cushion, then directly under the coverlet where she finds the object.

I then try a series of three displacements: I put the coin in my hand and move my closed hand from A to B and from B to C; Jacqueline sets my hand aside, then searches in A, in B and finally in C.

In other words, it is only in this last stage of sensorimotor development that the permanence of the object no longer depends on its remaining in the same place as last seen. Only then is the object freed from perception of it and action done to it because only then is its continued existence lodged in the form of a concept.

The autistic child, however, cannot bear it if the object does not always appear in the same place, or events do not occur in the same order. Is it not reasonable to assume that this is so because he cannot believe in the persistence of an object if its place is not the accustomed one? Might this not reflect an ultimate effort to establish the constancy of objects that he needs for his security?

As Piaget [1954] puts it, "Whereas we think of the ball as able to occupy an infinitude of different positions, which enables us to abstract it from all of them at once, the child endows it with only a few special positions without being able, consequently, to consider it as entirely independent of them."

Going beyond Piaget, on the basis of our experience with autistic children, we may say that as long as the child is not convinced of his own existence as a constant, he cannot believe in permanence of any kind. As a matter of fact, at the root of the child's wish that nothing should change in the external world is his desperate wish that nothing should change in or about himself, since he is convinced that any change would be catastrophic. It is based on his conviction that he is helpless to preserve his integrity in the face of change, of his not being a self with an inner consistency that will survive outer change.

Some of Piaget's observations show that even where persons are of tremendous emotional significance to the child, their constancy as persons is not established until that of the child himself is fully secured.

At fifteen months and nine days Lucienne is in the garden with her mother. Then I arrive; she sees me come, smiles at me, therefore obviously recognizes me (I am at a distance of about one meter and fifty centimeters). Her mother then asks her: "Where is papa?" Curiously enough Lucienne immediately turns toward the window of my office where she is accustomed to seeing me and points in that direction. A moment later we repeat the experiment; she has just seen me one meter away from her, yet when her mother pronounces my name, Lucienne again turns toward my office. . . . At twenty-eight months and three days Lucienne, hearing a noise in my office, says to me (we are together in the garden): "That is papa up there?". . .

We know the little game which consists in saying to children "Go look in my room and see if I am there," and we know how often the child yields to the suggestion [Piaget, 1954].

Thus from the time the child is able to perceive an object as such, till when he is nearly three years of age, the object in its familiar place (papa at the window) is more readily accessible to his mind emotionally and probably also intellectually than the flexible person in the flesh, in an unaccustomed place (papa next to me). I have referred before to Harlow's experiments [1958] with terrycloth mothers who remain always in the same place and hence have superior permanence compared to the mother who moves. His findings suggest that the mother-at-a-fixed-place offers greater immediate security to the infant monkey, though such a mother, fixed in space and emotionally unresponsive, prevents the monkey infant from becoming a real monkey.

The mothers of autistic children are often described as cold and rigid, if not also intellectual. Certainly they are not free-moving in the realms of emotion or at least not in relation to their autistic child. In their emotions, then, many of them are nearly as frozen, nearly as rigid when they deal with the child as was Harlow's terrycloth mother. Piaget, we may assume, did not let his daughter relegate him to a faraway existence at the office window, but helped her to transform a security based on his being fixed at a certain place, for a security based on emotional attachments to a father who moved about freely.

In discussing the infant's inability to recognize an object apart from its customary place, Piaget [1954] remarks that the child's image of the object has fewer "moments of freedom" than our own. For him there is not a doll, a watch or a ball, each of which is permanent, unique no matter where he sees them. He has only discrete images such as "ball-under-the-armchair," "watch-under-a-cushion," "papa-at-his-window."

The autistic child who has experienced too few "moments of freedom" about himself as a person cannot transfer such a concept from himself to the object. Therefore he cannot grant to the object what was not granted to him by his experience in life.

The small child takes the flexible rhythm of day and night for granted. When he becomes aware of the change in seasons, his concept of a self persisting despite changes in the environment is well established. So he can transfer this constancy to the sequence of day and night even when they differ in length.

One of our autistic boys insisted that all days were equal in length, that the sun always rose and set at exactly the same time and place. Similarly the twice yearly change around daylight saving time threw him for weeks into a state of despair. His minimal hold on the world depended on everything remaining the same, because only then could he predict that another day would dawn. The constancy of the sun, of light, of the recurrent sequence of night following day were foreign concepts to him, because there was no constancy to his personal existence.

At a later stage of development even the normal child on entering puberty, is upset by the changes in his body, and even more so the emotionally disturbed child. Though his feeling for the permanence of his body was well established—and because of it the permanence of objects—too much change in his body threatens this feeling for the permanence of things. As his body suddenly changes, so does the world and his place in it. And if this can happen to children who for years have enjoyed a sense of permanence, consider how terrific a threat it must be to the autistic child's very existence.

As long as nothing moves in the world around him, at least no new dangers have been added to the old. Through his insistence on sameness the autistic child makes his most immediate surroundings a bit predictable, but without any comprehension or belief in the permanence of objects. This eliminates the need to understand the nature of the object. If the object is an-object-in-a-certain-place I need not know its intrinsic nature to predict the vagaries of its existence.

The tragedy is that one's predictable image of the world depends on having acquired a mental concept of the permanence of objects, and no substituting of sameness in the external world for it will do. Causal connections based not on the persistence of objects no matter where, but on their fixity in the external world, lead to autistic concepts of causality (only my thoughts or doing can move objects; if one bad experience happened when I wore a green dress, everything green will destroy me). It leads to a world such as Joey created.

Why can the autistic child not achieve a concept of the permanence of objects, though his desperate insistence on sameness shows he needs it? Or let us look at what Piaget [1954] deduced as necessary for achieving this concept. "The permanence attributed to the object as such . . . remains related to the subject's action. In other words, the visual images the child pursues acquire in his eyes a certain solidity to the precise extent that he tries to follow them." Thus to be able to imagine an object he cannot touch or see anymore, the child must have acted upon it in the past. The more, then, the infant's ability to act on his own is inhibited by anxiety (in this case, the act of visual pursuit), the less will he be able to establish in his mind the permanence of the object.

Moreover, it is not enough that "the visual images the child pursues" should prove to be constant. He must have reason to wish them to be constant. For example, the child will need to have the repeated experience that though the mother "disappears," she comes back again. If he cries for her or goes to look for her, or later on just waits for her, she will be there again. But he will also need to wish she would always be there, because of the comfort he finds in her presence. It is this wish for her presence, even when she is absent, that makes him establish her image in his mind so that she won't ever be "all gone." It is this permanence of the image in the mind that lends credence to the permanence of the object when it goes out of reach and out of sight.

With those we dread, or about whom we are deeply ambivalent, we are glad to have them "out of sight, out of mind." Those we love we keep permanently "in mind." If the child has at least one person who is permanently in mind, he can adjust his concept of reality from "no one is here," to "mother is not here, but she will return." And this accommodation to reality he will then extend to other persons and objects of less meaning to him.

On the other hand, if significant persons in the child's environment project him into too contradictory emotions, or utter despair, then if these figures lack permanence he is reasonably safe when they are not directly active. Thus in order to have some periods of respite, the autistic child denies that anything has permanence but dead objects that do not move, or that are not moved away from their customary place. Unfortunately, if no one has permanence then neither has he. This then adds an inner source of fear to those originating on the outside. As a result the child becomes frozen in autism by his contradictory view of the world: to gain even temporary safety from threatening figures on the outside, he denies them all permanence; but if only the immovable has permanence, then he himself does not. His existence is threatened at every turn.

Casting these thoughts not in Piaget's frame of reference, but the one that permeates this book, we might say that to believe in the permanence of objects, the child must first of all interact with the environment. This he must do until personal experience convinces him that he is best off if objects have a permanent existence though they can be and are moved about. He can then drop his egocentric stance (only what I see or touch exists) for a reasoned one based on past interaction between self and object (it has disappeared before but will come back again). On the other hand, if reality does not in some way meet his private longings he will not accommodate to it. He will persist in the "egocentricity [which] is the distorting assimilation of reality to the individual's private interests" [Piaget, 1954].

In our experience it is just this trust in the benign intentions of reality that the autistic child lacks. After all, the ingestive apparatus of the child accommodates itself to solid foods, for example, not only because he is hungry and the food is nutritious but because it tastes good and because eating is made attractive by the mother. Since the autistic child has not found interaction attractive, on the contrary finds it dangerous, he does not accommodate, and remains unwilling or unable to engage in it. Thus to the question of why can he not accommodate himself to reality, assimilate it, and acquire a concept of the permanence of objects the answer seems obvious from our viewpoint: because self-preservation requires that he should not accommodate to a reality he believes is destructive.

Consider, for example, the motor behavior of Julian, a ten-year-old autistic boy. How gingerly, and with deep insecurity he approaches even those aspects of reality one would normally expect him to find most familiar of all, such as the act of standing up. Yet when he wishes to move from even a low platform to the floor he "feels" for the ground with his feet, makes contact only slightly at first, then raises his hips, sliding his buttocks over the platform edge, and finally stands up, very slowly.

In all this Julian resembles an infant, still basically unfamiliar with his body and its movements, who has just learned to manage a change of body position to erect posture. And this, despite the fact that there have been countless occasions on which he could have been "learning" how to do such a thing. But clearly no learning took place. Though in each instance, and for literally thousands of times, the erect posture is successfully reached, as in getting out of bed every day, the achievement is never expected. It is always approached with tremendous caution, anxiety and effort, and each time found an unexpected surprise and remarkable achievement. The question is: why did no learning take place? Why did the repeated experience of achievement not result in better body mastery, in confidence, in a more complete inner representation of the body, in a more secure body ego?

It is not that these children lack some kind of body image or concept, have no orientation in physical space. How else could we explain their not bumping into things or hurting themselves in their apparently heedless and uncontrolled outbursts of motor activity?

Perhaps the clue lies in Julian's "feeling" for the ground though he has felt for it and reached it again and again in the past. He does it because he is not yet convinced the ground is there, because he doubts that anything is within his reach. Just as his mother was beyond his emotional reach so does everything else seem to be. And if something does turn out to be within reach, like the floor, it is each time an unexpected surprise.

The term "convinced" takes us outside of Piaget's frame of reference, since he is little concerned with the degree of belief in one's knowledge. But as Wolff [1965] has pointed out, without enough of this quantitative factor children may be much more vulnerable. Here I refer to the whole continuum from negation to doubt to speculation to reasonable certainty, to conviction. Children who *distrust* the stability of their environment may well have at their disposal the kinds of cognitive structures needed for object permanence, but they don't believe it.

More explicitly, this means that during the sensorimotor stage of development the autistic child cannot accommodate to reality by assuming the viewpoint of another person—for example, that of the mother who continues to exist though out of sight. He cannot see his own viewpoint (no one is here) as only one among many that are possible and try to coordinate it with these others.

While sensorimotor *achievements* (crying, grasping, creeping) are confined to actions in reality, sensorimotor *cognition* entails an inner representation of that reality. It is inevitably a private affair, a nonshared event. Only by testing it in interaction with other persons and objects can we correct errors in our private perception. If the child cannot do this or will not, he cannot transcend the sensorimotor stage of development.

In Piaget's words, "Intelligence, just because it undergoes a gradual process of socialization, is enabled through the bond established by language between thoughts and words to make an increasing use of concepts; whereas autism, just because it remains individual, is still tied to imagery, to organic activity, and even to organic movements. The mere fact, then, of telling one's thought, of telling it to others, or of keeping silence and telling it only to oneself must be of enormous importance to the fundamental structures and functioning of thought in general, and of child logic in particular" [Piaget, 1955].

Here I might reflect back on how Marcia formed circles with her mouth. Her thought, because still tied "to imagery, to organic activity, and even to organic movement," was still autistic. Only as Karen slowly entered her life did Marcia become willing to leave her private world, to share the experience of drawing a circle with Karen, and then to reproduce it with her mouth. But not until language entered the relation, and naming the circle was added, did Marcia leave autism, not only for social interaction but also for independent intellectual growth. Then she could not only form a mental image of a circle, but express it, or represent it in external symbolic form. And because she was also physiologically mature, she could almost immediately move on to a level of conceptual intelligence that enabled her to draw the human figure.

Here again, parallel thoughts of Harlow's come to mind. His experiments with raising monkey infants in varying ways—in isolation, with their peers only, and with their mothers—demonstrate the kind of development that can take place in emotional isolation as well as the kind that isolation rules out. This led him to speculate on what social isolation may do to humans.

> I think it is possible that social isolation in the human being really does not have as serious effect on intelligence as measurements would indicate. What it does is that it destroys the capability of the infant to socialize. If the infant cannot socialize, it cannot then develop an adequate language. If it cannot develop an adequate language it is going to test at a less adequate level than its theoretical capability [Harlow, 1961].

Since the autistic child is inhibited from acting on his own and hence from interacting with the world, he cannot leave his egocentric position. Without a concept of the permanence of objects and human relations the universe lacks order and appears totally chaotic and unpredictable. The only other principle by which order can reign is to make sure that everything remains always the same.

What then, is characteristic of the next stages in development, according to Piaget? What must happen if the child is to move out of the last stages of sensorimotor development toward preoperational thought— stages that the autistic child masters only in isolated aspects, inefficiently, or not at all?

During the preoperational subperiod the child acquires the ability to understand and to plan how to deal with reality through inner, symbolic manipulations, i.e., thought. Before this, as he proceeds through the six stages of sensorimotor development, the child learns slowly to link together, one by one, the sequence of actions or perceptions in which he gets involved. This Piaget likens to a slow-motion film where one static frame is viewed after another. The child does not yet compress them into a simultaneous, all-encompassing image of what all these frames, in sequence, are about. For that, he must first be able to represent in his mind a displaced object not visible to him any more [Flavell, 1963].

Once the child can do that he need not depend on still having physical hold of the object, or on seeing it right now. Instead he can conjure up objects or events in his thoughts and assemble them there. This enables him to grasp in a single internal epitome a whole sweep of events. It is a much faster and more mobile device, which can recall the past, represent the present, and anticipate the future in a single brief act. With this the child can infinitely better manipulate reality because he can plan, and then act on his plans.

Thus the requirement for true thought, or reasoning, is the capacity for representational thought. And for representational thought the child must be able to imagine (represent) an object he can no longer see or feel. Hence the crucial importance of the concept of the permanence of objects.

Piaget's analysis of the steps leading to abstract thought was most convincing to us. As noted earlier, we could not accept the notion that autistic children are congenitally unable to think abstractly, because they certainly can. But they seem unable to move freely from one thought to another. That is why—unless their deepest emotions are involved—they get stuck at one thought at a time. Their thoughts move exceedingly slowly, seem without inherent connection. It is as if, in Piaget's terms, they view single frames one at a time, one thought at a time, and not a comprehensive story.

Unfortunately for our purposes Piaget, like Bosch, pays little attention to the emotional development of children; his interest is in their intellectual development. Nevertheless, when we applied his developmental scheme to our understanding of autistic children, we were greatly impressed with the parallels between his observations and theories on normal children and our thoughts on infantile autism. Reading Piaget, one is struck with the degree to which autistic children do not seem to have truly mastered the last stage of sensorimotor development in which the constancy of objects is acquired as a concept; how inadequately they achieve the tasks typical for what Piaget calls the preoperational period of development; not to mention the all important cognitive structures achieved only during middle childhood, the so-called subperiod of concrete operations.

On the other hand, there seems little doubt that all autistic children we know had mastered all but the very last of the six stages of sensori-motor development, though in varying degrees.

For example, all of Piaget's data suggest that once a task has been mastered, the child is already pushing on to a new one. From the fifth stage of sensorimotor development on, the child intentionally provokes novelties, even if he does not know what will happen. In other words, novelty is conceived of on the inside, before the fact, and does not have to be encountered by accident on the outside.

But one of the striking things about autistic children is how frantically they avoid novelty, which presupposes of course that they have some concept of what novelty entails. And since the interest in novelty is typical from the fifth stage on, the child must have reached this stage sufficiently to know what is involved in it, so as to shun it.

In most cases the autistic child's ability to manipulate objects, and use their bodies, far transcends the sixth stage of development. But their ability to manipulate abstract thoughts, as opposed to thoughts relating to their emotional preoccupations, is below normal. It seems to have gotten stuck at the sixth stage of sensorimotor development, the stage that normally begins at eighteen months. This is roughly the age at which the autistic child is almost uniformly recognized as being deviant in his development.

Marcia's early use of language may illustrate further. When she began to talk, she would name objects someone else pointed out but she would not, except in rare instances, name the picture of the object unless she was able to touch it at the same time, and she had to follow a certain sequence in her naming in order to be successful. When we persuaded her to start somewhere in the middle of her series, her first tendency was to ignore the place where we had pointed and to begin at her usual place of departure. When she did start at the place where we pointed, she complied with great difficulty and would immediately start over at the beginning of *her* series. Once, when we repeated this several times she got very angry, began to twiddle and stopped naming objects for perhaps three minutes. But then she spontaneously began again by herself, in the order most familiar to her.

The constancy of Marcia's external world seemed to require not only visual contact, but tactile contact as well. Objects seemed to have a better established reality meaning when she followed her own sequence instead of ours. Object constancy had not been fully divorced from its context of personal action (hers), either in touching or in sequence of naming.

This again suggests certain parallels with Piaget's thoughts. During the first stage of sensorimotor development the object exists for the child only as long as he acts on it; there is only a "sucking object" or a "looking object" or a "grasping object." Coordination during the second stage establishes the identity between the sucking and the looking object to the extent that the child looks at what he grasps, and sucks what he looks at. When two actions are thus applied to a single object simultaneously or in sequence, the object for the first time gains a certain independence from any one of the actions done to it. Only when a great variety of actions have been applied to the same object, and the schemata representing the actions have been firmly established does the child dispense with touching, sucking, looking at and grasping an object. Only then does he act as if he accepted its permanence through only one of the many possible avenues of perception that identify it.

Thus for Marcia it seemed less a failure to establish the permanence of the object, than a failure in acquiring the freedom to move quickly and easily from one proof of its permanence to another.

What is just as characteristic of autistic children is the often incredibly wide range of their *décalage*, when compared to the normal. Décalage refers to the differences in a person's ability to apply cognitive structures to different tasks; to some tasks he will apply genetically much higher cognitive structures than to others.

Our observations suggest that while the autistic child is arrested in his development at the last stage of his sensorimotor development, he does not function all across the board at the same level of arrest. There may be a high level of development in one area and total failure at a much lower level. And this, though the lower level would be a prerequisite, in normal development, for the more complex forms. The logical sequence of development in autistic children seems to be different.

This was so for the mute autistic girl who in infancy was raised by her mother with dogs (see pages 348–349). During her first two years with us she did almost nothing but grunt and lay little blocks into complex patterns. But she was able to infer from certain goings-on that another child in the group was starting her menstrual cycle. Surely, in one sense, this child was somewhere in the middle of her sensorimotor development, but in another sense she was capable of very advanced symbolic activity. We must therefore assume that in part, at least, she had gone far beyond the period of sensorimotor development.

The same was even more patent in Gwen, a speaking autistic girl with a great spread of abilities. Gwen had acquired highly complex social skills, such as anticipating the social needs of other persons, including an uncanny ability to endear herself to those who had no emotional meaning for her while anxiously shunning those who did. At the same time she was totally incapable of attending to external objects for any length of time, and was sadly lacking in her comprehension of the use of objects.

How could any theory of development account for the following discrepancy? Gwen, when she wanted to draw, would disregard which end of the pencil to draw with, even after she saw clearly that her pencil (when used with the eraser end) made no marks. At the same time she was well able to perceive that when someone at the dinner table had bread in his hand he would soon want butter. She would not only pass the butter along, but would mutely enroll the help of another person whom she used as a social means to pass the object.

Many such discrepancies in our children are hard to pin down in terms of Piaget's theory, since they require us to assume a degree of décalage that cannot easily be explained by his theory. For example, Debby, a seven-year-old mute autistic girl, is putting a jigsaw puzzle together with great skill. When almost done, she discovers that one piece is still missing. Immediately she searches around, but her search is a directed one, not a random trial and error. At first she looks beneath the puzzle. When she cannot find it there, she immediately looks under the chair. This again is not a random search, because she goes directly to the spot where it is likely to be. When she does find it, she immediately puts it into its proper place in the puzzle.

To do this, after searching, requires that she straighten herself out and return to a task she had abandoned in order to initiate the search. To first search, and then return to an earlier task implies an awareness of the permanence of the missing puzzle piece. It implies also the mental image of the uncompleted puzzle. It implies imagining the space in which the missing object might be found. And finally, it implies the acceptance of a causal world in which the missing piece must be found as it really is and not as it might be "reproduced" through a twiddling, a clucking or some other autistic activity.

Observation suggests that many autistic children, like Debby, are perfectly well aware of the constancy of objects, that they know about relationships like "above," "below," "underneath," "to the right," "to the left," etc. In other words, they have conquered representational space. They are aware (selectively) of external causes, and submit themselves to these causes.

Perhaps then the "failure" in development should be fixed at a point of transition between the first creation of a world of inner representation, and the use of those representations as symbolic tools of thought. The children's use of symbols is weak and spotty. Their inner world of representation is not stable enough. When there is a radical alteration in the outside world they feel threatened, and may revert to much more primitive forms of behavior in an effort to re-establish its permanence. Or to put it differently, the child's failure seems to lie not in the actual establishment of the object's constancy, but in acquiring the freedom not to have to constantly re-establish its permanence.

Conversely, while many autistic children have not achieved the notion of object permanence, physical space or physical causality, they can nevertheless engage in a degree of symbolic activity which should not occur, according to Piaget's timetable, until a much later date.

Piaget does not enter the personal reasons for such abilities or their absence. But there seems little doubt that while experience, particularly the social experience, matters greatly, the child's emotional involvement in the task plays a great role. Given the autistic child's social isolation and the immense variety in the degree of his emotional involvement in tasks—total disregard for some phenomena, total concentration on others, witness Marcia's total emotional involvement in forced elimination, or Joey's in the flow of electricity—they seem to show an immensely wider latitude in décalage than is assumed in Piaget's system. Certainly Joey's astonishing understanding of electric motors and his total inability to play the simplest of games shows the décalage between the cognitive structures he could muster for his defensive needs and those he lacked for the most childish interactions.

Piaget [1950] is convinced that nonegocentric thought can develop only from repeated interpersonal interactions, especially those involving arguments and disagreements in which the child is actually forced, again and again, to take cognizance of the role of the other.

Here again the paradigm of breast feeding may illustrate. While at first the infant may view the breast he sucks from as part of himself, the separate existence of a variable object, the mother, is much easier to grasp than the separateness of a static object like the bottle. Milk from the breast may at times flow more easily than at others, need more strenuous sucking at some times than others. Later on the breast may recoil from his biting or chewing, as the bottle does not. Any or all of these may help the infant to conceive that there is a variable outside his control which is dependent on another being, while the flow through an opening in the bottle does not to the same degree force him to recognize a variable outside of himself.

But while social interaction is what does away with childish egocentrism, the autistic child cannot interact with the world. He feels both: that he is helpless to react when he is acted upon (the enemas inflicted on Marcia), and that his actions control the universe (as Joey's rocking of his body made the earth rock, or his eyes blinking made the light go on and off; indeed at this stage, Joey's view of the world was not at all beyond the infant's egocentric conviction that his crying, not the mother, produces milk). Thus Piaget's system accords entirely with the notion that it is the autistic child's unwillingness or inability to engage in social interactions that pegs his thinking and acting to the self-centered level of autism.

This is clearly seen in the area of language and communication, where he appears to make little real effort to adapt his speech to the needs of the listener. It is seen most graphically when a child is given the task of looking at objects from a given position and asked what they would look like when viewed from a different one. Until the stage of preoperational thought has been fully mastered the most common response to this task is to insist that it looks from any second position just as it does from the child's own perspective [Piaget and Inhelder, 1956]. Compare this with how the autistic child of any age cannot view an event from any perspective but his own.

But Piaget's thought coincides even more specifically with our conviction that it is the autistic child's single-minded preoccupation with a specific issue (in our opinion, his unremitting fear of destruction) that arrests him on the level of autism.

According to Piaget one of the most pronounced characteristics of preoperational thought is its tendency to center attention on a single, striking feature of the object of its reasoning to the neglect of other important aspects and by so doing, distort the reasoning. The child is unable to de-center. He cannot take account of features that could balance and compensate for the distorting, biasing effect of the single centration [Flavell, 1963].

Hence while Piaget is concerned mainly or only with how intelligence develops and not with the emotional aspects of behavior, his conclusions about what causes the type of thought we observe in autistic children are concordant with ours. It is hoped that this study may suggest what emotional interactions are needed if the child is to grow beyond autism.

I have described at length three of our efforts to provide such emotional interactions. To the extent that we succeeded and the children turned their backs—not to us now but the void, not away from their feelings, and ours, but thee-ward—they set foot in our world. But in this now common world they saw also, with Blake, that

> . . . thought is life
> And strength and breath
> And the want
> Of thought is death.

Bibliography

ALEXANDER, F., and T. M. FRENCH. *Psychoanalytic Therapy.* New York: Ronald, 1946.

ALPERT, A., and E. PFEIFFER. Treatment of an Autistic Child. *Journal of the American Academy of Child Psychiatry,* 3:591-616 (1964).

ANTHONY, J. An Experimental Approach to the Psychopathology of Childhood: Autism. *British Journal of Medical Psychology,* 31:211–225 (1958).

ARIETI, S. *Interpretation of Schizophrenia.* New York: Brunner, 1955.

————. (ed.) *American Handbook of Psychiatry.* New York: Basic, 1959.

BALINT, M. Early Developmental States of the Ego, Primary Object Love. *International Journal of Psychoanalysis,* 30:265–273 (1949).

————. Friendly Expanses—Horrid Empty Spaces. *International Journal of Psychoanalysis,* 37:235–241 (1955).

BATESON, G., D. D. JACKSON, J. HALEY, and J. WEAKLAND. Toward a Theory of Schizophrenia. *Behavioral Science,* 1 (1956).

BECK, S. J. *Psychological Processes in the Schizophrenic Adaptation.* New York: Grune and Stratton, 1965.

BENDA, C. E. Childhood Schizophrenia, Autism, and Heller's Disease, in P. W. BOWMAN and H. V. MAUTNER (eds.), *Mental Retardation.* New York: Grune and Stratton, 1960, pp. 469–492.

BENDER, L. Autism in Children with Mental Deficiency. *American Journal of Mental Deficiency,* 63:81–86 (1960).

BENEDICT, R. Myth, in *Encyclopedia of the Social Sciences.* New York: Macmillan (1933), vol. 11, pp. 178–181.

BERGMAN, P., and S. K. ESCALONA. Unusual Sensitivities in Very Young Children, in *The Psychoanalytic Study of the Child.* New York: International Universities Press, 1949, vol. 3–4, pp. 333–352.

BETTELHEIM, B. Individual and Mass Behavior in Extreme Situations. *Journal of Abnormal and Social Psychology,* 38:417–452 (1943).

————. The Special School for Emotionally Disturbed Children. *Forty-seventh Yearbook of the National Society for the Study of Education,* 145–171 (1948a).

BETTELHEIM, B. Closed Institutions for Children? *Bulletin of the Menninger Clinic*, 12(4):135–142 (1948b).

_____. Harry—A Study in Rehabilitation. *Journal of Abnormal and Social Psychology*, 44:231–265 (1949).

_____. *Love Is Not Enough—The Treatment of Emotionally Disturbed Children*. New York: Free Press, 1955.

_____. *Truants From Life—The Rehabilitation of Emotionally Disturbed Children* New York: Free Press, 1955

_____. Childhood Schizophrenia As A Reaction to Extreme Situations. *American Journal of Orthopsychiatry*, 26:507–518 (1956).

_____. Psychiatric Consultation in Residential Treatment: The Director's View. *American Journal of Orthopsychiatry*, 28(2):256–265 (1958).

_____. Feral Children and Autistic Children. *American Journal of Sociology*. 64(5):455–467 (1959).

_____. *The Informed Heart—Autonomy in a Mass Age*. New York: Free Press, 1960.

_____. Training the Child Care Worker. *American Journal of Orthopsychiatry*, 36(4):694–705 (1966).

_____, and E. SYLVESTER. Milieu Therapy—Indications and Illustrations, *Psychoanalytic Review*, 36(1):54–68 (1949a).

_____. Physical Symptoms in Emotionally Disturbed Children, in *The Psychoanalytic Study of the Child*. New York: International Universities Press, 1949b, vol. 3–4, pp. 353–368.

_____. Delinquency and Morality, in *The Psychoanalytic Study of the Child*. New York: International Universities Press, 1950a, vol. 5, pp. 329–342.

_____, and B. WRIGHT. Staff Development in a Treatment Institution. *American Journal of Orthopsychiatry*, 25(4):705–719 (1955).

BION, W. R. Language and the Schizophrenic, in M. KLEIN, P. HEIMANN, and R. E. MONEY-KYRLE (eds.), *New Directions in Psychoanalysis*. New York: Basic, 1955, pp. 220–239.

BLEULER, E. *Dementia Praecox oder die Gruppe der Schizophrenien*. 1911.

_____. *Dementia Praecox or the Group of Schizophrenias*. 1st Eng. trans. New York: International Universities Press, 1950.

BLOOM, B. S. *Stability and Change in Human Characteristics*. New York: Wiley, 1964.

BOSCH, G. *Der Fruehkindliche Autismus*. Berlin: Springer, 1962.

BOWLBY, J. *Maternal Care and Mental Health*. Geneva: World Health Organization, 1952.

_____. The Nature of the Child's Tie to His Mother. *International Journal of Psychoanalysis*, 39:350–373 (1958).

BRODBECK, A. J. An Exploratory Study of the Acquisition of Dependency Behavior in Puppies. *Bulletin of the Ecological Society of America*, 35:73 (1954).

BRUCH, H. Studies in Schizophrenia, *Acta Psychiatrica et Neurologica Scandinavica Supplementum*, 34:130 (1959).

BUEHLER, K. *Die Krise der Psychologie*. Jena: Gustav Fischer, 1929.

_____. *Sprachtheorie*. Jena: Gustav Fischer, 1934.

CALL, J. D. Newborn Approach Behavior and Early Ego Development. *International Journal of Psychoanalysis*, 45:286–295 (1964).

CARPENTER, C. R. A Field Study of the Behavior and Social Relations of

Howler Monkeys. *Comparative Psychology Monographs*, 10(2):1–168 (1934).

CASSIRER, E. *The Philosophy of Symbolic Forms:* Vol. I: *Language.* New Haven: Yale U. P., 1953.

COLLIAS, N. E. The Analysis of Socialization in Sheep and Goats. *Ecology*, 37:228–238 (1956).

CUNNINGHAM, M. A., and C. DICKSON. A Study of the Language of an Autistic Child. *Journal of Child Psychology and Psychiatry*, 2:193–202 (1961).

CUTSFORTH, T. D. *The Blind in School and Society.* New York: *American Foundation for the Blind*, 1951.

DARR, G. D., and F. C. WORDEN. Case Report Twenty-eight Years after an Infantile Autistic Disorder. *American Journal of Orthopsychiatry*, 21: 559–569, 1951.

DAVIDS, A., S. DEVAULT, and M. TALMADGE. Anxiety, Pregnancy, and Childbirth Abnormalities. *Journal of Consultant Psychology*, 25:74–77 (1961).

DESPERT, J. L. Discussion of L. Kanner, Irrelevant and Metaphorical Language in Early Infantile Autism. *American Journal of Psychiatry*, 103 (1946–7).

DURFEE, J., and K. WOLF. Anstaltspflege und Entwicklung im ersten Lebensjahr. *Zeitschrift fuer Kinderforschung*, 42–43 (1933).

EISENBERG, L. The Autistic Child in Adolescence. *American Journal of Psychiatry*, 112:607–612 (1956).

————. The Fathers of Autistic Children. *American Journal of Orthopsychiatry*, 27:715–724 (1957).

————. Private Communication. 1965.

————, and L. KANNER. Early Infantile Autism, 1943–1955. *American Journal of Orthopsychiatry*, 26:556–566 (1956).

EISENBUD, J. The Hand and the Breast with Special Reference to Obsessional Neurosis. *Psychoanalytic Quarterly*, 34:219–248 (1965).

EKSTEIN, R. The Space Child's Time Machine. *American Journal of Orthopsychiatry*, 24:492–506 (1954).

————. On the Acquisition of Speech in the Autistic Child. *Reiss–Davis Clinic Bulletin*, 1 (1964).

————, and J. WALLERSTEIN. Observations on the Psychotherapy of Borderline and Psychotic Children, in *The Psychoanalytic Study of the Child.* New York: International Universities Press, 1956, vol. 11, pp. 303–311.

————. and D. WRIGHT. The Space Child. *Bulletin of the Menninger Clinic*, 16:211–223 (1952).

————. Comments on a Psychotherapeutic Session with the Space Child. *International Record of Medicine*, 167:592–600 (1954).

ERIKSON, E. H. *Childhood and Society.* New York: Norton, 1950.

————. The Problem of Ego Identity. *Journal of the American Psychoanalytic Association*, 4:56–121, 1956.

————. *Identity and the Life Cycle.* New York: International Universities Press, 1959.

ESCALONA, S. K. Patterns of Infantile Experiences and the Developmental Process, in *The Psychoanalytic Study of the Child.* New York: International Universities Press, 1963, vol. 18, pp. 197–244.

————. Some Determinants of Individual Differences. *Transactions of the New York Academy of Sciences*, Series 2, 27(7):802–816 (1965).

EVANS, B., and C. EVANS. *A Dictionary of Contemporary American Usage.* New York: Random House, 1957.

EVELOFF, H. H. The Autistic Child. *Archives of General Psychiatry*, 3:66–81 (1960).

FANTZ, R. L. Pattern Vision in Young Infants. *Psychological Record*, 8:43–47 (1958).

FELDMAN, S. S. Blushing, Fear of Blushing, and Shame. *Journal of the American Psychoanalytic Association*, 10:368–385 (1962).

FERREIRA, A. J. The Pregnant Woman's Emotional Attitude and its Reflection on the Newborn. *American Journal of Orthopsychiatry*, 30:553–561 (1960).

FEUERBACH, A. VON. *Beispiel eines Verbrechens am Seelenleben des Menschen.* Ansbach, 1832.

FLAVELL, J. H. *The Developmental Psychology of Jean Piaget.* Princeton: Van Nostrand, 1963.

FREEMAN, W. Psychosurgery, in *The American Handbook of Psychiatry.* New York: Basic, 1959, vol. 2, pp. 1521–1540.

FREUD, A. Psychoanalysis and Education, in *The Psychoanalytic Study of the Child.* New York: International Universities Press, 1954a, vol. 9, pp. 9–15.

————. The Widening Scope of Indications for Psychoanalysis. *Journal of the American Psychoanalytic Association*, 2:607–620 (1954b).

FURER, M. The Development of a Preschool Symbiotic Psychotic Boy, in *The Psychoanalytic Study of the Child.* New York: International Universities Press, 1964, vol. 19, pp. 448–469.

GARRARD, S. D., and J. B. RICHMOND. Factors Influencing the Biological Substrate and Early Psychological Development, in R. H. OJEMANN (ed.), *Recent Research on Creative Approaches to Environmental Stress.* Iowa City: U. of Iowa Press, 1963.

GESELL, A. The Tonic Neck Reflex in the Human Infant. *Journal of Pediatrics*, 13:455–464 (1938).

————. *Wolf Child and Human Child.* New York: Harper, 1940.

GLAUBER, I. P. Federn's Annotation of Freud's Theory of Anxiety. *Journal of the American Psychoanalytic Association*, 11:84–96 (1963).

GOLDFARB, W. Receptor Preferences in Schizophrenic Children. *Archives of Neurology and Psychiatry*, 76:643–652 (1956).

GOLDSTEIN, K. Abnormal Conditions in Infancy. *Journal of Nervous and Mental Disease*, 128:538–557 (1959).

GOSHEN, C. E. Mental Retardation and Neurotic Maternal Attitudes. *Archives of General Psychiatry*, 9:168–175 (1963).

GROOS, K. *The Play of Man.* New York: Appleton, 1901.

GUNTHER, M. Infant Behavior at the Breast, in B. M. Foss (ed.), *Determinants of Infant Behavior.* London: Methuen. 1961.

HARLOW, H. F. The Nature of Love. *American Psychologist*, 12:673–685 (1958).

————. Affectional Responses in the Infant Monkey, *Science*, 130 (1959).

————. The Maternal Affectional System, in B. M. Foss (ed.), *Determinants of Infant Behavior.* New York: Wiley, 1961, vol. 2, pp. 3–33.

————, and M. K. HARLOW. Social Deprivation in Monkeys. *Scientific American*, 207 (5):136–146 (1962).

HARTMANN, H. *Ego Psychology and the Problem of Adaptation.* New York: International Universities Press, 1958.

HEBB, D. O. Drives and the C.N.S. *Psychological Review*, 62:243–254 (1955).

HERODOTUS. *The Histories of Herodotus of Halicarnassus,* New York: Heritage, 1958.

HESS, E. H. Imprinting. *Science*, 130 (1959).

HINSIE, L. E., and J. SHATZKY. *Psychiatric Dictionary*, 2d ed. New York: Oxford U. P., 1954.

HOFFER, W. Mouth, Hand, and Ego-Integration, in *The Psychoanalytic Study of the Child*. New York: International Universities Press, 1949, vol. 3–4, pp. 49–56.

HOOKER, D. *The Prenatal Origins of Behavior*. Lawrence: U. of Kansas Press, 1952, pp. 62–82.

HUSSERL, E. *Ideen zu einer reinen Phaenomenologischen Philosophie; Jahrbuch fuer Philosophie und Phaenomenologische Forschung*. Halle: M. Niemeyer, 1913.

ITARD, J. M. G. *The Wild Boy of Aveyron*. New York: Century, 1932.

———. *The Wild Boy of Aveyron*. New York: Appleton, 1962.

JACKSON, L. 'Non-Speaking' Children. *British Journal of Medical Psychology*, 23:87–100 (1950).

JASPERS, K. *Philosophie*, II. Auflage. Berlin: Springer, 1948.

JOSSELYN, I. M. Concepts Related to Child Development, #1: The Oral Stage. *Journal of the American Academy of Child Psychiatry*, 1:209–224 (1962).

KAMP, L. N. J. Autistic Syndrome in One of a Pair of Monozygotic Twins. *Psychiatria, Neurologia, Neurochirurgia*, 67:143–147 (1964).

———. Private Communication, 1965.

KANNER, L. Autistic Disturbances of Affective Contact. *Nervous Child*, 2:217–250 (1943).

———. Early Infantile Autism. *Journal of Pediatrics*, 25:211–217 (1944).

———. Irrelevant and Metaphorical Language in Early Infantile Autism. *American Journal of Psychiatry*, 103:242–246 (1946).

———. *Child Psychiatry*, 2d ed. Springfield: Charles C Thomas, 1948.

———. Problems of Nosology and Psychodynamics of Early Infantile Autism. *American Journal of Orthopsychiatry*, 19:416–426 (1949).

———. The Conception of Wholes and Parts in Early Infantile Autism, *American Journal of Psychiatry*, 108:23–26 (1951a).

———. Discussion. *American Journal of Orthopsychiatry*, 21:569–570 (1951b).

———. General Concept of Schizophrenia at Different Ages, in *Neurology and Psychiatry in Childhood*. Baltimore: Williams and Wilkins, 1954a, pp. 451–453.

———. To What Extent Is Early Infantile Autism Determined by Constitutional Inadequacy? *Proceedings of the Association for Research on Nervous and Mental Disease*, 33:378–385 (1954b).

———, and L. I. LESSER. Early Infantile Autism, in *Pediatric Clinics of North America*. Philadelphia: Saunders, 1958 vol. 5, pp. 711–730.

KEELER, W. R. Discussion. *Psychiatric Reports of the American Psychiatric Association*, 7:66–88 (1957).

KING, P. D. Theoretical Considerations of Psychotherapy with a Schizophrenic Child. *Journal of the American Academy of Child Psychiatry*, 3:638–649 (1964).

KLEIN, M. *The Psycho-Analysis of Children*. London: Hogarth, 1932.

———. *Contributions to Psycho-Analysis*. London: Hogarth, 1950.

KOHUT, H. Introspection, Empathy and Psychoanalysis. *Journal of the American Psychoanalytic Association*, 7:459–487 (1959).

LANGEVELD, M. J. *Studien zur Anthropologie des Kindes*. Tuebingen: Niemeyer, 1956.

LEWIN, B. Sleep, the Mouth and the Dream Screen. *Psychoanalytic Quarterly*, 15:419–434 (1946).

LINN, L. Some Developmental Aspects of the Body Image. *International Journal of Psychoanalysis*, 36:36–42 (1955).

LOOMIS, E. A. Autistic and Symbiotic Syndromes in Children. *Monographs of the Society for Research in Child Development*, 25(3):39–48 (1960).

LORENZ, K. *King Solomon's Ring.* New York: Crowell, 1952.

———. *Das sogenannte Boese.* Wien: Borotha-Schoeler, 1963.

LOVAAS, O. I., J. P. BERBERICH, B. F. PERLOFF, and B. SCHAEFFER. Acquisition of Imitative Speech by Schizophrenic Children. *Science*, 151:705–707 (1966).

LOWENFELD, B. Psychological Problems of Children With Impaired Vision, in W. M. CRUICKSHANK (ed.), *Psychology of Exceptional Children and Youth*, 2d ed. Englewood Cliffs, N.J.: Prentice Hall, 1963, pp. 226–310.

MAHLER, M. On Child Psychosis and Schizophrenia: Autistic and Symbiotic Infantile Psychoses, in *The Psychoanalytic Study of the Child*. New York: International Universities Press, 1952, vol. 7, pp. 286–305.

———. On Early Infantile Psychosis. *Journal of the American Academy of Child Psychiatry*, 554–568 (1965a).

———. On the Significance of the Normal Separation-Individuation Phase: With Reference to Research in Symbiotic Child Psychosis, in SCHUR, M. (ed.), *Drives, Affects, Behavior*. New York: International Universities Press, 1965b, vol. 2, pp. 161–169.

———, M. FURER, and C. F. SETTLAGE. Severe Emotional Disturbances in Childhood; Psychosis, in S. ARIETI (ed.), *American Handbook of Psychiatry*. New York: Basic, 1959, pp. 816–839.

MARAIS, E. N. *My Friends the Baboons.* New York: McBride, 1940.

MEAD, M. in J. M. TANNER and B. INHELDER (eds.), *Discussion on Child Development*. New York: International Universities Press, 1958, vol. 3.

MINISTRY OF HEALTH, U.S.S.R. Order Prohibiting Lobotomy. *Nevropat. i psikhiat.*, 20:17 (1951).

MONTAGUE, A. Constitutional and Prenatal Factors in Infant and Child Health in M. J. E. SENN (ed.), *Symposium on the Healthy Personality*. New York: Josiah Macy, Jr. Foundation, 1950.

MULLAHY, P. A Theory of Interpersonal Relations and the Evolution of Personality in H. S. SULLIVAN (ed.), *Conceptions of Modern Psychiatry*. New York: Norton, 1953, pp. 119–147.

NIEDERLAND, W. G. The Role of the Ego In the Recovery of Early Memories. *Psychoanalytic Quarterly*, 34:564–571 (1965).

OGBURN, W. F. The Wolf Boy of Agra. *American Journal of Sociology*, 64:449–454 (1959).

———, and N. K. BOSE. On the Trail of the Wolf-Children. *Genetic Psychology Monographs*, 60:117–193 (1959).

PAVENSTEDT, E. The Effect of Extreme Passivity Imposed on a Boy in Early Childhood, in *The Psychoanalytic Study of the Child*. New York: International Universities Press, 1956, vol. 11, pp. 396–409.

———. Observations in Five Japanese Homes. *Journal of Child Psychiatry*, 4:413–425 (1965).

PIAGET, J. *The Psychology of Intelligence.* New York: Harcourt, 1950.

———. *The Origins of Intelligence in Children.* New York: International Universities Press, 1952.

———. *The Construction of Reality in the Child.* New York: Basic, 1954.

———. *Language and Thought of the Child.* New York: Meridian, 1955.

PIAGET, J., and B. INHELDER. *The Child's Conception of Space*. London: Routledge, 1956.

PIOUS, W. L. The Pathogenic Process in Schizophrenia. *Bulletin of the Menninger Clinic*, 13:152–159 (1949).

QUINN, J. A. *Sociology: A Systematic Analysis*. Philadelphia: Lippincott, 1963.

RAPAPORT, D. The Theory of Ego Autonomy: A Generalization. *Bulletin of the Menninger Clinic*, 22:13–35 (1958).

RAUBER, A. *Homo Sapiens Ferus, oder die Zustaende der Verwilderten*. Leipzig: Julius Brehse, 1888.

RIBBLE, M. A. Anxiety in Infants and its Disorganizing Effects, in N. LEWIS and B. L. PACELLA (eds.), *Modern Trends in Child Psychiatry*. New York: International Universities Press, 1945, pp. 11–25.

RIMLAND, B. *Infantile Autism*. New York: Appleton, 1964.

ROCHLIN, G. Loss and Restitution, in *The Psychoanalytic Study of the Child*. New York: International Universities Press, 1953, vol. 8, pp. 288–309.

RODRIGUÉ, E. The Analysis of a Three-year-old Mute Schizophrenic, in M. KLEIN, P. HEIMANN, and R. F. MONEY-KYRLE (eds.). *New Directions in Psychoanalysis*. New York: Basic, 1955, pp. 140–179.

RUBINFINE, D. L. Maternal Stimulation, Psychic Structure, and Early Object Relations, in *The Psychoanalytic Study of the Child*. New York: International Universities Press, 1962, vol. 17, pp. 265–282.

SALIMBENE OF PARMA, in J. B. ROSS and M. M. McLAUGHLIN (eds.), *A Portable Medieval Reader*. New York: Viking, 1944.

SANDER, L. W. Issues in Early Mother-Child Interaction. *Journal of the American Academy of Child Psychiatry*, 1:141–166 (1962).

SARASON, S. B., and T. GLADWIN. Psychological and Cultural Problems in Mental Sub-Normality: A Review of Research. *Genetic Psychological Monographs*, 57:3–289 (1957).

SARVIS, M. S., and P. GARCIA. Etiological Variables in Autism. *Psychiatry*, 24: 307–317 (1961).

SCHACHTEL, E. G. On Memory and Childhood Amnesia. *Psychiatry*, 10:1–26 (1947).

———. *Metamorphosis*. New York: Basic, 1959.

SCHAIN, R. J., and H. YANNET. Infantile Autism—An Analysis of 50 Cases. *Journal of Pediatrics*, 57 (4):560–567 (1960).

SCHALLER, G. B. *The Mountain Gorilla—Ecology and Behavior*. Chicago: U. of Chicago Press, 1963.

SCHEERER, M., E. ROTHMAN, and K. GOLDSTEIN. A Case of 'Idiot Savant,' *Psychological Monographs*, 58 (1945).

SCOTT, J. P. Genetics and the Development of Social Behavior in Mammals. *American Journal of Orthopsychiatry*, 32:878–888 (1962).

———. The Process of Primary Socialization in Canine and Human Infants. *Monographs of the Society for Research in Child Development*, 28:3–44 (1963).

———, and J. L. FULLER. *Genetics and the Social Behavior of the Dog*. Chicago: U. of Chicago Press, 1965.

SECHEHAYE, M. A. *Symbolic Realization*. New York: International Universities Press, 1951.

SELYE, H. *The Stress of Life*. New York: McGraw-Hill, 1956.

SENSORY DEPRIVATION. A symposium held at Harvard Medical School. Cambridge: Harvard U. P., 1961.

SILBERSTEIN, R. M., and H. IRWIN. Jean-Marc-Gaspart Itard and the Savage of

Aveyron: An Unsolved Problem in Child Psychiatry. *Journal of the American Academy of Child Psychiatry*, 1:314–322 (1962).

SINGH, J. A. L., and R. N. ZINGG. *Wolf Children and Feral Man*. New York: Harper, 1940.

SMOLEN, E. M. Some Thoughts on Schizophrenia in Childhood. *Journal of Child Psychiatry*, 4:443–472 (1965).

SNELL, B. *Der Aufbau der Sprache*. Hamburg: Claassen Verlag, 1952.

SONTAG, L. W. The Significance of Fetal Environmental Differences. *American Journal of Obstetrics and Gynaecology*, 42:996–1003 (1941).

SPITZ, R. A. Hospitalism, in *The Psychoanalytic Study of the Child*. New York: International Universities Press, 1945, vol. 1, pp. 53–74.

————. Anaclitic Depression, in *The Psychoanalytic Study of the Child*. New York: International Universities Press, 1946, vol. 2, pp. 313–342.

————. The Psychogenic Diseases in Infancy, in *The Psychoanalytic Study of the Child*. New York: International Universities Press, 1951, vol. 6, pp. 255–275.

————. Autoeroticism Re-examined, in *The Psychoanalytic Study of the Child*. New York: International Universities Press, 1962, vol. 17, pp. 283–315.

————. The Derailment of Dialogue. *Journal of the American Psychoanalytic Association*, 12:752–775 (1964).

————, and K. M. WOLF. Autoeroticism, in *The Psychoanalytic Study of the Child*. New York: International Universities Press, 1949, vol. 3–4, pp. 85–120.

STERN, C., and W. STERN. *Die Kindersprache*. 2d. Aufl. Leipzig, 1920.

STERN, W. *Die Psychologie der frühen Kindheit bis zum sechsten Lebensjahre*. Leipzig: Quelle and Meyer, 1923.

SZUREK, S. A. Psychotic Episodes and Psychotic Maldevelopment. *American Journal of Orthopsychiatry*, 26:519–543 (1956).

————, and I. N. BERLIN. Elements of Psychotherapeutics with the Schizophrenic Child and his Parents. *Psychiatry*, 19:1–9 (1956).

TANNER, J. M., and B. INHELDER (eds.), *Discussions on Child Development*. New York: International Universities Press, 1958.

VAILLANT, G. E. John Haslam on Early Infantile Autism. *American Journal of Psychiatry*, 119:376 (1962).

————. Twins Discordant for Early Infantile Autism. *Archives of General Psychiatry*, 9:163–167 (1963).

WAGLER, L. *Die Bilanz einer hundertjaehrigen Hauserforschung*. Nuernberg, 1928.

WEILAND, H. I., and R. RUDNIK. Considerations of the Development and Treatment of Autistic Childhood Psychosis, in *The Psychoanalytic Study of the Child*. New York: International Universities Press, 1961, vol. 16, pp. 549–563.

WINNICOTT, D. W. Transitional Objects and Transitional Phenomena. *International Journal of Psychoanalysis*, 34:89–97 (1953).

WOLFF, P. H. *The Developmental Psychologies of Jean Piaget and Psychoanalysis*. New York: International Universities Press, 1960.

————. Private communication, 1964.

————, and B. L. WHITE. Visual Pursuit and Attention in Young Infants. *Journal of Child Psychiatry*, 4:473–484 (1965).

Index

INDEX

abstract thought, 240–1, 391–2, 454–5
accommodation, 443, 450
action, self motivated, 16 ff., 51, 53–5, 328–9
  absence of, 55
  and cognition, 444
  and imprinting, 29 ff.
  and object permanence, 450
  and self awareness, 177–8
  and speech, 79–80
  critical age for, 29 ff.
  degrees of absence, 75–6
  in infancy, 34 ff.
  parental response to, 29–30
action, self-protective, 74
adaptation, 59, 400, 443
  in autistic behavior, 286
  break down of old, 286
  fetal, 286
  infant-mother, 28–9
  in infancy, 27
  language, 458–9
  maternal, 26–9
  neonatal, 395
adolescence, 33–4, 83, 294
affective contact: *see* emotional reactivity; relatedness
affirmation, 143, 428
affirmation by repetition, 424
affluence and parental giving, 280–1
age, admission: *see* Orthogenic School
age, denial of, 193 n.

aggression, 201
  freeing of, 102–3, 202 ff.
  oral, 143
Agra (India), 346
alertness in newborn, 16
Alexander, F., 184
alienation, 111, 136, 284
  see also body
all-or-none principle, 41, 200, 446
Alpert, A., 249
alter ego, 300, 313–15, 325
Amala (wolf girl), 345 ff.
ambivalence, 89–91, 216
  maternal, 125–9
anaclitic, infancy as, 15
anal development, arrested, 118
anality, in treatment, 296–7
anal stage, precursers, 262–3
anal zone, defensive nonfunctioning, 118
Andy, 379–81
animal behavior: analogies to, 365
  prodromal, 128–9
animal intelligence, 50–1
animal-like behavior, 350, 370
animals: as alleged nurses, 346
  identification with, 349
Anna, 7, 374–7
anorexia, 99, 102, 111, 118, 127, 163, 377
  end of, 148
  neonatal, 18
Anthony, J., 421
anthropology, social, 347